# THEY CAME TO THE MOUNTAIN

Antelope Valley and the San Francisco Peaks from a lithograph made in 1867. Taken from William A. Bell's *New Tracks in North America,* London, 1869.

# THEY CAME TO THE MOUNTAIN

## The Story of
## Flagstaff's Beginnings

BY PLATT CLINE

Published by
NORTHERN ARIZONA UNIVERSITY
with NORTHLAND PRESS / FLAGSTAFF

A Flagstaff
Bicentennial-Centennial Commission
Official Publication

*for Barbara*

# Contents

# Illustrations

# Foreword

"WE FORGET," wrote Henry David Thoreau more than a century ago, "that [the past] had any other future than our present." And in *Walden* Thoreau identified himself as one who rarely read newspapers, arguing there was never anything in them which was new. If you have read about one war or one birth or one death you have read about all of them.

Platt Cline, journalist and historian, brings both views into question. He has not forgotten. He remembers well we are the direct cultural descendants of our forebears, and old newspapers have provided the principal source of this remembrance. He has felled, hauled, and milled the abundant forests of the *Arizona Miner,* the *Prescott Morning Courier,* the *Arizona Champion,* the *Flag,* the *Coconino Sun,* and other weeklies and dailies to erect an edifice he calls *They Came to the Mountain.* This book is a product of Cline's unabashed love affair with Flagstaff, Arizona, county seat of Coconino County and the heart of Arizona's tree-covered mountain domain. It is also his effort to understand who we are by knowing who we have been.

Like many other communities in Arizona, Flagstaff had its nebulous beginnings in the comings and goings of sundry surveyors, explorers, and others who passed by en route to elsewhere, all drawn to the general vicinity because of reliable springs in the area. Water is the magnet which attracts human life in the arid Southwest, and where there is a mountain, there are usually springs. This is not to say that before mid-nineteenth-century attempts to open wagon roads and railroads from Santa Fe and Albuquerque to the Pacific Coast there were no people here. Indeed, men, women, and children whom we know as "Indians" had arrived hundreds or even thousands of years before. But non-Indian Flagstaff had non-Indian beginnings, and its evolution from a railroad camp and timber town to a city would likely have proceeded as it did whether earlier Americans had lived in the region or not.

The concern, then, of *They Came to the Mountain* is with the formative years of one of Arizona's major communities. These are chiefly the years from the 1870s, and especially from the coming of the Atlantic & Pacific Railroad in 1882, to the formation of Coconino County in 1891 and the election of Flagstaff as its seat of government. The theme, implied throughout, is that of continuity. In reading of those who lived in the past we are continually reminded of ourselves. Our generation has not been spontaneous after all. We are much as our ancestors have made us. We are different as well, but given the perspective of a hundred years we remain surprisingly unchanged.

Flagstaff, as the reader will discover, owes its beginnings—and, in large part, its continued existence—to sheep, cattle, timber, transportation, and tourism. The arrival of the railroad assured the town of its future place in history, and in 1976 the city lies as a large hub at the center of a wheel more than eighty miles in diameter and whose spokes are the tracks of the Santa Fe Railroad and major highways leading in from the west, northwest, north, east, south, and southwest. Even to the southeast there is a paved highway linking Flagstaff to summer recreation country in Coconino National Forest. The mercantile business, so important to the town in the 1880s, continues unabated in that role in the 1970s.

There are other continuities as well. A growing center of population of nearly a hundred years ago continually had to seek larger and more secure sources of water. This is a situation with which all modern Flagstaff residents are also familiar. Less well known, perhaps, is the fact that the first Flagstaff colonizers, members of the 1876 Boston parties, arrived on the scene after having attended rallies in Boston at which they heard the boundless virtues of the region extolled. The cost to attend the rallies was ten cents. The cost to join the westward trek to the promised land was far greater to those whose hope and enthusiasm conquered wisdom and prudence. Cline treats the promoters of the Boston parties with compassion, certainly with more compassion than many people who invested their money, time, and energy in the forlorn enterprise. But again, those of us who have witnessed untold numbers of schemes involving the promotion of Arizona real estate in the 1960s and '70s to unwary Easterners and Midwesterners will come away with a sense of déjà vu.

Another kind of continuity is the genealogical one. It was in Flagstaff that many families founded their fortunes and their fame whose descendents are still among us in Arizona. There are the Babbitts and the Riordans. There are others who will be known to northern Arizonans, but who are less familiar to an outlander from the desert south such as myself. And finally, there are the legions of just plain folks, the butcher, the baker, and candlestick maker, who are the real backbone of history, the true source of continuity, to whom author Cline has bent every effort to give their due. Many of their progeny as well can doubtless still be counted among the population of Flagstaff or of the forty-eighth state.

*They Came to the Mountain* is not a comparative study. It is intended to tell us about Flagstaff and no other place. The reader, however, will be drawn to make his own comparisons. Flagstaff, while it had its booms, was never really a boom town. While it had its share of violence, death, and the occasional administration of justice by Judge Lynch, this was no Tombstone and it never had to be "too tough to die." Its growth was steady. Its early citizens appear, by and large, to have been solid. They probably represented a fairly good slice of middle class Anglo America of a century ago. They seem to have come as settlers intending to put down roots rather than as drifters seeking to exploit the terrain and then to move on.

The railroad camp out of which modern Flagstaff grew was almost as a veneer over the firmer stuff of which ranching, agriculture, and lumbering is made. These quieter pursuits required a high degree of cooperation and mutual help among the citizens. In short, they seem to have demanded at least rudimentary forms of social and political organization among the populace, forms which in other Arizona communities were sometimes whole generations in developing.

At least as early as the summer of 1882, the townspeople were fussing over the need for schools, churches, and fraternal organizations. The first Protestant preacher raised $25 from among "the boys" of the local saloons with which to buy a lot for a church; the ladies organized a local chapter of the Women's Christian Temperance Union. The Roman Catholic Church sent a Jesuit to oversee the religious needs of that particular segment of the community, and nearly every male of voting age seems to have taken an interest in politics on either the Republican or Democratic side of the fence. Newspapers were begun. A jail, albeit a flimsy one, was constructed. People organized and joined local chapters of the Grand Army of the Republic, the Masons, Eastern Star, Odd Fellows, and Knights of Pythias. There were balls and parties and picnics. In 1884 the Literary Society was organized and the wife of Judge J. C. Hicks gave a lecture on "Conditions, Fertility and Uses of the Cork Tree." By the late 1880s, Flagstaff had a public library.

None of this sounds like a wild and wooly western town of movie matinee and television fame. It sounds instead like a piece of already well-established middle America transplanting itself beneath the shadow of the San Francisco Peaks, "The Mountain" to which men came. And the transplant has been a success. Today's Flagstaff boasts three astronomical observatories, a university and a

renowned museum of anthropology and natural history, the Museum of Northern Arizona. As Cline remarks, "the community's attitudes and values favoring
[such institutions] were already evident in the 1880s."

Platt Cline's concern for the present and his love for his home have led him
to examine our common past. We are in his debt for having brought us, too, to
the mountain.

*April 1976*                                    BERNARD L. FONTANA
                                                Arizona State Museum
                                                The University of Arizona

# Preface

THIS BOOK IS A RECORD of significant events in the Flagstaff community during its formative decade, the 1880s, and among other things is also an attempt to define and interpret the actions of special people in a unique situation in the wilderness of Arizona Territory during that time.

Perhaps my chief qualification for attempting this project is that I spent the greater part of my adult life as reporter, editor, and publisher of the *Coconino Sun* and its offspring, the *Arizona Daily Sun,* which I helped found in 1946. For many years, it was my daily task to record the life of this community, attempting always to understand the forces and qualities which made it what it was.

I was fortunate in having been born and raised in a time and place which gave me firsthand knowledge of western frontier communities. My birthplace, Mancos, Colorado, was also a livestock, sawmilling, and mercantile town. Life in most small western towns was relatively unchanged from the 1880s until the end of the First World War; so, having spent some formative years in that period, I approached the study of Flagstaff's history with some understanding of what people were like and how they lived in early days.

Coming to Flagstaff in 1938, and knowing the day I arrived that, the Lord willing, I would spend the rest of my life here, I devoted myself to the community which I hoped to make my own. Necessity took me to the Holbrook newspaper for four years, and that was a good experience and gave me more understanding of the small western community. I loved Holbrook and its people, too. Returning to Flagstaff, I spent fascinated hours reading years and years of the yellowing files of the *Sun* and its predecessor, the *Arizona Champion,* back to the beginning. I looked upon the Flagstaff community's surviving pioneers as I had looked upon the oldtimers of my birthplace. Flagstaff's history became my own. I identified myself with the community, an immensely rewarding experience, but one which would also become a source of sadness as the breaking-up times came.

Another of my qualifications for this task was my acquaintanceship with some of those who played parts in pioneer times. I knew Ed Whipple, Lotta Beal Gillette, John Love, Tim Riordan, and Arizona's last Territorial Governor, Richard E. Sloan. I visited with or interviewed C. J. Babbitt, Henry F. Ashurst, Ralph and Bert Cameron, Lee and Zeke Newman, Billy Roden, Stanley Sykes, Prescott's Morris Goldwater, and Mrs. Sophia McLaws, who came to Joseph City as a bride with that community's first wagon train of settlers in 1876. I corresponded for many months with the widow of Apache County's famous sheriff of the 1880s, Commodore Perry Owens. I was privileged to enjoy the friendship of Billy Switzer, George Hochderffer, Charlie Stemmer, Al Beasley, and Judge Edmund Wells of Prescott, who camped at the future site of Flagstaff in 1864. I knew scores of Flagstaff's second generation and those who came in the 1890s, and was blessed with a special relationship with Dr. R. O. Raymond. I loved many of these people, and treasured them all.

The people of Flagstaff, or at least an extraordinary number of them, had extraordinary qualities, and not only the qualities always demanded of men and women who would be pioneers. The record of their living and doing which I attempt to depict herein suggests that many had a special vigor, a special self-confidence coupled with a self-respect which showed itself as a certain modesty. They were ambitious, but few of them were money or power grubbers.

As occasions arose down the years, I asked oldtimers why they chose to spend their lives here. The question never brought a quick or glib answer. They would search for words to express what they deeply felt. Usually they made references to climate and opportunity or family connections, but always phrased as a prelude to the real reason, an identity with and love for their community, which came out in varying degrees of elaboration and explanation. They didn't come to Flagstaff preparatory to moving somewhere else, as so many do now. They came here, most of them, to live, as in a later time I did. They took time to be neighbors, and most of them took time to have fun, and time to savor their good fortune in finding the community which fed their needs. As individuals they generally knew what they wanted, and together as a community, they always knew what they wanted. Alas for that departed time.

These extraordinary people, not all of whom by any means could be described as community leaders or public figures, gave the life of our community its special flavor. Some of this ebbed away with the passing of the pioneers, with changing conditions, and new challenges. But a lot of it persisted for quite a long time. This quality was made up of a lot of things and may be indefinable, but it is my hope that the reader will find clues to it in this book.

Zane Grey, the western novelist whose superficial romances were widely popular in the teens and twenties, on his seventeenth visit to Flagstaff in 1927, lamented the passing of the cowboy, the click of boot heels, the jingle of spurs. A bit later he wrote that he would never return to Arizona, that the West was gone, and that commercialism had conquered. Grey mistook the artifacts of the days of the open range for the spirit of the community. There was much more to it than that.

The major attack on Flagstaff's unique spirit came with the nationwide flood of homogenized mass culture, diminution of distances, instantaneous communication of distractive trivia, the erosion of the values of self-reliance and personal dignity on which the pioneers of Flagstaff had built their lives and their community.

Further dilution of the community's unique quality was wrought by some of those who flooded in in later years, many looking simply for any place to live, and some of whom were indifferent or hostile to Flagstaff's special qualities. But among these throngs, happily, were a number who sensed that there was something here besides opportunity and climate in a gorgeous setting.

Vestiges of our town's unique flavor are still discernible, despite the rising tide. Many of our people, newcomers as well as oldtimers, relish and cherish it. Let us hope that a taste survives for our children and grandchildren. To help achieve this, along with my wish to salute those with whom I have shared the Flagstaff experience, I wrote this book.

*February 7, 1976*            P. C.

NOTE TO THE READER:

In some quoted passages, punctuation has been added for clarity, and where variations in spelling appeared, the most generally accepted form has been used. In the case of proper names appearing in old records with different spellings, the one consistent with the most reliable record has been used, notably in the cases of T. F. McMillan, J. H. Tourjee, and G. B. Maynadier. Acknowledgments, sources and bibliography appear at the back. Those interested chiefly in the narrative may wish to skip biographical detail appearing in parts of Chapters IV and V, and all of Chapter VI.

# BEFORE THE BEGINNING

# Sierra Sin Agua

THE DOMINATING PHYSICAL FEATURE of northern Arizona is the San Francisco Peaks, which rise to a summit of 12,670 feet, highest point in the state. They thrust their great mass abruptly out of the Colorado Plateau, which extends northward through the southeastern half of Utah, eastward as far as Fort Wingate, New Mexico; southward to the great escarpment of the Mogollon Rim, and westward to the Grand Wash Cliffs near Kingman. The Peaks are the eroded rim of the crater of an extinct volcano which is horseshoe-shaped with the opening to the east.

From the summit on a clear day, landmarks as distant as two hundred miles may be seen. When I first came to Flagstaff in the 1930s, I was told that San Francisco, California, could be seen from the top of the Peaks, and that because of this the Peaks were so named. But of course the Bay area of California is some six hundred miles away and cannot be seen from the summit. The Peaks were actually named in honor of Saint Francis by friars when they established a mission at the Hopi Indian village of Oraibi in 1629—one hundred and forty-seven years before the California city received its name, in honor of the same saint. The Peaks are clearly and strikingly visible from Oraibi, some sixty-five miles distant, sometimes seeming to be suspended in the sky.

The major Peaks are four in number and the loftiest is Mt. Humphreys, which was named in 1872 for Brig. Gen. Andrew Atkinson Humphreys who, as a captain, served with the Army Corps of Topographical Engineers during the 1850s. When several expeditions were sent through the area seeking routes for wagon roads and a railroad, Humphreys evaluated the survey data. Later he became a general and Chief of the Corps and was honored by having this important landmark named in his honor.

Although Humphreys was essentially a desk soldier, he later served with distinction in the Civil War on the Union side. He led a brigade at Gettysburg that stood in the path of a major Confederate attack and earned himself the nickname of "the fighting fool of Gettysburg." I have found no record, however, that he ever viewed the peak which bears his name, or even that he was ever in Arizona. All honor to him for his considerable services to the nation, but it would perhaps have been more fitting to name this highest peak in Arizona for someone who had made a greater contribution in the immediate area. From Flagstaff, it is possible to see only a corner of Humphreys Peak because Mt. Agassiz is in the way. Humphreys is part of the northwestern rim of the ancient crater. Many local residents believe they are looking at Humphreys when they are actually viewing Agassiz or Fremont Peak. A Flagstaff street also bears Humphrey's name.

Mt. Agassiz, or Agassiz Peak, is 12,340 feet in elevation. A ski lift runs up its western slope today to a point not far below the top. The ride up on this lift, which runs in the summer months too, is one of the greatest sightseeing experiences in the area. Agassiz Peak was named in honor of Jean Louis Rodolphe Agassiz (1807–1873), who made fossil studies for a railroad survey through the area in 1867–68. He was a Swiss and a famed zoologist who taught at Harvard. A Flagstaff street is also named for him. When Gen. William J. Palmer submitted his railroad survey report in 1868, he referred to a "high extinct volcano, known as San Francisco Mountain, but whose name for distinction we changed to Mt. Agassiz."

Immediately east of Agassiz is Fremont Peak, elevation 11,940 feet, the second of the two peaks so plainly visible from Flagstaff. It was named in honor of John Charles Fremont (1813–1890), the so-called "pathfinder" of the west. An unsuccessful candidate for President in 1856, when he was defeated by James Buchanan, he was later appointed governor of the Arizona Territory and served from 1878 to 1882. He played absolutely no part in anything that ever happened in sight of the San Francisco Peaks and, according to Will C. Barnes's *Arizona Place Names,* he "never saw the peak which was named in his honor." Fremont Peak should be renamed, but the chances of this happening are remote.

The peak at the eastern extremity of the crater rim is called, locally at least, Doyle Peak. Fittingly, it was named for Allen Doyle (1850–1920), who was a stockman, guide, and an authentic pioneer in this area. He drove a herd of cattle here from Prescott in 1881 and stayed to become famous as a guide for many notables, including the western writer, Zane Grey.

Now, sweeping our eyes over this great mountain mass before scrambling to the top for a throat-clutching view, we are reminded of how appropriate is its second, unofficial name—*Sierra Sin Agua,* that is, "Mountain Without Water." There are no flowing streams except in very wet years and then only for a few months of the year, due to the extreme porosity of the volcanic material of which the mountain is composed. It is important to keep this absence of water in mind to understand the historic and prehistoric use and development of the area.

As to the name Sierra Sin Agua: A couple of generations ago it was fairly generally believed by scholars that Luxan (1583) and Farfan (1598), members of early Spanish exploring parties, were referring to the Peaks when they mentioned in their journals the lack of streams near mountains encountered on their journeys from the Hopi villages into the Verde Valley looking for Indian mines. However, Katharine Bartlett of the Museum of Northern Arizona studied the matter carefully, and concluded that neither the Espejo party including Luxan, nor Farfan had approached the foot of the Peaks on their expeditions. I find her lucid, learned discussion convincing. So our Peaks are not the Sierra Sin Agua of the sixteenth century. But the name is nevertheless most appropriate, as they are indeed "Mountains Without Water," or at least without permanent streams.

There are, however, springs—the biggest and most reliable near the foot of the mountain being Leroux. It was named in honor of Antoine Leroux (1801–1861), a scout and guide who accompanied several expeditions through the area long before the beginning of Flagstaff. In the Inner Basin, the crater of which our Peaks are the rim, are many springs, and some of them are very good ones indeed. At the time of the earliest settlers, some of these springs were flowing, and over the ensuing years all have been developed extensively as sources of water for the city. The most productive is Flagstaff Spring, which will flow a million gallons a day for several months in good years. The first spring discovered was Jack Smith Spring, named for the man who found it. It will flow six to seven hundred thousand gallons a day in late June and July. Other springs in the Inner Basin supplying water to the city have been given such names as Snowslide, Doyle, Raspberry, and Little Bear Paw, over the years.

When winter precipitation is good, the city will get three million gallons of domestic water a day over several months from this source. It is probably our best water, and certainly our cheapest, because no pumping is necessary to bring it down from the mountain to the city mains. In a year of heavy snows, like that of 1972–73, the springs may produce twice as much water as the pipeline to the reservoirs north of the city can handle, and thus there is a loss of three to four million gallons a day. This considerable supply of excellent water is available to our city today only because of development over a period of many years. Before the coming of the Americans in the 1870s, the overflow from the Inner Basin springs came intermittently in a small stream flowing east out of the open end of the horseshoe-shaped crater. Leroux and other springs on the south side of the mountain fed a seasonal stream, the Rio de Flag, which ran down the valley through the site of our city. It now flows only during times of heavy runoff.

There are other names for the Peaks, too. The Hopi Indians, who live in mesa-top villages sixty-five to seventy-five miles to the northeast, and whose trash heaps indicate a continuous inhabitation of the area for possibly one thousand years, call the mountain *Nuva-teekia-ovi,* which means "the Place of Snow on the Very Top." The Hopis believe that the mountain is one of the principal abodes of the kachinas, supernatural beings which are represented by the popular kachina dolls. The Hopis go to the Peaks for certain plants and other objects for use in ceremonies, and at the very highest point on Humphreys Peak there is a crude rock cairn which has been used by Hopis for centuries as a place to deposit prayer feathers, and perform rain and blessings-bringing rituals.

The Navajos, those latecomers who were probably not in the immediate area at all prior to A.D. 1700, call our mountain *Do'ko'oslid,* which means something like "blue western mountain" or "abalone shell mountain." The Havasupais, whom the Hopi call Ko-ho-nina from which the name of Coconino County is derived, call the mountain *Hvehassahpatch,* which means "big rock mountain."

Now come with us briefly to the top of the Peaks; for, despite the fact that we cannot see the Pacific Ocean from their summits, the view, or rather views, are well worth the climb. Looking down to the south and southeast, we glimpse sections of Flagstaff, a part of the view being blocked by the considerable mass of Mt. Elden, 9,280 feet high. From where we stand we note that the top of Elden is a bit cluttered by antennae and reflectors of various kinds, all no doubt electronically useful, and they really don't detract materially from the beauty of the mountain. This mountain was named for one of the very earliest settlers in the area, John Elden.

Extending from as far as we can see to the east-southeast, to the south, and then far on to the west are the triple slashes through the forest and hills which mark the routes of Interstate Highway 40 and the Santa Fe Railway mainline. Far to the southeast over the top of Elden, we sight the White Mountains along the Arizona-New Mexico border, more than one hundred and fifty miles distant.

Now directing our view to the south, Mormon Mountain rears its bulk thirty miles away on the west side of Mormon Lake. Both lake and mountain gained their names from the establishment in 1878 of a dairy by Mormon settlers from the Little Colorado Valley—the Colorado Chiquito. Far beyond we see Baker Butte, which extends southward out from the Mogollon Rim, of which it is a part, some sixty-five miles away. It is said that it was named for James Baker, who brought sheep into the area in 1868. Yet farther south we see the Mazat-zals, and beyond them the Superstition Mountains east of Phoenix.

Turning further, we view Bill Williams Mountain thirty miles distant to the southwest across open parks and beautiful forest. Both the mountain and the town at its northern foot were named for the famed Mountain Man and trapper, Bill Williams. About halfway between where we stand and Williams, we glimpse the network of railroads, highways, the water tanks, buildings and other structures marking the Navajo Army Depot, which was one of the major storage places for munitions for the Pacific Theatre during and after the Second World War.

Turning our eyes straight to the west, we see at a distance of eighteen miles another great mass, Mt. Sitgreaves, a pretty good mountain in its own right if it didn't have so much competition in the area. Its elevation is 9,388 feet. It was named for Capt. Lorenzo Sitgreaves, who led an expedition through the area in 1851 to establish a route between New Mexico and California. Another pretty good mountain is Kendrick, about twelve miles to the northwest. Kendrick is 10,418 feet in height and, like the Peaks, Bill Williams and Sitgreaves mountains, is volcanic in origin. It was named in honor of Maj. Henry L. Kendrick, who was in charge of the military escort for the Sitgreaves expedition. Streets here are named for both Sitgreaves and Kendrick.

Swinging around to the north, we see the gorge of the Grand Canyon sixty-five miles away, with the great North Kaibab Forest stretching away from the North Rim. On a clear day it is possible to see well down into the Canyon, perhaps the most famous natural wonder in the world. Any view of the Canyon is great, but a good way to appreciate fully its tremendous scope is to view it from atop the Peaks.

Looming on the horizon to the northeast, about one hundred and twenty miles distant, is Navajo Mountain, deep in the heart of Indian land. From where we stand, it looks like an island, or perhaps it suggests the back of a huge whale sighted far out at sea. Its southern slopes are in Arizona, but its mass is in Utah. Beyond, the mountains near Maryvale, Utah, can be seen on clear days.

Turning again, now to the east, we see quite clearly the Little Colorado River Valley some twenty-five to forty-five miles away, and far beyond the Colorado Chiquito loom the mysterious Hopi Buttes, some ninety miles distant across the Painted Desert.

Below us, nine miles to the east, is one of the most arresting sights in our whole great vista—a cone of black cinders with an orange and red rim suggesting the colors of the sunset. We are told that it was named Sunset Peak by the famed one-armed soldier, explorer, and scientist, Maj. John Wesley Powell, in 1879. It is now known as Sunset Crater. From where we stand, its rim is nearly six thousand feet below us, glowing like a live coal among burned-out cinders. Such are the unsurpassed panoramas that the San Francisco Peaks provide of Arizona's high country, of the country of the Sierra Sin Agua.

It has only been in the past few hundred years, of course, that Europeans have known of this vast, kaleidoscopic land. The Indians were in this area at a very early time, certainly as early as the sixth or seventh century of the Christian era, and probably much earlier, perhaps four thousand or more years ago. Various groups, bands or tribes have come and gone, brought in or forced out by many factors, including weather changes and the presence of other groups or bands, friendly or hostile. Some of the Indians that we find on every side of us in northern Arizona today, such as the Hopi and the Havasupai, are related remotely in time to the very earliest inhabitants of, or travelers through, our area. Others, such as the Navajo and Apache, came much later, from the north and through the passes of the Rockies.

Through the late nineteenth century and up to the present time [1976], the Indians have made a noticeable and interesting impact on our culture. Perhaps this impact is so much a part of living in this area that many tend to take it for granted. This comes home to us when we have visitors from other parts of the nation or the world and we try to tell them about our red neighbors. Certainly there are few homes today in Flagstaff which do not boast some item of Indian manufacture, whether it be Hopi basketry, kachina dolls, pottery or jewelry, or Navajo rugs and jewelry, and many people here are proud to have friends who are members of these various tribes. The literature relating to the Indians is rich and interesting; there are literally hundreds of books dealing with them.

Early travelers and the first settlers in the area were much impressed by the profusion of Indian ruins and pottery shards found all around the Peaks, especially on the south, southeast and east, suggesting an extensive prehistoric population. Elden Pueblo at the foot of Elden Mountain, and the ruins in Walnut Canyon a few miles to the southeast, were favorite picnicking and excursion spots for early residents, and these and many other Indian ruins in the general area are now well known to tourists and sightseers, as well as to archaeologists and other scientists.

The late Dr. Harold S. Colton, founder of the Museum of Northern Arizona, spent more than forty years in archaeological and ethnological research here, and was long recognized as a leading authority in these fields. And, after an extensive and careful study of these ancient sites, he calculated the probable prehistoric population of the area at various dates. His estimates for the early population of what is now Flagstaff, plus the areas southeast and east of the Peaks out to the Little Colorado River, were: A.D. 600, 300; A.D. 800, 380; A.D. 975, 875; A.D. 1085, 3,764; A.D. 1160, 8,416; A.D. 1250, 612, and A.D. 1350, none.

That twelfth century figure of over eight thousand is startling—a greater population than the area was ever to have again until the middle of the twentieth century!

Colton's estimates also show that the increase in the prehistoric population in the twelfth century was very rapid, and the subsequent drop to the zero point was equally rapid. After that vast increase in population followed by the zoom downward, the only people in this area for centuries thereafter were a few nomadic hunters and seed-gatherers, transient war or hunting parties, and Indian travelers. The Indians did quite a bit of getting around, and commerce and other contacts between and through the various tribes was widespread, and continues to be so today.

Along the rocky ridges overlooking the Little Colorado River, crude stone implements and evidence of the manufacture of such implements have been found. These may be extremely ancient, perhaps many thousands of years old. At Grand Canyon and at Walnut Canyon, small animal effigies made by twisting a single split willow wand into the form of a deer or similar animal have been found that are believed to be magic fetishes left by hunting parties in the area as early as four thousand years ago.

Much later, and speaking in very general terms, well along in the Christian era we find three major Indian cultures in or converging on this area. The Cohonina came from the west and generally moved around the north side of the Peaks; the Sinagua came from somewhere—no one is quite sure where— and moved around the south and southwest sides of the Peaks; and from the northeast came the culture known today as the Kayenta. Still later, and during the height of the twelfth century population boom, a few members of a fourth culture—the Hohokam from the Valley of the Sun far to the south—moved in, settling in small villages east of the Peaks. The area, then, was a cultural frontier.

"Ko-ho-nina," as noted above, is the Hopi name for the Havasupai Indians, who today live in beautiful Cataract Canyon, a tributary of the Grand Canyon, and who may be related to the prehistoric Cohoninas around the west and north sides of the Peaks.

The name Sinagua, which we have cited before but in another connection, was coined by Colton for the peoples who lived on the south and southwest sides of the Peaks—as far as we know the original inhabitants of Flagstaff. They came from the southeast, a branch of the Mogollon culture. The name Sinagua would probably be more appropriate for our county than Coconino, but of course, it was not coined until well into the 1900s and long after Coconino County became a political entity.

The third culture, Kayenta, is the name given by archaeologists to a major branch of a wide-ranging prehistoric people called the *Anasazi*—the "Ancient Ones" in Navajo—whose center of activity was in the northeastern corner of what is now Arizona and the Four Corners area. All these cultures met around the Peaks, learned from each other, and combined to a considerable degree, with the Sinagua dominating during the century when agricultural activity and productiveness reached its maximum.

Now what caused the tremendous growth in population during that century, climaxing in about A.D. 1160? Dr. Colton has proved to the satisfaction of most archaeologists that it came about largely because of the eruption of Sunset Crater a few years before or after the time of the Norman Conquest of England in A.D. 1066. Ash, cinders, and lava ejected by the volcano covered Indian dwellings which were excavated in the early 1930s, and their charred wooden beams were dated by the then newly discovered tree-ring method. Prevailing winds during the eruption carried the ash generally in a broad ellipse running northeastward and southwestward about thirty to thirty-five miles in its long dimension and about fifteen to twenty miles in width. When the volcano subsided, some one thousand square miles of land had been covered with black, basaltic sand.

The Sinaguans who were living in the area at the time of the eruption moved away from the danger point, but soon came back again when the ash and cinders had ceased to fall. Digging around, they found that the ground was moist under the black sand; that this moisture tended to remain; and that they could now plant and raise crops in areas which before had been quite barren. Very soon a land rush was underway and Indians of the various groups came in to acquire some of the now very fertile land. The coming of these groups, coupled with the vast increase in available food, Dr. Colton tells us, resulted in the area's population explosion in the eleventh and twelfth centuries.

This prosperous situation must have lasted for a few generations. Then more and more land returned to barren desert as the wind and rain did their work of carrying away the life-giving volcanic mulch. In due time, and rather rapidly, farming in much of the area again became impossible. Dr. Colton has also postulated that the increase in population brought about a different style of living—

now in closely grouped pueblos rather than in scattered individual dwellings. This crowding, coupled with the lack of sanitation, brought an increase in disease which played a part in further reducing the population. Many of the people moved southward into the Verde Valley. Others went elsewhere, and possibly some contributed their blood streams to the groups we know today as the Hopi.

The earlier dwellings had been pithouses, half-subterranean, the tops being built of logs and dirt. These pithouses have been found all around the Peaks, and there must have been many in the Flagstaff valley which parallels the Rio de Flag through our city today. One was found during the excavation for a home along Fort Valley Road not far from one of today's shopping centers. Dr. Colton found he had been driving right over the top of one for many years at the entrance to his property farther north on Fort Valley Road, and promptly excavated it. No doubt cultivation of the valley from the beginning of modern times—the 1870s— up to the early 1940s destroyed evidence of many others.

Long-used Indian trails went from watering place to watering place in northern Arizona. A major Indian trail led from the Hopi villages southwest-ward to the crossing of the Little Colorado at its juncture with Canyon Diablo, thence on westward by Turkey Tanks and to the springs along the southern foot of the San Francisco Peaks. Another went from the villages to the crossing of the Little Colorado at a point near the present city of Winslow, then south-westward to Sunset Pass, Chavez Pass, and on westward, with alternate routings to the Verde Valley. The trail around the Peaks must have led to Elden and Leroux springs, and no doubt southward down the Flagstaff valley to what later was known as Old Town Spring. Other trails fed into these trails, and they in turn fed into others.

There must have been a lot of prehistoric traffic back and forth along the general line of the thirty-fifth parallel, for the same reason that it is the route of the railroad and major highways today—it comprised the shortest distance and easiest travel between east and west across the area, except when hostile Indians made detours far to the north or south more feasible. In the nineteenth century, alternatives were the Gila Trail, which went from El Paso to the vicinity of Las Cruces, New Mexico, thence westward across southern Arizona to Yuma; and the Old Spanish Trail, which went from Santa Fe up across southwestern Colorado, crossed into Utah near the Green River, ran westerly across Utah, thence southwest to the Virgin River, and on into California.

With the departure of most of the prehistoric population following the dis-appearance of the volcanic mulch, and after a severe twenty-three-year drought in the late 1200s, the Peaks were free of the presence of man except for occasional Indian travelers, or hunting or war parties, until the coming of the Spanish in the sixteenth century. They established no settlements or posts in the area, with the exception of missions in the Hopi villages, but they did explore it repeatedly and thoroughly.

The first Europeans to see our mountain were undoubtedly members of Coronado's expedition in 1540, which came up from the south through eastern Arizona to the Zuñi villages. Coronado sent a small party, under the leadership of Don Pedro de Tovar, to visit the Hopi villages. Tovar's group must have been well aware of "the Place of Snow on the Very Top." Tovar sent Don Lopez de Cardenas to investigate the Indians' stories about the vast chasm slashing across the plateau west of Hopiland. He was led to the South Rim of the Grand Canyon by Hopi guides, and unquestionably he and his small group had a good long look at the mountain dominating the southern horizon, a mountain which nearly a century later would be named for Saint Francis.

The next expedition into the area was that of Antonio de Espejo, a Spanish merchant who was living in what is now the northern part of Mexico, and who led a small party into the Rio Grande region in the fall of 1580. On arriving at the pueblos, Espejo learned that the missionaries left there earlier were dead. The Espejo party then went westward to Zuñi, where they found three Mexican Indians who had come there forty years before with Coronado's party. And here they also heard of minerals to the west. It is more than likely that Espejo had set out on his trip with the idea of prospecting for silver.

Espejo's party of nine whites with Indian guides then visited the Hopi mesas in early 1583, after which Espejo and four companions continued on west and south. Espejo's route has been carefully studied and retraced by Miss Bartlett, whose conclusions regarding the Sierra Sin Agua have already been cited. She tells us that Espejo's party probably went southwestward from the Hopi village of Awatovi to Comar Spring, then by Pyramid Butte and on to the crossing of the Little Colorado (called by the Spanish Rio de Lino or River of Flax) at Sunset Crossing, the present-day Winslow. Here they turned a bit more west and continued on to Sunset Pass, then to Chavez Pass and to Hay Lake. Circling north, they went along the south shore of Mormon Lake, then turned to the southwest and passed by Rattlesnake Tank. Following Beaver Creek downstream to a point north of what is now Camp Verde, they marched up the Verde Valley. A member of the party named Luxan later wrote:

We ... marched four leagues to the mines. ... Midway we found a large and copious river which flowed from north to south, which we called el Rio de los Reyes [River of the Kings; this must have been the Verde River]. Close to it was a cienega into which flowed a stream of water. Rustic people with crosses on their heads waited for us. Many of them came with us to the mines which were in a very rough sierra; so worthless that we did not find in any of them a trace of silver, as they were copper mines and poor. So we determined to return to camp at once.

Miss Bartlett states that Espejo's own account says that the mines were rich, and she notes that silver is found with copper in modern workings in the area, which must have been near Jerome. Nevertheless, the Espejo party retraced their steps to Awatovi and New Mexico. Dr. Colton tells us that this was the first recorded expedition of white men in the San Francisco Mountain region.

In 1598, Juan de Onate moved into northern New Mexico to conquer and settle the country. After arriving at the pueblo we now know as San Juan, Onate traveled in August to the Hopi villages to receive their submission to the king of Spain. Here he heard of rich mines off to the west and dispatched his Captain of the Guard and of the Horses, Marcos Farfan de los Godos, with eight whites and Hopi guides to investigate. Miss Bartlett says that Farfan's probable route followed the Indian trail probably taken by Espejo fifteen years before, from Awatovi to Sunset Crossing and on southwest through Sunset and Chavez passes. Farfan apparently did not visit Mormon Lake but turned more to the west, visiting Stoneman Lake. He went down Dry Beaver Creek and into the Verde Valley and then up to the site of the Jerome mines.

Indians guided the party to a spot where there was a shaft sixteen and a half feet deep from which Indians mined the colored ores they used for body paint and for coloring blankets. Farfan wrote that "the mine has a very large dump where there were many and apparently very good ores. . . . The vein is very wide and rich and of many outcrops containing ores." Members of the party took claims for themselves and their companions who had remained at Awatovi. Farfan noted that "the veins are so long and wide that half of the people of New Spain can have mines there." He then described the locale in terms that seem to exactly fit the Jerome area. The Farfan group returned to Awatovi and their leader, Onate, and the entire party then retraced their route to New Mexico.

No doubt they saw and wondered about our mountain, and it seems likely that sometime thereafter some so-far-unreported expedition was sent out to look for mines here.

The Franciscans established a series of missions in the Hopi villages in 1629. They were San Bernardino at Awatovi, San Bartoleme at Shimopavi, and San Francisco at Oraibi. There were also chapels at some of the other villages. Pine and fir timbers from Black Mesa and possibly the San Francisco Peaks were hauled to the villages for roof beams in the major structures erected by the Franciscans. In 1680, the Hopis joined the other southwestern pueblos in driving out the Spanish, and the Hopis remained free of them thereafter. The New Mexico pueblos were reconquered in 1692. The Franciscan buildings were destroyed at the time of the revolt. The beams at Oraibi were carefully saved and used to roof one of the kivas (underground ceremonial chambers). Here they remained until the twentieth century. Then the roof was removed and the beams piled up in one of Oraibi's streets, where they remained for many years, still showing the elaborate, European-style carving placed there either by or under the direction of the Franciscans back in 1629-40. Parenthetically, a Hopi friend of the author's whose home is on the site of the old mission, has a prized possession—a small bell with Spanish markings and dates, which he wears tied to his knee with buckskin thongs when he performs in ceremonies. Visiting with him years ago, he volunteered the information that someone in the village had a Spanish chest from the time of the *To-ta-achee* (long robes). We were unable to find it, but he had seen it. Further discussion revealed that he was talking about a Spanish cavalryman's breastplate—a Spanish chest!

In 1776, Father Francisco Garces crossed the northern part of Arizona north of the Peaks. He went from Cataract Canyon eastward to a crossing of the Little Colorado north of Cameron and on to Hopiland, where he met with hostility. This was a journey of exploration with the idea of ultimately establishing a chain of missions between Santa Fe and California. A year before, in 1775, Fray Silvestro Velez de Escalante, Franciscan missionary at the Zuñi villages in New Mexico, journeyed to Hopiland, arriving at Walpi on June 25, and at Oraibi June 27. Here, seeking information about the route westward, which along with a bit of proselytizing were the main reasons for his journey, he learned that a young Ko-ho-nina Indian was in the village. The Ko-ho-nina told Fray Escalante about the area to the west, and made him a map of the route to Cataract Canyon, his homeland. Fray Escalante thus would have been quite well prepared for a trip through the San Francisco Mountain country, but instead he returned to Zuñi.

The following year, on July 4, 1776, Fray Escalante, with two companions, Fray Francisco Atanasio Dominguez and Capt. Miera y Pacheco, set out from Santa Fe to find a route to the missions in California. They went northward up through southwestern Colorado, thence into Utah, and circled far to the north, touching the shores of Utah Lake. Then they decided to abandon the journey to California, swinging south again and to the Colorado River, where they crossed at a place which has since been named The Crossing of the Fathers in their honor, and returned to New Mexico by way of the Hopi villages. No doubt they had many sights of the Peaks.

Unquestionably there was other travel in and through the Peaks area from time to time in those earliest days. New Mexico had many *ricos* or wealthy land and stock owners who were well able to fit out expeditions not only to explore and prospect for minerals, but to travel through to the California settlements. Individuals and small parties, too, must have used the trails in the area, but of this there is only one record. A large rock near the Big Carrizo some twenty-two miles east of present-day Holbrook bears this weathered inscription:

1811

SILBESTRE ESQUIBEL

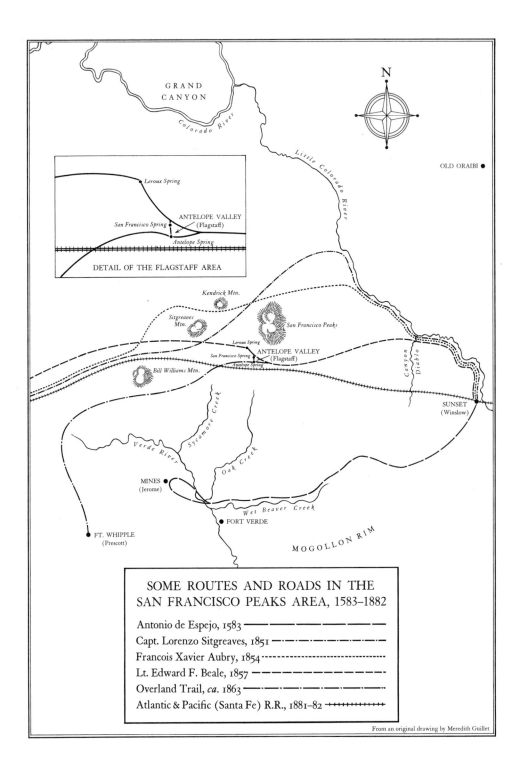

GRAND
CANYON

*Colorado River*

*Little Colorado River*

N

OLD ORAIBI ●

**DETAIL OF THE FLAGSTAFF AREA**

*Leroux Spring*

ANTELOPE VALLEY
(Flagstaff)

*San Francisco Spring*

*Antelope Spring*

Kendrick Mtn.

*Sitgreaves Mtn.*

San Francisco Peaks

*Leroux Spring*

*San Francisco Spring*    ANTELOPE VALLEY
(Flagstaff)

*Antelope Spring*

*Bill Williams Mtn.*

*Canyon Diablo*

SUNSET
(Winslow)

*Sycamore Creek*

*Verde River*

*Oak Creek*

MINES ●
(Jerome)

*Wet Beaver Creek*

● FORT VERDE

● FT. WHIPPLE
(Prescott)

MOGOLLON RIM

**SOME ROUTES AND ROADS IN THE
SAN FRANCISCO PEAKS AREA, 1583–1882**

Antonio de Espejo, 1583 ——————
Capt. Lorenzo Sitgreaves, 1851 —·—·—·—
Francois Xavier Aubry, 1854 ·············
Lt. Edward F. Beale, 1857 — — — —
Overland Trail, *ca.* 1863 —··—··—··—
Atlantic & Pacific (Santa Fe) R.R., 1881–82 ++++++++

From an original drawing by Meredith Guillet

# CHAPTER II

# The American Expeditions

THE FIRST AMERICAN of whom we have a record who thoroughly explored our area was Antoine Leroux of Taos, a companion of Kit Carson, friend of Old Bill Williams, and an outstanding figure in the ranks of the twelve to fifteen hundred mountain men who trapped, fought Indians and explored the West in the half-century preceding the Civil War. He was to guide several of the major expeditions through the San Francisco Mountain country, and was rightfully acclaimed as one of the most reliable, skilled and experienced scouts and advisors.

Leroux was born about 1801, and grew to manhood in Saint Louis, Missouri. We are told by Forbes Parkhill that he was predominantly of French blood, with a trace of Spanish, and probably of Indian. With other young men in Saint Louis at that time, he heeded the call of the distant west, and went to Taos, where he married Juana Catarina Vigil and made his home. Leroux was not one of the improvident trappers who consistently blew their earnings in a big annual spree at Taos.

Hs was a Mountain Man and a scout; but he was also comparatively well educated. He spoke French and English fluently, wrote well, and had a working knowledge of Spanish. He must also have had a knowledge of some Indian dialects. A good businessman, he managed to accumulate a substantial estate. During the 1820s and 1830s, he ranged far and wide over the great unknown area lying between Santa Fe and California. While trapping on a northwestern Arizona stream in 1837, he came upon Old Bill Williams, the famed trapper and Mountain Man. Leroux named the stream Bill Williams Fork, and the mountain northeast of it Bill Williams Mountain, in honor of his friend.

In 1846, he was guide for Col. P. St. George Cooke, who led the Mormon Battalion from Santa Fe to California; served with Lt. J. H. Whittlesley in a campaign against the Utes in 1849; worked with the U.S. Boundary Commission in 1849–51; in 1849–50, he and Kit Carson accompanied Maj. William N.

Grier in pursuit of Indians who had abducted a woman and her daughter; and he is given as source of data appearing on a map of the Southwest prepared in 1851 by Col. John Monroe.

In 1851, he guided Capt. Lorenzo Sitgreaves on a survey for a road from Zuñi to the Colorado River, the first official expedition to visit the San Francisco Mountain area; in early 1853, he guided Capt. J. W. Gunnison through Colorado seeking a railroad route; in 1853–54, he was guide for A. W. Whipple in his explorations for a railway route from Fort Smith, Arkansas, to Los Angeles, another group which visited our area. In 1854, on his way home from California, he discovered the prehistoric ruins in the Verde Valley now known as Montezuma's Castle and Montezuma's Well, locating them on what he called the San Francisco River, erroneously supposing that it originated in our mountain. It was really the Verde River.

Edward F. Beale, who made four journeys through this area, had the highest regard for Leroux. When Beale was traveling cross-country to assume his duties as superintendent of Indian affairs in California and Nevada in 1853, his party overtook Leroux on the trail, and Beale wrote: "We considered ourselves fortunate in receiving the services of so experienced a guide." Only a spell of illness at one time, and his commitments to the Whipple expedition at another, prevented him from becoming Beale's guide, but he assisted Beale in securing supplies in Taos for one journey. Leroux died June 30, 1861, at his hacienda, we learn from Parkhill. He was buried a month later, August 1, in the nave of the parish church, evidence of the esteem with which he was regarded.

Leroux could be described as father, perhaps grandfather, of Flagstaff, because he was first to become intimately acquainted with this area, and it was on his advice that the expeditions followed the general routing through here which they did. A street in Flagstaff is named for him. The finest spring at the foot of the San Francisco Peaks was named in his honor, and no doubt he joyed in that recognition. An exposed layer of sandstone in the Painted Desert also bears his name, and a wash or fork just west of Holbrook also has the name Leroux.

He deserves recognition beyond what he has received, and it would have been justice to name a major landmark for him. As we proceed with this narrative, his qualities and primacy in exploring and guiding in this immediate area will become apparent. The people of our city today know little about him, and this is their lack; and they might well devise some adequate means of commemorating him, and this they owe the memory of the first white man to claim this area as his province.

In compliance with a resolution of the United States Senate, an expedition under the leadership of Captain Sitgreaves, Corps of Topographical Engineers, U.S. Army, was sent out in 1851 to explore the Zuñi and Colorado Rivers. He was to go down the Zuñi to its junction with the Colorado, determining its course and character, "particularly with reference to its navigable properties, and to the character of its adjacent land and productions."

The party was organized at Santa Fe, and included in addition to Sitgreaves, Lt. J. G. Parke, also of the Topographical Engineers; S. W. Woodhouse, M.D., physician and naturalist; R. H. Kern, draftsman; Leroux, the guide, plus five Americans and ten Mexicans as packers. Sitgreaves bought as many mules for the trip as he could, but not securing a sufficient number, requisitioned from the assistant quartermaster at Santa Fe forty additional with pack saddles and other accouterments. He also obtained some provisions from army stores. His start was delayed waiting for an expedition against the Navajos to be launched, the plan being to take advantage of the protection afforded by this force part way on the journey.

Bvt. Maj. H. L. Kendrick, of the Second Artillery, was detailed with thirty men as an escort for the Sitgreaves party. Sitgreaves finally launched his expedition September 24, consuming, as he reported, in the meantime part of the limited supplies available for the expedition. "The mules likewise suffered from the delay, for there was scarcely any grazing in the immediate vicinity . . ." he wrote. "The mules of Major Kendrick's command were still more unfit to undertake a difficult march, many of them having been taken out of wagons after a journey of several weeks' duration." Sitgreaves' party numbered fifty.

He quickly determined that the Zuñi is not a river but a rivulet. On the fourth day of march they came to the Little Colorado. They followed roughly along the thirty-fifth parallel, passing near the site of present-day Holbrook; then on to Sunset Crossing, close to the site of present-day Winslow. They there turned northwestward and followed down the Little Colorado. They passed a number of ruins of prehistoric Indian dwellings. On their fifteenth day of march from Zuñi they came to the precipitous falls which eliminated any idea that the Little Colorado could ever be navigable down to where it joins the Colorado River. Sitgreaves wrote "the river falls over a succession of horizontal ledges . . . forming a beautiful cascade of one hundred to one hundred and twenty feet in vertical height." He named it Grand Falls.

Here, after a discussion with his guide, Leroux, which dealt not only with the roughness of the terrain and the precipitous canyon ahead, but also the condition of the animals and state of supplies, the group turned off toward San Francisco Mountain with the idea of striking the Colorado River below the great canyon and then exploring upward as far as practicable. As they moved toward the mountain, they came on ruins of many stone houses; they had discovered what today are known as the Wupatki ruins, now a national monument. As they moved away from the stream, they had a serious problem of finding water for the animals. They came upon an encampment of Indians, presumably Ko-ho-ninas. After having traveled two days without water, they sent the mules back to the river to drink, and returned with every possible container filled. Two more days of marching and they were again in dire need of water. They saw many antelope and other game, and Sitgreaves was impressed by the beauty of the area. They were moving around the north and northwesterly sides of the mountain. At camp No. 17 they came to the brow of a cliff overlooking a green vale five or six miles in extent, and they were certainly seeing what is known today as Fort Valley. Descending, their guide took them to a spring, which a couple of years later was named Leroux Spring in his honor by Whipple. After resting, they moved on westward, passed near Bill Williams Mountain, and on to the Colorado River. Their closest approach to present-day Flagstaff was Leroux Spring, seven miles northwest of the city. However, members of the party, particularly the guide, Leroux, might very well have ridden down the valley to take a look to the south and southeast.

The most interesting part of the Sitgreaves account is Dr. Woodhouse's two reports, one on the natural history of the country, in which he describes the flora and fauna, and the other his medical report. Those interested in the plants and animals of our area acknowledge a great debt to Dr. Woodhouse for his pioneering observations. As to the medical report, there are a number of interesting entries worthy of inclusion in this narrative. First, Dr. Woodhouse was bitten by a rattlesnake early on the journey. Purely in the spirit of scientific research, he decided to try the western remedy for snake bite, namely potent spirits, so he imbibed a half-pint of whisky, then followed up with a quart of brandy! He was intoxicated, became ill, but recovered his senses in five or six hours. He then continued proper medical treatment, but during the rest of the trip was handicapped by having one hand of little use due to the bite. Nearing the Colorado River and the end of the expedition, Woodhouse was shot through the leg with a Yavapai arrow.

His summary of illnesses and accidents on the trip is most interesting. Nearly all of the party at one period became ill from an exclusive diet of mule meat "without condiments of any kind." Many had influenza. Diarrhea was common. One man was treated for cholera, and others had minor ailments. Three were treated for gonorrhea, five for syphilis, two for secondary syphilis. One man died from concussion after being hit on the head with a rock by another member of the party. One was crippled by an arrow wound, then beaten to death with clubs in the hands of Yuma Indians. Most interesting was that Leroux was seriously wounded by arrows launched at him by a group of "Cojninos" Indians. One struck him behind the ear and broke some bones. Another, also armed with a stone point, entered his forearm near the wrist joint, and the head became firmly embedded in the bone. The doctor finally had to cut down to the bone, then use dental forceps to remove the arrowhead. Leroux suffered great pain for many weeks, but recovered.

Leroux's own account of this scrape is interesting. It appears in the diary of Baldwin Mollhausen, who accompanied the Whipple expedition two years later, and is too lengthy for full inclusion here. Leroux kept his rifle swinging in the direction of the hiding Indians, and called for his companions, who came to his rescue. He told Mollhausen, "I could not use my arm again during the whole journey, for wounds made with sharp stones are more difficult to heal than when made with iron."

One of the most extraordinary figures to appear in northern Arizona during the nineteenth century period of exploration was Francois Xavier Aubry, a Santa Fe merchant of French-Canadian descent. Aubry was born in Quebec in 1824. When he was eighteen, he traveled to Saint Louis, supply point for emigrants and others traveling west. Here he gained valuable experience working in a store operated by two other French-Canadians. Using his credit with his former employers, he struck out for himself, freighting merchandise to Santa Fe, quickly selling it, and returning to Saint Louis for more. His trips were made in record-breaking time. While his freight moved slowly by wagon, he traveled on ahead by horseback, frequently averaging seventy-five miles a day.

Aubry had a gift for what today would be called public relations. He would announce that he was about to start for Santa Fe and would take mail for any and all; in Santa Fe he would announce in the papers that he was enroute to Saint Louis, and would do the same. Pleased at the stir he had created by his quick journeys, he declared that he would go from Santa Fe to Independence in eighteen days, and bets were placed. On the way he was attacked by a gang of Mexican bandits, was held up a half-day by hostile Indians, and four days by extreme cold weather, lost a half-day because of a snow storm, killed three mules by hard riding—and galloped into Independence just fourteen days from Santa Fe, four ahead of his schedule. Some time later he announced that he would make the same journey in ten days. He was attacked by Indians, had to walk thirty or forty miles, killed five horses by hard riding, and was without food for three days—but completed the trip in eight and a half days! Later he decided to break his own record, and arranged for mounts to be available for him at various points. He galloped away in a driving rain and mud. He broke down six horses, slept only a few hours, walked twenty miles, and ate only six times—but he galloped into the streets of Independence at the expiration of only five days and sixteen hours! On this eight-hundred-mile trip he had averaged one hundred forty miles a day! The newspapers widely acclaimed his feat, and he became known as the Skimmer of the Plains.

Aubry was highly successful as a merchant but preferred exploration and adventure. In 1852, he drove thirty-five hundred sheep, one hundred mules, ten large wagons, and many horses from Santa Fe to San Francisco via the Gila Trail through southern Arizona. The venture was highly successful financially. He then determined to make the return trip along the thirty-fifth parallel with the avowed intent of demonstrating its feasibility for construction of a railroad. On June 20, 1853, he set out with a party of twelve Americans and six Mexicans, plus two tourists, one a man from Santa Fe, the other from Independence, who went along, Aubry said in his journal, "for a pleasure trip." They used only pack animals, and had no wagons or carriages. They were almost constantly harrassed by Indians. In one battle, twelve of the party were wounded, they killed twenty-five Indians, and Aubry suffered six wounds from arrows. Water became scarce and for a month they lived on a diet of mule flesh. After further fights with the Indians, Aubry wrote:

> Our condition is bad enough. I have eight wounds upon me, five of which cause me much suffering; and at the same time, my mule having given out, I have to walk the whole distance. Thirteen of us are now wounded, and one is sick so that we have only four men in good health.

The measure of this remarkable man is to be seen in this journal entry. He had eight arrow wounds, but only five of them hurt! He walked much of the way—and was ready in a few months to repeat the trip and prove, at his own expense, that a route across this wilderness was feasible. He followed roughly the thirty-fifth parallel, marching eastward to the Little Colorado, and thence on to Zuñi and Albuquerque.

Aubry was an intelligent man and had a fair education. He kept diaries on all of his travels, and it is from them we learn the details of his trips through northern Arizona. Reaching Albuquerque on September 10, he had completed the trip under unbelievably difficult conditions in eighty days. At the end of the journey, he wrote:

I set out in the first place upon this journey, simply to gratify my own curiosity, as to the practicability of one of the much talked about routes for the contemplated Atlantic and Pacific railroad. Having previously travelled the southern or Gila route, I felt anxious to compare it with the Albuquerque or middle route. Although I conceive the former to be in every way practicable, I now give it as my opinion that the latter is equally so, whilst it has the . . . advantage of being more central and serviceable to the Union.

At Albuquerque, Aubry was sought out by a member of Whipple's party and questioned about the country he had crossed, and Whipple took along a copy of Aubry's journal. Aubry felt that the trail he had made was unsuitable for Whipple's purpose.

In the fall of 1853, Aubry and a group of other Santa Fe businessmen gathered a band of fifty thousand sheep and set out on the same Gila route he had used the year previous. They arrived in Los Angeles early in January, 1854. Traveling on up to San Francisco, he announced that he would return to New Mexico along the thirty-fifth parallel again, and that he would attempt to establish a wagon road. On July 6, 1854, his party of sixty men, including eleven who had been with him the year before, left San Jose and headed east. He had one wagon, and a boat to be used in crossing the Colorado. He crossed his 1853 trail at several points, and also that of Whipple. This time it seems he passed far north of the San Francisco Peaks. He does not mention seeing them. He arrived in Santa Fe on August 18, just forty-three days after leaving San Jose.

At the end of his trip, he went to the store of some friends, and ordered a toddy and glass of water, and became engaged in an altercation with Richard H. Weightman, an attorney and former publisher of a Santa Fe newspaper. After words were exchanged, Weightman tossed a glass of whisky and water in Aubry's face. Aubry drew a gun, Weightman a knife. In the struggle, Aubry was fatally slashed in the abdomen, and died in a few minutes. Weightman was freed by a jury which found that he had killed in self-defense. A spring in Coconino County is named in Aubry's honor. A canyon, cliffs, hills, and a landing on the Colorado River, all in Mohave County, are also named for him. Other explorers recognized the value of Aubry's efforts, and later, Lt. Edward F. Beale, surveying a wagon road from Fort Defiance to the Colorado River, used one of Aubry's men as a guide.

The location of a railroad or railroads extending across the West to California was a matter of great political importance in the 1840s and 1850s. Slavery was an issue, of course. The economic benefits of direct connections with the vast new areas in the West were apparent. California Senator Gwin, in 1853, introduced a measure to authorize construction of a railroad along the thirty-fifth parallel. The measure failed, but served to focus attention on the route. An interesting point is that Gwin quoted Joseph R. Walker, mountain man, trader, and explorer, in support of the route. Walker was said to have traveled from Los Angeles to Santa Fe along the thirty-fifth parallel in 1851, making the trip in twenty-five days, and the return trip in thirty-two days.

In 1853 Congress authorized Secretary of War Jefferson Davis to cause surveys to be made by the Corps of Topographical Engineers to ascertain the most practicable and economic route, and appropriated $150,000 for the purpose. Davis planned three surveys. One, which concerns us here, was to be conducted by Lt. Amiel Weeks Whipple of Massachusetts, from Fort Smith west approximately along the thirty-fifth parallel. The others were to be conducted by Capt. J. W. Gunnison along the thirty-eighth and thirty-ninth parallels through Colorado and Utah; and by Isaac Ingalls Stevens, newly appointed governor of Oregon, even farther north near the forty-seventh and forty-ninth parallels. After the reports on these various surveys were in, the Topographical Bureau found that it needed further data on a fourth route along the thirty-second parallel. The most southerly of the proposed routes, it would go through Texas, southern New Mexico and Arizona, and on to San Diego. It was particularly attractive to the southerners, including Secretary of War Jefferson Davis, and a bit later his favoring it over the other routes tended to discredit all of the work done by the Topographical Engineers. Perhaps the most likely route, considering all factors, if a railroad was to be built through the West prior to the Civil War, would have been that along the thirty-fifth parallel, which would have served the middle states as well as the south. At any rate, we are here concerned with Lieutenant Whipple's survey because it came directly through our area, and his recommendations as regards railroad construction were later rather closely followed when the actual planning of the thirty-fifth parallel route was underway.

Whipple was a competent and experienced explorer and engineer. He saw service on the Mexico-United States boundary survey and other important projects, and many years later was at the Battle of Bull Run as chief topographical engineer. Promotions followed. He made a balloon ascension over the Confederate lines, thus becoming a pioneer in American military aviation. He was mortally wounded at the Battle of Chancellorsville in 1863 and shortly before he died was promoted to major general. Camp Whipple, later Fort Whipple, at Prescott, was named in his honor.

In 1853, when he was named to head the thirty-fifth parallel exploration, he received far more applications for membership in his company than he had places. The party, when finally organized, included Dr. J. M. Bigelow, Ohio, physician and botanist; Jules Marcou, Massachusetts, geologist and mining engineer; Dr. C. B. R. Kennerly of Virginia, physician and naturalist; A. H. Campbell of Virginia, principal assistant railroad engineer; H. B. Mollhausen, a citizen of Germany, topographer and artist; Hugh Campbell of Texas, assistant astronomer; William White, Jr., Pennsylvania, assistant meteorological observer and surveyor; George G. Garner of Maryland, assistant astronomer and secretary; N. H. Hutton, District of Columbia, assistant engineer; John P. Sherburne, New Hampshire, assistant meteorological observer and surveyor; Thomas H. Parke of Pennsylvania, assistant astronomer and computer; Walter Jones, Jr., District of Columbia, assistant surveyor; in addition to Whipple. Whipple's company left Fort Smith July 14, 1853, and after four months reached Albuquerque, where they were joined by Lt. Joseph C. Ives and others who had come ahead to establish a cardinal astronomical point for the survey and make other observations.

At Albuquerque, Whipple employed Leroux, and Whipple was well aware that he was fortunate to have him in his company. Leroux had made a quick trip into Colorado to assist Captain Gunnison on part of his survey, then hurried back to New Mexico to keep his appointment with Whipple. While an expedition such as Whipple's could no doubt have found its own way along the thirty-fifth parallel, progress could be greatly speeded by an experienced and dependable guide. Leroux knew the water holes and springs; he knew the Indians who occupied the area; and of vast importance was that he knew the terrain. Whipple depended heavily on him, deferring again and again to his judgment, and was not disappointed.

After spending a month preparing for the trip, the party of about a hundred men set out on November 8 and headed westward. They passed Laguna and Zuñi, and soon crossed into Arizona. In due time they came to the valley of the Little Colorado, and in his journal Whipple made some favorable entries about the area which twenty-two years later were to play a material part in convincing about a hundred New Englanders that a plan to colonize the area was feasible. On December 3, Whipple wrote:

> With water for irrigation, such as in this region artesian wells might afford, the soil would yield abundantly. This valley is at the same altitude as that of Rio Grande at Albuquerque. Hence there is probably less rain

here than at Zuñi and crops would require artificial watering. The advantages of the country for grazing, however, cannot well be surpassed. With
two hundred mules, besides beef cattle and sheep, we were able to camp
where we please, without fear of want of grass. Formerly New Mexico,
according to Gregg, exported annually 500,000 sheep for mutton alone.
Twice that number could doubtless have been sheared. The wool, allow-
ing two pounds per fleece, and that it is worth forty cents per pound,
would be worth $800,000 and would pay every year to a railroad company
a handsome freight . . . there scarcely need be a limit to the number [of
sheep] that may graze upon this region. Nature has furnished grass, sufficient water, and a climate most favorable to this purpose.

December 5, he noted:

Taking an early start, the pack train following the guide and the
wagons as usual in rear, we proceeded about eleven miles over a slightly
undulating prairie, covered with gramma de china, to the bed of a river
coming from the north, to which we gave the title of Leroux's fork. . . .
[This is just west of present-day Holbrook, Arizona.] The valley of
[Colorado Chiquito] is very wide, reminding us forcible [sic] of the bottom land upon Rio Gila. Like that, the soil is good, and with irrigation
from the river, might be cultivated to advantage. . . . Camp is beautifully
situated in a cottonwood grove, upon the bank of Rio Colorado Chiquito.

And the next day, he added:

The valley of the river continues to be several miles in width, and the
soil, like that of Rio Gila, would doubtless be excellent for maize or cotton. The stream is now small, but rapid; its waters are fresh and clear,
and sufficient for the irrigation of a considerable portion of the low lands
that border it . . . great quantities of broken pottery have been found.

On December 7, Whipple wrote that they were moving toward the snowy
peaks of San Francisco which had been visible for several days. The party
camped from December 8 through December 12 at a site just east and a bit
north of present-day Winslow. On December 13, the wagons and most of the
party continued on down the river toward the crossing near present-day Leupp,
where Canyon Diablo joins the Chiquito. Whipple, with five companions and
Leroux, plus thirteen soldiers, rode on west. They rode all day, camped for supper, and then set out again by night, but after an hour and a half were forced by
a storm to stop for the night. They awoke to find that it had snowed a few

inches. Soon they were at the brink of a very steep canyon, which Whipple named Canyon Diablo. He estimated its depth at one hundred feet; actually, it is about two-hundred-fifty-feet deep. He noted that it could be bridged for a railroad. His reconnaissance party then rode northward along the canyon's rim to the crossing toward which the wagon train was bound from further east. At this point, Whipple noted that "the valley is here wide and thickly covered with good-sized alamos [cottonwoods]."

Here Whipple sent a messenger back to Lieutenant Ives instructing him to conduct the survey on down the river to the crossing. Whipple and his reconnaissance group then turned again westward toward the peaks of San Francisco Mountain. They went through the cinder hills, and saw a large herd of antelope. Resuming their journey the next day, December 17, they moved toward the southeast foot of the mountain. Whipple made various entries as to feasibility of railroad construction along the line he was taking, pointing out that the only obstacle so far met with was Canyon Diablo, and adding:

> To search for water, this being our third day without it, we turned the southwest point of San Francisco mountain and avoiding the valley on the left, kept upon the spurs close at its foot. After traveling about seven miles, we reached a permanent spring that poured from a hillside and was lost in the grassy plain below. In honor of the guide, it was called Leroux's spring. It is the same to which he conducted Captain Sitgreaves two years since, but by a different route, passing around the north and the western base of the mountain.

This spring is located above Fort Valley, seven or eight miles north of Flagstaff. On December 18, Whipple wrote:

> Two years ago when Leroux was here with Captain Sitgreaves, the hills were covered with savages, who occasioned them considerable annoyance by hostile demonstrations. But thus far, since leaving the Navajo country, we have not seen the fresh track of a wild Indian. The snow is untrodden except by beasts and birds, which afford plenty of game. Antelope, deer, hares, and turkeys are abundant; also a singular species of striped squirrel.

The party then turned back toward the train:

> Following the course of the open, meadow-like valley, irrigated by the waters of Leroux's spring, we passed southeast and east about four miles

and discovered a small stream flowing towards the great southern valley and forming probably the main branch of the Rio Verde. [This it was not, but almost certainly Rio de Flag which ran southeasterly down through the present site of the city. Leroux believed this small stream to be the headwaters of what he called Rio San Francisco, or the Verde.] It is fed by springs. From the San Francisco Springs [probably the springs near the Museum of Northern Arizona plus the others on down Rio de Flag including, possibly, what later was called Old Town Spring] we passed over a spur from the hills, and encamped near the southeast point of the mountains, having traveled about six miles.

The above constitutes the first record we have of an American setting foot in the immediate Flagstaff area.

Whipple's reconnaissance group then traveled on back to the Chiquito-Canyon Diablo crossing near present-day Leupp to rejoin the rest of the party. Ives had led the group back up stream a mile or so to a better camping spot. The entire party then moved westward, and on December 23, reached Cosnino Caves and Turkey Tanks, where it was decided to halt and rest the men and mules for a few days. Here they celebrated Christmas Eve. Mollhausen, the German draftsman and naturalist who was a member of the expedition, tells about it in interesting detail. A huge fire was built, speeches were made, and a jovial pail of toddy was prepared. Each plunged his tin mug into the pot and came back for more:

> We then sat down in a circle around the fire and smoked and drank again; toasts and jokes followed one another rapidly, hearts became lighter, the blood ran more swiftly in the veins, and all present joined in such a lively chorus as echoed far and wide through the ravines, and must have sadly interfered with the night's rest of the sleeping turkeys. A little way off the Mexicans were celebrating the festival in their own style with the gunpowder we had given them, and shot after shot, and then whole salvos, sounded through the still air, till the concussion shook down the snow from the branches. Of course they did not fail to accompany these demonstrations with the songs of their country, and at last they became so excited that they determined to have a bonfire.
>
> Into a close cedar thicket where the branches touched the ground, they threw firebrands; the pointed leaves or needles, rich in resin, caught fire immediately, the flames blazed over the tops of the trees, and sent millions of sparks into the sky. It was a most beautiful spectacle!

The Mexicans sang their songs; the Americans joined in with Negro melodies; there were fresh beakers and more songs, and soon, Mollhausen tells us, the mirth became faster and more furious. Two Mexicans who had been prisoners of the Navajos came before the group and performed a Navajo dance:

. Old Leroux, with a face considerably redder than the fire alone would have made it, smoked his pipe, and, as he looked on complacently, observed—"What a splendid opportunity it would be for the Indians to surprise us tonight!" But a surprise would not have been easy, for no customary precaution was neglected. . . . As the night advanced, the store in the mighty bowl drew to an end; the ranks around the fire began gradually to thin; one after another vanished behind the curtains of his tent and by the time the fire had burned low, deep stillness reigned over the camp.

Mollhausen adds that the next day was spent in perfect quiet, in thinking over past times and distant homes where the church bells were now summoning all to the religious celebration of the season:

While deep in the woods the woodpecker hammered away at the decaying trunks and the small birds seemed to warble their thanks for the lovely summer day [sic], and the shelter afforded them by the thick cedar bough from frost and snow, we looked up at the sublime summits of the San Francisco Mountains, and needed no temple made with hands wherein to worship our Creator.

The next day, December 26, they broke camp and set out for the southern point of the mountain. Mollhausen records:

As soon as we had the wooded hills behind us, and were following an opening towards the west, we saw the mountain displayed in all its beauty. We were about ten miles from the base of the principal one and could clearly distinguish its formation. Four great peaks, covered with dazzling snow, rose high above the rest, and though numerous summits thronged around and seemed connected with them—perhaps had grown out of them—that only tended to complete their unmistakably volcanic character.

They rode on, and the snow became deeper. They shot squirrels, saving perfect specimens for the collection, and eating the others. The second day's march brought them to a small brook "that contained, especially in the hollows, plenty of good water, and we watered our cattle here before we went on to look for Leroux Spring." They must have been at the springs along Rio de Flag in the immediate vicinity of the site of Flagstaff, because he says that the brook was one of the sources of the San Francisco River and, as stated above, we know Leroux believed the Rio de Flag to be headwaters of the stream which is today known as the Verde.

In the afternoon they reached a level ravine which soon led them into a spacious valley bounded on three sides by woods but on the north by the San Francisco Mountains, two of which, Mollhausen wrote, "rose like enormous Colossi before us, whilst the snowy peaks of the two others only peeped over from the west." After reaching Leroux Spring, the company made camp. They remained in the vicinity of the spring for about ten days while Whipple explored the surrounding area, seeking a route down the western slope that would be feasible for railroad construction. Mollhausen reports that the men would take blocks of lava and heat them in the campfires, then roll them into the tents for warmth.

On December 30, Whipple, with several companions and the guide Leroux, with a soldier escort, set out on a reconnaissance to the west. On January 1 they camped near New Year's Spring, described as a pool ten or twelve feet in diameter, with water twenty inches deep below a stratum of ice three inches thick. It was probably in Pittman Valley at the foot of Mt. Sitgreaves. They then followed the trail of Captain Sitgreaves, made two years before. They worked their way on west, circled back, and on January 6 were again at New Year's Spring, where they found the main body encamped. Whipple wrote:

> The peaks of San Francisco Mountain are again white with snow. A sheet of the same also tips the summits of Mt. Kendrick and Mt. Sitgreaves. But the valley westward, with the grassy slope and border of pine and cedar forests, forms a pleasing contrast to the wintry-looking region which we are now prepared to leave behind.

Whipple had found a pass south of the San Francisco Mountains. The party continued their explorations westward. After reaching the Colorado River, they turned north and crossed at the Needles, which Whipple named; then journeyed west to the Mohave River, and on to a point where they came to the old Mormon wagon road to San Bernardino. There, most of their labors were over. They reached Los Angeles on March 24, 1854, having been four and a half months on the way from Albuquerque. In his report, Whipple stated:

There is no doubt remaining that for the construction of a railway, the route we have passed over is not only practicable but in many respects eminently advantageous.

The desk soldiers at the Bureau of Western Explorations and Surveys, using Whipple's estimates, calculated the costs of his route at nearly $170 million, far higher than the others. In the final report, this was revised to around $94 million.

When the data was in from the several surveys for a transwest railroad route, it became evident that a number were feasible. Each had some advantages, but none, at least in the minds of a majority of Congress, was clearly and over-whelmingly superior. This coupled with increased pre-Civil War tensions and Secretary Davis' apparent preference for the most southerly route along the thirty-second parallel, led to a political deadlock, preventing agreement on con-struction anywhere. Out of this situation, along with growing demands from California and other areas for government assistance in improving communica-tions through the west, plus recognition by some foresighted leaders that further railroad reconnaissance should be carried on under any label or guise, came ap-proval of the Pacific Wagon Road Program. Here was something on which Congress could agree. The law authorized $50,000 for a road along the thirty-fifth parallel from Fort Defiance to the Colorado River.

John B. Floyd, who had succeeded Davis as Secretary of War, selected Edward Fitzgerald Beale to establish and improve this route. It was an excellent choice. Beale was born in 1822 in the District of Columbia. His father had won a Congressional Medal for gallantry in the battle on Lake Champlain in 1814. Young Beale attended the Naval Academy, graduating in 1842. He sailed on the frigate *Congress* under Commodore Stockton for California, but twenty days out, was sent back with important dispatches. Promotions followed. He was with the small body under Lieutenant Gillespie that joined Kearny's column just before the disastrous battle of San Pasqual in the Mexican War. He, with an Indian servant and his friend, Kit Carson, crept through enemy lines and car-ried the news of the party's plight to Stockton. Within two years, he made six journeys from ocean to ocean. In 1848 he brought the first authentic news to Washington of the gold discovery in California, along with some samples. In 1850 he was promoted to lieutenant. A few months later, he resigned and as-sumed the management of large California properties belonging to Stockton and W. H. Aspinwall. He was named superintendent of Indian Affairs for Cali-fornia and Nevada in 1853. He made a preliminary survey for a railroad through southern Colorado and Utah. He was named brigadier general of the California militia. At this point in his career, he was chosen for the wagon road survey which concerns us here. Following the survey, he was appointed surveyor general of California and Nevada. In 1876, he was named Minister to Austria-Hungary. Later, he was strongly but unsuccessfully supported for the post of Secretary of the Navy. But he is best known, of course, for his successful experiment in using camels as pack animals in the vast arid areas of the American West.

Beale was a man of superior intelligence, great physical stamina, great courage; he was educated, daring, curious. He carried good books with him on all his travels. His reports are lively, witty, and factual. He enjoyed good food and drink, and dispatched the best hunters in his parties to keep the larder supplied with game and fowl. Arriving at Mt. Floyd in western Coconino County, which he named in honor of the secretary, he drew out a flask of brandy, and with some mint gathered at a spring, prepared a julep in observance of the occasion. Arriving at Fort Defiance on a hot August day at the beginning of the survey, he was delighted to see the captain's servant uncover a tub of ice, while at the same time the captain produced a flask of red-eye. He was a strict disciplinarian and customarily got his party up at three or four in the morning and on the road by five. They would march until midmorning, have a short rest for food, and continue until late afternoon. There is a Beale Point in Grand Canyon, Beale's Springs in Mohave, and a Beale Mountain and Beale Spring west of Flagstaff. There is also a Beale Street and a commemorative monument to him and his camels in Kingman. Along with others we mention from time to time in this narrative, he is worthy of greater commemoration. Because Congress provided that the eastern terminus of this section of the road be Fort Defiance, Beale and a part of his group rode there, then back to Zuñi for the actual start, leaving that point August 31, 1857, and heading westward. The caravan consisted of a couple of dozen camels, eight wagons, and a couple of ambulances loaded with surveying equipment and Beale's personal effects, and drawn by mules; a band of three hundred fifty sheep and fifty-six men.

While exploring Death Valley with his close friend Kit Carson in the mid-1850s, Beale had had the idea of establishing a camel corps to facilitate transportation and communication in the arid wilds of the West. According to his biographer, Stephen Bonsal, he later told his son that while out with Carson, he had been reading Abbé Huc's *Travels in China and Tartary* by firelight. He suggested the plan to Carson, who was skeptical. Beale became enthused, and succeeded in convincing the Secretary of War that the plan should be given a trial.

An expedition was sent to the Middle East and eventually seventy-nine camels were purchased. They were shipped to Texas, and in due time placed in use on the wagon road survey.

While Beale's job was to survey a wagon road, he was fully aware that he was also performing a reconnaissance for possible railroad construction, and his comments include references to the feasibility of such a route. His caravan, camels and all, followed the general line of the thirty-fifth parallel. Near present-day Holbrook, Beale named a peak Mount Whipple in honor of his predecessor on the route. This was probably Woodruff Butte. Moving along the Little Colorado, the party ascended a long slope. Under date of September 4, Beale wrote:

> We came suddenly to its termination, from whence we enjoyed a magnificent view. The whole river [Little Colorado] for miles was spread out before us; and far in the distance, over the green tops of the cottonwood trees, San Francisco Mountain, rising apparently out of a vast plain, stood as a landmark which was to be our guide for many days.

The next day he noted that despite many long hours of travel, the view was unchanged, and that San Francisco Mountain looked no nearer. Following, he noted that the camels were so quiet and gave so little trouble that "sometimes we forget they are with us." Along the Little Colorado, he noted much beaver sign. They saw abundance of game, including elk, antelope, deer, and coyotes in large numbers. They also saw large Indian signal fires far to the south. Beale was greatly impressed by the abundant grass and noted that if the Indians were removed or kept in check, the country would immediately gain a large population. The party followed down Canyon Diablo to its junction with the Little Colorado in order to cross, as had its predecessors.

Moving on westward toward the mountain, Beale was greatly impressed by its beauty. They came to Turkey Tanks and what Beale called Cosnurio [Cosnino] Caves. Beale noted that the sharp lava rock had no effect on the feet of the camels. At breakfast camp on September 11 he noted that fresh Indian tracks had been seen, and that they were now at the base of San Francisco Mountain, "which looks down frowning upon us." A shower or two fell. His journal then reports:

> Leaving breakfast camp at 1, we travelled rapidly over a lovely country of open forest and mountain valley, which continually drew exclamations of delight and surprise from every member of the party. . . . As we

passed successive vales and glades, filled with verdant grass knee high to our mules, dotted with flowers, and the edges skirted by gigantic pines, they constantly gave vent to their delight in fervent ejaculations of praise.

Here they arrived at what must be the site of present-day Flagstaff:

> After going a few miles, we found it necessary to ascend a mesa, which was rough with stones on the sides, and with flat rock on top. Crossing this, we descended into a pretty valley, where we found some holes of water; but these not being sufficient, I sent out a man to explore, and in a quarter of an hour we heard his two shots, which was the signal agreed upon, announcing the discovery of running water. Following the direction, we crossed a low hill, and found the water rising from a marshy place, and running or rather trickling through high grass, down a short cañon not over a hundred yards in length or more than fifty in width. The sides of this cañon are some ten feet high, and of solid rock and should this become an emigrant trail, by throwing a dam across the lower end, water sufficient for ten thousand head of cattle may easily be obtained. . . . San Francisco spring we found nearly dry.
>
> Today we saw besides other game, such as bear, deer, and antelope, some partridges resembling in plumage and habits our own bird at home. . . . Some elegant squirrels were killed today, very large and beautifully furred, a silver grey with rich brown down the back. . . . Our camp is cheerful tonight, and brilliant with numerous fires. The night being cool, the mule guard and camp guard have built various fires around the spaces guarded, and these in addition to the mess fires, give a very pretty effect, especially as each fire has a dozen logs of the fattest pine upon it.

Here Beale complains that they had no guide because the one they hired in Albuquerque was "the most ignorant and irresolute old ass extant." He must often have wished he had been able to engage the services of Leroux. The next day he noted that the morning air was keen, but the sky bright and clear:

> Leaving our last night's camp, which I called Stacey's spring, after one of my party, and travelling west by south [north] seven miles, over a country of the same character as that of yesterday, we came to the beautiful valley [Fort Valley] of Leroux's spring, in which I encamped to water and graze the animals for two hours and a half. The road to the spring, from our last camp, is rough with loose stones of volcanic origin

for half the way; but the grass is luxuriant throughout as elsewhere. The timber still retains its large size and abundant quantity. I measured today a pine nineteen feet in circumference and of very great height.

Leroux's spring is one of transparent sparkling water, and bursts out of the side of the mountain and runs gurgling down for a quarter of a mile, where it loses itself in the valley. . . . We left Leroux's spring at 4 and a half P.M. and encamped at 7. Our road for the evening lay entirely through a heavy forest of pine, and was rough with loose stones. The grass, however, was as good as usual and very abundant. The road was over a rolling or rather undulating country.

The next day, September 13, they passed to the north of Mt. Sitgreaves, and between it and Mt. Kendrick. To the southward Bill Williams Mountain was in sight. They saw many antelope, and Beale described the area as one of the loveliest they had seen. Here they continued on westward, and in due time arrived at the Colorado River on October 18, 1857.

Beale had high praise for his camels, and in his report to Secretary Floyd said that they carried loads of seven hundred pounds with no difficulty, that they could live on food which the mules would not eat, and could travel for long periods without water. While mules and horses became tender-footed in rough country, not a single camel had such trouble, even in the sharp lava rock of the San Francisco Mountain area. He recommended extension of their use for official purposes throughout the West. A problem of handling camels was that most of the men who came in contact with them had no idea of how they were to be handled, and at least at the beginning, disliked them because they were strange. With the coming of the Civil War, the camel corps was discontinued, and in time the animals were either sold to private individuals or escaped to roam the wilds. Some of the wild ones were said to have been sighted as late as 1900.

Beale went on to "Los Angelos," where he remained until January 1, 1858, when he commenced the winter journey back across his own route. They departed from the Colorado River on January 24, the party consisting of twenty men and fourteen camels plus mules and wagons. In the early morning hours of January 27, they were attacked by Indians. They killed two, and lost a mule and had another seriously wounded. On January 31, he noted that they were moving well along and traveling in a straight line for San Francisco Mountain, "the snow-covered peak of which made an excellent guide. Our way today has been over a country of great beauty and exceedingly rich in grass and cedar timber." From time to time they found evidences of a trail which Beale took to be Whipple's. They traveled south of Mt. Sitgreaves and headed for Leroux Spring. On February 2, he noted that they had entered the noble forest of San Francisco:

> The old mountain covered with snow, relieved by the dark green patches of pine and the plain at its base, with its black forest of gigantic timber, presents a beautiful sight as the sun is setting this evening.

The next day they traveled through about a foot of snow. On February 3, he wrote that after traveling all day they came to their old camp at Leroux Spring. The next day, his birthday, they passed by San Francisco Spring and moved on around the south side of the mountain:

> Our camp is a beautiful one this evening; a clear space of three miles around and skirted with lofty pine trees. We amused ourselves as we strolled through the pine forest this morning, in shooting squirrels, which are abundant here and of a very beautiful species.

The next day they were at Cosnino Caves, and he noted the profusion of water at Turkey Tanks. They continued on toward the east without major incident, and arrived on February 22 at the end of the journey, having completed the return trip from the Colorado River in twenty-eight days. He reported:

> A year in the wilderness ended! During this time I have conducted my party from the Gulf of Mexico to the shores of the Pacific Ocean, and back again to the eastern terminus of the road, through a country for a great part entirely unknown, and inhabited by hostile Indians, without the loss of a man. I have tested the value of the camels, marked a new road to the Pacific, and travelled 4,000 miles without an accident.

In the letter of transmittal accompanying his report, Beale noted that he had covered the route between Fort Defiance and the Colorado in both late summer and midwinter without difficulty, and that he had found more or less water in summer, and more or less snow in winter:

> As far as the San Francisco mountain the road needs scarcely any other improvement than a few bridges. In one place alone a bridge at Canyon Diablo would save twenty-five or thirty-five miles travel, and on the whole road its length might be shortened by . . . one hundred miles. As this will inevitably become the great emigrant road to California, as well as that by which all stock from New Mexico will reach this place

[California] it is proper that the government should put it in such a condition as to relieve the emigrant and stock drivers of as many of the hardships . . . as possible. . . . I presume there can be no further questions as to the practicability of the country near the thirty-fifth parallel for a wagon road, since Aubry, Whipple and myself, have all traveled it successfully with wagons, neither of us in precisely the same line, and yet through very much the same country. . . . Starting with a drove of three hundred and fifty sheep, that number was increased by births upon the road, but not one was lost during the journey.

Nor had he lost a man nor had a single case of sickness:

Even in midwinter, and on the most elevated portions of the road [Flagstaff] not a tent was spread, the abundant fuel rendering them unnecessary for warmth and comfort.

Beale urged appropriation of $100,000 more to build bridges, shorten the road, and make other improvements. He was to repeat his journey in 1858–1859. But before we get to that we must deal with 1st Lt. Joseph Christmas Ives.

Ives was born in New York City in 1828, lived in New Haven, attended Yale College, and graduated from the U.S. Military Academy with the rank of second lieutenant. He soon transferred to the Topographical Engineers and served as assistant to Whipple in the 1853–1854 survey along the thirty-fifth parallel. In 1857–1858 he commanded an expedition sent to explore the Colorado River, which we will deal with shortly. His "Report Upon the Colorado River of the West" won him high acclaim, as did other writings and maps. In 1859–1860, he served as engineer and architect of the Washington National Monument, then became astronomer and surveyor for the commission surveying the boundary between California and other United States territories. Appointed captain in 1861, he declined, and joined the Southern cause. He became a captain of engineers in the Confederate Army, won promotions, and became aide-de-camp to President Jefferson Davis. He aided General Beauregard in the defense of Charleston.

Ives was well educated, intelligent, a keen observer, curious about the various Indian peoples and their customs, had an eye for beauty, and also had a sense of history. He was a very good writer, and his reports are justly acclaimed, even if at times he tends to be a bit literarily self-conscious.

Refusal of the Mormons led by Brigham Young to obey federal laws, caused the government to send an army into the Territory of Utah in 1857. The problems of supplying an effective armed force quickly became apparent. The War Department organized a number of expeditions to locate supply routes. Already engaged in a Colorado River reconnaissance was the party led by Lieutenant Ives. A shallow-draft steamboat, the U.S.S. *Explorer,* had been built in Philadelphia, dismantled, shipped to the mouth of the Colorado River and reassembled at Yuma. The *Explorer* steamed up the river to the mouth of Black Canyon, the last of the mighty gorges carved by the Colorado in its long course from the Rockies. Here Ives decided that he had reached the limit of navigation and divided his party, sending some members back down the river on the steamer and leading the rest overland to the eastward. His survey aboard the *Explorer,* however, convinced him that by using the river to transport supplies inland, the overland distances to such points as Salt Lake City, and Forts Defiance and Buchanan could be substantially reduced.

Ives's overland party included Dr. John S. Newberry, a surgeon, geologist, and naturalist; Prussian Baron F. W. von Egloffstein, topographer; and Baldwin Mollhausen, the German draftsman and artist, who had been with Ives on the Whipple expedition five years before. They also had a lieutenant and an escort of twenty soldiers. On March 23, 1858, Ives's party left the river in the vicinity of the Needles and moved along the general line of Beale's wagon road, roughed out only a few months before. They then approached Grand Canyon near Diamond Creek, and there Ives became the first recorded Anglo-American to trod foot in the bottom of the great chasm.

At their eightieth campsite near Bill Williams Mountain on April 25, Ives noted the profusion of game and pasturage. Moving toward San Francisco Mountain, he was as enthralled by the beauty of the area as Beale had been:

> To eyes that have been resting upon the deserted and ghastly region northward, this country appears like a paradise. We see it to the greatest advantage. The melting snows have converted it into a well-watered garden and covered it with green meadows and spring flowers.

Ives mentioned that the mules were in difficulty because of sore feet, due to the jagged volcanic rock. On April 30, he wrote:

> The route continued through an open park, dotted with flowery lawns and pretty copses, and then reached the edge of the great forest that surrounds the San Francisco mountain, and entered its sombre precincts. It was delightful to escape from the heat of the sun and travel through the cool underwood. Across the dark shady glades a glimpse would some-

times be caught of a bright tinted meadow glowing in the sunlight. Antelope and deer were constantly seen bounding by, stopping for a moment
to gaze at us, and then darting off into the obscure recesses of the
wood. . . .

Under the southwest base of the San Francisco peak we camped at a
spring, known to be permanent. It is in a sheltered nook almost buried in
the side of the impending mountain. There is abundant grazing. The
water is cold and delicious. The surrounding forest furnishes shade in
summer and material for warmth in winter, and at all seasons of the year
the place doubtless affords an excellent camp. [This was no doubt at
Leroux Spring.]

The next day a roaring gale swept the area with snow and sleet, and Ives
noted:

Dense and black masses of clouds are still drifting past the San Francisco Mountain summit and the surrounding slopes, and icy cold blasts
reach us at intervals from that quarter.

On May 2, they proceeded with relief toward the distant Little Colorado,
which Ives refers to by the very old Spanish name of Flax River. He recorded
that the mules were in very bad condition. Here the party divided, one group
headed by the lieutenant going on eastward toward Fort Defiance with the sore-
footed mules, and Ives and his staff northeastward to the Hopi villages. Here
they enjoyed Hopi hospitality, including a first taste of piki bread, the tissue-
thin bread which is a staple of Hopi diet. The Hopis in turn enjoyed a taste of
wheat bread and molasses.

Ives arrived at Fort Defiance on May 23, having been on the road about sixty
days. The scientific contributions of this expedition were important; each member of the party was an expert in his field. The drawings and maps are remarkable, and Newberry's geological reports were a major step in the study of the
area. Historian William Goetzmann states that Newberry was the first geologist to observe the Grand Canyon and its subsidiary canyons, "and though the
expedition moved so rapidly that he had to run to pick up specimens, still he
was able to trace out a typical stratigraphic column that went deep into the
earth and far back into the ages." Egloffstein, the topographer, had devised a
new method of shading his maps, a method so successful that it was used by
many topographers thereafter.

Now we return to Beale, that indefatigable, inveterate explorer and frontiersman. While Congress failed to appropriate funds for further improvement

of the wagon road along the thirty-fifth parallel to California, the Army Appropriations Act of 1858 included $50,000 to construct bridges and improve the road from Fort Smith, Arkansas, to Albuquerque, and $100,000 to complete the road from Albuquerque on westward along the thirty-fifth parallel.

Beale was at Fort Smith in mid-October organizing the party and arranging for the work to be done from that point to Albuquerque. He placed an assistant in charge of the bridge work east of Albuquerque. He was in Albuquerque by March 3, 1859, to organize the rest of his expedition. Among other things he purchased two hundred fifty head of sheep to be driven along, some to supplement the larder, the others to be taken on through to California. On March 29 the party headed westward from Zuñi. Minor changes were made in the route. At the Little Colorado his hunters bagged four beaver and party members caught some fish. On April 4, he noted that "San Francisco [mountain] with its frosty head, in sight this morning . . ." On April 12, he wrote:

> We are now at the foot of the San Francisco mountain, and a light snow is falling, which melts almost as rapidly as it falls. Travelled seven miles and encamped in some cedars by the roadside. We are glad once more to see the green grass.

The next day they traveled to Cosnino Caves and stopped at noon and found a stream of water filling the whole bed of the creek. The day following, April 14, they worked removing large rocks from the road and grading it, and in the evening rode on six miles and ascended a rocky mesa, changing the line of the road a bit. This must have placed them in the immediate Flagstaff area. Beale noted that water holes which they had dug the previous year were full, and that his hunter had killed an antelope.

On April 15, continuing the road work, they moved on and arrived at Leroux Spring after traveling seven miles. Beale recorded:

> The weather delightful; no one could pass through this country without being struck with its picturesque and beautiful scenery, its rich soil, and its noble forests of timber; the view from our camp of this morning is unsurpassed in the world; the soil is rich black loam, the grass, gramma and bunch equally mixed, and the timber, pine of the finest quality, and greatest size; water at this season we find everywhere, nor is there at any time any lack of it at this place.

On April 16, the party traveled westward four miles; the next day, they rode on five or six miles and came upon a spring. They camped to develop it, and

Beale again wrote about the beauty of the area; "with deer and antelope bounding over its green turf . . . the magnificent San Francisco mountain, capped with
eternal snow, renders the landscape perfect; the [hunter] killed an antelope."
They were probably in Government Prairie.

On April 18 occurred a memorable event. Members of the party were busy
digging out a basin for the spring when two men were seen approaching from
the west on camels, whom Beale recognized as S. A. Bishop, and the camel
driver, AliHadji (later well known in Arizona as "Hi Jolly"), who had accompanied Beale on the 1857–1858 trip. Beale had sent a man ahead to California
via El Paso with instructions to have a camel caravan with supplies meet the
Beale party when they arrived at the Colorado River. They were to have an
escort of seven hundred soldiers. But when it became evident that it would take
too long for the escort to arrive, Bishop had outfitted an expedition of forty men
and came on. They were met by a force of a thousand Mohaves and a battle
ensued. Bishop's group routed the Indians and remained in their village a few
days, defying them. He sent twenty men back, left six at the river, and with the
remaining fourteen came on to meet Beale. Two days out he was attacked by
two hundred Mohave warriors, anxious, Beale says, to wipe out their previous
defeat. "These," Beale wrote, "with his small party many of whom were beard-
less boys, but *frontiersmen,* he routed, killing four at the first fire." As Bishop
approached the river on his way to meet Beale, four men who had been making
fruitless attempts for nearly a year to get mail over the road joined him, then
fled when they got a look at the band of warriors, leaving the mail with Bishop's
party. The mail was placed on a camel and brought along to the meeting in
Government Prairie west of San Francisco Mountain. Here it was taken back
west again, again on camelback. "Thus the first mail of the thirty-fifth parallel
was brought on my camels both ways," Beale wrote.

On April 28, Beale recorded that his party was forty miles from the Colorado
River and that the Indians had shot one of his mules and stolen another. "It will
be curious if I do not find some way of circumventing these fellows before
morning," he wrote, adding that arrows had narrowly missed one of the horse
guards.

And on April 29, he reported:

We played a very good joke on the Indians last evening, which
brought our accounts quite square with them; about sun down after they
had killed the mule and stolen the one mentioned yesterday, I caused the
mules to be hitched up, and camp made ready in as much apparent con-

fusion as possible, knowing the devils were watching every move we made, it was managed that we got off at night, so that they could not see the men we left behind concealed in the rocks, after going a few miles as if we had been frightened off, and were moving to seek open ground, we encamped and built our fires; all this must have amused Mr. Indian vastly. . . . The men left lay in the rocks until daylight when, just as we had expected, our red brothers came down to see the mule they had killed, and what damage beside they done us, when our party fell upon them and killed four, returning to camp before it was ready to start in the morning, bringing bow, arrows, and scalps as vouchers; it was a good practical joke—a merrie jeste of ye white man and ye Indian.

The party moved on and in due time were met by three or four white men who informed Beale that the military escort had made a treaty with the Indians and things were more peaceable along the river. On May 4, they swam their mules across the river and started for the settlements for provisions for the return trip.

On July 2, they started eastward again. Two weeks later, the party again arrived at Leroux Spring, and here F. C. Engle, a member of the party, wrote:

> Leroux Spring, which rises in San Francisco mountain, flows into a valley in its western side; its stream conducted by a trench down to one of the stations of the mail company; in the trench, which is about 500 yards in length, several deep holes have been dug and walled around; the water of the spring is as clear as crystal, pure and cold; throughout the year it yields an unfailing supply.

So we learn that a mail company had a station or camping spot in the vicinity, and that some effort had been expended developing a reliable source of water for stock below Leroux Spring in what we now know as Fort Valley. On July 18, Engle wrote:

> At 7 A.M. our train consisting of three light wagons left Leroux Spring. We left at the spring two heavy wagons and an ambulance in charge of Mr. Bishop whose . . . party . . . is to work upon some portions of the road between Leroux Spring and the Colorado River. . . . Passing out of the valley we travelled about two miles through a belt of timber . . . our trail was marked on the trees by three "blazes." . . . Leaving the timber we entered the valley of "San Francisco Spring" [probably at the present-day site of the Museum of Northern Arizona and the Thomas McMillan

residence]. In this valley the grass was luxuriant and water abundant. There is a beautiful spring about midway, to the left, another about two hundred yards further on, on the opposite side. When abreast of "San Francisco Spring" we left the main road and struck off to the right. Passing the spring, which were [*sic*] full of excellent water, we crossed the valley and encamped for breakfast. Scarcely had we reached the spot [probably the present-day site of Flagstaff] when a herd of antelope bounded across the plain . . . our hunter . . . started in pursuit and returned in a short time with a noble buck. For a while here the rain poured down in torrents.

The party then located a boat which had been hidden by the mail company, then marched on to Turkey Tanks–Cosnino Caves, and camped. By July 29 they were in Albuquerque, having covered the entire distance in only one hundred eight hours of marching time, which is not only a commentary on the stamina and skill of Beale and his companions, but graphic evidence of the excellence of the route. In his letter of transmittal to Secretary Floyd accompanying his report, Beale wrote:

> Without intending to draw invidious comparisons between the various routes from our western border to the Pacific Ocean in favor of that by the 35th parallel, I think I can, with safety, say that none other offers the same facilities for either wagon or railroad.
>
> It is the shortest, the best timbered, the best grassed, the best watered, and certainly, in point of grade, better than any other line between the two oceans with which I am acquainted.

Beale's expeditions were a major part of the groundwork which resulted, in 1866, in the chartering of the Atlantic & Pacific Railroad. In due time the line was built, and its routing along the south slope of San Francisco Mountain resulted in the founding of the community which today we know as Flagstaff. Beale's fast, final trip over the wagon road in the summer of 1859 brought to a close the series of explorations, reconnaissances, surveys, and road building projects along the thirty-fifth parallel under government auspices. The government, particularly Congress, very soon had something else more pressing to think about; secession of the Southern States, and then the beginning of the bloody, fratricidal Civil War.

No doubt during the years following Beale's last expedition, scores, perhaps hundreds, of emigrants, travelers, mail and dispatch carriers, traders, stockmen, soldiers, and others, rode or drove along the Beale wagon road. We know from the *Arizona Champion's* files, for example, that a Samuel C. Miller, later a leading citizen of Prescott, camped on the site of what is now Flagstaff with a party from California in the summer of 1861. And we know from the Prescott *Miner* that the U.S. Post Office Department moved in November 1864 to set up a mail route between Albuquerque and Prescott, with twelve relay stations, one of which was at Leroux Spring. This once-a-week service, incidentally, apparently started early in 1865, but was soon abandoned. For in May 1866, the *Miner* reported that "the route from here to Albuquerque was abandoned some months since, after a few irregular trips." Heavy snows and hostile Indians were given as the cause, but the newspaper also indicated that mismanagement played a part.

Another traveler through the area who left a record was John Marion, publisher of the *Arizona Miner,* who accompanied Gen. George Stoneman on an inspection tour of military posts in the territory in the fall of 1870. In his journal for September 2, he noted:

> Got an early start as usual. Traveled across Leroux valley, in which we found plenty of excellent water, and an immense hole in the ground—an extinct crater—which, no doubt, in times past, vomited forth huge streams of molten lava. After leaving the valley, our route led around the western base of the San Francisco Mountain, through the largest, straightest kind of pine timber. It was late in the afternoon when we arrived at Antelope Springs on the northeast side of San Francisco Mountain, and encamped near an old abandoned stage station.

Marion's statement that Antelope Spring was on the northeast side of the mountain, it may be noted, is incorrect. He may have gone around to the north, but the Beale wagon road, which he presumably followed, is on the south side.

While after Beale's final trip there were no more officially sponsored and recorded expeditions, there were some other events during the 1860s of importance to Arizona and to our San Francisco Mountain area.

First, on February 20, 1863, Congress passed the Arizona Territorial Bill which became law February 24.

Second, on December 29, 1863, the new territorial government was established within the bounds of Arizona.

Third, on July 27, 1866, the Atlantic & Pacific Railroad was chartered by Congress to build a line westward to the Pacific.

And in 1867–1868, General Palmer, thirty-one-year-old Union war veteran and railroad executive, would conduct actual construction surveys along the route.

John A. Gurley had been appointed governor of the new territory but died soon after his appointment, and was succeeded by John N. Goodwin, who set out with his official party to formally establish the territorial government. A number of the new territory's officials entered Arizona through Yuma. The governor, however, with the secretary of state, chief justice, associate justices, district attorney, surveyor general, and postmaster, assembled at Fort Leavenworth for the trip westward. They set out on September 26, accompanied by three companies of soldiers. The story of their journey is interesting and has been told many times. The caravan moved across the line into Arizona, and on December 29, the ceremony of organizing the government of the new territory was held at Navajo Springs. They left the next morning, and moved on westward along the Beale road. On New Year's Eve they camped in a grove of cottonwoods on the Little Colorado River. On January 10 they crossed around the mouth of Canyon Diablo, as had so many of their predecessors moving along this route. In the distance they could see San Francisco Mountain, the higher reaches snow-covered. They camped near Cosnino Caves, as had Sitgreaves, Whipple, Beale, and others. Then they came to the site of present-day Flagstaff. They visited San Francisco Spring and camped for two days. Associate Justice Joseph P. Allyn entered in his journal the comment that the mountain was the most beautiful he had ever seen.

The group of officials then turned southwestward and traveled to Volunteer Spring, which today is within the boundary of Navajo Army Depot, a dozen miles west of Flagstaff. They passed the southern base of Bill Williams Mountain, reporting deer and turkey, and bagging two of the birds. On a tree they found a note for the commander of their escort, signed by a Lieutenant Pomeroy, stating that they should be watchful for hostile Indians. They moved on and in due time came to an old camp used by the troops. Probably this was Camp Pomeroy. Ray Brandes tells us that in November 1863, General Carlton set up a temporary camp in Coconino County. It was along the trail between Bill Williams Mountain and Chino Valley and the only one ever established in what is now Coconino in the days of the Indian wars. This camp was named after Pomeroy and consisted of a small guard and a mule team. Brandes tells us that they were soon run off by Indians. This preceded establishment of Camp Clark (1863) which in turn preceded establishment of Fort Whipple (1864). The governor's party arrived at Whipple January 22, 1864, and immediately set up in business.

The railroader and engineer who was to survey the thirty-fifth parallel route in 1867–1868 was William Jackson Palmer, born in 1836 of Quaker parents. At seventeen, he worked as rodman on a railroad. He then traveled in England, and then served as secretary and treasurer of a coal company, from which he moved to the Pennsylvania Railroad as private secretary to J. Edgar Thomson, president. When the Civil War came, he organized a Pennsylvania cavalry company and became its captain, and a year later became a colonel. By the end of the war he held rank of brevet brigadier-general. Years later, in 1894, he received the Congressional Medal of Honor for conspicuous bravery under fire.

Following the war, Palmer became treasurer of the eastern division of the Union Pacific, which for a time became the Kansas Pacific. He was in charge of surveys to extend the railroad's lines through the West along either the thirty-second or thirty-fifth parallels, and his survey through northern Arizona became the route followed by the Atlantic & Pacific, which later became the Santa Fe. After 1870, Palmer was no longer associated with the Kansas Pacific, becoming eventually involved in the Rio Grande Western in Colorado which he sold in 1901. He died near Colorado Springs in 1909.

In his surveys of the two routes through Arizona, Palmer almost from the beginning was convinced that the route along the thirty-fifth parallel was most feasible. In the letter of transmittal with his report, he declared:

> The results along the 35th parallel proved to be of such a favorable character that, with its great advantage in distance and accessibility from nearly every section of the Union to start with, its claims have been found decidedly to out weigh those of the extreme southern line.

Palmer pointed out that the distance from Kansas City to San Francisco via the thirty-fifth parallel route was two hundred sixty-three miles shorter than by the thirty-second parallel, and from Kansas City to San Diego was one hundred eight miles shorter than by the other route. He also noted that the thirty-fifth parallel route, that of Beale's wagon road, was superior because of better grades, freedom from hostile Indians, supplies of timber, ballast, and water. He considered alternate routings around the San Francisco Mountain, one running around to the north, the other to the south, where the railroad was eventually built.

The crossing of the summit near where Flagstaff stands today he named Tonto Pass, which he described as immediately south of a high extinct volcano, known as San Francisco Mountain, but whose name, for distinction, he changed to Mt. Agassiz.

Our examinations proved that the waters of Leroux, Antelope, and San Francisco Springs, here-to-fore considered among the sources of the Verde, are entirely cut off from any outlet in that direction, and that they sink in the wet season in a basin 7 miles northeast of Antelope Springs, where the course of their drainage is eastward towards the Little Colorado.

Palmer was enthusiastic about the climate in the area:

The people of the eastern half of our continent have scarcely a conception of the physical pleasure of mere existence in the pure air and fine weather of this elevated northern plateau. For healthfulness, it is conceded to have no superior. In our engineer parties, numbering, with attaches, some 150 young men, and exposed to numberous [sic] hardships, there was not either going or returning, a single case of real sickness, and all came home much heartier and more robust than when they started. This covered a winter in the mountain regions of Arizona.

His enthusiasm mounted as he discussed agricultural resources:

In crossing the Mogollon Range, we have the finest country met with, perhaps, on our entire route. It is the famous San Francisco Mountain country, magnificently timbered, well watered, and covered winter and summer with the most nutritious gramma grass. Its soil . . . will produce, without irrigation, wheat, barley, oats and potatoes, in the heaviest crops. The summit and slopes of this range are dotted everywhere with beautiful little grassy parks, openings in the virgin forest of gigantic pines which cover the mountain.

Palmer then quoted Dr. C. C. Parry, geologist and naturalist of the survey, who also raved about the invigorating atmosphere, grassy parks and numerous springs. Palmer added:

The most attractive place of summer resort on the line of the road will be met with here on Mt. Agassiz. It has every attraction; health, scenery, sky, water, elevation, climate, and proximity to the greatest natural curiosity known on this continent—the "Grand Canon" of the Colorado River, from which it is distant some 40 or 50 miles.

He concluded his report with a plea for federal assistance in construction of the thirty-fifth parallel line and, with other arguments, pointed out that its availability would greatly reduce the need for soldiers to keep the Indians under control, as fewer men could be moved back and forth by rail to points where they were needed at much reduced cost.

Construction of the western railroads was delayed by the depression of the early 1870s. The historian Samuel Eliot Morison tells us that "stock speculation, over-rapid expansion of the agricultural West, and a world-wide drop in prices brought on the panic of 1873 and a depression which lasted three years." One result of unemployment and hard times in New England was that about one hundred young men, most of them from Boston, decided to better themselves by journeying far out west to northern Arizona and establishing a colony. They were to come in two groups in 1876 and we will deal with them here as the Boston parties.

# CHAPTER III

# The Boston Parties

UNDOUBTEDLY THE MOST OFTEN REPEATED, most widely circulated story relating to the Flagstaff community's beginnings has to do with the purported raising of the flag by the Boston Party here in the wilderness on July 4, 1876, in observance of the nation's Centennial. Research into the origins of this story brings to light much interesting data, perhaps the most interesting and surprising being that a townsite was laid out during the early summer of 1876, drawings were held for building lots, corner posts were erected, at least some beginnings were made toward erection of cabins, officials were elected to direct the community's affairs, and finally, a name was chosen for the new town—and it wasn't Flagstaff!

Our story starts in Boston in 1873, when a large and elaborately illustrated book appeared under the authorship of Samuel Woodworth Cozzens, *The Marvellous Country; or Three Years in Arizona and New Mexico, The Apaches' Home.* The subtitle of this extraordinary book is quite extraordinary, too: "Comprising a Description of This Wonderful Country, Its Immense Mineral Wealth, Its Magnificent Mountain Scenery, the Ruins of Ancient Towns and Cities Found Therein, With a Complete History of the Apache Tribe, and a Description of the Author's Guide, Cochise, the Great Apache War Chief, the Whole Interspersed with Strange Events and Adventures." That's quite a menu, and the author strives "marvellously" to fulfill its promise.

Cozzens lived for a time in southern Arizona in the late 1850s and early 1860s. He was appointed judge of the First Judicial District at Tucson on April 5, 1860, by L. S. Owings, governor of the provisional government of the Territory of Arizona. On his way back East, Cozzens visited northwestern New Mexico as far west as the Zuñi villages. There is no evidence that he ever visited northern Arizona. *The Marvellous Country* recounts dramatic and hair-raising adventures, one of the most fascinating being his account of going off into the Apache country with Cochise as sole companion, being introduced to the other famed Apache, Mangus Colorado, by Cochise; and his various narrow escapes from torture and death. There are several passages in the book dealing with our area. From the top of a mountain near Zuñi Cozzens describes the view as follows:

> Farther to the westward, the San Francisco peak stood like a mighty giant vigilantly guarding the priceless treasures concealed within its bosom; while its aerial summit like a great white plume, seemed gracefully suspended in the blue ether of heaven's bright dome, and offering a most grateful relief to the eye while tracing the enormous ravines, steep mesas, deep canons, volcanic peaks, arid deserts, and overthrown rocks on the vast country lying to the westward, and stretching into such boundless immensity of space that one utterly failed to comprehend its magnitude, while it required but little stretch of the imagination to fancy that beneath the far-distant horizon could be seen the bright, sparkling waters of the blue Pacific, as they gently kissed its sandy beach of a thousand miles away.

Well! That's quite a lot to see from Zuñi! And hear this!

> Occasionally a lovely green valley could be seen peeping out from its yellowish-gray surroundings, like a beautiful emerald in a setting of topaz, or resembling an oasis on the white, sparkling sand of the desert.

To us today, this is pure fantasy; but the valley of the Little Colorado did present a more inviting view a century ago than now; most of the cottonwoods and willows which lined its banks are gone, and so is the high grass which covered much of the area before it was destroyed by overgrazing in the 1880s and 1890s. But it never was as Cozzens described it—from a hundred miles away!

Let us continue with Cozzens. While he was with the Zuñis, he said they met a group of Moquis (Hopis) who had found a starving and nearly dead American along the trail; they were bringing him to Zuñi as the nearest place of assistance. He was Parley Stewart, a Missourian

> ... who had left his home two months before for the purpose of going to Los Angeles, California, by the thirty-fifth parallel route. Near Los Angeles he had a son living, whose wife and child were accompanying him, in addition to which his own wife and six children the youngest being a girl of thirteen years of age, made up the party, in all ten persons; four grown men and six women and children ... they had passed to the south

of what they supposed to be the Moquis country, and a couple of days journey beyond it, without seeing any signs of hostile Indians, when upon coming to a beautiful valley abounding in fine grass, through which ran a stream of clear, beautiful water, they determined to halt for a few days, for the purpose of giving their weary animals a little much-needed rest.

Here follows the most significant passage, as far as our story of the Boston parties is concerned:

From Mr. Stewart's description of the place, the cacique, as well as the Moquis, thought it was without doubt upon one of the tributaries of the Colorado, perhaps upon the Colorado Chiquito [Little Colorado] itself, for he described the valley as very large, and the pasturage as fine; magnificent great oaks were scattered throughout, and the banks of the stream, the water of which was clear and very cold, were entirely free from underbrush, yet skirted by trees of great size, which afforded a most refreshing shade, while the base of the rough and rugged mountains that formed the setting of this jewel in the desert, seemed to be covered with a fine growth of pine, cedar, and fir trees. After toiling for months over the hot, dry and dusty road across the plains, exposed to the burning heat of a solstitial sun, is it any wonder that this quiet, beautiful valley, with its grateful shade, luxuriant herbage, and cool water, seemed to be to the tired and travel-worn wayfarers a little Eden which no serpent had yet intruded?

Is it any wonder that they should determine to pause here for a while, and enjoy the beauties with which Nature's hand so lavishly bestowed her good gifts?

The Stewart party failed to keep watch at night, were attacked by a band of Indians, and the only survivor of the massacre was Parley himself, who then wandered about starving until he was rescued by the Hopis. The details of this story are blood-curdling, but more important to our narrative is the impression Cozzens gave about the valley of the Colorado Chiquito. He certainly made it easy to believe that a garden of Eden existed there; remember what he claimed he saw from the mountain near Zuñi shortly before!

Cozzens' book containing these fanciful descriptions of a fertile valley in the Little Colorado country, was well received in New England, and soon he was in demand as a speaker. New Englanders found it inviting to believe that far, far away in northern Arizona lay a beautiful, fertile, well-watered valley suitable for settlement. Thousands of men were out of work as a result of the great panic of 1873; many stories were in circulation regarding quickly made fortunes in the gold fields and along the lines of the railroads then under construction, and the Arizona frontier was relatively quiet for the first time in decades, as General Crook and his cavalrymen and Indian scouts had pretty well tamed the dread Apaches. Arizona seemed an attractive goal for many young New Englanders— and here was Judge Cozzens, introduced and endorsed by a number of responsible citizens, writing and telling about The Marvellous Country way out there along the thirty-fifth parallel in northern Arizona.

By late summer 1875, the Arizona Colonization Company was formed in Boston, with Cozzens as president, James M. Piper, secretary, and S. C. Hunt, treasurer. Meetings were held to attract and enroll young men. Paid notices were inserted in the newspapers, and news reports regarding the meetings were published. A check of the files of the Boston *Herald* between October 1 and December 26, 1875, brings to light at least nineteen advertisements or articles regarding the movement, an average of one every four or five days. Typical of these notices is the following which appeared October 12:

ARIZONA!!

The next regular meeting under the auspices of the

Arizona Colonization Company

will be held at

JOHN A. ANDREW HALL,

TUESDAY EVENING, Oct. 12 at 8 o'clock, when full information will be given in regard to the intentions of the Company; the prospects for mechanics, miners and farmers who wish to improve their present condition; the resources of Arizona; and the means of getting there; Judge S. W. Cozzens and other gentlemen acquainted with this region will be present.

J. M. PIPER, Sec. A.C.C.

An admission fee of ten cents to pay hall rent was usually charged.

A notice appearing in the same newspaper a week later stated that Hon. A. J. Bailey would preside, and that addresses would be made by Judge Cozzens, Capt. George H. Pettis, late of the First California Infantry, for five years stationed in Arizona, "and several others." A notice appearing a few days later stated that Alderman Robert L. Spear of Somerville would preside, that Captain Pettis would again be on the program, and that "Maj. E. W. Griggs and other

gentlemen well informed on the subject of Arizona, its immense mineral resources, its delightful climate, fertile valleys, etc.," would speak. Obviously the
movement was given help by the association of various prominent citizens with
its leaders.

It appears that everyone concerned was acting with good intentions, believing that conditions in northern Arizona were as projected by the enthusiastic
but poorly informed Cozzens. It also seems clear that everyone connected with
the movement believed that someone else actually had firsthand knowledge of
the area, and that none of them had. Cozzens, Piper, Hunt, Major Griggs, and
others who led the movement, were later accused of staging an elaborate money-
making fraud. But they seem to have been simply victims of their own enthusiasm and failure to secure reliable data about the area; and certainly, they made
no money.

As the movement attracted adherents, interest became widespread throughout New England. Probably the clincher came when the Boston *Daily Globe*
editorially endorsed the men heading the project:

> We have been earnestly asked by many attracted to [the proposed es-
> tablishment of a New England colony in Arizona] to look into it and
> judge of its merits. This we have done to some extent, and while we do
> not wish to be understood as endorsing any private enterprise, we do not
> hesitate to say that we have every confidence in the gentlemen promi-
> nent in this and believe that their statements can be implicitly relied on.
> . . . These gentlemen, we believe, mean business, mean to go out as colo-
> nists themselves, are not speculators, but earnest, well-meaning men who
> desire to build up a new place and open up new resources for the mutual
> good of themselves and their companions.
>
> Their scheme contemplates the establishment of a township in a
> valley which they know, and which we have every reason to believe,
> from the examination of government reports, to be eminently desirable.
> It is the valley of the Rio Colorado Chiquito, near San Francisco Moun-
> tain. Of this region Whipple, in his report to the government of his sur-
> vey of the 35th parallel railroad route, says, "where were extensive forests
> abounding with game, wide grass valleys affording pasturage to innum-
> erable herds of deer, crystal brooks alive with trout, their fertile banks
> well cultivated and now lined with ash and timber. That this solitude has
> not always been unbroken by man was shown by the numerous ruins of
> stone houses and fortifications that covered the heights surrounding."

That this civilization is not there now is due to the ravages of the blood-thirsty Apaches, who within the last two years, have been completely sub-jugated and driven into reservations by the United States troops under General Crook. And so it is that this region is again open to settlement, and a new civilization, and that it is rapidly being occupied we are abun-dantly satisfied by examination of late files of Arizona papers. From these papers we also obtain more conclusive evidence that the almost uni-versal belief in the wealth of Arizona's mineral resources, had been under, rather than over, estimated.

The projected region selected for this colony is on the line of a pro-jected railway, which will, of course, follow civilization; is in the path of Whipple's survey, and is marked "wood, water, and grass abundant"; the Colorado Chiquito is a permanent river; the territory is on the same parallel as the northern part of South Carolina, is about 5,000 feet above the level of the sea; and the climate is represented to be mild and delight-ful. Of its advantages for grazing Whipple says in his report: "This sec-tion cannot be surpassed. With two hundred mules, besides beef cattle and sheep, we were able to camp where we pleased without fear for the want of grass. Nature has furnished grass, sufficient water, and a climate most favorable to this purpose." This much we feel justified in saying for the projectors of the scheme, and the scheme itself.

In its issue of Monday, October 25, 1875, the Boston *Daily Globe* published a letter from an interested citizen asking pertinent questions about the proposed colonization project. The questions were handed to a reporter, who took them to "one of the gentlemen prominent in the Arizona movement," and "found him ready to answer any and all questions that could be asked, supporting his replies by references to government reports, late files of Arizona papers, maps, and whatever testimony of travelers or others he had been able to accumulate." A few of these responses will suffice to illustrate the optimistic mood of the project's sponsors:

*How many miles from the end of the railroad to the proposed location?*

It needs little spirit of prophesy to state that in a very few years a rail-road will be at our very doors, and the whistle of the locomotive will startle the echoes of the beautiful valley of the Rio Colorado Chiquito. At present we state our distance from the railroad at six hundred miles.

*How long will it take to go there from New England?*

About thirty days as we propose to go, that is, by "prairie schooner," taking with us supplies for sixty days after arrival.

*If, as I suppose, the colony intends to start this fall, will they not suffer from cold, until suitable shelter can be provided?*

At the altitude in this region, situated 5,000 feet above the level of the sea, the nights are cool, throughout the year, the days being sometimes quite warm, but so clear is the atmosphere that one suffers much less oppression from heat than here. This is the testimony from all sources.

*What facilities will there be for erecting houses?*

The same as in any other newly opened country plentifully supplied with timber. . . . Let me read from Whipple's report, page 46: "The banks of the Chiquito are skirted with cottonwood trees. Leaving the valley we immediately enter upon small cedars, which increase in size and number, until reaching the base of the San Francisco mountain they intermingle with, and finally give place to, immense forests of stately pines and Douglas spruce. No finer timber grows in the interior of our continent. For 130 miles there is a constant succession of these forests."

*At what season do they plant in that section?*

As the Indians in this latitude have always raised two crops in the year, it will be seen that the best time for planting seeds will be a question for farmers to settle on the spot. Some planting will be done immediately upon the arrival of the colony. Whipple says, page 17, "We traversed this region in winter, but the climate was that of spring, and vegetation was already rapidly advancing."

*How far is it to the nearest white settlement?*

About sixty miles from Randalville, a settlement of thirty families made last spring. About 130 miles from Prescott. No danger from poor lo.*

*What are the chances for finding mineral deposits in the immediate vicinity?*

The question surprises me. No man who reads need ask it. History for 300 years is full of marvellous stories in regard to the mineral wealth of Arizona . . . look at this government mineral map; you will find more gold and silver indicated than in any other state or territory. Why shouldn't it be rich? It lies between the known wealth of Nevada and the

*Satirical reference to Alexander Pope's line, "Lo, the poor Indian! whose untutor'd mind. . . ."

historic mines of Mexico in the same ranges of mountains. . . . General
X. E. Chamberlain states to us, last week, that he had often seen kettles in
use by the Indians for cooking, which were hammered out of virgin
silver. Late Arizona papers are full of applications for patents to new
mines, and accounts of discoveries of new leads and deposits. None but
the most skeptical can hesitate for a moment to believe such accumulated
testimony.

*Do you gentlemen propose to go with your colony?*
Certainly sir . . . otherwise how shall we reap any benefit?

*What benefit can you expect more than any other colonist?*
Precisely this, sir: If a man starts out alone from Boston, not only is it
very difficult for him to get to our location, but, alone, there, he must suffer many privations and delays before civilization reaches him. We propose numbers to make civilization . . .

The unidentified member of the group who gave these answers also said that
their purpose was to make money by homesteading or locating claims; that they
would establish a town site, cut it into lots, and each of the first one hundred
men would receive one of the lots; that they could homestead one hundred sixty
acres each, at very minimum cost; and that the scheme was not backed by a
railroad company. "No sir, no railroad company has a dollar in it . . . We make
our own contracts and mean to execute them."

Many meetings—perhaps a more descriptive term would be rallies—were
held. Enthusiasm mounted. In mid-January 1876, the Boston *Globe* reported
that little had been heard from the Arizona Colonization Company during the
previous two months, but that they had been busy organizing. Cozzens addressed a meeting "informing the audience that he spoke only of those things
whereof he knew." He showed some specimens of placer gold taken only fifteen
miles from San Francisco Mountain. The man who brought the gold, whose
name was not given, with seven others joined the venture. "The first party of
fifty men proposes starting in February," the paper noted.

It is not impossible that traces of gold might be found in the general area.
Marble Mountain, twenty-six miles north of Flagstaff, also known as The
White Horse Hills and White Horse Mountain, could conceivably produce
some evidence of gold. A geologist, Karen Verbeek, tells us that "the latite pipes
on the western side of Marble Mountain contain minor amounts of limonite
and hematite, and traces of silver and gold." These minute amounts of gold
might show up as placers in stream beds and washes.

On February 11, the *Globe* reported that such large crowds were attending the meetings that there was no standing room left. "Little new can be said except that the company is accumulating corroborative evidence of their original truthfulness. . . . Party of first fifty is nearly made up." Some two weeks later, the *Globe* reported that a farewell party was held, Judge Cozzens addressed the group, an oyster supper was served, and that the colonists had then gone to take the 6:00 P.M. train to New York. "Fifty men strong and determined who intend to make a home for themselves and families . . . farming, stock raising, and many who will devote themselves to mining entirely."

In McClintock's history of Arizona is reprinted an article about the Boston party "from an unspecified eastern publication." A study of the item suggests that it probably appeared in the New York *Herald,* about March 1 or 2:

> A band of 150 men [actually about 50] arrived here yesterday and took the first train . . . on their way to Arizona. At the base of the San Francisco Mountains they intend to establish a colony. Each man takes provisions for ninety days, and his personal outfit of tools and clothing to a total prescribed weight of 300 pounds, transportation for which and for himself to the end of the long journey is furnished by the Arizona Colonization Company—a Boston concern—at a cost of $140 per man. At the end of the railroad the colonists are to be joined by the company's engineer, Mr. G. B. Maynadier, who went ahead about a week ago to provide transportation from that point. Mr. Maynadier was the chief engineer of Henry Meiggs' Andes Railroad in Peru and is said to be thoroughly acquainted with Arizona. The part of the country in which the proposed settlement is to be made is said to be very rich in the precious metals and at the same time very advantageous for agriculturists. A company is forming in San Francisco with a capital of $10,000,000 to work locating mining claims on the west side of the mountain to which the colonists are going. Within about thirty days at least eighty more men, with the families of some of those who have already gone, will go from Boston to join the Colony.

On March 7, the Boston *Globe* reported that the hall was filled to overflowing with more men anxious to learn of "the marvellous country." It stated that the second party would be forwarded as soon as fifty men were obtained, and that they hoped to get underway before April 1. "There is little doubt that the sons of New England will make a strong foothold in this well-known rich territory and Boston will have the credit of starting the enterprise."

Other articles followed. Requests for information about the colonization plan were so numerous that the company started publication of a little newspaper, *The Arizona Bulletin,* which was distributed at meetings.

The second group made their departure about May 1. The plan was to send out additional groups of fifty men, one each month or so, until hundreds, even thousands, had made the long journey and settled in northern Arizona, "The Marvellous Country."

We have gone into considerable detail regarding these preliminaries, to enable us to understand why a hundred New Englanders would launch themselves into the wilderness with absolutely no firsthand information regarding their destination—the valley of the Colorado Chiquito and San Francisco Mountain. This is very definitely not the way the West's most successful colonizers, the Mormons, did business. They would send out parties of scouts, locate watering places and camping spots, and before a band of colonizers was put on the road, they knew, or at least their leaders knew, pretty well what they were going to encounter.

The Mormons had made various reconnaissances and explorations of northern Arizona in early days. Charles S. Peterson tells us that they would have settled in the area as early at the mid-fifties if their Elk Mountain Mission had not been driven from Moab by irate Indians. Church leaders never lost sight of the possibility of settling in the area, and unquestionably they knew a lot about it. In 1873, the Mormons made an abortive move toward establishing a Little Colorado River colony. Its failure was not the result of a lack of knowledge of the area, but perhaps a lack of determined leadership in the mission itself. The leaders in Salt Lake City, including President Brigham Young, hadn't given up. "However, the plan to settle the Little Colorado was postponed—postponed for a far longer period than Brigham Young anticipated when he announced in a public meeting in August of 1873 his intent to lead a new colony south immediately after October conference," Peterson says. It was to be three years before colonization of the Little Colorado would be resumed. In 1875 the church sent out two exploring parties, both of which returned with information indicating that colonization of the Little Colorado was feasible.

Plans were made for another attempt at establishing colonies in the area during the winter of 1875–76. Most certainly the church leaders in Salt Lake City were aware that a group of men in Boston were first talking about, then preparing for, an emigration to the area. Church leaders kept themselves well informed on everything relating to the general western area and their own interests. While important news reports were moved about the country by telegraph, much of the bulk of the daily and weekly news dispatches circulated in the form of newspapers, and most papers had regular departments summarizing interesting and important news gleaned from other newspapers. We may be sure that President Young and others had seen copies of newspapers carrying articles about the Arizona Colonization Company.

This unquestionably was a factor causing church leaders to expedite plans for another attempt at colonizing the Little Colorado. On January 23, 1876, two hundred men from northern Utah were called to the project. On January 29, they met in Salt Lake City with President Young, who told them to start as soon as possible. The Mormons were on the road long before the first Boston Party had its farewell oyster supper and started its long journey. On March 15, the Mormon vanguard arrived on the Little Colorado with thirty teams. There they met two Mormon missionaries who had been working among the Indians—and who certainly knew the area. By March 26, the Mormons had traveled upstream, arriving in the valley of the Colorado Chiquito where they were to settle. They were under the leadership of Lot Smith. John Bushman, one of the Mormon leaders, has this to say about his group's knowledge that the Boston Party was on the way: "Teams were arriving from Utah every day. We were informed that there was a large company from Massachusetts coming to colonize in this country, and we were advised to make claim to all the land we could. This company came later and went to the San Francisco Mountain. . . ."

The Mormons founded four settlements, including sites near present-day Winslow, then known as Sunset Crossing, and at present-day Joseph City, which they first called Allen's Camp. Sunset had some importance as a point where the mail and stage line crossed the river on the route between Prescott and Albuquerque.

As early as March 3, the Prescott *Miner* published the following item regarding the Boston Party:

> By telegraph: Boston, Feb. 29. A party of 45 young men left Boston for Arizona last night. They are the advance guard of a colony forming here to settle in the Little Colorado River.

On April 14 the *Miner* reported as follows, under dateline of "Little Colorado, A.T., March 27, 1876":

> Editor *Miner*:
> I am pleased to be able to inform you of the arrival here of S. Brown, of Salt Lake City, with the advance guard of two hundred men of the

Mormon colony intending to make a settlement on this river. They bring with them seed and teams to put in a crop this Spring; they also have topographical instruments and a great variety of mechanical tools and skilled mechanics to use them who can do anything from the stocking of a plow to the building of a woolen mill. I understand it is the intention of this colony to put up a woolen factory as soon as suitable arrangements can be made, and I think it is a good investment, considering the cost of transportation of wool to the East and then that of manufactured woolen goods, back again for the use of the people, who raise the wool. Again, this is the center of a range capable of sustaining 2,000,000 sheep, including the Moggollons [*sic*] and western slope of the Rocky Mountains.

Felix Scott

The above letter reached us a little too late for last week's issue which makes it rather old for this, but it's good and newsy and we should like to hear often from the same source on progress of the Saints in their new colony in Arizona. Since the date of this letter, we learn from John Rarick that the whole colony has arrived with 160 teams and settled along the river from Sunset Crossing thirty-five miles up to Walker's ranch, and as soon as they unhitched from their wagons they hitched on to plows and already have considerable wheat and other grain planted.

A week earlier, the *Miner* had reported that Salt Lake City papers advised that a colony of Mormons was en route to Arizona "under a promise from Brigham Young that they shall be protected in the enjoyment of houses, lands and as many wives as they desire. . . ."

By the time the Mormon settlers had arrived, the first contingent of the Boston party was a couple of hundred miles or so east of the Colorado Chiquito, slowly trekking westward toward the land of promise. The Mormons certainly knew the Boston party was on the way, but apparently the Boston party had no knowledge whatsoever that the Mormons not only had already arrived, but were even contemplating such a move.

The Mormons were first on the Colorado Chiquito, for whatever it was worth. They had the farming land, some of which they were to abandon in time because of its unsuitability for cultivation. Only by the most heroic efforts were even these expert colonizers able to establish and maintain themselves in the area. In the years to follow, the dam for irrigation purposes at the Joseph City (Allen's Camp) site was to be repeatedly washed out and rebuilt, until the ninth dam was built and placed in use in 1924. Whatever its long term value, the

Mormons, by late March 1876, were in possession of the area on the Little Colorado, and on the routing of the transnorthern Arizona railroad.

In mid-March, articles giving some details regarding the Boston party's organization, destination, and progress, appeared in the San Francisco *Call,* the Tucson *Citizen,* and other newspapers around the nation. The forty-five men comprising the first party [see Appendix A], under the leadership of Maj. E. W. Griggs, had arrived at the end of the railroad at La Junta, Colorado, March 4. Most of what we know about the party's progress and membership comes from the letters and journal of George E. Loring, a twenty-two-year-old Boston watchmaker, a member of the group.

From La Junta, Loring wrote his wife that the railroad had been completed to that point only three weeks before, and that his group had purchased seven teams. "Nights are very cold but everyone is in high spirits at breakfast . . . gay and happie as can be. . . . Mann [Horace E., destined to be a long-time resident of Phoenix] and myself are partners. We have bought many good things together. I find him a very nice fellow very lively & active pleasant & good habits. . . . We have two banjoes, two violins, tamberines, bones and some good voices, so we have some lively music. We have a German with us of the very same class you will see acted on the stage. The boys have lots of fun with him. We start in the morning for Trinidad. . . . It will take us five days to travel their [*sic*]. . . . We buy provisions for three months and all of our tools. I have got a dog."

One member of this party was the nine-year-old son of Griggs.

On March 15, Loring wrote his wife that going through the mountains they had to put twelve mules to each wagon. "Uncle Dick Wooten is a noted man in Colorado. . . . He is an old scout trapper & Indian hunter he and Kit Carson travelled together. He is now sixty years old. Came to this part of the country when he was nineteen years old. He keeps a toll gate. Keeps the road of the mountain in order. He showed us his old Pepper Box that he had killed Indians and heaps of game with."

On March 28, the New Englanders arrived at Albuquerque. Here they crossed the Rio Grande, using fourteen mules hitched to each wagon to pull through the flooding stream. Loring noted that "some of the boys had a fight." A few days later an article regarding the party appeared in an Albuquerque newspaper:

## A BOSTON COLONY

Some fifty men from the New England states, principally from Boston, passed south through town on Saturday last. They constitute the ad-

vanced guard of a new settlement, projected on the Colorado Chiquito in
Arizona. . . . All [*sic*] the present time there is considerable settlement on
this river. The nearest post office is Camp Apache, Arizona, some 69
miles distant. The settlers now there have a man employed to carry the
mails. He makes the trip once a week. Should, the 35th parallel road be
built through, this settlement will be on the line of the road. . . .

On the same day, April 1, a humorously skeptical article appeared in the
Tucson *Citizen*:

### ARIZONA EMIGRANTS

In the *Citizen* of Mar. 4, we published a telegram from Boston stating
that a party of 45 young men had left that city on the 28th ultimo, for
Arizona, this being the advance guard of a colony coming to settle in the
Little Colorado section. In the New York *Herald* of Mar. 1st we find the
following item. Whether these Boston colonists are all one and the same
party we know not, but if they are the right kind of material and are prepared for a little temporary roughing they can hardly fail to do well ultimately in this territory. However from reading the *Herald*'s item, we are
afraid that these emigrants have got things very much mixed and have
about as romantic and false ideas of what they are going "into a wilderness for to see" as the boy who jumps into his mother's washtub, after his
first perusal of Robinson Crusoe and sails out on his native river to realize
the fantasies of an excited imagination. The *Herald* says: In August last
the lectures delivered by Judge S. W. Cozzens awakened a strong desire
among many unemployed men in that city to try their fortunes in what
he represented to be a land of unbounded mineral and agricultural
wealth. A company having for its object the colonization of a choice part
of that far off country was readily formed with Judge Cozzens as President, J. M. Piper, Secretary and S. C. Hunt, Treasurer. Mr. J. D. Maynadier, the Chief Engineer of Harry Migg's [*sic*] great railroad construction in Peru, was engaged by the company and started for Arizona about
a week ago to arrange for the transportation of colonists from the end
of the A.T. & S.F.R.R. and to pick out a location for a town at the
base of the San Francisco Mountains which is the objective point of the
colony. . . .

If we would be permitted to offer one suggestion to these colonists, it
would be that if they haven't got Judge Cozzens along with the advance
party coming to settle at the San Francisco Mountain, they should imme-

diately sent back a delegation to bring him. Don't take any promise of his coming after and fetching along fresh supplies and recruits. These colonists need Judge Cozzens with them first, last and all the time. He has been here, he knows the country, is fully posted, and is just the man to advise and consult with and to hold responsible for future developments.

The New York *Sun* of Mar. 1st in connection with a reference to this party of emigrants, says that a company is forming in San Francisco with capital of $10,000,000 to work located mining claims on the west side of San Francisco mountain. We think there is a mistake here, and that instead of these claims being on the side, they are on the top rock of the supreme summit on San Francisco Mountain.

On April 15, Loring wrote his wife that the party was snowed in near Inscription Rock, and some of the men took advantage of the stop to inscribe their names. He mentioned that they had gathered buffalo chips for their fires, explaining to his young wife that "buffalo chips are composed of fine grass dried in the sun," and adding that his mule had run away.

Under dateline of April 18, from "Randalville, A.T.," apparently a temporary name given to one of the Little Colorado settlements, the Prescott *Miner* announced the arrival of the Boston Colony. Under the heading "Items From Little Colorado," the paper reported:

> Quite a stir is being made along the river by the arrival of the Boston Colony—50 men and six wagons. Part of their train was left six miles back of the Zuñi villages, they being unable to proceed on account of their mules being in such poor condition. I understand another Company was to leave Boston on the 15th. inst. There are several hundred Mormons settled along the river . . . quite a number of families . . . going to work in earnest. . . . They intend to have 800 acres under cultivation this year.

Under the same heading but with a dateline of April 25, from Beaver Creek, the same newspaper reported:

> The advance of the Boston party is now on the Little Colorado . . . 45 men . . . they say the country, from what they have seen, has been misrepresented to them. They bought their teams & outfits in LaJunta. . . .

Horace E. Mann, Loring's bunkie, told in later years about the party's arrival at the Colorado Chiquito and finding the Mormons there. After recounting the story of the party's organization and the long journey west, he said:

They saw their last house in passing McCarty's ranch on Silver Creek, and turned due westward, with their goal nearly in sight. The men were forced to walk, as the teams were loaded with their baggage and supplies. . . .

The colonists received a blow that took the heart out of them when they reached St. Joseph [now known as Joseph City]—the goal toward which they had toiled for weeks and the spot in which their plans were centered. For a party of Mormons had beaten them to the tract and were building a stockade and dam for irrigation.

The valley of the Colorado Chiquito was not only already occupied, it was occupied by Mormons about whom the New Englanders had heard disturbing tales. A party of westbound emigrants had been massacred in a remote part of Utah, Mountain Meadow, years before. And Mormons were known to be strange people with strange customs and beliefs. The valley itself was no less forbidding; it didn't look at all like a New Englander's idea of a fertile farming area. It seems unlikely that they would have settled there, even if the Mormons had not beaten them to it.

So the first Boston group crossed the Little Colorado River, now to them a river of shattered dreams, and moved along its west bank to the crossing around the head of precipitous Canyon Diablo. Near this place they camped, and some of them inscribed their names or initials on a big rock there, joining the others who had done the same over the years. Loring, his buddy Mann, and some others floated down the Little Colorado on a raft from Sunset Crossing to near the juncture with Diablo; others accompanied the wagons.

On April 27, Loring wrote his wife that "The Old Gov. [obviously, the party-leader, Griggs] is nearly crazy he has been flying around today he did not know whether to go to Prescott or back to Albuquerque or to the Mountains he wanted one of the boys to blow his brains out . . ." The next day, Loring wrote his wife that nine men had gone on ahead of the party to Prescott to collect money sent to them there, and that they intended to rejoin the party. And on April 29, he wrote that nine additional men had started for the mountains with six day's provisions, seeking another place in which to settle. He wrote that his yeast was getting low so he had to make crackers. "I bet you when a man has fed of flour and water for sixty days it makes him think of the good things at home you *bet*."

One of the men who had gone on to Prescott gave a report to the Prescott *Miner*:

THE BOSTON COLONY—Pardon Spencer, of Rhode Island, who came as one of the Boston colony, arrived here last evening and represents the party quite dissatisfied with the representations made to them by Judge Couzins [*sic*], and that they will not attempt to remain on the Little Colorado. He looks for a majority of them here soon. They view the matter just as the *Miner* has constantly represented, a good country for individual enterprise and the investment of capital, but not adapted to colonization.

On May 1, Loring wrote that three of the men had returned from the mountains—no doubt the San Francisco Peaks—and that they had found a nice valley four miles from the mountain, with plenty of wood and a spring. He said they were anxious to move "for a more desolate place [than] we are now stopping in cannot be found." The party's leader, Griggs, said he would start that night with a team to carry provisions to those gone before. Loring and Mann insisted on going along, but to do this, they had to do all their cooking in advance, as no utensils could be carried except a frying pan. So they stayed up until 1:00 A.M., departure time, doing their cooking. He estimated that they were forty-five miles from the mountains.

In Mann's reminiscences, he said that after camping at the Canyon Diablo crossing, he and five others, one of whom was Loring, took a light wagon and two mules and started toward the San Francisco Mountain. This no doubt was the group headed by Griggs.

On May 5, Loring wrote that they were in splendid country, heavily wooded, and that they found an Indian ruin in a cave, and found "old pottery all over the country." This may have been the ruins in Walnut Canyon. He reported that Griggs came in at night "and said they had found a beautifull valey [*sic*] seven miles nearer the mountains and we were going to start in the morning for it. . . ." He also wrote that one of the men had killed an antelope and given him the liver. "What a meal we were going to have for supper. . . . We passed some splendid timber all day large pine trees. . . . We had to keep our fire low for fear of being jumped by Indians." Saturday, May 6, he wrote that, "I woke up hearing the wild turkeys gobbling. H. [Mann] and I took our rifles and left the road for a hunt we passed over some splendid looking valleys (but without water) and through some of the best timber land in the land we saw lots of turkey sign but nary a turkey. We saw quite a number of deer but could not get near enough for a shot." A day later, he reported: "We were disappointed in the valley [Griggs' first San Francisco Mountain site—probably Antelope Valley] they had another one in view . . . their is quite a number of deer around here. H & I are afraid our provisions will give out. We only allow ourself two large thin rashers apiece for one day ration. We are so short of flour we thought it a case of necessity to hunt today. So after our humble breakfast we started out but did not strike the right place for game. We got in the woodland and traveled ten miles in hope of striking some valley. I went up to a high mountain to take a view. All I could see was trees. It was black with trees as far as the eye could reach. I got to camp at 3 pretty tired. The men are all out of tobacco and they smoke leaves and coffee anything that burns. I have not used any for some time do not miss it much. Half of the men's shoes are worn out. Having our trunk delayed so puts us in want of a good many things. Made supper of deer bones. The wood smokes everything up . . . the [coyotes?] barked around our camp all night."

On Wednesday, May 9, Loring wrote of their arrival at the second site, located by Griggs "seven miles nearer the mountains. . . . We started out for . . . the end of our journey for the present. We found it a very pretty valley at the base of the mountains it is five and a half miles long and will average a mile and a half in width. It is surrounded by hills covered with trees on all sides. It has several springs in it of good water as ever was drunk. Part of the land might be used for agriculture if the climate will admit which I doubt. . . . H went out with his rifle in the afternoon I had cooked a couple of pieces of dough for our supper. We tugged into camp a deer which weighed 125 lbs. I don't know what we should have done without it as we only had four or five pounds of flour left. We gave all in camp a meal from it (there are twenty of us here). I had some onions so we had fried onions with our meat went to bed with a full bellie. It seems good after a man has gone hungry."

Where were the other twenty-five men of this first party? Some had gone to Prescott; some may still have been at the Canyon Diablo camp; some had gone back to Zuñi for the trunks; and some by this time may have simply quit and turned back toward civilization.

Maynadier, the engineer, who probably should have been in charge of the party rather than Griggs, laid out a townsite. Then a drawing was held for lots. Some of the men busied themselves setting corner posts, and some sort of plats or maps were made, because Loring refers to such a record. Some of the men started building cabins.

Loring does not give sufficient clues in his letters to locate the camp and townsite of the first Boston party. But another member of the group, Captain Richard Robbins, in a letter to The Boston *Daily Globe* on May 29, stated that it was in a valley "called by Lieutenant Whipple Leroux Valley." He describes it as ". . . on the *southwest* [author's emphasis] side of the mountain and at the foot, about three miles long and two wide, being surrounded by low foothills covered with a splendid growth of pine timber. The soil is fine for agricultural [*sic*] and the grass splendid for the grazing of stock. Natural fine springs were situated in different parts of the valley, giving us plenty of good water. . . ."

Loring's friend Mann stated to historian McClintock and others in later years that the small advance guard rode on ahead to Leroux Spring, which is in Fort Valley. He also recalled the Maynadier surveyed a townsite, each of the members being allotted a tract.

It seems certain that Loring, Mann, and the others in the first Boston party camped, raised the flag, laid out a town, and chose building sites at a point in Fort Valley seven or eight miles northwest of present-day Flagstaff.

Diaries and journals kept by two members of a Mormon group visiting the area eleven months later, in April 1877, support this. John Bushman, who had come to the Little Colorado settlements with the Mormon parties in 1876, and noted in his diary the passage of the Boston party that spring, returned to Utah, then made another trip to Arizona in the spring of 1877. His journal, composed later from his diary, records that his small party came from the northwest and "arived at fort valey By the San francisco Mountain" [*sic*] on April 13. "In the west end of this valey the Boston Colony that came west in July 1876 built a stockade fort, and laid out a Town, But they only remained a short time, and abandoned the Place [*sic*]." His group remained at Leroux Spring waiting for another party to catch up. He walked through the valley on April 15, and noted the rich black soil. The second Mormon contingent, led by a man named Hunt, arrived on April 20, enroute finding some strayed animals belonging to Bushman and the others, and substituting a fresh team for one of their own exhausted ones. On April 23, while the rest of the party rested, Bushman and three other men made a reconnaissance along the line they would take when they resumed travel. They rode southeast, and at eight miles and fifteen miles distance from their camp found two nice valleys. The first was probably Antelope Valley. "They [would be] good stock ranches some springs and a little running water in the first one." The "little running water" was probably Rio de Flag. They saw some antelope and deer, and returned to camp.

In the Hunt contingent was Ida Larson. Her diary, edited by her sister May in 1933, recorded on April 20: ". . . We reached the San Francisco spring [the Mormons frequently called Leroux Spring San Francisco Spring] before dark. Here we found our friends, all well, waiting for us. We think we can all travel together from here on. This is a beautiful valley at the foot of San Francisco Mt. There was a lone soldiers grave, and a Flag pole or staff. . . ."

On April 24, the men hunted for strayed animals, and found them all by 4:00 P.M. The assembled party immediately started on their final lap for the Little Colorado settlements, covering five miles, then camping because of the late hour. The next day, April 25, after traveling two and a half miles, they came through what Bushman described in his diary as "a very rich valley and camped at a spring for dinner. The Boston colonists put up a liberty pole 1876. [This would be the second Boston party's July Fourth, 1876, flagstaff, at the Clark ranch in Antelope Valley.] Snowed and blowed hard." Within a few days they arrived at their destination.

To return to Loring. On Wednesday, May 10, he wrote another letter to his wife from the group's campsite: "We had enough bones today for a soup so I dug about 300 oinions [sic] they grow wild and about as large as a red cherry it takes two hours to dig a mess but they are good after they are cooked you bet." The next day, he noted that the group expected the Prescott team would be back with provisions and mail Saturday. "Very disagreeable day for me." He was homesick. On May 12, he wrote that he and his friend Mann spent the day building a log hut. Sunday, May 14, he noted that he had little red blotches on his skin that itched and burned. Later he found he had body lice and boiled his clothes.

On May 20, the group at "San Francisco Mountain, Arizona," wrote a letter to Mr. John Campbell, requesting that it be published in the Boston *Herald*. It appeared June 18, 1876, probably traveling by courier or stage from either Prescott or Sunset Crossing to Albuquerque, and thence on east:

COZZENS' ARIZONA COLONY. Statement by 22 of the Deceived Colonists—Warning and Advice to the Credulous.

The Cozzens colony in Arizona has again been heard from, this time in a statement from 22 of its members, who seem to have realized that the Arizona of "Judge" Cozzens' imagination was not the reality, and that they had been badly sold, awaking from their golden dreams, many of them, to find themselves penniless in a strange and new country. The following is a copy of the statement of the 22 disgusted colonists forwarded to Mr. John Campbell of this city:

San Francisco Mountain, Arizona Territory, May 20, 1876.

Mr. John Campbell—Dear Sir: We, the members of the first party of the Arizona Colony Company, having arrived at our destination, and from our own observation that everything in regard to land for farming, climate and minerals has been misrepresented so far as we have been, and the reports of Lieutenants Beale and Whipple are incorrect and over-drawn, greatly tending to misrepresent this country in every way. We consider the Arizona Colonization Company nothing but a swindle, and we take this method of expressing ourselves, solely to prevent others from venturing on an uncertainty. This country is heavily timbered, and is full of rock called "malpais." There is no farming land at all at our location. Having been 90 days on the road, instead of 45 as were told we should be, some of the men in consequence are entirely destitute of money and pro-visions and with the exception of a few men connected with the leaders, the party will leave in a few days for California and for other parts of Arizona. In fact it is a humbug.

The statement is signed by [twenty-two members of the party].

In a note, Mr. Charles M. Harriman says to Mr. Campbell, "Please publish this in the *Herald* and you will have the thanks of all of the signers. We should have had more names, but nine men have already left for California. I shall go to Prescott and see if I can find something to do. If I don't succeed I shall then go to California."

A few days before the above was written, one colonist, the Rev. William Taplin, managed to get himself lost. Loring mentions that the man left camp with only three biscuits. On May 19, the Prescott *Miner* reported:

LOST AND FOUND—Rev. Wm. Taplan, chaplain of the Boston Col-ony, on Saturday last left the party with which he was traveling in the direction of San Francisco mountains to try to shoot game, and expecting to rejoin them at a place called San Francisco Spring. On coming to the spring, he found that they had been encamped there but had moved on up the Valley. Mr. Taplan remained at the spring over night, and early in the morning started on the supposed trail of his comrades; after walking all day he became bewildered, seems to have partially lost the power of reason, and was not again conscious until Wednesday morning. He had then been without food since Saturday and realized that he had walked a long distance, and suspected he was on the Prescott trail, which he con-tinued to follow, and soon came to a ranch in Chino Valley, where he was cared for and furnished means at Mr. Banghart's to reach this place, which he did yesterday forenoon. Here he met several of the Boston boys, and after resting and refreshing himself started back to San Francisco

Mountain to let his companions, who must be searching for him, know what had become of him. San Francisco Spring is at least seventy-five miles from Chino Valley, and how much further he wandered is not known.

On Friday, May 26, Loring wrote a most interesting letter:

> It rained today for the first time. It was the first time I seen a rain since leaving Boston In the evening we had a town meeting, voted for three men to draw up a constitution, a sheriff, town cleark [*sic*], two overseers of the poor and a poundmaster. We elected our Captain [Griggs] to that responsible office with great excitement. We then voted for the name of the town. Some were very anxious to have it named New England. Most every man had a name that he liked better than any other he had ever heard. There was thirty of us so we had to have a majority of sixteen to carry the day. After a good deal of voting we got it down to two names New England and Agassiz after the great man the mountain was called on the new maps and a town with such a future before it would be well worthy to be named after so great a man. And so at last the want of sleep caved some of the N.E. men in and the town was named Agassiz.

The next day he wrote that a thundershower had put out the fire which had been raging in the forest around the camp for a week. On Monday, May 29, he wrote that three of the men left for Prescott and took letters to mail. "I spent the day thinking what a fool I had been to leave my wonderful baby and my dear wife." He added that he had cut four large posts and hauled them to his lot.

One of the letters sent to Prescott to mail was undoubtedly the one from Captain Robbins, referred to above. The letter appeared in the Boston *Daily Globe* Sunday morning, July 8, more than five weeks later. The significant point is what some of the more experienced and responsible men were thinking while they were still at the village of Agassiz. He datelined his letter "Agassiz, A.T., 75 miles northeast of Prescott, foot of San Francisco Mountain, May 29, 1876," and addressed it to the editor of the *Globe*:

> Sir: Thinking that Bostonians may perhaps be interested in our colony and its doings, I will endeavor to give you a short sketch of our location and new town. First, I would mention that our trip was long and tedious on account of the extreme cold weather and late spring. We suffered very much for the want of water, as the snows had not melted and filled

the streams, that we found dry instead. The grass was dead and we could get no grazing for our animals. The few inhabitants of the territory living along our road universally reported it the coldest and latest spring they had known for twenty years. The valley of the Little Colorado we found to be much below our expectations as an agricultural country, the best part having been taken by the Mormons. It was therefore universally agreed that the original plan should be changed and the location for the town be made in a valley near the foot of the mountain. A prospecting party was sent out and they selected the site of a town the valley called by Lieutenant Whipple the Leroux Valley. It is on the southwest side of the mountain and at the foot, about three miles long and two wide, being surrounded by low foothills covered with a splendid growth of pine timber. The soil is fine for agricultural [*sic*] and the grass splendid for the grazing of stock. Natural fine springs are situated in different parts of the valley, giving us plenty of good water which, with plenty of game in the shape of deer, antelope, turkey, and rabbits, assure us that starvation is impossible, if we but use the energy every man should possess. The only drawback that can be feared to the farming of the valley successfully is, as many fear, the extreme shortness of the season, the elevation being high and in consequence the early autumn and late spring rendering it, perhaps, impossible to have crops mature. This is a matter only of opinion and must be taken as such only to be proven by time. We have been here only a very short time and have made no prospecting trips, as to minerals. I myself found about five miles from our camp a piece of gold-bearing quartz-float. Under a strong glass minute particles of the ore were claimed to be seen by old miners. Float, you must understand, are broken pieces of quartz that have become detached from the main ledge and in some way scattered over the surface. By following up this float one may possibly discover the ledge. It takes time to do this and I propose to follow it up very soon. I saw also what are claimed to be silver indications. Adjacent to our valley are several others equally as large and fine. The climate is fine, beautiful and invigorating. I know of no place so well suited as this country for a man of small means to better and improve his condition; but he must come to a new country, a country that his head, hand, and individual endeavors are going to make blossom as the rose and bear fruit. He must expect to find everything here as different as possible from the East. People, life, climate, soil, grass, the way of doing things, the ideas, the food, all things are just different in the West from the East as day is from night. A man must adapt himself to circumstances to the place—to the people—and make out of the country what is in it. . . . An eastern man coming here must expect to be disgusted, but he must stick and get used to it. Let a Western man tell what is here in plain, honest, unvarnished, truthful words, and let an Eastern man hear it and come here, and he would swear that he had been swindled; but let him stay, and in one year he would not go back, and would speak just as the Western man had. This is the actual experience of nine tenths of the people in the territory. It is a rough, independent life, for which our Eastern men are not fitted without a year's education. Any man who will come to a new country, hang around for two months without trying to do anything, and then go home, is hardly fit to give an opinion, when the people here say that they don't know what can be done until tried. It is a new country, and until thoroughly tested it cannot be said that it will or will not succeed in this or that. Personally, I propose to remain and see it out. In coming here an Eastern man cannot expect to find the home comforts ready for him, but plenty of chances to make the comforts. He must not expect to find houses ready for him, but he must go to work and put them up. First a log house and in time a finer residence. He must not expect to find nuggets of gold laid round for him, but he must go into a systematic search for the mineral, and with hard work he will find them. Until their log houses are done they must be content to roll themselves in their blankets and with the starry heavens for their roof sleep, as our soldiers did, the sleep of the weary. The trees afford plenty of logs for [cabins] and the forests and vales plenty of game for the killing. The other evening we had a meeting and chose seven officers and named the town "Agassiz." The extremely long journey, as mentioned before, has brought us here with but barely one month's provisions, and therefore some of the men are obliged to go to Prescott to earn money to purchase. Some think it useless to remain as they fancy crops cannot be raised on account of the short season. Some think that as others go, they will. I am going to Prescott on business for the company and will therefore have quite a number with me. It is just as we expected—many coming from the luxuries of a large city, homes well established, cannot get up heart to stay and rough it here. I repeat that I confidently believe that a man of moderate means can do better here, if willing to accept the situation and work and rough it, than he can anywhere else. It lies entirely with the man. I have no doubt that those who have written home exaggerated reports will in a year or two wish themselves back. I will keep them informed of our doings. . . . I remain your obedient servant, Captain Richard Roberts [Robbins].

When this letter was republished by the Prescott *Miner,* the editor mentioned that Captain Robbins was formerly of the United States Army "and well known in this city."

On May 30, Loring wrote "I did a heap of work, work I never did in the East. I dug a post hole at each corner of my valuable lot three feet deep. I had to blast them out with a crow bar using muscle for powder. The posts where [*sic*] seven feet high about six inches through. I peeled every post I blistered my hands a good deal. I packed my trunk for an early start in the morning. Every man is disgusted with this section. The mountain is covered with a burnt rock an indication of no mineral watsoever [*sic*] and the climate is too cold for agriculture. The frost hangs on untill [*sic*] late and comes on very early in the season and their is considerable snow in the winter and that spoils it for stock." The next day he wrote that he drove tacks in his shoes "to keep the soal [*sic*] from dropping off." He added that "every man but two where [*sic*] going. One of these two was our old chaplain whose mind is affected and the other one . . ." —here the letter becomes illegible.

A couple of days before the Agassiz town meeting was held, the Prescott paper reported that a detachment of eighty more of the Boston colony was moving slowly along, having started their journey westward on May 1. According to Loring, all of the first party—perhaps about thirty men, the other fifteen or so having gone either to Prescott earlier or turned back eastward—with the exception of the two he mentions above, left for Prescott May 31–June 1. By June 5, they arrived there after a difficult hike. The Prescott paper reported:

> Some thirty of the Boston colony came in from San Francisco Mountain on Monday, had their picture taken in a group, and have scattered, some going to California, thence back to Boston, some to the mines, and some have found employment here.

In further letters home, Loring was very hard on Griggs and his nine-year-old son. He expressed admiration and liking for Maynadier, and added: "Don't believe a single word you hear in Boston about the company or the country . . . don't you build up any plans at all. Two thirds you hear in Boston is a damned lie." On June 27, he wrote that Hunt, treasurer of the colonization company and leader of the second party, had arrived in Prescott June 26, and "reported the second party must be at the mountains by this time and probably all of them will be here before long . . . his party had a splendid outfit and delight-ful weather on the way out. He is very much disappointed in finding no pros-pect for a colony or any signs of gold in the San Francisco Mountains."

A month later, Loring wrote from Phoenix that the Arizona Colonization Company had made no money out of the venture, and had sold the teams to pay the drivers. In September, he wrote that Cozzens was never seen or heard of north of Tucson. He said he had been told by Hunt, leader of the second group, "that they got rid of Major Griggs, leader of the first group, by giving him a mule to leave the country with." In August, he received a letter from home stating that "most of the first party have returned." Loring settled in Phoenix, in due time opened a variety store which included a watchmaking department, became Wells Fargo agent for that station, and prospered. In later years he had business reverses, and moved to California. He died in 1932.

The reader will note that nowhere in Loring's letters is there any mention of the raising of a flagstaff in the village of Agassiz—and according to Loring, not more than two members of the first party could have been at Agassiz on the traditional flag-raising date of July 4, 1876, as the others had left May 31–June 1. However, Loring didn't mention that the Mormons had beaten them to the Colorado Chiquito, either. Loring's bunkie, Mann, who was to remain in Ari-zona as a prospector and miner, and spend many years in Phoenix and Douglas, did make statements about the flagstaff. His story appears in Arizona historian McClintock's account, and also in a Douglas *Dispatch* interview in 1927. He said that he and five others left the main group at Canyon Diablo, camped at a small spring "just south of San Francisco mountain where Flagstaff is now." While waiting for the main party to come up, they hunted and explored, and traveled up a little valley to the north and northwest to the "big LeRoux Springs," below which they found the remains of a burnt cabin and of a stock-ade corral, which he surmised might have been used as a station of the trans-continental mail route.

Many yards out in the valley and away from the remainder of the forest was a lone tree and a plan grew in the brains of the eastern youths.

Setting to work, they lopped off every branch of the tree and smoothed it. They placed a leather loop at the top. A young man whom Mann remembers only as Tillinghast owned an American flag and, as the conquerers stood at attention, the flag was run up the pole. Years later, after the arrival of the railroad, the town was given the name of Flagstaff, Arizona.

The date of the flag raising was late in May, 1876, the exact date for-gotten by the pioneers now residing here. . . .

The party took up land and surveyed a townsite of what is now Flag-staff, but then decided to continue on to Prescott. . . .

Neither Loring nor Mann mentioned that they found anyone other than their own party in the San Francisco Mountain area during the time of their visit. From other sources, we know that there were at least three settlers in the general area that year, Thomas F. McMillan, Frank Hart, and Charles O'Neill, and we know that McMillan arrived in May 1876—the very month the first contingent of the Boston party was here. And a few weeks later the second Boston party raised its flagstaff on this ranch.

The second Boston party [see Appendix B], which left Boston accompanied by Hunt, the company treasurer, had much better equipment for such a jour-ney, and Hunt was without doubt a better leader than Griggs, who fell apart when he found Mormons encamped on the Colorado Chiquito. Griggs also angered some of his fellow colonists by having brought his nine-year-old son along, and making sure the boy was as comfortable as possible under the condi-tions prevailing. And he completely lost whatever control he had ever had when he threatened in desperation to shoot himself when the group was camped in the cold and wet at the mountain, and running short of provisions.

The second party took the same route to La Junta. According to William M. Breakenridge, they had a carload of mules and wagons, and a lot of supplies. An official of the forwarding company sent for Breakenridge, and asked him to unload the stock, match it up into teams, and get the party organized for their trip westward. Breakenridge says that none of the party knew anything about stock. He tells us that Hunt, the leader, was a school teacher who was tuber-cular, and was making the trip to regain his health. Hunt hired Breakenridge to help at a salary of $300 per month. The party had five tons of supplies and bag-gage, and few of the men had the allotted 300 pounds. He organized the stock into two six-mule teams with two wagons to each team, and soon had the stock broken to drive with a jerk line. Breakenridge hired two teamsters and a night herder. He says there were forty-five men in the party, and that besides two months' provisions some of them had tool chests, shotguns and rifles, a few hoes and garden rakes, and one eight-inch plow—to colonize a country with.

They moved out, and after the usual difficulties with bad roads, stock, horse-thieves, and general inexperience, addressed a letter to the Boston *Globe*. They recounted some of their adventures, then asked that an accompanying paper be published "as an offset to some of the despatches lately going the rounds of the press, representing our enterprise as a failure." This is the paper:

> In Camp Near Las Vegas
> May 24, 1876
>
> Whereas, two of the second party of colonists from Boston for Arizona, viz., S. Curtis Thayer and Edward C. Webster, left us this morning of their own accord; and, whereas, they made both before and after leaving statements that we believe and know to be false in regard to the expedition and the company; therefore Resolved,
>
> First, That we wish to make it known to our friends East and the public generally that we have no sympathy with the men aforesaid, having learned nothing since leaving Boston to discourage us from our undertaking or our change in purpose.
>
> Second, That we rejoice in the departure of these men, as many of the dissensions [*sic*] in camp and on the march have been the result of their constant fault-finding and unwillingness to fulfil their written obligations to the company.
>
> Third, That thus far the Arizona Colonization Company have fully carried out their promises, and have done all in their power to forward our interests in this expedition.
>
> Fourth, That a copy of these resolutions be sent to the Las Vegas papers and The Boston *Globe* for publication.
>
> 
>
> (signed)   A. F. Abbott, *Chairman*
> F. T. Chase
> T. H. Bray
> J. G. Sinclair
> J. W. Hemmingway,
>       *Com. on Resolutions*
> 

And forty-three other.

Dennis B. Mahoney was the only man in the outfit that declined to sign. Want of time only forbids me giving you more details of our trip and the prospects we hear of before us. At a more convenient season I will write more at length.

S. C. H.

No doubt "S. C. H." was Samuel C. Hunt, party leader.

The New Englanders arrived at the Mormon settlement of Allen's Camp June 23, according to the Prescott *Miner* reprint of a letter in the Salt Lake

Thomas F. McMillan, first
settler (1833–1906).

George E. Loring, member
of first Boston party (1854–1932).

City *Deseret News*. After reporting on progress of the Mormon colony, the item stated that "the same night the letter was written a company of Bostonians were camped at the settlement. They purposed [*sic*] settling on the Little Colorado, but had arrived in time to be too late. That was the second company from the same city that had passed along, one hundred in all, none of them having families." The fact that the New Englanders were along the Little Colorado on June 23 is verified by the diary of John Bushman. The diary states under date of Friday, June 23, 1876.: "A company of 50 emigrants came here going west from Boston." Breakenridge pertinently remarks that "if there had been no Mormons there our party could not have located, as they were not prepared, and had only provision enough to last them through to Prescott."

On July 1, Loring had written his wife from Prescott again, saying that Hunt had arrived a few days before, and that he said he had left the second party at Randalville. "He seemed very much disappointed in the country, they are all down on Cozzens fearfully. . . ."

An item in the *Miner* later in July, stated that Hunt had gone back to the San Francisco Mountain country about the first of July to resume his leadership of the second contingent.

After leaving Allen's Camp, the second party had moved on toward the San Francisco Mountain. Breakenridge says they camped at "Larue" Spring, but members of the party who later became residents of Flagstaff said they camped at the spring on what later became the Clark Ranch. This would have put them in the area of China Canyon, between present-day Flagstaff junior and senior high schools. They were in the area for several weeks. We are told that it was a hunter's paradise, with plenty of deer, bear, antelope, and turkey. "The men in the party were not very good shots, and although they got some game, they soon had most of it scared away from the vicinity," Breakenridge writes. He mentions that one day some of the men left camp and hiked to the summit of the peak and camped there all night. Those below could see their campfire plainly, he added.

If this group had left Allen's Camp seventy-five miles eastward June 23 or 24, or even a day or so later, they could easily have been at the present site of Flagstaff by July 4—and raised a flagstaff here, as members of the party subsequently declared they did. The precise location of this flagstaff, however, later became a part of a larger controversy involving other flagstaffs and the naming of the community, as we shall see.

After the second party had rested their teams and celebrated the glorious Fourth, they set out for Prescott under Hunt's leadership. They were still an organized group, still traveling together, still had all their wagons and stock and members. They had been better organized in the beginning, better equipped, and apparently had more responsible and capable leadership. They arrived in Prescott July 26, so they must have left the Peaks area around July 18–20. The following report of their arrival in Prescott appeared in the Prescott *Miner* July 28:

Second Boston Party—The second party of Boston colonists of 47 men, 7 wagons, 20 mules and two horses, arrived here, on Wednesday, from San Francisco Mountain where they had gone with the expectation of finding the first party, of fifty, comfortably housed and busy with the crops, but instead they neither found men, crop, nor land suitable for their purpose, and, like their predecessors, kept on into Prescott, where they seem to be at a loss to know just what to do. The owners of the teams constitute the Company who undertook to bring the Colony to Arizona, under a mis-apprehension of the character of the country, having received their infor-mation, like the balance of the Colonists, from one Judge Cozzens who represented the country well adapted to colonization, and as they all found the contrary to be the fact on their arrival at San Francisco Moun-tain, those who had paid their money to be brought here concluded that it would only be fair for the Company to take them back to the end of the railroad, or on into California. This the Company appear to be un-willing to do, having as they consider discharged their part of the work in bringing them here.

If the party really desire to form a Colony and engage in farming, the better plan, as it seems to us, would be to look about for a suitable place rather than give up and start back, simply because they have been de-ceived as to one particular location. We have always considered Arizona, as a whole, unfit for colonization, and that individual enterprise was best suited to it, but we understand there are valleys large enough, and un-claimed lands in sufficient bodies to support quite a colony either on Salt River or the head of the Gila, and if these people are particularly anxious to live in communities, it seems as if a wise thing for them to do would be to examine these localities before deciding their enterprise a failure. They are nearly all young men of good health and muscle, and if they decide to give up the community notion and rely upon individual effort, there is certainly nothing very discouraging in the fact that San Francisco Mountain is not a garden of Eden. Thousands have come and are coming from Kansas and other countries under quite as unfavorable circumstances as those from Boston, and yet they all seem to find something to do, and are not discouraged nor sorry that they came to Arizona.

Writing to his mother in Boston from Phoenix on August 4, Loring said: "I think the second party thought as we did, *only more so*. When they heard we had left the mountain, they said we did not amount to anything, no pluck, no stick to us. When they reach the Paradize [*sic*] they lost their stick and pluck very quick . . . they will all go through to Cal . . . there is no work in P. . . ." But they didn't all go through to California; at least two of them, G. A. Bray and John A. (Slow) Wilson, returned to the Flagstaff area in a very few years. And Bray's cousin, T. H., also a member of the second party, remained in Prescott and in due time had a prosperous mercantile business.

Accounts dealing with the first party suggest a lack of leadership and organization from the start. The members seemed to do a lot of wandering about. A few went ahead to Prescott, and apparently never returned. And it seems that some turned back eastward before they got to the mountain. The chaplain, Taplin, was lost for days and showed up in Prescott, as recounted earlier; then he journeyed back to the San Francisco Mountain, and refused to leave when the others did. However, he shows up a bit later in Prescott, delivering milk. Another member, Abraham Gagnon, apparently set out alone for Prescott and never made it. His body was found, according to the *Miner* of June 30, "on the old government road leading from Chino Valley to Bear Spring, some three miles beyond Banghart's ranch. He was lying on his back under a juniper tree, with his head pillowed on a stone, and his pistol still in his hand," and according to the coroner's jury had shot himself "while in a state of mental aberation [*sic*], superinduced by want of water and food."

The first party was never once all together in one place after they left the Mormon settlements on the Little Colorado, as compared with the better led and organized second party. We recall that when the meeting was held to organize the town of Agassiz, there were only thirty present, the other fifteen having departed in one direction or another.

But not everyone agreed with the Bostonians' assessment of the Peaks area. This item appeared in September 1876, in the Prescott paper:

*Not So Bad a Country*—George Brower, who, with Mr. Chenowith and family, of Salt River, and other, made a trip last month around the base of San Francisco and Bill Williams' mountains, reported some fine land and an excellent quality of grass in that region. George informs us that the location selected and abandoned by the Boston colonists a desirable place for stock raising, and contains sufficient arable land for all the purposes of raising vegetables and forage to sustain quite a large population. He thinks the time is not far off when this land and the very extensive belt of the finest timber in the world contiguous to it, will be a prize worth seeking.

How right George Brower was. Within four years of the time of the Boston parties' visits, a number of men had made themselves prosperous raising sheep in the area. Within five or six years, a sawmilling fortune was founded, and before ten years had passed, there were a number of prosperous mercantile establishments. And there was the railroad.

# THE
# BEGINNING

# CHAPTER IV

## *The First Settlers*

MOST OF OUR NEW ENGLANDERS have now vanished over the horizon, headed for California or back home to Boston, having learned at first hand that colonizing a wilderness is tough, especially if you don't really know what you're doing. But in the years before and immediately after the Boston parties' ill-starred venture, there were others who saw a potential in the San Francisco Peaks area who did know what they were doing.

In 1869, the Union Pacific and Central Pacific completed construction along the forty-second parallel, spanning the continent with a railroad. This did not dampen the demand for lines on other routes, but rather otherwise. The practicability of such major construction had been proved, and it had also been demonstrated that areas served by the railroad were quickly settled. That same year, General Palmer submitted his report on his detailed surveys along the thirty-fifth and thirty-second parallels. He strongly favored the northern route, which is of special interest to us. Three years before, Congress had chartered the Atlantic and Pacific Railroad to construct a line along this route. The panic and depression of the early 1870s put a stop to all such ambitious projects, but only for a time. Railroads would be built along both the thirty-fifth and thirty-second parallels, but not for a decade.

During those years there was a more or less constant stream of travel along Beale's wagon road, and the Peaks must have been combed over time after time for evidence of mineral. One man who prospected the area thoroughly in 1864 was Edmund W. Wells, who came with others from Colorado. Failing to find any indication of mineral, he moved on to Fort Whipple, where he worked in the quartermaster and commissary departments. He became an important figure in the development of Arizona, served as U.S. District Judge, Arizona Attorney General, member of the Constitutional Convention, and was an unsuccessful candidate for governor following statehood.

The San Francisco Mountain area was certainly not terra incognita; probably hundreds of men scouted and hunted around its springs and parks during those years. No doubt many were fully aware of the area's tremendous advantages for stock raising, although the difficulties attending establishment and operation of ranches were formidable. We are fortunate to have information about one party which traveled from Fort Union, New Mexico, to Prescott, via San Francisco Mountain in 1869. The group was headed by Jerre W. Sullivan and George Hance. The record appears in the June 1, 1923, issue of the *Coconino Sun,* in a discussion of old county legal records by L. S. Williams, who wrote:

> I may be mistaken, but I believe there are but two men living [in 1923] who saw the townsite of Flagstaff in its virgin state, before a house was built, a tent erected or a street laid out. . . . If I am correct in this statement, both of these men are living in Arizona today, Mr. Jerre W. Sullivan and Judge George Hance, both of Yavapai county. . . .
>
> Last year Mr. Sullivan related a pleasing incident to me relative to his first visit to what is now the splendid little city of Flagstaff. In the fall of 1869 the Sullivan-Hance party was organized at Fort Union, New Mexico, for an expedition to Prescott. There were nineteen members of the party, which included the late Captain John Hance, a brother of Judge Hance, and who passed away several years ago at Grand Canyon and is buried there at the spot he loved so well. The party proceded through New Mexico and arrived at or near the present townsite of Flagstaff on the afternoon of November 20, 1869. It was snowing, and although the leaders were apprehensive about the weather, they concluded to camp for the night. As near as I could determine from Mr. Sullivan's description, the camp site was either at the rocky point of Elden around which the present road to Winslow winds, or it was near the rocky pointed curve immediately opposite the Arizona Lumber & Timber company's plant. Mr. Sullivan was certain they camped near a rocky point within a mile of the present townsite. The party was short of fresh meat, and turkey tracks had been observed that afternoon in the snow. Two men took their guns and had proceeded less than a mile, when they came upon a flock of turkeys and succeeded in bagging the flock. When they were counted it was found they had killed nineteen, a turkey for each member of the party. Mr. Sullivan states they were a little short of cranberry sauce and celery, but that they had the rest of the trimmings.

A week later, Williams added:

If you will ask Mr. Sullivan he will tell you that when the Sullivan-Hance party broke camp on the morning of November 21, 1869, they passed over the present townsite of Flagstaff, along the old trail to a point near the present railroad station of Maine; thence through Garland Prairie and across the head of Sycamore Canyon, then skirting the southeastern foothills of Bill Williams, they descended the rim by the old government trail; then across the head of Hell's Canyon and into Chino Valley, and on into Prescott. It is doubtful that a dollar has been spent upon this old road since F. N. Gray was appointed over-seer in 1879, and yet you could leave Flagstaff in a wagon today and follow with comparative ease the same route taken by the Sullivan-Hance party in 1869.

The next report we have of happenings around San Francisco Mountain is tremendously interesting, and tantalizing—if we only knew the sequel to this item in the Prescott *Miner* of June 15, 1872:

## NEW COLONY.

Despite the efforts of savage Indians and their white allies to retard the settlement, development, and progress of our new Territory, the white stock is increasing all over its broad bosom, and will continue to increase and flourish.

Thursday last, we received a call from Alva Smith, an old resident of Prescott, who left here in 1868, and has, until a short time ago, resided in Colorado Territory, where, he says, whites are plenty and Indians scarce.

Mr. Smith and 16 other enterprising American citizens have just come through in wagons and on horseback from Colorado, and settled at the base of San Francisco Mountain, about 65 miles north from Prescott, on the line of the proposed Atlantic and Pacific Railroad, in a country in which timber, grass, game, water, &c., are plenty and good.

With them is a young physician, Dr. J. Anderson.

Mr. Todd will return soon to Colorado, to bring his family and sawmill to his new home.

A. H. Henderson, a surveyor, is now at work laying off farms.

Professor J. W. Glass is collecting specimens for a museum in Denver. Already, the party has planted corn, potatoes, &c. and a better satisfied lot of men cannot be found.

Mr. Smith says others are coming on behind from Colorado, Montana and elsewhere, with minds made up to stay in Arizona. We, of course, extend the right hand of welcome to all who may come here, and feel rejoiced to know that hundreds are coming to share with us the peace and other good things population and railroads will bring this, up to the present, war ridden, Government snubbed Territory.

A careful search of the *Miner*'s files for many months following fails to give us any more information about this party. It's probable that the growing depression and consequent drop in prices, and the fact that the construction of the railroad would obviously be delayed for some years, caused the party to disband or return to Colorado. Where was their site at "the base of San Francisco Mountain"? We don't know. It's possible that it was west of present-day Flagstaff, maybe somewhere around Volunteer Spring in what is now [1976] Navajo Army Depot. But it could have been around in Black Bill or Doney parks on the east side of the Peaks, or in Fort Valley. Wherever it was, we have found no evidence of their attempted settlement.

An interesting figure who ranged in the area around San Francisco Mountain, Bill Williams Mountain, and Oak Creek Canyon as early as 1875, was Jesse Jefferson Howard, known for many years as "Bear" Howard. Ed Whipple, who knew him well, told in an interview appearing in the *Coconino Sun* December 7, 1928, how Bear Howard got his nickname: "His partner had been pulled out of a tree and killed by a bear the year I came here [1880], and thereafter old Howard made it his life's work to hunt bear and in some measure to repay for his partner's life. Bear Howard built the shack around which Carl Mayhew's Oak Creek summer hotel [Mayhew's Lodge] now stands. . . ." On a hunt in the Peaks area in 1875, he came upon a little stream which he followed to its source in the Inner Basin, where he found a large spring. Along with others, it was developed in the 1890s, and today is one of our sources of city water. Bear Howard's descendants are the Purtymans of Sedona-Oak Creek.

These and scores of other adventurers who became thoroughly familiar with the San Francisco Mountain and its environs did not establish themselves permanently, and it remained for the coming of the sheep to lay the groundwork for a permanent settlement. Sheep were very big business in New Mexico from early Spanish times. By the beginning of the 1800s, the ten or twelve leading families of New Mexico had such large holdings that they did not know how many sheep they owned, and Francisco Xavier Chavez, first governor of New Mexico after Mexico gained her independence from Spain, in 1822 owned more than a million sheep and others had almost as many. During the 1850s, more than a half million sheep were driven from New Mexico to California, some going via the Gila Trail through southern Arizona, others nibbling their way along the thirty-fifth parallel. Some of these sold for as much as $16 per head when they arrived in the rapidly growing California settlements. A lot more would have gone along the route passing near San Francisco Mountain if it had not been for hostile Indians, particularly the Navajos and Yavapais. Following Kit Carson's roundup of most of the Navajos in Canyon de Chelly in 1866, the Navajo threat was considerably lessened, but not entirely removed. Shortly thereafter, it became comparatively safe to run stock in northern Arizona, although stockmen would lose many sheep and cattle to Indians well up into the 1890s. The movement of sheep up through the 1860s was from New Mexico south into Mexico and westward into California. A disastrous drought in California in the early 1870s reversed this movement, and soon thousands of sheep were being moved out of California to the east, seeking water and range. By the mid-seventies, Arizona's reputation as sheep range was becoming well known. Thousands of head were driven in, first into the western part of the Territory, then as additional range was needed, into the northern portion by 1875.

One of these stockmen was John Clark, born near Augusta, Maine, March 13, 1839. He lived for some years in Massachusetts with a sister. In 1869, he set out for California via the Isthmus of Panama. Arriving in California, he worked on a dairy farm near San Jose, then got into the sheep business. In 1875, he drove five thousand sheep across the desert into Arizona, no doubt because of the California drought, entering Mojave County. In a severe storm, three thousand of the herd perished. He spent the winter on the Big Sandy, and in the spring of 1876, drove his herd to a range near Bill Williams Mountain, and then a year later moved southeast of present-day Flagstaff and settled in what became known as Clark Valley, part of which is now covered by Lake Mary.

Clark narrowly escaped being killed by a grizzly bear on the site of Flagstaff. In the biographical section of McClintock's history of Arizona, appearing in 1916, the bear story appears, apparently as told the interviewer by Clark himself:

> With a companion he had camped for the night, when he noticed a large silver tip bear making for camp. He only had a revolver, while his companion had a rifle. The latter concealed himself behind some bushes and when the bear was only a few feet from him stood up and took aim with his rifle but becoming nervous, he missed the animal and the bear, scared by the noise, did not see the man who had fired, but made straight for Mr. Clark. When the animal came within distance Mr. Clark fired all his six shots from his revolver into the animal, which apparently fell

dead. By the time his companion came toward him the bear had aroused, however, and chased them both up a tree, and as Mr. Clark was the last one up, with the bear in close pursuit, bruin caught his boot and pulled it off his foot. It remained at the foot of the tree for hours but finally lay down and died from the effects of the revolver shots. It certainly was a close call for Mr. Clark.

When he examined the heart, he found it shot to pieces.

Clark remained in Clark Valley until 1887. He had done remarkably well. In one year, 1883, he sold five thousand sheep for four dollars a head. In 1887 he purchased three hundred and twenty acres just north of town from his twin brother Asa, who arrived in 1883, and who had purchased the land from Thomas F. McMillan. From the time of Asa's acquisition of the property on, it was always known as the Clark Ranch. John Clark quit the sheep business and went into cattle, and also engaged in mercantile business in the Flagstaff Commercial Company. At one time he owned a butcher shop. He was married January 8, 1888, to Elizabeth M. Cook, also a native of Maine, educated in Massachusetts. He was Republican, and in 1900 was a candidate for county supervisor, but was defeated. He was for many years a leading figure in the Flagstaff community. He belonged to the Odd Fellows and the Baptist Church. He served as president of the local Pioneers' Society, and with Dr. D. J. Brannen took part in its organization in 1905. When John came to Flagstaff in the mid-1870s, he sent home glowing reports of opportunity here. Accordingly, Asa came out and joined him in 1883. John Clark died August 10, 1923.

Also in 1875 came William Henry Ashurst, some records say with John Clark. He was the father of Henry Fountain Ashurst, who was to serve Arizona in the U.S. Senate for thirty years. The elder Ashurst was born in Macon, Missouri, in 1844. With his parents he crossed the plains and mountains to California in 1856, and settled at Red Bluff. He worked in the mines. In 1871 he married Sarah Bogard, and in 1873, the young couple set out for Arizona driving a herd of sheep. They spent two years on the trail. Their famous son, Henry, was born in Nevada. The Ashursts first located in the Bill Williams Mountain region. For a short time he was a partner of John Clark. In 1876 he moved his stock to Anderson Mesa, southeast of present-day Flagstaff. His holdings there later became known as Ashurst Run, and Ashurst Lake is named in the family's honor. In 1882 he sold the sheep and purchased four hundred cattle from Henry Wingfield of Camp Verde. He served in the Fourteenth Territorial Legislature in 1887 as representative from Yavapai County. Roscoe G. Willson,

Cabin home of the William Henry Ashurst family on Anderson Mesa, occupied from 1878 to 1890. On one occasion the parents and small children hid in the nearby rocks to escape from a band of marauding Indians.

whose writings about early stockmen are well known, tells us that Ashurst was neat and well dressed, never swore, but had a fiery temper, drank brandy, and smoked and chewed tobacco. There were ten children.

In 1919 Henry returned to the site of the old Anderson Mesa home. In his diary he wrote that the family lived there every summer from 1878 to 1890, and from 1878 to 1883 they also wintered there. He wrote feelingly about the dreadful day when Indians galloped by on the warpath, and the family hid in the rocks. He visited the grave of his little sister Margaret, who became ill in the winter of 1879 and died. The mother had prepared the body for burial, the father had dug a grave and made a coffin, and the children had walked through the snow to the burial site. In later years, the Ashursts moved to Flagstaff so the children could attend school. The father died in a mining accident in Grand Canyon in January 1901. Mrs. Ashurst died in 1924.

Oldtimers have been in agreement down through the years that the first permanent settler in the immediate Flagstaff area was Thomas Forsythe McMillan, who arrived certainly no later than May 1876, the date shown in minutes of the organization meeting of the Pioneers' Society of Northern Arizona on April 12, 1905. Yavapai County records show that he and two others gave notice in February 1876, that they were claiming ten acres of land and all of the water in the Little Colorado in the vicinity of present day [1976] Joseph City for "milling and agricultural purposes," probably too small a parcel for either farming or stock raising. This suggests that McMillan was already established somewhere in northern Arizona at the time. We know he came from California, bringing a herd of sheep. He first settled on what in later years was known as the Clark Ranch, which encompassed areas we know today as City Park, Flagstaff junior and senior high schools, Clark Homes, and the residential area extending northward. His cabin was near a spring which was located in what we now know as China Canyon, a narrow, rocky defile between the two schools. McMillan used the canyon for a corral, closing off the north and south ends with pole or rail fences.

McMillan's son Donnelly, on a visit to Flagstaff from his home in Kingman, told this writer in an interview appearing in the *Arizona Daily Sun* August 28, 1954, that his father took up a large tract which included the areas of the city mentioned above, and on out Antelope Valley including the springs. In a sheep deal in 1883, McMillan traded the southern portion of the property to Asa Clark. Clark had W. A. Switzer, a pioneer who came in 1883, build a house for him. After surveys were made, it was discovered that it was on a school section and hence not available for patent. Asa battled over the title for four years, then sold his equity or interest to his brother, John, who after fifteen years of effort and litigation, finally acquired title. Later it became city property.

McMillan's grandson, Thomas C. Fleming, says that McMillan left the Clark Ranch area after a year or two and moved northward to the section we now know as Cheshire Estates. Finding the ground there a bit boggy, he moved again, this time locating permanently and homesteading the area which is now owned by the Museum of Northern Arizona. There, in 1886, he built a two-story log structure, where he dwelt for many years. The building still stands, and has been carefully preserved. It is now occupied by members of the museum staff.

McMillan's obituary, which appeared in the *Coconino Sun* on September 8, 1906, gave his age as seventy-three, indicating that he was born in 1833. However, the 1880 census for Yavapai County gave his age as forty-three, which would mean that he was born about 1837. He was an only child, native of Mount Pleasant, near Nashville, Tennessee. His mother's maiden name was Jane Turner. His aunt was Sara Childress, wife of President James K. Polk; one of his ancestors was General Forsythe of the Revolutionary Army, and a cousin, Benton McMillan, was at one time Governor of Tennessee. His parents died of yellow fever when he was a child, and he was reared by an uncle in Nashville. Unhappy and venturesome, he left home and went to northern California to prospect for gold; he then went to Australia and engaged in sheep raising for several years, then returned to California before moving to northern Arizona.

After building the big house at his homestead in 1886, McMillan went to San Francisco, where he married Katherine Donnelly Anderson, a widow, and brought her and her six-year-old son, Arthur Anderson, to Flagstaff in February 1888. His daughter, Mrs. Mary Fleming, wrote in a memoir dated November 7, 1941, that they arrived in a blustering snowstorm, and were met at the train and taken to the ranch in a sleigh driven by Jim Goodwin.

McMillan played a major part in bringing about the establishment of Coconino County, and served on the first elected board of supervisors. He built the Bank Hotel Building which stands at the corner of Santa Fe Avenue and Leroux, and was active in community affairs.

Mrs. Fleming tells us that her father was not a church member, "but he taught us the commandments of God, the Lord's Prayer, and to do unto others as you would have others do unto you. He also knew all the nursery rhymes, and one we especially liked was 'Old man Tucker was a fine old man, he washed his face in a frying pan, he combed his hair with a big cart wheel, and died with a toothache in his heel.'" The children were the stepson, Arthur J.

Anderson; Donnelly J. McMillan; Mary Edith McMillan Fleming, and Thomas Benton McMillan.

McMillan died September 5, 1906, and his obituary described him as "straightforward and plain spoken, an exemplary citizen, and his death will be mourned by all who knew him." The impression we have gained from oldtimers is that he was a man of dignity, great integrity, and reserved in his dealings with others. An interesting sidelight on his personality, however, is to be found in the gentle, loving and sensitive letters he wrote to his small stepson at Christmas, signing them Santa Claus. They are in the possession of his grandson, Thomas Fleming.

Mrs. McMillan raised her family and skillfully handled the property after his death. She died March 5, 1923, having managed to keep most of the original homestead, the Bank Hotel property, ten city lots, and a number of life insurance policies. The *Coconino Sun* reported on March 23, 1923, a couple of weeks after her death, that her estate was valued at $51,000, all of which she left to her four children and grandchildren.

At this point it may be noted that McMillan, who was on hand when the flag-raising Boston parties passed through the Peaks area, was also associated with what appears to be the first official naming of the community. At a meeting of the Yavapai County Board of Supervisors in October 1880, Thomas F. "McMillain" was appointed as voting registration officer of "Flag Staff." Several days later, the supervisors received a petition "from A. Jackson and eight others, asking that the settlements on Oak Creek be formed into a voting precinct . . ." The board ordered "that the petition be granted and that that portion of Yavapai County known as Oak Creek Valley be and the same is hereby established into a voting precinct . . ." The board appointed Madison Burch, inspector; S. C. Dickinson and B. F. Copple, judges, for the new Oak Creek precinct. Meeting a couple of days later, the board considered requests for formation of more precincts, and took action: "It appearing to the board necessary that precincts be established at the following places, to wit: Stoneman's Lake, Flag Staff, Batesville, Bumble Bee, it is ordered that voting precincts be and the same are hereby established at the above named places, to be known as above named and officers of election were appointed for such precincts as follows: Flag Staff, James O'Neal [*sic*], inspector; John Eldon [*sic*] and T. F. McMullan [*sic*], judges."

A month later the board passed on demands for $5.00 for James Alexander and the same amount for James Black, clerks, for their services in the election held at Flag Staff. Both were allowed. Demands from Oak Creek included those of Francis McClaren, Madison Burch, S. C. Dickinson, Mitchell Burch, for $5.00 each, also approved.

When the Prescott *Miner* on November 12, 1880, published the results of the November 2 election, it was found that polls were not opened in two precincts, and that three had not yet reported, one of which was Flag Staff. Oak Creek was in with its totals, however, showing that thirteen ballots had been cast. A week later the returns from Flag Staff finally came through, showing a total of eleven ballots.

This is most significant and important data, because it documents the fact that Flag Staff had been officially recognized as the name of the community at San Francisco Mountain by the Yavapai Supervisors in October 1880, approximately seven months before the day in May 1881, when as will be noted later, P. J. Brannen is said by some to have given the community its name. And in fact, the area had been Flagstaff at least as early as 1878.

In early September that year, Jonathan L. Harris, under contract with the General Land Office, conducted a survey of the area now occupied by the City of Flagstaff, a thirty-six-square-mile expanse described as Township 21 North, 7 East, Gila and Salt River Meridian. Harris's survey, with the accompanying map and field notes, reveals significant facts, the most interesting being that the McMillan property was then known as Flagstaff Ranch. Harris makes two references to Flagstaff, one, to "the house at ranch known as 'Flagstaff'" and "at a distance of 250 links W the line of cultivated ground at 'Flagstaff' commences. . . ."

Where did surveyor Harris get this data? No doubt from the people living here—probably McMillan, Clark, and possibly others. Harris's map shows quite clearly that the Flagstaff area he mentions was bounded on the north by what today we know as Havasupai Road, on the east by Humphreys and Fort Valley Road, and extended westward into what today we know as City Park. The cultivated land Harris shows ran from about Havasupai Road southward to Navajo Road. The ranch house or cabin he shows would be located in the area of the football field at Flagstaff High School.

Harris's map also tells us that the old Beale wagon road, down which the famous camel caravan trailed, came into our area from the east roughly between Linda Vista Drive and Swiss Road in East Flagstaff. It ran not far south of Linda Vista to where it crossed Fourth Street. About half way between Fourth Street and Monte Vista Drive it forked, and the Beale road ran northwesterly, while the southern fork, marked Overland Road on Harris's Map, ran north of today's Coconino High School grounds, crossed Cedar Hill, and then turned southwestward, passing by Antelope (Old Town) Spring, around the foot of Mars Hill, and continuing westward. Harris shows another road running northward from the Overland Road very close to present-day Navajo Drive and coming into what was then the McMillan establishment, house and corrals, an area which today [1976] is in the vicinity of the Museum of Northern Arizona.

Huge flocks of sheep being driven through the Peaks area en route to New Mexico as a result of the California drought of the mid-1870s, included breeding ewes of a superior strain, which could be sold in New Mexico for nearly double. Sometimes sheepmen would combine their bands and together drive them across Arizona. Richard J. Hinton's *Hand-Book to Arizona* (1877), perhaps the most reliable and best written of the several guide books on Arizona appearing during that period, said, "General Kautz, commanding the department recently [reported that] . . . in the San Francisco mountain country he saw and heard of many large bands of sheep and cattle. Notwithstanding the dryness of the season, the grass is very fine in that region, particularly on the eastern side of the mountain." General Kautz must have made his observations in 1876.

The Daggs brothers were early sheepmen in the area. Two of them, J. F. and W. A., drove their flocks on through to the Silver Creek range in Apache County. They were later joined by another brother, P. P., and together they operated as Daggs Brothers until 1890. In the early 1880s, they established Flagstaff as their headquarters. It is said that some years their flocks numbered fifty thousand.

Arriving in this area about the same time as McMillan, though probably a few months later, were James O'Neill and Frank Hart. O'Neill established a homestead at the springs south of Flagstaff which bear his name. Later, operators of the big sawmill at Flagstaff bought his place, and built a pipeline to supply their mill. This water was also available to the Flagstaff community when other supplies were inadequate.

Frank Hart settled in the area on the west slope of the San Francisco Mountain north of Leroux Spring and into the area which we know as Hart Prairie. He left Flagstaff about 1888.

Coming to Volunteer Springs about twelve miles west of Flagstaff in 1876 or 1877 was Walter J. Hill, driving a band of sheep. He was born in Vermont in 1854. In a dozen years, his herds had increased to the point that he was described in 1887 in the *Arizona Champion* at Flagstaff, as the largest sheep owner in Arizona. His wool clip for some years averaged a hundred thousand pounds, which suggests that he had from twenty to thirty thousand head. He was active in community affairs, and in 1888 became the first Master of Flagstaff Lodge

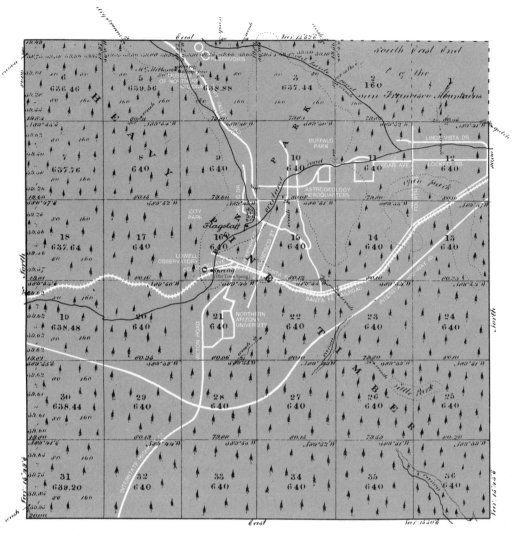

Map of Twp. 21 North, R. 7 E., Gila and Salt River Meridian (Flagstaff area) made in 1878 by J. L. Harris, deputy surveyor. Modern streets and landmarks have been superimposed to locate points on the original map. In his field notes Harris refers to "the house at ranch known as 'Flagstaff'" which appears above and left of center.

No. 7, F.&A.M. Ed Whipple, who came to Flagstaff in 1880, said in an interview appearing in the *Coconino Sun* December 7, 1928, that Hill was shot down on the Colorado River by a holdup gang when he was after horse thieves. "He later recovered and moved to California. His place was at Bellemont, where he built the tank for ice, and then went into the sheep business. At one time he was rated as one of the wealthiest men in the country, but finally went broke."

Following the establishment of the Mormon settlements on the Little Colorado at Allen's Camp and Sunset in 1876, John W. Young, son of the president of the church, Brigham Young, and one of his counselors, sent an expedition to Leroux Spring to establish title to the water there. The trip was made by three men in 1877. They built a small log cabin near the spring. Later, Young established a camp in the valley near the spring, and hearing rumors of Indian troubles, built a fort which has given the valley its name. Young's camp was originally headquarters for about sixty tie-cutters, working under contract on construction of the Atlantic & Pacific Railroad in 1881–82. There Young later established the Moroni Cattle Company, which about 1883 became the Arizona Cattle Company. The Mormons called Leroux Spring "San Francisco Spring," which has caused some confusion, as other explorers and pioneers gave that name to the spring which is near the site of the Museum of Northern Arizona, and in early days supplied water for the McMillan homestead. The Arizona Cattle Company was commonly known as the "A-1 Bar outfit" because of its brand.

Another early settler was John Elden, for whom Elden Mountain, Elden Spring, and Elden Pueblo were named. His daughter, Helena Elden Lindsey, in an article appearing in the *Coconino Sun* December 31, 1926, wrote that her father brought sheep into the area in 1875. He may have been here that year, but it is more likely that he brought the sheep with him when he returned to the area from California with his bride, arriving in February 1877. They made the trip by covered wagon, and when they reached the foot of the mountain, Elden built a log cabin which became the family home, and there three children were born: Helena, Eloise Felicia, and a boy, John.

George Hochderffer, who came to Flagstaff in 1887, was a friend of the Eldens, and tells the tragic story of the boy, John, in his autobiographical book, *Flagstaff Whoa!* He wrote that Elden Spring had a very limited flow, and the band of sheep and sixty head of cattle owned by Elden took all of it. One day a stranger, said later to have been Bob Roberts, with a herd of mules came and started to water at the spring. He was told to go on to Antelope or San Francisco springs, as there was not enough water. As he was leaving, he swung around and fired a random shot, hitting and killing the six-year-old boy. Elden was not home at the time. Hochderffer says that this was probably the cause of Elden selling his sheep and leaving the country which he loved so dearly. The child was buried near the cabin, and his grave has been visited down through the years many times by local residents. It is marked with stones.

Coming to northern Arizona in 1877, and locating at Clear Creek on the Verde in 1878, was the John W. Newman family, members of which were to live active lives in various northern Arizona communities. One of the sons, Lee, visiting in Flagstaff in 1947, told the writer about a visit to this area in early days. He and brother Jeff, in the summer of 1879, took a camp outfit and rode to Rogers Lake, and then on to the site of Flagstaff. They found some work had been done at one of the springs, and saw signs of old camps. He remembered seeing a tall pine tree, about eighteen inches in diameter and sixty feet high, with the limbs all trimmed off, west and north of the spring about a hundred yards. He did not know which spring, however.

On December 28, 1877, the *Miner* reported:

> ELK.—H. Crowell, Sam Dean and Wm. Cannon returned this morning from a hunting trip north, to the San Francisco Mountains, bringing with them several deer, and four large elk which were very fat, and would weigh at the least calculation 400 pounds each. Elk meat, when fat, is said to be excellent, and as that brought in by these gentlemen happens to be of that kind, we predict they will have but little trouble in disposing of their whole load.

In the same issue the *Miner* reported:

> Johnny Rogers, who lives on the outer rim of civilization, beyond Bill Williams' mountain, with no human inhabitant between him and the Ava Supias [Havasupai Indians], is in town spending the holidays and enjoying a season of relaxation from the excitement of the chase and the duties incumbent on a mountain ranchman. He tells us that he never heard of the new mining district discovered beyond him by Spencer and O'Leary until he came to town, but that there is plenty of room between him and the Colorado River and Cataract Creek for extensive mining operations, provided the mineral is only there. The Ava Supia Indians, of Cataract Creek sometimes visit his ranch, and he finds them, like all other Indians, to bear watching.

Saxton Seth (Boss) Acker was born in Michigan in 1845. He came West in 1869 to California, and then in 1877 to Arizona. In an interview appearing in the *Coconino Sun* December 21, 1928, he recalled first seeing Mormon Lake in 1877, while riding for cattle. About 1879 he moved to the Flagstaff area from Prescott. He was married in 1893 in Flagstaff to Charlotte May Wirts, who was born at Hudson, Michigan, in 1864, and came to Flagstaff in 1891 as school teacher. In 1895 the Ackers moved out to the Apache Maid Ranch fifty miles south, and remained there until 1910, when they moved back to Flagstaff. They had two daughters, one of whom died as a young girl. Daughter Alma taught in Flagstaff schools for many years.

Acker was commonly known as "Boss," a name given him when he bossed cow outfits during his years as a stockman and range rider. He was six feet four inches in height, and weighed well over two hundred pounds, a big man in every sense of the word. He served four years as Coconino County treasurer, Mrs. Acker being his deputy. She later served as assistant county superintendent of schools, and from 1917 to 1923, was head of the county school system. She also taught at Beaver Creek, Camp Verde, Middle Verde, and two years at Emerson School in Flagstaff. She was first matron at the Normal School, now Northern Arizona University. Acker died June 21, 1932, in Flagstaff.

Allen Doyle, who came to northern Arizona in 1876–77 and established a cattle outfit at Marshall Lake in 1878, and whose name is commemorated by Doyle Saddle and Doyle Peak, was a man of extraordinary qualities—extraordinary because he really exemplified the qualities of honesty, self-reliance, independence, and the pioneering spirit which have come to characterize the western frontiersman of legend. This remarkable man was a prototype for the heroes of countless western short stories, novels, and films, which have combined to form a significant element in the folklore and myth of America. He was the friend, and favorite guide and companion of the western writer of yesteryear, Zane Grey; his experiences appear in fictional form in *The U.P. Trail* and others of Grey's books. He was also the friend and guide of Jimmy Swinnerton, noted Arizona artist and cartoonist. He guided countless expeditions into the wilds of northern Arizona over a period of many years.

Doyle was born in Detroit, Michigan, in 1849, left an orphan at five years of age, at seventeen went west, and, working with railroad construction crews, was a participant in the driving of the silver spike which in 1869 completed construction of the first transcontinental railroad, the Union Pacific. He worked as a cowboy in Wyoming, made a living hunting buffalo, drove ox teams, and eventually came to northern Arizona. On Christmas Day 1877, he was married

in Prescott to Sarah Allen of Kansas, member of a pioneering family, early settlers in the Verde. They had five children, two of whom died in infancy. The
survivors were Lena; Lee, who also became a guide and professional hunter,
and Burton. Son Lee was location manager, guide, and consultant for many
movie companies working in this area in the 1920s and 1930s. He was owner of
"Rex, King of Wild Horses" and Rex's many successors, all familiar to western
movie fans of a generation ago.

Al Doyle's church connection was Presbyterian, and his political affiliation
Republican. A week before his death on November 7, 1921, he had a long visit
in Flagstaff with his old friend, Zane Grey. The *Coconino Sun*'s report of his
funeral said the procession to the grave was four blocks long.

Mrs. Doyle died May 8, 1923, at her Flagstaff home. In her obituary appearing in the *Coconino Sun* May 11, 1923, we learn that she was the first white
woman to cross Grand Canyon, making the trip shortly after Bright Angel
Trail was finished.

One of the colorful characters who came to this area very early was Abraham
Lincoln Smith, born July 16, 1864, in western Missouri. He arrived here in
1877, and spent much of his life in Oak Creek Canyon. On July 18, 1941, the
*Coconino Sun* published a little sketch about him, the data coming from Frank
M. Gold, longtime Flagstaff attorney:

> Link since his residence here had worked in a little of everything and
> always made somewhat of a success at all of it. Main occupation has been
> trapping, following his trap lines along Oak Creek and throughout
> Verde Valley.
>
> Old timers characterize Link as an extremely humorous man. He has
> a high pitched voice, which speaks commonsense and the truth. One
> story told about him was during a celebration in Flagstaff. Young cow-
> boys were attempting to rope goats, without success.
>
> "Get me a rope and cowpony," Link shrilled, "and I'll show these
> young up-starts how it is really done." A rope and cowpony were soon
> found. Link yelled to turn the critter loose. One twist of the rope and that
> goat hit dirt.
>
> Now old Link is 77 years old and still in good health. He states he has
> never been in the hospital except to carry someone out and has never
> spent two bits on medicine.
>
> Perhaps the best story told about old Link happened during last elec-
> tion when a young hopeful asked for his vote. Link came right back and

said: "Gosh darn you! You wait until you have a few more hairs in your nose and then I'll vote for you."

Link and his wife will celebrate their golden wedding anniversary in Clemenceau Sunday. They have six children who are expected to take part in the celebration and all the children live around these parts. The oldest is 49 and the youngest is 27. They include Roe N. Smith, Charles Smith, Mrs. Nellie Hart, Ira Smith, Mrs. Della Piper and Mrs. Ella Heydorn.

Another pioneer who arrived in northern Arizona in 1877, and in the Peaks area in 1878, was John Auterson Marshall, who was to play a useful role in the growth of the Flagstaff community, serving as water superintendent for thirty-two years. He was born in Nova Scotia in 1859, and at sixteen went to San Francisco, and worked in logging camps and at sawmills in northern California and Nevada. He was a skilled blacksmith. His grandson, Howard Weidner, told the writer in March 1973, that Marshall came to northern Arizona with a group of Mormon immigrants in 1876 or 1877 although not a member of that church, and ran their beef herd at Mormon Lake. He met Martha Allen, a sister of Sarah Allen who was to marry Allen Doyle, at Silver City, and later renewed their friendship when the Allens had located on the Verde. They were married in Prescott in 1877, and a year later came to the Flagstaff area. He homesteaded on Anderson Mesa in 1892, later patenting the land. Marshall Lake was named for him.

The Marshalls had two children; Charles, who was a barber in Flagstaff up into the 1950s, and Josephine, who became Mrs. Hayes Weidner. Hayes succeeded his father-in-law as water superintendent when the elder man retired in 1929. Howard said that his grandfather ran a blacksmith shop in a little cabin near Bright Angel Lodge on the south rim of Grand Canyon in early years, and that the cabin still stands, now used as an office. He was a pioneer member of the Flagstaff volunteer fire department, and a founding and charter member of the Knights of Pythias. He died September 23, 1932, four years after the death of Mrs. Marshall. His obituary appearing in the *Coconino Sun* September 30, said: "There was general sadness over the passing of John Marshall. A gentle, kindly man, a loving husband and father, a fine neighbor, an able, hard-working, conscientious public official. He was extremely valuable in the city water department and gave it many of the best years of his life."

An item in the Flagstaff *Champion* in November 1888, regarding the death of a young man, Philip Hull, Jr., stated that he had come to Flagstaff with his father "nine years ago" which would make it 1879. Ed Whipple once recalled that Hull raised horses in Pittman Valley.

Charles Hugo Schulz, for whom Schulz Pass and Schulz Springs were named, came to Flagstaff in 1880, driving a band of sheep from Texas. He was born in Buffalo, New York, in 1854. He served four years in the 1890s as member of the Coconino County Board of Supervisors, during which time the courthouse was built. The hill just west of the city on which Lowell Observatory is located was at one time known as Schulz Mountain. However, the name was changed to Mars Hill shortly after the observatory was founded in 1894. Schulz increased his sheep holdings until at one time he was considered the largest sheep owner in Arizona. He retired in 1911 and moved to Phoenix. He died in 1934.

Ed Whipple came to Flagstaff in 1880 before the coming of the railroad, probably with the idea of establishing a business in preparation for that event. In his *Coconino Sun* interview appearing December 7, 1928, he said: "Soon after my arrival I opened a saloon and restaurant combined. I was later a carpenter, a deputy sheriff for a number of years, and in fact, I have been almost everything. It was some years after I came that I opened up the only undertaking establishment here, and have been here from that time on." After forty-five years, he turned the business over to his son-in-law, W. L. Compton.

Whipple was born in Adams County, Iowa, December 25, 1856. He ran away from home as a young man, and headed west for the buffalo range country, lived with the cowboys, and learned to ride. He was on hand when the Indians attacked Medicine Lodge, Kansas. Later, he was chased across the range by a band of fifteen Indians. In 1878, after experience driving big cattle herds, Ed crossed the plains to Colorado, and from there to Albuquerque, where he went into the freighting business. In 1903, he married Mrs. Sofia Jensen, who had a six-year-old daughter, who is still living in Flagstaff in 1976, Mrs. Flora (W. L.) Compton. Whipple was foreman when structures were erected on the campus of the Normal School in the 1890s. He also built Lowell Observatory's first telescope dome in 1894.

His *Sun* interview gives much firsthand information about early times:

When I came here [1880] there were very few people in the country. In fact, I believe I can name all those who lived on the mountain at that time. There was John Clark at Clark Valley, now Lake Mary, who ran sheep. Then there was old Bill Ashurst, father of U.S. Senator Henry F. Ashurst, at Ashurst Lake. Gray and Dow ran cattle over the country where Flagstaff now stands. In fact, they furnished beef for the crew that built the railroad. Tom McMillan was at Clark's pasture, northwest of town. Frank Hart lived at the head of Fort Valley where the spring is, and had a great number of sheep. The Daggs brothers were located at Stoneman Lake, with sheep also. Dave Hart, Les Hart's father, lived at Oak Creek ... Old Man [probably Philip, Sr.] Hull was in the horse business, with headquarters at Pittman Valley; Pittman, after whom the Valley was named, also lived there at that time.

There was John Rogers, after whom Rogers Lake was named, who had his headquarters where the town of Williams now stands.

Whipple also mentioned Bear Howard and John Elden and continued:

I believe that is all of the people who lived in the country at that time ... I brought eight people in my party from Albuquerque, including a lawyer, a surveyor, a cook, a freighter, none of the names of whom I remember. Also there were W. W. Dunbar, Fred Ellis, Charles Hawes and my uncle Elijah Fitch....

Whipple died December 26, 1939, one day after his eighty-third birthday, as result of a self-inflicted .32 bullet wound.

Another oldtimer who came to Flagstaff in 1880 was John Heinz Love, born in Nebraska on February 19, 1865. He had little schooling, and left home in his early teens, arriving in Flagstaff when he was fifteen. He lived for a time with Asa Clark, on the property now occupied by the high school and near the site of McMillan's first cabin. He worked as a railsplitter for William Ashurst, and spent most of one winter snowbound at Mormon Lake, an experience which seriously affected his health, as he lived for many weeks on salt meat and little else. He was noted as being an extraordinary walker, and frequently traveled very long distances by shank's mare. Love acquired the reputation of being an excellent housecleaner, and commanded premium wages for his efforts; routinely he would do the annual housecleaning for the big homes of the community. About October each year, he would go down to his ten-acre place near Page Springs, returning about April. He was associated with Babbitts's curio business for a time, and then during the nineteen-tens and -twenties, worked with Babbitts in various capacities, frequently serving as greeter and general handyman during the Saturday night openings of the big store. In later years he spent his winter at Long Beach and Pasadena. He married Johanna Leissling. Love died December 21, 1942. He was a kindly, humorous man, and contributed in his own special way to the character and flavor of the Flagstaff community.

By 1880, two years before the coming of the railroad, the community of Flagstaff had started. It had acquired a name; it had a population, as the decennial census that year shows. In the twenty-ninth enumeration district, which included the San Francisco Mountain area, sixty-seven persons in twenty-seven households were counted between June 1–21. There were only three adult women and five female children. The three families were those of Elias W. Pittman, fifty-four, stock raiser; wife, Charlott [sic], fifty-four; two sons and a daughter; Allen W. Miller, thirty, stock raiser; wife Harett J. [sic], twenty; two sons and a daughter one month old; and George E. Johnson, forty-three, sheep raiser; his wife, Elizabeth, thirty-three; two sons and three daughters, the youngest eleven months old. There were many single men, but some had employees living with them. The list includes the names already familiar to us, and some not so familiar, such as Robert J. Talley, thirty-seven, and Jessey Field, employees of McMillan; teamster James Goodwin, thirty-eight; and sheepherders Manuell Valardo, thirty; James White, twenty-seven, and William Spencer, sixty.

The twenty-eighth enumeration district, which included the outlying areas to the south and east, reported two hundred and eighty people, one hundred of whom were women. Of these, thirty-nine were wives, the remainder being either children or unwed. Again, the list contains some familiar names and names that are lesser known, including Henry Fulton, twenty-five, sheep raiser; Charles Archer, fifty-five, and Mose Casner, forty, who raised horses.

By the time the last of these first settlers had arrived, the Atlantic & Pacific Railroad, chartered by Congress in 1866, had had many up and downs. It had built a few miles of track, and had gone through some drastic reorganizations and refinancings. It had one very valuable asset, and that was the charter to build a railroad along the thirty-fifth parallel, under the terms of which it was to receive title to alternate sections of land on both sides of the right-of-way north and south for forty miles. There was an additional strip extending another ten miles, from which sections would be given to the Atlantic & Pacific in exchange for lands within the forty-mile belt which had already been preempted or were otherwise not available.

The reorganization and re-reorganization is a complicated story. For the purpose of this narrative, it suffices to say that the Atlantic & Pacific came under control of the Atchison, Topeka and Santa Fe. In early 1880, the rejuvenated Atlantic & Pacific prepared to start construction from Albuquerque to the Colorado River, and in 1881, E. E. Ayer, a Chicago industrialist, secured a contract to supply ties and other lumber and timber for the railroad, and made plans to erect a sawmill at San Francisco Mountain.

These decisions were made in board rooms and offices far distant from the quiet forest glades around Antelope and San Francisco springs, but they were to have a tremendous and lasting impact, very quickly sending scores and then hundreds of settlers into the area, crystallizing the formation of the community of Flagstaff.

# CHAPTER V

# The Coming of the Railroad

SOME OF THE MEN who directed the affairs of the rejuvenated Atlantic & Pacific in early 1880 bore names which would become familiar to northern Arizonans in the years to come: E. F. Winslow was vice president, and the community of Brigham City, founded by the Mormons on the Little Colorado, would be renamed in his honor; Henry R. Holbrook was chief engineer, and the future seat of Navajo County would bear his name; the leading division engineer was Lewis Kingman, whose name would be given to the Mohave county seat. C. W. Sanders, chief engineer, gave his name to Sanders. Chalender, west of Flagstaff, which at one time rivaled Williams in size and activity, and had a post office from 1883 to 1897, was named for George F. Chalender, superintendent of motive power for the company. But Thomas Nickerson of Boston, president of the line, seems to have been bypassed when stations were being named.

Kingman's duties were important. He was to make the final survey, and set the line for the track from Albuquerque to the Colorado River, decisions which would have a lasting effect on the entire vast area. He started from Albuquerque with a party of twenty-one men and five wagons in April 1880, and rather quickly located the line as far west as the future site of Holbrook, a place first known as Horsehead Crossing and a bit later Berado's Crossing.

On April 2, 1880, the Prescott *Miner* reported:

> Many of the most valuable watering places, cattle ranges and timber claims are being taken up in the vicinity of Bill Williams and San Francisco Mountains, near the line of the 35th parallel route . . . and there no longer exists a doubt in the mind of any intelligent man but what the A. P. will cross Arizona within the next eighteen months.

On May 14, 1880, the *Miner* ran an engraving of a locomotive and cars in full tilt down the track, with the heading: "The [Railroad] Coming; The A.T .& S.F.R.R. Still Booming," and reported:

Louis [*sic*] Kingman, Assistant Engineer of the above Company, came in this morning to purchase supplies for his locating party, and brings the cheering intelligence that the graders are still at work this side of Albuquerque. The report that the graders had been called off arose from the fact that a small party were grading in the Querino Canyon, in Arizona, when the news of Indian troubles reached them and as they were only 50 strong, they went back and joined the graders beyond Wingate.

Mr. Kingman has made a permanent location of the line as far as the mouth of the Puerco, on the Little Colorado [today's Holbrook] and is now on his way, with five wagons and 21 men, to the Colorado River, where he will establish a point for crossing, either at the Needles or above, and will proceed thence to locate the line permanently in this direction, so as to get out of the hot region of the Colorado before the very hot weather sets in. He expects to reach the point nearest to Prescott within the next 35 or 40 days, and will probably put in the rest of the summer in selecting the best route around San Francisco Mountain. His wagons are now near Hell's canyon on their way to Mineral Park, while his packing outfit is encamped in Williamson Valley.

The Beale wagon road was still in use from the Rio Grande through northern Arizona to the Colorado River; here and there the line varied from that laid down by Beale and his camel corps years before; but in the main, the old routing prevailed, simply because it represented the shortest distance between two points, insofar as such a straight line was feasible for travel. Considerable portions of it were included in the Yavapai County road system. Under date of July 7, 1879, the following minute appears in the proceedings of the board of supervisors: "In compliance with a petition to that effect, Road District No. 15, commencing at a hill one-half a mile north of Campbell's and Baker's ranch near Point of Rocks, thence by way of Chino Valley, Hell Canyon, Bill Williams Mountain, San Francisco Mountain to the west boundary of Apache [Navajo] County, was established, and G. N. Gray was appointed overseer thereof."

On June 12, 1880, the Albuquerque *Daily Golden Gate* reported that John W. Young was in town en route east to negotiate with Atlantic & Pacific officials for construction of one hundred twenty-five miles of roadbed through Arizona. He had just come from the Little Colorado settlements, which he said now had a population of about two thousand. He said the land was productive, and that the new settlers were doing well and were contented and happy. He added that the Mormons were not interested in prospecting, believing that more money is lost than is made in that vocation, but that his people would work for wages in mines for others.

By mid-June, the bridge over the Rio Grande was nearing completion, and sixty miles of grading was ready for ties and rails. Progress was slowed by a shortage of laborers. By early August, sixty men were laying track, and the contractors were bringing in boarding cars to accommodate more workers. Soon track was going down at the rate of about three-quarters of a mile a day. Grading parties were well into Arizona. The Prescott *Miner* expressed the hope that the line would be completed to the Colorado River by January 1882, and "When this shall have been accomplished commerce will open up anew, business revive, mining take a sudden start, immigration come in, money become plentiful, property advance in price, labor be in demand, towns spring up, our valleys and hills be settled, and general prosperity follow." With the coming of fall, contractors announced that they would continue grading during the winter as weather permitted, but that track-laying would halt until spring.

It was apparent that the routing would be close to the line established in 1867 by General Palmer, and many years before that by Beale's wagon road. In the vicinity of San Francisco Mountain, it would cross Antelope Park near Antelope Spring, which very soon would become known as Old Town Spring.

Here and there were men aware of the opportunities offered by construction of the railroad. Among these were Patrick B. Brannen, successful Prescott general merchant, and his twenty-five-year-old nephew, Peter James Brannen, natives of Ottawa, Canada, as were the other Brannens. P. B.'s brother was Dr. Dennis J. Brannen, who was to become Flagstaff's first physician, arriving in 1882. Peter Brannen's brother was Joseph M., who came to the area later. Either during the winter of 1880–81 or very early spring, 1881, the Prescott merchant and his young nephew selected a site for a general merchandise store near Antelope Spring, and freighted in from Prescott a supply of merchandise and a tent in which to display it. After a few months the tent was replaced by a log cabin and lumber structure, which would burn in due time along with nearly everything else at Old Town. There were already many men working along the line, tie-cutters were busy in the woods, and the rapidly growing stock-raising business also offered a market for supplies of all kinds. P. J. Brannen played an active part in the community from the beginning, and was the first to observe that a better site for the town was a half mile or so east, at a level spot near where the railroad would set a box car as depot after arrival of the rails here in August 1882. Accordingly, in 1883, he built a $10,000 cut stone building directly across the track from the depot. That structure, partly destroyed by fire a time or two, but rebuilt each time, stands today on the northeast corner of Santa Fe Avenue and San Francisco Street; it is now [1976] occupied by a bar, Joe's Place.

Before Flagstaff was incorporated in 1894, P. J. was widely referred to as "Mayor" Brannen. In addition to his active management of the pioneer general store, he homesteaded the Brannen addition, which is that part of our community lying south of the railroad tracks and east of San Francisco Street. He left Flagstaff in 1892, moving to California. By 1912, he was engaged in business in San Pedro. There he had a mercantile business, an insurance agency, and was also active in real estate. He died August 3, 1939, and his name is commemorated in our community by Brannen Avenue, Brannen Circle, and by the housing project, Brannen Homes.

Another who saw opportunity at Antelope Park at the time was Ed Whipple. No later than the spring of 1881, he opened a combination restaurant and saloon, also in a tent, and also quite near Antelope Spring. Both his establishment and the Brannen store faced southeast, and bordered on the railroad right-of-way, near the foot of what was later named Mars Hill.

In its March 25, 1881, issue, the Prescott *Miner* also took note of another potential opportunity:

> PRAISEWORTHY.—The Directors of the 35th Parallel R.R. certainly deserve much credit for employing none but white labor in building their great transcontinental railway from the Atlantic to the Pacific. Mongolian labor is below par with these people.
>
> A saw mill in the Bill Williams or San Francisco country would be a regular mint for the next two or three years. Who is the first to reach for the golden apple?
>
> The railroad people are putting up several buildings at different points between the Little Colorado and Big Chino Valley, hauling their lumber all the way from Prescott.
>
> Lumber is being hauled from Prescott to the San Francisco mountains, 100 miles, where forests of pine are innumerable.

Although the editor of the *Miner* was not aware of it, plans already were underway to establish a sawmill in the area.

By this time a hundred men were laying rails, seven hundred were employed at grading, and track had been completed to a point one hundred twenty-seven miles west of Albuquerque. During the previous season, engineer

Kingman had completed the work of establishing the line at the eastern and western ends of the route, and was now closing the gap through the middle part of northern Arizona. His survey crews, numbering twenty men, were camped at the McMillan corral near the spring in China Canyon by mid-April 1881. We are fortunate that a member of that party wrote an account of his experiences, and it appeared in the *Coconino Sun* July 20, 1901, just twenty years later. The writer was J. M. Erskine, and here is his story:

One afternoon about the middle of April, 1881, four light wagons, with a few provisions and some 10 men, drove up to the spring on what is now Mr. John Clark's place, about half a mile north of town. There was a similar party already camped there, which had arrived some four days previous. This was the first and second installments of the Atlantic & Pacific Railroad Company's surveying corps, of which the writer was a member, Mr. Kingman being the chief.

It did not take the 20 men long to know each other, and in a short time all were enjoying themselves, as the weather was simply delightful, and we enjoyed the fine fresh water, something we had not had in a very long time.

The writer had started for Tombstone the fall before, but along in January on the way to Silver City, N.M., the Apache Indians caught the next stage to me, and as the Indians were worse farther west, I came to the conclusion that Colorado was good enough for me. But upon reaching Albuquerque the opportunity presented itself to join the A. & P. Survey corps in Arizona.

The next day we went to the then terminus of the railroad, which was at Bluewater, N.M. The day following our stock came out and after a day spent in fitting harness, dividing loads and crews, the long drive was commenced. It came to the writer to be one of the first to herd the stock at night. This was not a very pleasant job as rustlers were getting in their work whenever they could. Besides there were some good Navajos that were none too good to steal horses. I only lost two horses that night; but from that time on I was not called on to stand guard.

We left the Little Colorado with all the water we could haul, hoping that when we got to Canyon Diablo we would find plenty. Upon arriving at that point we found only a small amount, and the rocks were simply alive with rattlesnakes. We concluded to leave the water to them, and dealt out to each animal one bucketful of water, a small amount for tired animals. The next morning we did the same, then made as rapid a drive as we could to Turkey Tanks, where we found plenty of water.

The next day we struck the site of what is now the city of Flagstaff. This being the division on which we were to work, all hands turned to hauling ties from where the lumber mill now stands to build our quarters, there being some dozen Mormon families there that the famous John W. Young had sent there a few weeks prior to cut ties at 15 cents each— bacon at 40 cents a pound.

Then it began to snow, and we kept in our tents. The tents were none too good, and we had to keep busy to keep warm. Luckily we had a good supply of blankets. The storm kept up for two weeks and there was over two feet of snow on the level. The storm having stopped our freight, provisions began running low, and Mr. Kingman started with two four-horse teams for Prescott, then about the only town in Arizona outside of Tucson, and after an absence of some two weeks returned with a good supply.

We commenced our work by first laying out the bridge over the canyon six miles east of town. We had made our cross sections up to about where the lumber mill is now when the first installment of freighters and graders came in. Then, from quietness, all was bustle, getting work started.

One of the hardest tasks of all was to find water. Well do I remember a freighter coming up to our spring with a dozen tired mules. We informed him that was our private water supply and that he must hunt elsewhere for water. "Private be d—d," he said. He was going to water his famishing mules at that spring; without trouble if he could, but nevertheless they were going to be watered there. We took him at his word, as he was just that kind of fellow.

The spring in what is now Old Town came near causing bloodshed the night before I left. The traders had teams with tanks going all over the country hauling water.

A little circumstance came up that gave me a chance to quit and get to Albuquerque. I accepted the chance, as one of the main objects of my coming out was to see what the outlook was for mineral, and my partner, who had returned from a trip about Prescott and that country, reported that on account of the scarcity of water it would take years to develop a claim, so I threw up the sponge and started back east.

The day before I started the first saloon was opened [probably Ed Whipple's] just a short way east of our spring, we having made our quarters near where John Clark's stables are now. We had the hightoned residence of the country, being ties set on end, with wagon-sheetcovers for roof and pine boughs for a carpet, also for bed springs.

With plenty of the best provisions the company could furnish us, we lived high, and were able to help now and then some poor Mormon family, for I never saw people much poorer than the John W. Young people were.

I made the trip to Brigham City with one set of Mormon freighters, then made a contract to Holbrook section, and finally caught another outfit that carried me to the end of the road near where Gallup must now stand. . . . I remember an experience near Navajo Springs that might have cost us our lives had it not been that we used caution all through the country.

Our party consisted of five men and two women, all well armed. The water had been used up at the springs by a big bull outfit, so we were directed on to Squaw Springs, only a mudhole, occupied by some renegade Navajos and their stinking goats. We gave them five dollars in silver to let us occupy the place for the night. Before dark they came to camp to trade for arms, offering everything they had. But we refused to sell, and made them leave. That night we had two men out with the stock and one on watch at the camp, besides a good dog. Probably had we not used good care and been well armed we might have been up with the angels now.

I was thankful to arrive at Albuquerque and when the company offered me a section about where Ash Fork stands now, I simply declined with thanks.

On May 6, 1881, the *Miner* published the following item:

Mr. McCarthy is in from Price, King & Co.'s camp, Flagstaff. He reports lively operations in grading, cutting ties, etc., in that section.

As mentioned in the previous chapter, in 1877 John Young had established claim to the waters of Leroux Spring by sending a party of three men to build a small log cabin; perhaps also to serve as shelter for missionary parties traveling the Beale wagon road.

McClintock tells us that by early 1881:

About 60 graders and tie cutters were camped, mainly in tents, on Leroux prairie or flat, below the spring, according to Mrs. W. J. Murphy,

now [in 1915] of Phoenix, a resident of the prairie for five months of
1881, her husband a contractor on the new railroad. She remembers no
cattle, though deer and antelope were abundant.

In the early spring came reports of Indian raids to the eastward. So
Young hauled in a number of double-length ties which he set on end,
making a stockade, within which he placed his camp, mainly of tents.
Later were brush shelters within, but the great log house . . . was not
built until afterward. Thereafter was attached the name of Fort Moroni,
given by Young, who organized the Moroni Cattle Company. At the
time of the coming of the grade to Flagstaff, Young also had a camp in
the western end of the present Flagstaff townsite.

This was the origin of the fort which gave Fort Valley its name.

While grading crews in Arizona were swinging their picks and firing the
dangerous black powder and shoving dirt around with mule-drawn fresnos,
and tie-cutters were hacking away in the forest on both sides of the line, and
Erskine and his mates were running final lines under engineer Kingman's direction and replacing stakes pulled up by Indians or knocked over by game or
stock, an important decision which would have a great and lasting impact on
the Flagstaff area was being arrived at in Chicago by one of the nation's top
industrialists. He was Edward Everett Ayer.

Ayer was born in 1841 in Wisconsin. As a youth he had gone to California,
enlisted in a Union cavalry regiment, later joined an infantry regiment, and
saw plenty of service. Shortly before his twenty-third birthday, he completed
his enlistment and returned home to Illinois, arriving in mid-summer 1864. In
a very few years he became an important businessman, and one of his specialties was manufacturing and buying and selling ties and other railroading supplies. He made many very large deals, some involving as much as a million
dollars. By 1880 he had done a lot of business with the Santa Fe, and had friends
in its hierarchy. When the Santa Fe made its arrangements to absorb the
Atlantic & Pacific, Ayer knew the details. He was also busy making plans to
provide many hundreds of thousands of ties for the Mexican Central Railway,
then under construction. From Ayer's army experience in Arizona, he was well
aware of the tremendous forests in the northern part of the Territory.

Early in 1881 he proposed to the Santa Fe that he would build a lumber mill
in the San Francisco Mountain region to supply material for construction of the
line along the thirty-fifth parallel. He was also seeking a source for the ties and
telegraph poles he would sell to the Mexican Central. The Santa Fe gave him

an option on eighty-seven sections (square miles) of their timberland south and west of the mountain. He took a special car to New Mexico and out to the end of the line. He had an expedition of wagons for transport, an ambulance for his party to ride in, and upon request to his personal friend, Gen. Phil Sheridan, got an escort of eight or ten soldiers from Fort Defiance, as there were rumors of unrest among the Indians.

Ayer left most of the party a few miles from the site of future Flagstaff, and with three soldiers scouted the country for several days, sleeping on the ground and surveying the forest throughout the area. Satisfied that there was adequate raw material and water, he made the decision to bring in a mill. To fulfill his contracts with the Santa Fe and Mexican Central, he knew he would have to build a big one, capable of producing 150,000 feet of lumber a day. He hastened back eastward.

While Ayer was making arrangements for the extraordinary feat of moving a complete large sawmill into the wilds of northern Arizona, together with everything needed for its operation and the accommodation of its workers, con-tractors were pushing work on grading, and the rails were stretching westward. The big problem was lack of manpower. Largest contractor on the line was J. R. Price & Company, with fifty-four miles of roadbed underway. Their head-quarters was established in tents and cabins at a site about five miles east of present-day downtown Flagstaff. George Hochderffer camped at the site in 1887 on his way to Flagstaff, five or six years after the construction crews had moved on; he described it as "the most beautiful campsite of our journey west." There were the remains of a dozen houses of logs, roofless except a few had a covering of split timbers and dirt. Doors made of hewed-out slabs still hung in the doorways, and over most of them were nailed deer antlers. Some of the cabins had canvas roofs, and there must also have been many tents.

There were a number of other contractors along the line. A lot of men were involved, and about most of them we know nothing. No doubt there were some who worked hard, drew and blew their wages in regular sprees, then returned to more backbreaking work. There must have been men who carefully saved to buy farms or open little businesses back home in Virginia or Ohio or Vermont or Illinois. There must have been men who cheated other men in friendly card games; there must have been many yarns told around campfires, of fights with Indians, of Civil War experiences; there must have been lasting friendships made, and there were fights and killings and lynchings. Forty years later, in the November 11, 1921, issue of the *Coconino Sun,* we find a single paragraph about one of the many men who chopped the ties, swung the picks, built the railroad:

James Healey, veteran of the Civil War, is believed to be the first settler in Flagstaff now living here, though he is not quite sure whether Ed
Whipple didn't settle here before he did. Mr. Healey came here April 25,
1881, getting off the stage at the foot of Elden Mountain and hiking over
the hill to where we are now, and going to work for Bryant Brothers,
railroad tie contractors. Asked if he had noted many changes during the
more than 40 years since then, he said, nothing much, except everything
has changed.

Possibly the man driving the stage on which Healey came to Flagstaff was
Frank Heiser, born in 1850, who came to Arizona at age eighteen to fight
Indians as one of General Crook's cavalrymen. For years he carried the mail,
and also drove the stage between Prescott and Brigham City (Winslow). He
settled at Flagstaff, and spent many years working as a ranch hand. In the 1910s
he moved to Pasadena, where he died in April 1922.

Another one of the hundreds of men who did the actual physical work of
shoveling, digging, hauling, and driving the teams, was Frank Watson. All we
know about him comes from his brief obituary, appearing on December 10,
1926, in the *Coconino Sun*:

> Frank Watson, who had a leg amputated two weeks ago in an effort
> to check an infection, died Monday morning after receiving care at the
> county hospital for the past six weeks. . . .
>
> Mr. Watson came to Flagstaff with the Atlantic & Pacific Railway in
> 1881 as a teamster for the railway contractor, Bill Garland. He spent
> many years with Garland wherever new roads were to be graded. In later
> years he was at times employed near Flagstaff hauling logs. For the past
> few years he was caretaker for the Dan Francis country home north of
> town. . . .
>
> Frank Watson was born March 19, 1851, in Virginia. He spent much
> of his boyhood in Maryland helping his father, an oysterman. Those who
> knew him intimately say that he was a fine old man and that none more
> honest could be found. So far as known he never married and he leaves
> no relatives.

Healey, Heiser, and Watson, only three of many hundreds, mostly nameless
and faceless. Many of them who came to build the railroad were only boys, and
a considerable number of the others must have been veterans of Union and
Confederate armies.

What pay did the men receive? Wisbey tells us that during the construction of the Atlantic & Pacific in 1881–1882, tracklayers and graders were receiving $2.25 a day, and spikers and iron men $2.50. Stone masons received more. In June 1882, stone cutters were getting $5.00 per day, quarrymen $3.00, rock men $2.65, plug and feather drillers, $3.00; laborers, $2.45, and sailors to rig derricks, $3.00. The working day was ten hours and board was $5.50 per week. The Prescott *Miner* reported on May 13, 1881, that teamsters were receiving $35 per month with board. Bryant Brothers, for whom Healey worked, and Garland, Watson's boss, were in areas west of Flagstaff. Other contractors were Woodruff, Sims, Shinfield, and Fisher.

We learn from the April 1, 1881, issue of the *Miner,* that mail service along the line was becoming routine:

> We are indebted to Mr. Fred W. Williams for the following information: The mail for Chino Valley, San Francisco Mountains and Brigham City leaves Prescott Tuesday, Thursday and Saturday, of each week, at 9 o'clock A.M. Arrives at 11 A.M. Monday, Wednesday and Friday.
>
> W. H. Greenup, one of our oldest freighters, carries the mail between Snyder's Springs and Brigham; distance, 90 miles.
>
> The railroad people are making new trails, by which, it is thought, the distance between Prescott and Brigham will soon be reduced to 140 miles.
>
> Grain is scarce and dear on the route. Oats has brought 8 cents per pound in the San Francisco country. Kansas corn is worth 6½ cents per pound on the Little Colorado. Here are chances for the farmers of Yavapai county.

By mid-summer, Price, the contractor who had a camp near Flagstaff, was in Albuquerque purchasing a mowing machine and horse rake to cut hay for his stock, stating that the grass was now better than it had been known for years. A Prescott liquor house announced that it had sent to the railroad forty-two dozen bottles of excellent beer and that another large quantity would be sent along soon. As the work proceeded, the Albuquerque *Journal* became ecstatic, and in a long article appearing June 10, 1881, discussing various areas through which the rails were to go, said:

> Nowhere does the country afford lands better adapted to stock raising and agricultural purposes than the valleys of the San Francisco Mountains. Enterprises are here met half way. Nature has crowned this region with everything calculated for the happiness of man. The huntsman, the

agriculturist, the stock raiser and the lumberman alike find here the opportunities to rise swiftly above want to prosperity and comfort. The tourist, too, can find here ample enjoyment and refresh himself with the enchantment and wild beauties of nature. The weary wanderer whose toils have shattered health upon life's arduous pathway is healed by the quickening influences of the climate, and when these peaks become dotted with the modern inns of the Nineteenth century, and progress has wrought the changes incident to an advanced civilization, this locality will become a favored spot for the sons and daughters of our country. Let the people of the East, the North and the South sally forth and take early advantage of the great opportunities held out to the enterprising and industrious arm of man by this locality . . .

In June, John Young went to Salt Lake City to find laborers, and Simms, a contractor, went to California to recruit five hundred Chinese to help speed rail-laying. He apparently found them for subsequently Chinese labored on the Atlantic & Pacific across northern Arizona, some of them remaining in the towns along the line to run laundries, restaurants and other businesses. On August 5, the *Miner* predicted that the railroad would be completed to Flagstaff by January 1, 1882. And on the same date the paper published two interesting items from Bill Williams:

Mr. J. F. Scott, a potato raiser of Bill Williams Mountain, says his potato trees are looking well. Coming in he met wagons with Parker's sawmill, at Hell Canyon.

At Johnny Rodgers' old place, Berry Bros. have a large stock of general merchandise, which they sell at wholesale and retail. Six immense wagons, drawn by oxen, arrived from the end of the track, with goods for this firm. Thirteen ox teams recently passed on to McCormick's camp with supplies from the end of the track. Merchants, we hear, sell high up there. Kansas oats goes at 9 cents per lb., Arizona corn and barley for about six cents. The several contractors are pushing work.

The *Miner* also published an item stating that the Atlantic & Pacific would soon be bringing choice eastern apples to Prescott markets, and urging Yavapai farmers to consider producing fruit to manufacture wines. And undoubtedly it was about this that the following observation was made:

As yet there are no towns of any importance along the line of the Atlantic and Pacific west of Brigham City (Winslow).

Flagstaff has one store and five deadfalls [saloons] and is situated seven miles south of San Francisco Mountain on the railway line. They sell water and whiskey.*

On August 12, 1881, the *Miner* published a column written by P. J. Brannen. It was titled "Interesting News Letter" and it was, very. It was datelined Flag Staff, perhaps the first time the community's name was used as source of a news report:

### WOOL—MAN SHOT—ETC.

Flag Staff, August 9, 1881.

Ed. *Miner*—Please send a copy of the *Daily Miner* to my address here. In all probability I will be able to get some subscribers for your paper. You know we have an established government office at the front of which I am postmaster [sic]. Anything I can do for you towards getting subscribers for your paper will be done with the greatest pleasure.

Our little town is growing; several restaurants, stores and saloons are now in course of erection. We have now six of the latter.

Large quantities of wool are being shipped from this vicinity to the end of the A. & P. road. The principal wool growers of this section are Messrs. Hill, Hart, Oneal [sic] and Dagg [sic] Bros.

I presume you have learned, ere this, of our fellow townsman, Mr. Chas. Hawes, being shot. The circumstances of the case are these: Mr. Hawes was on his way to the end of the track for goods and picked up a man who solicited a ride. When a few miles the other side of Holbrook they camped, after partaking of a meal laid down to sleep. His partner, procuring a bull dog pistol, which was concealed in a box in the wagon, stood over Hawes and deliberately shot him through the head, the ball entering just below the left ear and coming out beneath the right eye, strange to say, not killing him. After recovering from the terrible shock Hawes made search for his pistol, but finding it missing he at once mistrusted who had done the deed. Looking out the back of the covered wagon he saw his partner preparing to dig out, saddling one of the best horses, thinking, of course, that he had killed Hawes, and intended to rob him of what money was on his person, but to his astonishment saw Hawes looking out of the wagon. Seeing that he was not going to succeed in carrying out his intentions, he confessed that he had shot him but

*The comment is scribbled on a scrap of paper contained in the Flagstaff folder in the Arizona Historical Society's library in Tucson.

claimed it was an accident, and wanted to know if he had not better go for saddles and went. He is still at large.

Mr. Hawes returned to Holbrook bleeding all the road [sic], but shortly after his arrival there they managed to stop the blood. He remained at Holbrook a few days then left for here, where he arrived on Saturday morning, eight days after being shot. He is doing well, and was in our store this morning. I think he is out of danger. Well, I have entered into a rather lengthy account of this tragedy but thought when I started in I might as well give you the whole particulars.

A large party of desperados passed through here yesterday with quite a band of stock. Each one of them had a couple of six shooters strapped to their person and Winchester rifles strapped to their saddles.

Must close for this time as the mail will shortly leave for Prescott.

Yours truly,

P. J. Brannen.

In the same issue, the *Miner* mentioned that scores of teamsters and teams were needed by merchants of Prescott and railroad contractors to take goods to the camps along the railroad line in the mountains. Reports of comings and goings to Flag Staff now became routine in the news columns of the *Miner*. It reported on August 26 that "Railroad teams continue to arrive and depart in such numbers that it would be hard to keep track of them." It also reported in the same issue: "It is rumored that the Navajos are saucy and mean. They will have to be whipped good, and that soon." Another item stated: "A man was found dead a few days since at Devil Springs, east of the San Francisco Mountain. It is thought that the Navajos committed the deed of killing." In the same issue appeared the following: "Brannen & Co. are sending huge quantities of goods to the line of the R.R. where they have a branch store, and are selling many dollars worth daily. Success to them. They are deserving." Another item: "R.R. Contractor Price came in from the camp yesterday. He is out of certain articles of provisions, which he is supplying from the Prescott market." Another item: "A buckboard departed this morning for Holbrook, on the Little Colorado, to which point the cars of the Atlantic & Pacific R.R. are now running."

Evidence that Flag Staff was becoming a town, with all of the consequent complications, is seen in the following item, also appearing on August 26: "Homer Fry, the gentlemanly and efficient bookkeeper of Price, King and Co., has been appointed a Justice of Peace and Notary Public for the Flag Staff precinct. He goes home with plenty of blanks and clothed with the authority to make matters run smooth, or else the offenders submit to the compiled laws of our Territory."

On September 2, the *Miner* reported that on August 26 seven men had been killed in a black powder explosion on the line west of Flagstaff. Three others were maimed. One man was blown five hundred feet in the air, another's mangled remains caught in the top of a tall pine tree. A man with a mule harnessed to a cart was blown to pieces and the cart demolished but the mule was unhurt. The bodies were gathered up in blankets and buried near the scene. About the same time the Yavapai County sheriff sent a deputy to make a trip along the line of the railroad to look things over. He was given kind treatment by Messers. Price, King & Co., and their people, the *Miner* reported.

In late August two men were killed on the Rio Puerco near Holbrook. They were tending bar. The murderer was not caught. The *Miner* stated:

> In this connection, duty to law-abiding people compels us to again call attention to the fact that along with the A. & P. Railroad, there have come into Northern Arizona many scoundrels—who are terrorizing the country north of us, and who will become more dangerous if not properly attended to. On them, preaching and good advice are utterly wasted. Born to die in their boots, there is but one straight, efficient mode of dealing with them. We cannot permit them to fasten on this section of Arizona a cloud similar to that spread broadcast over Southern Arizona by their desperate colleagues, the cow-boys. If the proper officers cannot put them down, then, citizens will be compelled to combine and set examples that will force upon them the conviction that Northern Arizona is not a healthy region for their kind. The peace and fair fame of these Northern Counties cannot be trifled with. The Apaches and other Indians threaten us; for their acts there may be some excuse, but none, whatever, can be set forth by white men who, too lazy to work when there is plenty to be done, pass their days and nights in the commission of savage crimes. Down with the scoundrels.

During the summer and fall of 1881, a sawmill was built near Bill Williams Mountain by the firm of Wilson & Haskell, with Luke Wilson as manager. By early August they had foundations ready for the machinery, and by the end of the month they were teaming the machinery from Prescott to Williams. "Soon the whistle from this forest-reducer will greet the ears of the army of graders and others who are preparing the way for the steel rail, upon which will swing back and forth the riches of east and west," said the *Miner* on August

26. On September 9, the *Miner* reported that a large tubular boiler, built at Zanesville, Ohio, was in the streets of Prescott enroute to Wilson & Haskell's mill at Bill Williams Mountain. In the same issue the *Miner* said the mill would be ready to operate the next week, and that 300,000 feet of logs were cut and ready for the saws. This mill also produced ties for the Atlantic & Pacific. However, by the fall of 1882, it was shut down, and by March 1883, it had relocated south of Prescott.

The Mormons had a mill, too. It had been erected about 1870 at Mount Trumbull in the Unikarets Mountains of northwestern Arizona, to cut lumber and timbers for the Mormon Temple at Saint George, Utah, fifty miles to the north. In 1876, when settlement was made by the Mormons on the Little Colorado, the mill was hauled to Sunset in September by Warren R. Tenney, who had operated it at Mount Trumbull. It was set up in the Mormon Lake area and soon was producing lumber. The site was named Millville. The mill, McClintock says, later became the property of W. J. Flake, a pioneer of the community of Snowflake. In the summer of 1882 it was taken to Pinedale, and in 1890 to Pinetop, in the southern part of what is now Navajo County. It was later taken to Lakeside.

The rails reached Sanders on August 31, 1881, but washouts swept away portions of the roadbed a number of times, and along with the unprecedented rain came Indian troubles—the Apaches were on the warpath. A band of renegades killed and scalped more than a dozen people near El Rito about sixty miles west of Albuquerque. This was one hundred twenty-five miles east of Sanders, but made it difficult to hire laborers. The Prescott *Miner* on September 9 reported that telegraph operators along the line between Albuquerque and Sanders threatened to leave their jobs if they were not furnished with guns for protection. Their fears were pooh-poohed, and they were described as tenderfeet from Chicago—but they got the guns.

On the same date the *Miner* reported that J. M. Sanford, near Bill Williams Mountain, had produced around thirty thousand pounds of potatoes, which would net him $6.50 per hundred pounds. "Quite a little fortune for a farmer, doctor, lawyer or any other high-minded individual," the *Miner* commented.

On September 23, the *Miner* reported that "Mr. Shenfield, R. R. contractor, left for his headquarters near Volunteer Springs [today's Navajo Army Depot] this morning. He is one of the most popular contractors on the line, therefore has no trouble in procuring help to do his work. He has recently contracted with the company to grade ten miles of road west of the tunnel."

The following news report appeared in the *Miner* on October 1:

*Killed and Wounded*

FLAG STAFF, A.T., Sept. 24th, 1881.

Ed. *Miner*:—Mr. H. J. Bishop, saloon and store keeper of this place, was shot and killed this morning by some men who were drinking and carousing at 7 o'clock A.M. They visited several saloons and demanded drinks, finally calling on H. J. Bishop. He refused to admit them, saying he did not want them around, when two of the party immediately fired on him, both shots taking effect. Bishop, however, before falling, fired three shots in self defence, wounding two men named Hall and McBride, the latter being hit by two of the bullets, one in the arm and the other in the shoulder. Hall and McBride, it is believed, are the ones who fired the shots killing Bishop. After wounding his assailants Bishop dropped down and expired. Both of the wounded men, it is thought, may die, but at writing are yet alive. In the event of their recovery it is hoped that the proper authorities will see that they are brought to justice, as well as other accomplices, if any, and punished to the full extent of the law, so that other outlaws and would-be murders may take warning by their example; otherwise a vigilance committee will be in order, and Judge Lynch shall prevail upon those gentlemen of satan to leave this section or take a swing in open midair suspended. Bishop having no relatives here, P. J. Brannen was appointed by the citizens here to take charge of his property. It is to be hoped that a good Deputy Sheriff and Constable will be appointed.

VIGILANTEE.

J. A. Park, Internal Revenue Collector, made an official trip to Flag Staff in October, and other places along the line. He reported in Prescott that "at Flag Staff, in a dance house, a few nights before, war was declared, and in the first engagement a man by the name of Charles Allen was shot in the knee. An armistice was then concluded, and for the time being all is quiet and serene in that city by the San Francisco Mountains."

But a few days later, the *Miner* published these items:

ANOTHER MAN SHOT.—Mr. William Taylor arrived in town to-day from Lail's Camp, on the line of the Atlantic & Pacific R.R., bringing with him Wm. Sheriff, who was wounded a few nights since through both thighs. The party who did the shooting was an employe of Mr. Lail, and at the time was drinking. He had no quarrel with Sheriff, but was after other parties, therefore it is claimed that the wounding was accidental. Mr. Sheriff is at the Sisters Hospital, where he will receive kind treatment.

### Berry Brother's Store Robbed

The store of Berry Brother's, near the Bill Williams' Mountain, on the line of the A. & P. R.R., was robbed a few days since by three men who gained admittance in the night under the pretext of wanting to purchase goods. There were three men in the store at the time of the robbery, but they were covered by the guns of the highwaymen. They took what money there was in the house, 7 guns, 7 pistols, silk hankerchiefs, clothing, etc. When they departed they gave notice that they would return in 15 days. Two of the desperate characters are known in Colorado and New Mexico as King Fisher and Comstock. We are indebted to Mr. Park, of the Internal Revenue, for the above information. He was near there when the robbery took place.

By late fall of 1881, Flagstaff had a population of about two hundred on weekdays, which doubled on weekends. There were about twenty frame buildings and perhaps as many tents. There was a dance hall, many saloons, and robberies and gun play were frequent occurrences. The *Miner* reported:

> At Flagstaff there is a dance house in which the proprietor has a large platform erected which he has furnished with several pistols and guns. When a valiant gets a little troublesome he picks him off at a single shot and that is the end of the creature.

Another item:

> James Alexander, a mere lad, took up last spring near the San Francisco Mountain a ranch, of which he planted several acres in potatoes. The yield amounted to 40,000 pounds, which he can sell for 10 cents a pound, amounting to $4,000. Not a bitter pill this.

In 1921, a week before his death, Al Doyle wrote a memoir regarding early days, a valuable source of information relating to the community's beginnings:

> Gophers were the only permanent residents and deer, antelope, rabbits and an occasional bear about the only transients in Flagstaff previous to 1881. That was the year before the railroad came through.
>
> The railroad got as far as Canyon Diablo in the fall of 1881. It took six months to build the bridge across that gorge. In the meantime a lot of tie choppers came on ahead to cut ties. . . .

Wherever water was to be found there was where these new western towns were located. The stakes for the railroad had been run, and the tie-choppers naturally settled where they could be close both to water and to the line. "Old Town Spring" was the logical place, and there they camped, in log houses, and there Brannen built his store and other small business places, including a bakery and several saloons, were located. . . .

Saloons and gambling houses were the principal places of business for some time following the founding of the town, and, indeed, for some time after the town had moved to its present location.

Previous to the coming of the railroad, travel east and west was all by way of the old Star Route stage line, which ran from Santa Fe, N.M., to Prescott.

West-bound express, mail and passengers were brought by stage part way, then in buckboards, and then on mules or behind the riders across the Mogollon mountains by way of Sunset Pass and Chavez Pass [both near Winslow], Stoneman Lake, Beaver Head, Camp Verde and into Prescott.

This route was abandoned before the railroad reached here, the new stage line from Winslow, which was the end of rails while the Canyon Diablo bridge was building, being along the old Beal [sic] trail, past the south base of Elden mountain, north of here, and out through Fort Valley and Government Prairie to Ash Fork, then south through Hell's canyon to Prescott. The superintendent of this line was Ben Baker, who had been superintendent of the old Star route between Santa Fe and Prescott.

Like all the early western stage lines, there was a good deal of trouble with bandits. There were several between Elden mountain and Prescott, Baker himself being held up once with a coach full of passengers, of course, also losing their valuables.

The popular conception of this country in the East at that time was that it was a rendevous for "cowboys," the eastern designation for bad-men. That is, in the East, they supposed all the bad man stuff was pulled by western cowboys. The fact is, however, that the average resident of the West was jealous of the reputation of the West and prompt to do his part in enforcing law and order, and cordially despised these bad men, who almost without exception, were young fellows fresh from the East, who had come here for adventure, or to get away from punishment for crime, and who let their hair grow long, while they practiced assiduously with their six-guns to become, as many of them did, proficient enough to use them as a means of livelihood.

About the only thing the bad men and would-be bad men did that they could be excused for doing was letting their hair grow long. They didn't do that as a mark of wickedness, but merely because it was the most convenient thing to do, there being no barbers here then.

I recall the sudden conversion of one of these eastern bad men. He was a young man, really a boy, from Iowa. His favorite recreation was trying to see how near he could shoot [at] others of the railroad construction gang without hitting them. They got tired of it and locked him in a box car, promising to hang him right after supper. They had supper and then about eighty of them, wild to end this particular bad man's foolishness, took him from the car, stuck up a wagon tongue and got all ready to string him up. One man, however, stepped out with his two six-guns and promised to kill as many of the crowd as he could if they proceeded with the hanging. He was soon joined by several more. Finally, fifteen against the rest, they bluffed it out on condition that the bad man would leave for the east the next morning, which he did.

Old Town spring was a lively camp while it lasted. There were a few men with families there, among them Marvin Beal, father-in-law of John Francis; J. H. Hawks, who ran the bakery, Beal's brother and a few others.

One pioneer who arrived in 1881 was John Lind. When he revisited Flagstaff in November 1926, the *Coconino Sun* interviewed him, and his story reveals some of the color and flavor of the early days:

> John among his reminiscences spoke of his 40 consecutive years here, during which he saw Flagstaff grow from a single log cabin to the largest city in northern Arizona. He and his family would be here yet, but Mrs. Lind's health demands another climate, and they left here four years ago.
>
> When John, originally from Cincinnati, came here from Winslow with his employer, a haberdasher, he arrived on the back of a little white pony which he borrowed, as he had none of his own, and the railroad—then the Atlantic and Pacific—was built only as far as Winslow. This road's completion to Flagstaff was delayed six months because the steel bridge for Canyon Diablo was a few feet short on both ends when it arrived and it took that long to manufacture another one of the right length.
>
> There was only one wooden building here, at what was then designated as Antelope Park. So John set out the stock, composed mostly of

miners' red flannel shirts, high boots and hats, in a tent. The settlement consisting of many tent saloons, gambling joints and the like clustered about Old Town spring.

The one log cabin was occupied by Dad Hawks, who waited on his customers strapped to a brace of pistols. There was but one other wooden building, a small shed where a big bear was kept.

Old Town spring, the only source of water, often got very low. Old Man Rumsey used to spend the night drowsing beside it, holding a dipper to catch its dribble, pouring his catch into a bucket as its weight every so often awoke him.

Antelope Park, as Flagstaff was then called, was selected by the Ayer Lumber Co., now the Arizona Lumber & Timber Co., as the site for their mill. The machinery and boilers were just arriving overland by wagon train when John came here. Later, with the arrival of the railroad, which selected a station site on the flat, the settlement moved also. . . .

The grassy parks soon drew stockmen; some of those who arrived during the earlier years with bands of sheep were John Marshall, Al Doyle, John Clark, Jack Smith, Tom McMillan, Frank Hart, W. H. Ashurst, Walter J. Hill, Uncle Jeff Howard and John Elden.

Later as the village grew, it became necessary to haul water to town. Leroux springs in Fort Valley never went dry. Charles Veit and Frank Cavanaugh used to bring it in with ox teams in barrels. They stopped and delivered wherever they saw a stick by the side of the road flaunting a white rag.

Jack Smith and Frank Hart found and located City springs in the crater of San Francisco Peaks.

The seasons seemed to be much more severe then than now, the snows more sudden and deeper. Johnny tells how he retired one night after taking a last survey of the heavens and noting a clear sky to arise next morning and find the ground level with 32 inches of snow. One dry summer, when lack of water had driven wild life to the crater of the Peaks, the Indians set fire to the forest on the mountain to drive the game down. John will never forget the awe-inspiring scene, he says.

On October 28, 1881, the Prescott *Miner* reported a rumor that another man had been killed on the line of the Atlantic & Pacific. "The numerous murders in this county are a disgrace, nevertheless they are indicative of lively times." In the same issue the *Miner* said that Prescott gamblers had a new game:

S. H. POKER.—This interesting game has attracted large numbers of people to the clubroom of Mr. Thorne today. Over three hundred thousand dollars changed hands during the forenoon. The game beat anything we ever beheld at the Centennial.

On November 11, 1881, the *Miner* published these items:

## A MAN ACCIDENTLY KILLED

Mr. Keely, a blacksmith, in the employ of Clifford & McCormick, Railroad Contractors on the A & P line, near the Bill Williams Mountain, was accidently shot on Sunday, causing death. It appears that some young men were handling a pistol, which was dropped on the floor, exploding, the ball passing through the body of Mr. Keely, inflicting a severe wound from which he died the following day. He was brought to Prescott today, November 2d, where he had a wife in delicate health, to whom the sudden and unexpected news fell with a crash and weight that was almost unbearable. We learn that deceased was a very industrious quiet gentleman, who bore an excellent reputation. He leaves a wife who is highly respected, and about to become a mother. She mourns the loss of an affectionate husband, who was taken away in the prime of life by the hands of divine providence, at a time when he was full of hope and looking to the future as of great promise.

## TWO MEN SHOT

News comes to the *Miner* from Clifford & McCormick's camp, on the line of the Atlantic & Pacific R.R. to the effect that on Tuesday night a desperate character made a fight, wounding two men, fortunately killing neither. The guilty party was arrested, and is now enroute to the County Jail. Shooting is too frequent by odds on the Atlantic & Pacific line, and vigorous measures will have to be resorted to in order to check it. We never counsel violent or hasty action, but as the emergency presents itself, we say let there be a little wholesale hanging of bad characters.

All the news was not of a violent nature. On November 18, the Prescott paper reported that the largest single shipment of wool ever made by any Arizona firm was made by C. P. Head & Co., from Holbrook via the Atlantic & Pacific; three hundred thousand pounds of wool, making a trainload of nineteen cars. But on the same date, the following item appeared:

## ANOTHER MAN SHOT

At Pittman Flat in this county, on Sunday last a dispute arose between a man named McGuire and Sam Ball, the pioneer of that section about a certain tract or piece of land. McGuire, we hear was about to appropriate the land to his own use and was in the act of fencing the same when Mr. Ball remonstrated and forbid him trespassing further. McGuire, we hear, drew a pistol and Ball a Winchester rifle when it went off inflicting a serious wound in McGuire's groin. So it goes; a man for breakfast, dinner, and supper every day on the line of the A. & P. R.R. Mr. Ball came into Prescott, and delivered himself into the hands of the authorities for examination.

In another column:

SHOT AN EAR OFF.—Mr. F. Lowry, agent for the Judson and Giant Powder, arrived today from the Atlantic & Pacific R.R. While enroute home he drove into Elliott's camp for the purpose of greasing his buggy. Just as he reached said camp the cook and one of the boarders had a dispute, when the cook merely shot the ear off his adversary. Mr. Lowry didn't like the looks of the natives of this particular camp, and elected to drive on without oiling his vehicle.

By December 3, the rails had stretched across the Painted Desert beyond the point subsequently named Adamana (after Adam Hanna, who came to Flagstaff in 1883 and later was a rancher in that Apache County area), and had reached the Mormon settlement of Brigham City, which the railroad renamed Winslow. By mid-December the track was going down at the rate of ten miles a week; by December 19 the railhead was on the east brink of that most formidable obstacle, Canyon Diablo. Work had started many months before on the bridge, which was to be 541 feet long and 223 feet high. It was fabricated by a steel company in the East, and shipped to the railhead. Stonework abutments were prepared of native stone. It was a deck bridge of eleven spans, varying from 30 to 300 feet each, and contained 1,489 cubic yards of masonry. Its cost was $200,000 and for that time and place, it was a remarkable achievement. It was completed in late June 1882, about a year after work on it began.

The railhead town, Canyon Diablo, was notorious as a rough, tough place, with saloons and gun play. A number of persons were buried in the cemetery there, but all traces have now disappeared except for the stones marking the resting place of Herman Wolf, an Indian trader whose place of business had been a few miles north, and who died at the turn of the century. When the writer visited the site of Canyon Diablo years ago, there were acres of bottle fragments glinting in the sunlight all around.

The following appeared in the *Miner* on December 30, 1881:

## JUDGE LYNCH
### *The Swift Retribution that Followed the Crime of a Flagstaff Saloon Keeper*

On Sunday last, at Pittman's Flat, a small settlement twenty-three miles this side of Flagstaff, on the A. & P. road, while Chas. Collins and another party, whose name we were unable to learn, were disputing over some trivial matter, Wm. Lewis, familiarly known as "Arizona Bill," walked up to Collins and without a word or any apparent reason drew a pistol and shot him in the neck, killing him instantly. Lewis was arrested and confined in a house close by for safe keeping and a guard placed over him, where he remained over night. On the morning of the day following, Monday, about two hundred armed railroad men gathered at the house and demanded Lewis, who was turned over to them by the guard. Having secured the prisoner, the mob took him to a tree close by and strung him up, after which they fired fourteen shots into his body. Particulars regarding the affair are very meager and unsatisfactory.

Lewis, previous to his death, was a deputy sheriff and was engaged in the liquor business at Flagstaff, where he was spoken of as a quiet and well-disposed citizen. He was also well known in Prescott, where he always attracted considerable attention by the manner in which he wore his hair, which fell in curls over his shoulders, and his tall, slender figure. Collins, the man he killed, was, we believe, a stranger in Arizona, and it is said was only eighteen years of age.

A couple of weeks later there was another lynching at Flagstaff.

While people were killing each other and getting lynched for doing so, and merchants were hauling huge loads of supplies from Prescott for the workers, and more supplies were coming from Albuquerque part way by rail, Edward E. Ayer had not been idle. He had put together a sawmill, shipped it out to the end of the track, and because he could not wait six months for construction of the Canyon Diablo bridge, manhandled and ox-teamed the mill over the canyon crossing and thence along the right-of-way westward to the chosen site west and south of the "Flag Staff" community.

It was an extraordinary undertaking, but typical of Ayer, who did many extraordinary things. A man of very great wealth, he became a benefactor of the Field Museum in Chicago and gave it a great collection of archaeological and ethnological items, and other objects of scientific and artistic value from all over the world. His valuable library, including original Spanish records dealing with the New World, was placed in the Newberry Library of Chicago.

Ayer's sawmill was not the first in the general area, but it was the first to provide a major economic base for employment and growth at the foot of San Francisco Mountain.

We learn from the files of the *Arizona Champion,* published at Flagstaff in January 1887, that Ayer's mill consisted of a Fraser & Chalmer's one-hundred-twenty-horsepower engine, with a twelve-foot drive wheel, and a battery of four big boilers, a double circular sawmill, a gang edger with like capacity, and equipment for manufacture of shingle, lath, and specialties. The problems of setting up and getting the plant running were immense. The file of old letters in the lumber company's archives include repeated tales of woe on the part of the general manager, whose name appears to have been Vanzulinzer. He complained about the lack of skilled labor, the need for all sorts of items, the lack of accommodations, and the shortage of water. In spite of difficulties, the erection of the mill progressed. It wouldn't be running by the time the railroad arrived at Flagstaff, but it wouldn't miss it far.

The Canyon Diablo Bridge was completed on July 1, 1882, and the first train rolled over it at 3:37 P.M. Meanwhile, grading had been pushed all along the line, and about a hundred thirty miles of roadbed was ready for rails. The builders had stockpiled about two hundred miles of rail and fastenings, and hundreds of thousands of ties were ready for use. The Prescott *Courier* reported on July 8, 1882, that more than six hundred thousand pine ties were cut and stacked in the San Francisco Mountain and Bill Williams Mountain areas. Two bridges crossing Johnson's Canyon near Ash Fork caused some delay, but contractors all along the line pressed ahead with grading and preparation of the roadbed.

On July 14, 1882, the *Miner* published the following:

## GOZARD

Whatever the word may signify, is the name of a new and flourishing town on the A. & P. R. R., San Francisco Mountain country. This town is located in the very heart of a dense pine forest which will produce millions upon millions of feet of lumber. Already two sawmills have been put up at Gozard with 100 horse power engines. The manufacture of

sash, blinds, doors, boxes, and in fact all kinds of wooden articles has commenced, and are being shipped to the Eastern cities. Three years, or even
two years ago the man who would have ventured the assertion that Arizona would be producing buckets, washtubs, doors, sash, blinds, etc., for
the Yankees of the East, would have been put down as a veritable crank.
Such is the case, however, and today these articles are being shipped from
the mountains of Arizona away down to the wooden nutmeg state, and
some 300 people find employment in thus doing. New settlements are
springing up all along the line of R.R., and hence we find our population
increasing as no other portion of Arizona. After all, railroads do a great
amount of good in reclaiming the western wilderness by those who have
nerve and courage to lead out as pioneers. A few years ago the whole
[area] between Los Angeles and the Missouri for a distance of nearly two
thousand miles was one vast unexplored wilderness. Now it is settled by
the most enlightened civilized people, and here and there we find beautiful towns containing temples of learning and Christianity. Barbarism all
along the line has yielded gradually to the advance of civilization.

Where was Gozard? We have been unable to find any other references, and
no Flagstaff oldtimer has been able to shed any light on where it was, who
established it, or what became of it. Possibly it was in the Bill Williams Mountain area, as the *Miner* frequently lumped together references to that mountain
and San Francisco Mountain.

On the same day that the story about Gozard appeared, the *Miner* had other
news from the front. One item said that Jim Alexander, who had been visiting
relatives in Prescott, was returning to Bill Williams Mountain, where he was
engaged in ranching, and another said that Tim Casey had left Prescott for
Pittman Valley, where he and his partner, Bob Connell, had a large wholesale
liquor store, suggesting that there was a lot of business activity in that area and
a considerable community. The news from Flagstaff (by this time the *Miner*
was making it one word instead of two) was routine:

## THE FLAGSTAFF KILLING
### *The Murderer and his Partner Lynched*

On the 6th of this month, a man named Brown, a sport, together with
his partner, for some frivolous offense, killed a man by the name of
Stone, and another—a looker on in Venice—by the name of Deitrich.
The two murderers, Brown and, we believe, Benjamine, escaped to the

Typical construction camp along the Atlantic & Pacific right-of-way in the vicinity of San Francisco Mountain during 1881–82.

An Atlantic & Pacific locomotive and cars on the Canyon Diablo Bridge shortly after construction during late summer, 1882. Note men standing on the cliffs at mid-lower right.

woods, but were followed by the citizens, and the last seen of them they were swinging to a pine limb, stark dead. The murdered men were inoffensive citizens, well liked by the people of Flagstaff.

The construction of the Canyon Diablo Bridge had held up the laying of track for more than seven months. With that major obstacle now behind them, the crews moved swiftly, averaging better than a mile of completed track a day. Construction engineer Kingman notified his superiors that laying track and surfacing was costing $529 per mile. Within a week after crossing Canyon Diablo the railhead was at Walnut Creek. On August 1 it reached Flagstaff, thirty-three miles from Canyon Diablo, and while we have found no record of how the little settlement responded, we may well imagine that there was quite a celebration along the one street and in the saloons. On September 1 the rails reached Williams; on December 6, Seligman; by March 27, 1883, Kingman.

Arrival of the rails at Flagstaff marked the beginning of vast changes. Within a couple of weeks another highly significant event occurred: On August 19, Ayer wrote his Chicago office: "It is noon and I have just got the boilers running and succeeded in blowing the noon whistle for the first time," thus marking the start of operations of the big mill which was to play such an important part in the life of the Flagstaff community, particularly during its first four or five decades.

As the railhead moved westward, so did the contractors and their workmen and the payrolls, and trailing in their wake came the gamblers, dance hall girls and other riffraff, like hogs following a swill wagon. Each community along the line had its turn at the dubious but exciting and profitable honor of being "Terminus, Atlantic & Pacific." On August 25, the *Miner* reprinted the following from the Albuquerque *Journal*:

### A. & P. FRONT

A correspondent writing to the Albuquerque *Journal* from the line of Atlantic & Pacific road, sends that paper the following interesting description of the places and country north of Prescott and progress of work on the railroad.

The slightly rolling plains are thickly studded with tall pine trees, some of them being from fifty to seventy-five feet in height. Most of the trees are void of limbs at the trunk, thus affording to sight-seers elegant views of the country for miles around. Occasionally the line crosses open and circular grassy parks of some two or three miles in diameter, enclosed by lofty pines, presenting a very handsome appearance, the work of nature's hand alone. Eight miles west of Cosnino the road winds along with light curves close to the foot of the Frisco mountains. Some of these rugged spurs are 12,000 feet above the sea level. The tops are seldom visible, owing to the dense clouds almost constantly overhanging them. The view from the summit would certainly be grand, radiating for many miles and embracing a fine stretch of territory. At a distance one would think the ascent could be made with but little difficulty, but at a nearer approach it seems almost impossible, the sides of the mountains being at many points almost perpendicular walls of solid rocks and boulders.

Flagstaff, known as "Home, Sweet Home" among railroaders, lies in the mountain district, ten miles from Cosnino. The name is supposed to have been given it by the "boys in blue" many years ago. Considerable has been said regarding the rough class of people that inhabit this place. Allow me to say that from observation and acquaintance made during a stay there of several weeks I am of the opinion that Flagstaff has a majority of peaceable citizens, with the usual minority of rowdies common to western settlements. The latter are mostly worthless tramps, who are not permanent residents anywhere. A man that attends to his own business will be treated as a gentleman in Flagstaff. Meddlesome and abusive characters are quietly warned to take their departure, and if ill treated only receive what they richly deserve. Revolvers are not brought into requisition at every little fracas, as is supposed by citizens of other towns. The leaders in the only disturbance I witnessed at Flagstaff were promptly arrested and taken to Prescott, where they will be dealt with by the laws of the country. Flagstaff has a number of wideawake and enterprising citizens. It has a board walk for "rambles on starry nights" I suppose, and a number of wholesale and retail dry goods and grocery stores.

A short distance from Flagstaff is the newly built steam saw mill of Mr. E. E. Ayres [sic], of Chicago. Further west is Parker's sawmill in full blast, turning out lumber rapidly, and 5 miles from Flagstaff Perkins' mill is at work full handed. At present the track layers are two miles west of Volunteer, and upwards of 360 miles from Albuquerque. Fifty miles have been laid since July 1. We are now within 20 miles of Williams, the probable terminus of the third division, and the iron horse should be there early in September. Everything works finely under the able management of Engineer Lawton, who is at present superintending construction. The road bed is in excellent condition, well settled and solid.

Mr. Haynes, our water service man, and a very important character with us, after many unsuccessful searches for a steady flow of good fresh water, has at last struck a bonanza at Volunteer, and now has two large tanks built, that supply trains with water, thus saving considerable delay and trouble by not having to haul water from a point eighty miles to the rear. The tie-spotter from Coolidge has arrived in Flagstaff, and with a force of fifteen men ties are turned out, notched and ready for laying at the rate of 6,000 per day.

G. H. Hereford has been appointed agent and operator at Cosnino, and A. E. Hornbeck at Flagstaff. P. E. Fisher, of the general passenger and ticket office at Albuquerque, is terminal agent, and is at present stationed at Volunteer.

On September 1, the *Miner* published the following items regarding Flagstaff:

Flagstaff now sports eighteen saloons and several general business houses, but a number of them are preparing to move toward the front as the track advances. Flagstaff, however, will always be quite an important place, being surrounded by a fine stretch of country and situated in the finest timber belt in the Territory. Messrs. Brannen & Co. report a steady increase in the merchandising business at that point, with no signs of it falling off as the track is pushed westward.

Ayer's immense saw mill at Flagstaff has started up, and is now turning out lumber at a rapid rate. The mill can turn out 6,000,000 feet of lumber per year, but when crowded can do still better. The company now have about 1,000,000 feet of logs on hand, while the immense pineries will afford an almost inexhaustible supply of material.

A week later, these items appeared:

Williams, on the A. & P. R. R., 56 miles from Prescott, has 100 houses, and over 500 population. Flagstaff has about the same number.

It appears to us that some of our friends are going a little fast in making investments at Williams. Prescott must be connected with the A. & P. railroad at a nearer point, and it will be, therefore don't go too fast. The tunnel is eight miles nearer Prescott than Williams, and still farther west we get to the line of the railroad much nearer than at the tunnel.

On October 13, the *Miner* published a long column of news from Williams, including the following:

Sam Ball, of Pittman Valley, while out hunting several days since, was surprised by the sudden appearance of a huge bear in closer proximity than was actually necessary considering the short acquaintance of the two, when Mr. Ball, not stopping to exchange compliments, fired at the bulk, wounding his bruinship, and then a hand-to-hand struggle ensued, in which Mr. Ball had his right arm broken and otherwise received several slight wounds, but finally dispatched his adversary with his hunting knife. At last accounts Mr. Ball was getting along splendidly.

The First Infantry Company passed through here to-day on its way to Whipple.

Judge A. O. Noyes returned from Flagstaff to-day, and speaks well of the town and its population.

Wild game is in abundance around these parts, and we invite the members of the Prescott Rifles to come out this way and enjoy a good hunt.

Geo. Rich, Deputy Sheriff of Williams, has resigned his position. He is supposed to have had a hand in the robbery lately committed upon the wholesale liquor firm of W. E. Talbot & Co., of Williams.

The machinery for the Turkey Creek mill left here yesterday loaded on several wagons.

Work was pressed all during the winter of 1882–83. By April 15, the rails were only forty-one miles from the Colorado River. The general superintendent of the Atlantic & Pacific, F. W. Smith, came through to Kingman from Albuquerque on a special train in eighteen hours. (In the 1970s, the time required for a passenger train to cover the same distance was seven and a half hours.) Track was completed to the bridge site on the Colorado on June 8, 1883. The bridge was completed after some difficulties with flooding and on August 8, 1883, the last spike was driven.

The Southern Pacific, which had reached Tucson on March 20, 1880, to be greeted by wild celebration and the firing of cannon, had reached the Colorado River April 19, 1883, and the company had built a depot and hotel and yards at Needles, the junction point of the two railroads, two miles up the river from the Atlantic & Pacific bridge. The Southern Pacific conveyed the line from Needles to Mohave, some sixty miles west of Barstow, to the Atlantic & Pacific by a contract in the fall of 1884 under a lease-sale arrangement, along with trackage rights to San Francisco.

A special train of two cars, containing Superintendent Smith and other notables, crossed the Atlantic & Pacific bridge in due ceremony following the driving of the final spike. The Atlantic & Pacific was officially opened to through passenger service on October 21, 1883, on which date a train left Albuquerque bound for San Francisco. It carried about two hundred passengers, and included a sleeping car and a mail car.

Thus came the railroad, and the real beginning of Flagstaff. The construction of the railroad brought about establishment of the big sawmill. It also brought about the rapid growth of the livestock industry in the area, and ushered in the beginnings of tourism, which was to become, in due time, a major factor. Vast economic changes would come with the years, and many, many years later, the scientific and academic factors would gain major importance; but Flagstaff's foundations were laid by the railroad, the sawmill, and the livestock industry.

# CHAPTER VI

# Pioneers of the Eighties

FOLLOWING CLOSE BEHIND the Atlantic & Pacific survey crews as they staked the line across the high plateau of northern Arizona in 1880, came the contractors and crews of workmen whose task it was to clear and grade the right-of-way, cut ties and timbers, build bridges, and lay track. These hundreds of men were in the San Francisco Mountain area for some months. Supplying their needs brought about establishment of a number of business firms in the little settlement at Antelope Springs, already known as Flag Staff.

During those months while Flag Staff was a construction boom town and then railhead, money, whiskey and blood flowed freely, acts of violence were commonplace, and the settlement in no way resembled the sort of community that a considerable number of people had in mind. Then the crews moved on down the line, drawing with them most of those who preyed on the youthful, the innocent, the generous and foolish; the thieves, tinhorns, soiled doves, who edged around the construction payrolls like coyotes circling a crippled steer. They left behind them at Flagstaff a different sort; those who sought opportunities in a new, growing community.

These settlers had started coming before the construction crews; they came in ever-increasing numbers, on horseback, in buggies and covered wagons, some on foot, and then with the completion of the railroad, by train. They were coming, each in his unique way, to contribute to what would be a unique community. The boom was over, but the years of growth, development and fulfillment were just beginning.

Here we offer brief sketches of some of these pioneers, including some whose acts were of special interest or significance to the community, some who were simply interesting as individuals, and others as a sampling of the hundreds who came and made the community. It would be impossible to summarize the lives or even list the names of all.

The first families with children to settle here were the Beals, brothers

Marvin, forty-three, and Frank, thirty. Natives of New York, they grew up in Illinois, then moved to Kansas, and together saw opportunity beckoning in Arizona. In the summer of 1881 they arrived here, built a log cabin near Antelope Spring close to the tent-cabin establishment of the pioneer merchant, P. B. Brannen, and Ed Whipple's restaurant and saloon. As railroad construction workers came in increasing numbers, and the big new Ayer sawmill started operation, and opportunity-minded seekers came into the area, the brothers opened a second saloon and eating place.

They were joined at Thanksgiving, 1881, by their wives and children, who had come from Kansas to Gallup by train, where they were met by Frank, driving a buckboard. The two-hundred-mile trip to Flagstaff over rocky roads and in winter weather was one of great hardship. Frank's wife was Anna, and they had a one-year-old son, Edward. Other members of the party were Marvin's wife, Martha, and children Nellie, Jennie and Edwin. Many years later one of Frank's and Anna's children recalled their mother telling that when the buckboard pulled up at the log cabin near the spring on that winter day in November 1881, "The men at the tie camp just stood around looking and she was afraid to get out of the wagon." No doubt the tie-cutters were a rough bunch, perhaps hungry for their first glimpse of a respectable woman in many months.

Frank and Anna became parents of Lotta in October 1882, the first child born in Flagstaff. Lotta and the other children attended the first school. Lotta later attended the Normal School, which in due time became Northern Arizona University. She married Kenneth Gillette. She died in 1972. A sister, Ruth, died at an early age.

Children born to Marvin and Martha Beal in Flagstaff included Lillian, Frank L. and Irene. Nellie married John Francis; Jennie married William Bayless; Lillian first married Everett Hanna, then William Freidlein; and Irene became Mrs. Fred Meyers.

Marvin and Frank Beal played substantial parts in the community's beginnings and growth, and were loved and respected by their fellow townsmen. Marvin died at his home in 1908, and Frank in 1910.

John William Francis, one of the community's stalwarts, came to Flagstaff in 1881 as a youth of twenty-five, accompanied by his brother, Dan, twenty-one. They were born on a farm near Chillicothe, Missouri. Another brother, Dr. R. M. Francis, joined them here later. John graduated from Kirksville Normal School in 1877 and taught school for two years, an unusual but apparently highly successful preparation for a strenuous life as lawman, stockman, merchant and community leader. John and Dan moved westward, stopping for a time at Trinidad, Colorado, where they earned a few dollars hewing railroad ties. Moving on down the line, they arrived in due time at Flagstaff. John served as Yavapai County undersheriff in the late 1880s, became sheriff after Coconino County was established in 1891, and was re-elected several times. He was also a deputy United States Marshal. But he was not only a famous lawman; in early years, he substituted for Mrs. Eva Marshall, the first school teacher in Flagstaff, and also ran a saloon. Later he was in business and ran stock. He served as a school trustee and played an active part in community affairs.

John Francis was a man of unusual attributes. He was loved and respected, but feared by those on the wrong side of the law. In his obituary, the *Sun* said that "when he went after a man, he went to get him. His failures to accomplish his mission were few. Cool, brave, unhesitating, quick as a flash on the trigger, and a dead-shot, there were few among the numerous badmen of those days who cared to measure gun skill with him, and many of them, wiser than they were good, surrendered without a fight when he caught up with them. Some others, less discreet, tried to shoot it out, and in those cases Sheriff Francis was invariably victor." As Yavapai undersheriff he took part in putting down the celebrated Tewksbury-Graham feud in the Tonto Basin, a story made famous by Zane Grey in *To the Last Man*.

One incident will illustrate the respect citizens and badmen alike held for Francis. A posse had holed-up a horsethief in the Mogollons, and its members advised him that if he didn't surrender, they would send United States Marshal John Francis in after him. He replied that Francis could come. Francis rode into the area, and after an exchange of fire from behind rocks, the thief shouted that it was time for breakfast, invited Francis and a deputy to join him, and stood in plain sight. Francis and the deputy stood up and approached. After eating heartily, Francis tried to convince the man he should surrender, which he refused to do. They left, but returned in due time. Francis saw the man walking without his gun, which leaned against the house some distance away. Francis called to him to surrender. Instead, he ran for the gun, and Francis dropped him with one shot. Years later Francis received a letter from a prominent businessman in Kansas City, stating that many years before his wild younger brother had gone West, and that in attempting to find him, they learned he had been shot while resisting arrest by John Francis. The Kansas City man invited the officer to visit him. In a few months he had occasion to be in that city, met the man, was taken to his home in a chauffeur-driven limousine, treated with every courtesy, and he gave the brother a complete report of the incident.

At the time of his death in 1925 of cancer, Francis owned several residential and business properties in Flagstaff, had a country home, two ranches in Doney Park and other interests. Mrs. Francis died in 1950. Both are buried in the Masonic Cemetery here. They were survived by three children, Lenore Ada, wife of Dr. M. O. Dumas; Marvine Josephine, wife of W. B. Raudebaugh of Flagstaff; and Irvin W., of Los Angeles.

Dan Francis, who rode horseback from Missouri to Flagstaff with his brother, also played an important part in Flagstaff's early history. With a partner, Hugh E. Campbell, he operated a meat market and in the course of time they branched out into the sheep business. In the early 1900s the Campbell-Francis Sheep Company had become the largest in Arizona, possibly in the entire Southwest. Land holdings at one time amounted to more than a hundred thousand acres. As a Democrat, Dan Francis was elected Coconino County treasurer. When he died in 1931, Judge E. S. Clark of Phoenix, an old friend from early days, said: "I know of no man who was more widely liked and respected in the state than Daniel Francis." He was survived by two sons, Dan Jr. and Lawrence; and two daughters, Mrs. Phillip Pendleton and Nan Francis.

Among the first to settle in Old Town were the J. F. Hawks family, which included three boys, George, Will and John, and three girls, Sadie, Mary and Anne. Sadie married Sam King, bookkeeper for P. B. Brannen & Co. Anne married Harry Kislingberry. George and Will were killed by a mob which broke into the jail after the two had been arrested in connection with the shooting of John Berry in a saloon brawl in January 1887. Hawks operated a hotel and bakery, and in later years was known as Dad Hawks.

Old Man Rumsey was an early comer to Old Town. He had a log cabin near Old Town Spring, and in 1885 got into trouble for fencing off the spring and attempting to claim it as his own. The Rumseys had two children, Frank and Susie, who were students in the first school.

One of the community's most useful and active citizens was Dr. Dennis James Brannen, who arrived in April 1882, a cousin of Peter J. Brannen, Flagstaff's first merchant. He was born near Ottawa, Canada, in 1858. When he was a child the family moved to Illinois. Dennis attended the University of Illinois, then went to Cincinnati where he attended the College of Medicine, graduating at twenty-four with highest honors. He practiced for a short time in Cincinnati and Bloomington, and then headed west for Flagstaff. He was appointed surgeon for the railroad company, and also for the Ayer Lumber Company. The old files of the newspapers in the 1880s and 1890s are full of his comings and goings up and down the line, caring for patients and answering emergency calls.

In the early 1880s, Brannen was offered an opportunity to take over a major

JOHN FRANCIS, pioneer teacher,
rancher, lawman (1856–1925).

DR. D. J. BRANNEN, the town's
first doctor (1858–1908).

hospital at Tucson, but declined in order to continue to care for his patients in northern Arizona. He established the community's first drug store, and had his office in the same building. In 1883, as the Democratic candidate, he was elected to the Thirteenth Territorial Legislature from Yavapai County, and was quickly recognized as one of the ablest members of that body. In 1893, Gov. L. C. Hughes offered him the superintendency of the state hospital at Phoenix, but he declined. But he did accept an appointment as territorial health officer for northern Arizona. In 1887, he was named Flagstaff postmaster, played a major part in organizing the Flagstaff Board of Trade, was president of the company which operated the first stage coach to Grand Canyon, and for a decade was in the cattle business. He also owned ranches and dealt in real estate, and had property interests in Illinois and California. He served as a member of the board of visitors of the Normal School. He was captain in the Arizona National Guard, was one of the organizers of the local lodge of the Order of Woodmen, and was active in the grand lodge. He was also active in the Elks. He served as president of the Santa Fe Pacific Association of Railway Surgeons, a member of the Association of Military Surgeons of the United States, was president of the United States Board of Pension Examiners under Presidents Cleveland, Harrison and McKinley. As if all this wasn't enough to keep him busy, he accumulated a fortune of several hundred thousand dollars. In the early 1880s, he married Kathleen O'Donnell. Following her death, he married Felicia A. Marley.

Brannen spent much time in Washington, District of Columbia, serving Arizona and particularly, Coconino County, in various ways. While visiting in the Capitol Building in 1908, he suffered a stroke and died a few minutes later. He was buried in Flagstaff. Dr. Brannen was an extraordinary man, of great talent and devotion. His medical practice, oldtimers said, always came first. Flagstaff owes much to him.

A stalwart citizen of Flagstaff in early times, one who contributed in a major way to the establishment of sound practices in county government, was Jesse Watkins Gregg, a native of Illinois who came in 1882. He was born in 1861, and in 1892 married Matilda Louisa Hoffman, member of another pioneer family which came West from Michigan by covered wagon. During three of his five years as a county supervisor, he was chairman of the board. He was successful in ranching and farming, raised horses and mules, but found time to take part in civic affairs. He played an active part in the Pioneers' Society from its founding in 1906, and was vice president at the time of his death. The Greggs' four children were Esther, who became Mrs. Joe D. Tissaw; Jim; Nellie (Mrs. A. G. Fransen), and Jesse.

In 1913, Gregg went into a Flagstaff saloon looking for one of his employees, John Rowles. He found him engaged in a drunken fight with another man, and placed his hand on his shoulder, suggesting that he stop fighting and come back to work. Rowles turned and struck him. Gregg fell to the floor. He died almost instantly, and it was found he had suffered a skull fracture. Rowles had worked for Gregg for more than a year, and was a highly valued employee, but was vicious when drinking. Rowles was tried for manslaughter and sentenced to prison.

Mrs. Gregg was a student in the first school in Flagstaff. Her classmates included United States Senator Henry F. Ashurst and many other pioneers. She lived a long and useful life, and died in 1938. Gregg's uncle, Al, came to Flagstaff at an early time. He was a faro dealer who had the reputation of being strictly honest, and it is said that he would refuse to let men gamble when their losses became too heavy. On one occasion he won $1,000 on one turn of a card in a game with J. J. (Sandy) Donahue, and an oldtimer who was present said that Donahue simply smiled and walked back to his own saloon. The Greggs have a family tradition that Uncle Al came to Flagstaff with Ed Whipple, and that en route they were caught in a blizzard and Whipple would have frozen to death if Al Gregg had not whipped him to keep him from succumbing.

Jerome J. (Sandy) Donahue came to Flagstaff in 1882. While he was a prosperous and profligate saloon keeper and gambling hall operator, he also served Coconino County as sheriff, and was considered an excellent and devoted lawman. His deputy for a few months was Henry F. Ashurst. George Hochderffer has written that Sandy would scour the county in a fancy buckboard with a spanking pair of blacks, seeking offenders, leaving Ashurst to attend routine duties in town. He was also the enthusiastic and able chief of the volunteer fire department. Senator Ashurst made the following entry in his diary while visiting in Phoenix in 1923, during a reunion of pioneers:

Amongst my callers was "Sandy" Donahue, once healthy and prosperous; but his strength has oozed away and he is now penniless. Vast sums of money have slipped through his fingers, for large was his bounty before his money took wings. He requested a loan of twenty-five dollars which I was glad to grant, for I cannot forget that he called me from cowboy life, thirty years ago, where I was eating sourdough bread, drinking rank coffee, and riding herd under the winter stars for pitiably small wages, to my first real "job," *viz.,* turnkey in the county jail, at sixty dollars per month, then a princely salary.

Three years later, Ashurst wrote:

> Met Mr. J. J. (Sandy) Donahue, once the local celebrity at Flagstaff, where he gathered objects d'art, kept a carriage, drank vintages, wore clothing cut a la mode, was sheriff of his county. Of his revenues derived from his Senate Saloon and his gaming tables, he gave bountifully to the needy and helpless. Now in his declining years, he labors hard for coarse fare, sleeps in bunkhouses, and travels in street cars.

Donahue in his young manhood had been a professional diver in the Great Lakes. He made, handled and spent many thousands of dollars. It is said that no man ever asked him for help without receiving it. Hochderffer says that Donahue once gave him $5.00, all the money he had with him, so that Hochderffer could buy a ticket to Flagstaff from Winslow. Donahue then went and borrowed a similar sum to buy his own ticket. At one time he owned two saloons in Flagstaff, and built the Commercial Hotel. Oldtimers say his famous bar, The Senate, was elegantly furnished. His prodigality finally broke him, along with the closing of the saloons. He was admitted to the Pioneers Home at Prescott in 1929. Hochderffer visited him there and said he had a bookcase full of good books. He died at Mayo Brothers Clinic in 1932 at the age of seventy-one. Oldtimers always speak with affection and friendliness in referring to Donahue, a big man with a big heart, who lived with zest, overlooked the faults of others, was generally kind, but a tough man in a fight. His name appears frequently in the news columns of the *Coconino Sun* down through the years. He was intelligent, imaginative, a man always willing to take a chance or give another man a chance. People took advantage of him, but not because he was foolish—rather, because he was generous of heart.

Judge A. P. Gibson came in 1881 from Hutchinson, Kansas. He built near the spring and his house burned, and he then rebuilt further up the hill. His family included Mrs. Gibson, William, Alice, Ostoria and Ida. Alice married George Hill, a pioneer mining man; Ida became the wife of William Hochderffer. William and his father owned the AP brand of cattle with headquarters at Tunnel Spring two miles west. Ostoria (Oscar) became a well-known and prominent Arizona attorney.

Oldtimers in the area were members of the family of John Wesley Newman, who was born in 1825 in Tennessee. They came to Arizona in 1877 from Nevada, and settled on Clear Creek in 1878. John died along the trail en route to Prescott that year. The mother, Jane Bennett Newman, moved the younger children to Prescott for school, the older boys staying at Clear Creek to take care of the cattle. There were eight children, and the oldest at time of death of the father was seventeen. The children were Martin, Jefferson Davis, Frances, Lee, Emma, Florence, Wallace and Zeke. In June 1947, when visiting Flagstaff, Lee told a *Sun* reporter that in 1879 he and his brother Jeff rode into this area, saw some evidence of work around a spring, and also noted a tall flagstaff. Lee said he visited the area again in 1880, and again in 1881. In 1884, Mrs. Newman and smaller children moved to Flagstaff for the youngsters to attend school. Newmans played parts in various northern Arizona communities. Martin moved to California; Jeff engaged in wool growing, then moved to California, then back to Arizona. Frances married J. D. Houck. Lee moved to Holbrook, went into the stock business, and served eight years as sheriff. Emma became Mrs. Joseph Dent, and after Dent's death married Frank Leslie, a longtime Flagstaff resident. Florence married Benjamin F. Taylor and they homesteaded on Beaver Creek. Wallace became a resident of Phoenix. Zeke lived in Holbrook for many years, was in the stock business, and was also a member of the Navajo County board of supervisors.

Arriving in Flagstaff in 1881, and later working for Ayer at the sawmill, was Charles E. Howard, born in Virginia in 1856. He continued at the mill until about 1890, when he went into the sheep business. He made his headquarters at Flagstaff, but for a time lived at Ash Fork to be in closer touch with his stock which ranged north of Ash Fork and Williams. He was married in 1906 to Mary Alverda Dresbach of Ohio. In later years they had homes at Mesa and Phoenix. He died March 14, 1922, at Phoenix. In his obituary the *Coconino Sun* noted:

> There was no better range neighbor to be found in Arizona than he and no truer friend to those with whom he had business relations and no man whose word was better than his lived in the state.

Also arriving in Flagstaff in 1881 was William Warren Willis, born in 1861 in Iowa. As a young man he went to New Mexico, and worked on construction of the Atlantic & Pacific Railroad before coming on to Flagstaff. He married Maria Johnson in Prescott. They lived in Flagstaff until 1929, when they moved to Holbrook. He did contract logging for the sawmills, and engaged in the stock business. He died in 1940.

Another citizen who came in 1881 was J. Y. Crothers. The *Coconino Sun* of February 25, 1892, reported that he had died February 24 at Prime's lodging house of pneumonia after an illness of a few days. The obituary said he came to Flagstaff in 1881, built the first house south of the railroad track, and engaged in the restaurant business. He was twice elected justice of the peace, and took a prominent part in public affairs. He was born in Allen County, Ohio, and was sixty-one at the time of his death. He left five daughters and two sons. Only one of them, Charles, lived in Flagstaff. The *Sun* described him as an exemplary citizen, as indeed he must have been, to serve as local judge during those difficult and violent times.

Another pioneer who arrived in the community in 1881 in a covered wagon drawn by a team of mules was Henry Claiborne Lockett. He was born in Missouri in 1856. When he was five, the family moved to Iowa. In 1878 he moved west as far as Kansas where he lived the life of a plainsman, catching and breaking wild horses. He drove his mule team from Kansas to Flagstaff, and was soon using it to haul railroad ties for the construction crews. A year after arriving, he secured property a couple of miles north of the community and raised hay and potatoes, gradually extending his holdings until he had about a thousand acres of farm- and timberland. He spent thirty-five years in the sheep business. A Republican, he was elected to the Territorial Senate in 1906. In 1893, he married Rosa Clark. They had three children, Rial C.; Virginia M., who was to serve as county superintendent of schools for years; and Mrs. Nettie A. Shill. Mrs. Lockett died in 1898. In 1904 Lockett married Miss Hattie M. Green of Phoenix. Mrs. Lockett, a civic leader for many years, and a writer and authority on Indians, died in 1962. Their two sons are Henry Claiborne, Jr., of Flagstaff and Tucson; and Robert Wallace of Flagstaff and Phoenix. One of the community's landmarks is the brown bungalow which the Locketts built in 1907, replacing a little white farmhouse in which they lived for years. It is on the west side of Fort Valley Road across from Northland Press [1976].

Lockett was one of the original promoters and stockholders in the Arizona Territorial Fair Association, was frequently called on for advice in Flagstaff's community problems, and was a member of the Elks and the Odd Fellows. He died in 1921 of cancer of the throat. His name is commemorated in our community by Lockett Road and Lockett Meadow.

One of the many extraordinary personalities who came to Flagstaff was Benjamin Doney, for whom Doney Park on the east side of the Peaks was named. He was born in 1842, and served aboard one of the Union vessels in the historic duel between the *Monitor* and the *Merrimac* at Hampton Roads, Virginia, in March 1862. He came to Flagstaff, according to Pioneers' Society records, in February 1882, during the building of the railroad as a construction foreman. He worked at a sawmill for some years, then homesteaded a ranch twelve miles northeast of Flagstaff. His little house was near today's Highway

89 in Black Bill Park, with two Lombardy poplars in front and a tin sitz bath on the porch. In the yard usually stood a red camp wagon. The house has in recent years been moved to the Pioneers' Museum, a short distance north of Flagstaff.

Doney received a pension of $60.00 per month as a veteran. Dr. Harold S. Colton wrote that Doney always had a loan at the bank. Once a month, as soon as he received his pension check, he would pay his loan plus interest. In a few days he would return to the bank and reborrow the money and then repay it the next month. He would hitch up his little red camp wagon with a stove pipe sticking out of the top and a door in the back, and drive to Flagstaff Saturdays, returning to his farm on Sundays. He was slight and lean, and walked vigorously. Colton says Doney was an inveterate pot hunter, and by 1900 had amassed a huge collection of prehistoric materials. He also prospected and looked for the "Lost Mines of the Padres," which Colton discusses with detailed knowledge and humor.

Doney joined other Union veterans in Flagstaff in organizing the local post of the Grand Army of the Republic. He died in 1932, at ninety, as result of injuries sustained in a fall from the porch of his house. His wife, Jessie, died in Los Angeles in 1920.

Adelaida Manvanares, who came to Flagstaff in 1882 as a young woman of twenty-three, spent a long and useful life in the community, dying in 1947 at the ripe age of ninety-seven. She was born on Christmas, 1849, in Santa Fe. In 1892, she married Frank Rodriguez, who died in 1921. Mrs. Rodriguez was survived by a son, Raymond. She lived to see four generations of her family.

One who came here as a tie contractor in 1882 and stayed, was David F. Hart, who was born in Connecticut in 1831. He joined the gold rush to California in 1849, then returned to Illinois. He married, then enlisted to fight in the Civil War, leaving his wife and two daughters. When he came home at the close of the conflict, he found all three had died. He moved to Kansas, then to Colorado, and then to New Mexico. He was in northern Arizona during the building of the railroad, and remained in Flagstaff until 1916, when he moved to Winslow. He had a wife and five children, four of whom survived him. He was a member of the Grand Army of the Republic and served Flagstaff Masons as one of the first Worshipful Masters. He died in Winslow in 1922 over ninety-one years of age.

Founder of one of Flagstaff's pioneer families was Charles A. Greenlaw, born in Canada in 1855. He was raised and educated in Maine in a lumbering area. In 1877, he moved to Minneapolis and engaged in the lumber business, then moved on west and lumbered in Colorado for a time. In June 1882, before the railroad arrived, he walked across Canyon Diablo and on to Flagstaff, and was employed at the Ayer sawmill. In 1886 he formed a partnership with his brother, E. F. Greenlaw; they established a large mill, and also became contractors for the successor of the Ayer enterprise, the Arizona Lumber & Timber Company. E. F. served in the Territorial House in 1895. Charles was married in 1884 to Ella Lamport, member of another pioneer family. They had six children: Eben, Vera, Allin G., Mrs. Mary (Dayton) Draine and twin sister, Mrs. Louise (Layton G.) Beamer, and Mrs. Eleanor (T. M., Jr.) Knoles. Greenlaw served as a member of the board of supervisors. He was a Mason, an Odd Fellow and an Elk. He died of a stroke in Phoenix in 1920. Mrs. Greenlaw died in 1946. The Greenlaw property, which remained in the family, is now the site of the shopping and business area in the eastern part of the city.

Jose C. Salas came to Flagstaff in 1882, before the arrival of the railroad. He was born in Pena Blanca, New Mexico, in 1866. As a builder and contractor, he built or assisted in building many structures in this community. He also worked on sheep ranches during early days. He died in 1946. His wife, Josephita, died in 1922. They had four sons and four daughters. Son Leo died in 1921, and Rio died in 1931. Surviving the father were Charles and Howard. The four daughters were Mrs. Fidel Garcia, Mrs. Veronica Carillo, Mrs. Dolores Genty and Mrs. Rosie Dennis.

Another family arriving in 1882 was that of J. A. and Eva Marshall. He became one of the justices of the peace, serving in 1883, the other being James M. Sandford. Mrs. Marshall became the community's first school teacher. They had two children, Cora and George. Marshall School was named in her honor.

Eric Denver, a native of Stockholm, Sweden, came in 1882 as a teamster hauling ties for the railroad. In 1884 he filed on a homestead near Bellemont, and lived there until his death in 1926. His wife was Julia Claywood, native of Missouri. They had a son, Ellas, and daughter, Mrs. Carl Herring of Phoenix. He built the Ideal Hotel, a landmark for many years. His obituary in the *Coconino Sun* said: "That his neighbors were his best friends is a tribute to his integrity of character."

M. A. Black, born at Council Grove, Kansas, in 1859, came to Flagstaff in 1882. He engaged in cattle raising and farming, and had a ranch in Black Bill Park on the east side of the Peaks for many years. He died in 1934. Survivors included his wife, a daughter, Mrs. Everett Meyers, and three sons, Otto, Myron and Matthew, Flagstaff.

Also coming here at a very early time were Matt Black's brothers, George

Washington and Samuel C. George was born in West Virginia in 1856, sixth of a family of eleven children. He spent his early years on the family farm in Kansas, then came to Flagstaff. He became a prominent figure in the cattle business, and for a time was a partner with his brother-in-law, James A. Vail. He invested in Flagstaff real estate and acquired a comfortable fortune, spending his later years in Los Angeles. He married the widow of a brother, Walter, and they had three children, Jim, Claud, and Mary Davis. His stepchildren were George J. and Chester. Following Mrs. Black's death, he married Mrs. Oliver Beatty of Ontario, Canada. He died in 1925. Samuel C. Black, another brother and also an early comer to Flagstaff, was a stockman. He married Mary Jane Taylor. Their children were Bernard C. (Bum), Mrs. Bertha Kinsey, Cerola Chisholm, and Lulu Sullivan. Samuel died in 1927, his wife in 1937.

James A. Vail came from Ohio in 1882 as a youth of twenty-one, driving ox teams from New Mexico hauling a sawmill outfit, which he put in operation west of Flagstaff and operated profitably for a few years. He also opened one of the community's saloons, and went through the fires of 1886 and 1888. He then erected the brick building which stands on the northwest corner of Santa Fe and San Francisco, and resumed his business. He became a substantial owner of real estate, and was also in the cattle business with his brother-in-law, G. W. Black. His wife was Mary Black. Their children were Edna, Grace, Ella, James, and William Theodore—the latter being named after William McKinley and Theodore Roosevelt. Perhaps it is unnecessary to point out that Vail was active in the Republican party. In 1890 he was elected to the Territorial Assembly and played an active part in the creation of Coconino County. He also served as a member of the board of supervisors, and was on the city council for four years. He attended the 1900 G.O.P. Convention as a delegate. He belonged to a number of fraternal groups. In later years he was in bad health and suffered business reverses. He took his life at his Flagstaff home about 1909.

Hugh E. Campbell was born in Nova Scotia in 1862. He worked in the Wisconsin woods, then came to Flagstaff in 1882. He and his partner, Dan Francis, ran a meat market, then built up herds of sheep as the Campbell-Francis Sheep Company, with many thousands of head of stock. In time their holdings placed them in the front rank of Arizona stockmen. In 1893, he married Madie Christman. Their children were Dan, who also became a successful stockman, and Mary Luella, who became Mrs. John B. Duerson. Duerson was a bookkeeper for the big sheep company. Campbell had two brothers who also lived here, Colin and W. H. Hugh Campbell served as head of the Arizona Wool Growers Association, was several times chairman of the State Fair Commission, represented

Coconino County in the State Senate, and attended the national Democratic Convention that nominated William Jennings Bryan. Campbell Hall, on the campus of Northern Arizona University, was named for him. He died in 1923 and was buried in the Flagstaff Masonic Cemetery.

Joseph Roger Treat was another Nova Scotian, born in 1860, who chose Flagstaff as home, arriving here in 1883. He worked for several sawmills and was foreman for the Arizona Lumber and Timber Company. He served as treasurer of Coconino County from 1905 to 1912, and in 1914 and 1915 was mayor of Flagstaff. It was under his leadership that the city opened negotiations with the railroad to build the first of the two fifty-million-gallon reservoirs north of the city at the foot of the Peaks. Treat spent some time in the lumber business in Mexico, leaving at the start of the Madero revolution. His brother, James M., was killed in a sawmilling accident. Joseph married his brother's widow, Mary. With a brother-in-law, James Lamport, he operated the first commercial stage to Grand Canyon from Flagstaff. Lamport was a brother of Mrs. C. A. Greenlaw. For a time, Treat also operated a sawmill at Lakeside. He died there in 1937, and was buried here with the Masons officiating. He had headed the local lodge in 1912. He was survived by his widow; a son, Dolph, and a daughter, Mrs. Augusta Larson.

Asa Clark, born in Maine in 1839, was the twin of John Clark who joined the gold rush to California and then settled in the Flagstaff area in 1876, one of the first stockmen in northern Arizona. The twins were among the youngest of a family of thirteen children. Asa married Rosaline Nutter. Urged by his brother John to move to Arizona, he arrived in Flagstaff in 1883, accompanied by one of his two sons, Charles. They lived for a time at the ranch in what was known as Clark Valley, settled by his brother John, an area now covered by Lake Mary. But soon Asa acquired from Thomas McMillan in a sheep deal the farm just north of the little Flagstaff community. The property soon became known as Clark Ranch, and it was because of the association of Clarks with the area that the name Clark Homes was given to the World War II housing project which now [1976] occupies the northern part of the City Park.

Asa conducted a clothing store, a shoe store and later a second hand store. Later his sons, Charles and John, operated the C. A. Clark & Co. establishment.

For many years Asa served as night marshal, paid by subscription of the merchants. His constant companion was a huge Newfoundland dog that made itself his guardian and added weight to his encounters and reckonings with rough characters. He also served as deputy under Sheriff John Francis. As a young man in Maine, Asa suffered an eye injury when corrosive sublimate which he was using to treat sores on a horse's legs caught fire and blew into his eyes. He suffered serious impairment of sight and in his later years was blind. He was a charter member of the Flagstaff Odd Fellows Lodge and active in community affairs. He died in 1927 at his home here, shortly before his ninety-first birthday. His son John had died two months before. Mrs. Clark died in 1937 at age eighty-seven. Surviving was their son Charles, for many years a resident of Grand Canyon.

Arthur W. Kinsey, born in Illinois in 1850, crossed the plains to California as a lad of ten or twelve with his parents in an immigrant train of prairie schooners. He came to this part of Arizona about 1883, lived for a time at Williams, then came to Flagstaff to work for the old A-1 Cattle Company, which had huge holdings north and east of Flagstaff, with headquarters at Fort Valley. He continued there for thirty-five years. He was married to Martha Griffith, a widow with two children, Charles and May. The Kinseys had two daughters, Mrs. F. J. Stein, and Miss Lura Kinsey, who taught school here for many years, and for whom Kinsey School was named. During the early 1900s, Kinsey was county road supervisor. Mrs. Kinsey died in 1915, and he in 1923.

Nelson G. Layton, a native of Indiana, came to Flagstaff in 1883, employed by the Arizona Lumber & Timber Company. He served Coconino County as probate judge, was superintendent of schools for two terms, and was then appointed state superintendent of public instruction. He spent his later years serving Flagstaff Masonic Lodge as secretary and building caretaker. He died in 1926.

William Henry Anderson was a native of Scotland who came to the United States in an early day, lived in Maryland during the Civil War, saw Stonewall Jackson's Army marching, knew some of the officers serving under Union General McClellan, saw Lincoln many times, and sold milk and apples to companies of Union soldiers, moved to Flagstaff in 1883 and in time made a success out of an occupation no longer deemed feasible here—farming. He was born in Aberdeen in 1849, and came to the United States in 1861. He moved to Illinois, then homesteaded in Kansas in 1870, and there he married Lorinda Allen, a native of Connecticut and a descendant of Ethan Allen, leader of the famed Green Mountain Boys in colonial times. In poor health, Anderson decided to move farther west. In 1880 he and his wife and son, Hugh, moved to Los Angeles. Then he went to work for the Southern Pacific, going to Gila Bend. Mrs. Anderson heard about Flagstaff and wrote to the Ayer Lumber Company for information, and received a glowing letter regarding Flagstaff from Jim Marshall, another pioneer.

In June 1883, Anderson and a friend made the trip to Flagstaff with a span of mules and a buckboard. Anderson located a ranch north of town and proceeded to farm. He produced fine potatoes and grain, and acquired the nickname "Spud." He was a hard worker, doing masonry, plastering, carpentering, and also raised horses. He was an experienced road builder and on one occasion worked the entire road from Flagstaff to Grand Canyon for $700. In 1912, he became the first county supervisor of roads. He was active in the Masonic Lodge, served as Worshipful Master, and was also Worthy Patron of the Order of the Eastern Star. He died in 1935. Mrs. Anderson died in 1936. They were survived by a son, John, and two daughters, Mrs. William F. Wallace and Mrs. Nathan Bankhead. Five other children preceded them in death. The Andersons were true pioneers, of the breed who proved in their daily lives that hard work and honest dealing brought honor and respect.

A pioneer who witnessed the entire panorama of Flagstaff's growth and development from 1883 to 1947, remaining active almost to the day of his death at ninety-one, was Arthur H. (Al) Beasley. He was born in 1856 in Illinois, moved to Kansas in 1871, and in 1883 started by train for the west coast. Along the way he heard other passengers talking about the pretty little town of Flagstaff. When the train stopped for water and to give passengers a breather, Al decided to stop over for a short visit. One of his jokes a half-century later was that he still hadn't decided whether or not to make his stay permanent. In 1885, he sent for his family, consisting of his mother, Catherine Beasley, four brothers and three sisters. Next to Al in age was sister Rhetta. He ranched for many years in the Fort Valley area. His sister Rhetta died in 1944. He was active in the Odd Fellows, rarely missing a meeting even in his advanced years. He was survived by two nephews and two nieces, one of whom was Mrs. G. Kent Rucker of Flagstaff.

Uncle Billy (W. H.) Switzer, who came to Flagstaff as a lad of fourteen in 1883, lived here for an incredible eighty-four years, dying a few days before his ninety-eighth birthday in 1967. His father, W. A. Switzer, mother, and the three children, left Kentucky by train for San Francisco in 1874. Later Billy would recall seeing huge herds of buffalo on the plains as the train puffed its way across the continent. From San Francisco they moved to Los Angeles. When Bill was fourteen, they decided to move to Williams, making the trip by train. They had to wait twenty-four hours at Needles for the bridge across the Colorado River to be completed. At Williams they lived in a tent. The father came to Flagstaff, and found that he could rent a house here and that the children would be able to go to school, so the move was made.

The father bought milk cows and Billy was placed in charge. He milked nine cows twice daily, and delivered milk around Flagstaff for fifteen cents a quart or fifty cents a gallon. The elder Switzer filed on a homestead in the area of present-day Switzer Canyon, where they lived for nine years, when the parents decided to return to California. Billy went along, got a job milking cows at a dollar a day, and saved enough to buy a ticket back to Flagstaff. He served three years as clerk of the board of supervisors, and was then county treasurer for three years. He purchased a saddle and harness shop, and later shifted to hardware, establishing the site of Switzer Hardware on North San Francisco Street in 1920. He married the former Nettie Lockwood, and they had nine children, seven of whom lived to maturity. They were Reba (Mrs. J. P. McVey), Ardelle (Mrs. Guy S. Sykes), Louise (Mrs. W. A. McCrea), Agnes (Mrs. Chester Anderson), Ruth (Mrs. Sidney Griffin), W. H., Jr. and Kenneth.

"We went to school in the log cabin schoolhouse north of the Armory building in 1884 and 1885," Uncle Billy recalled in a later day. "It was a tie-chopper's cabin. We sat on shingle blocks. Then they built the new school on what is now the college campus. I quit school to ride after cattle. I wanted to be a cowboy, but I milked cows and peddled the milk."

Billy was active in Democratic party politics, took a keen interest in school affairs, served as trustee, and played an important part in the affairs of the Masons. In 1964 when he was ninety-five, he was asked to prepare an account of some of his experiences. He sketched the family history, and concluded: "I love Flagstaff. I love its citizens. White people, black people, Indians, and Mexicans, they all speak to me and I to them . . . our children also speak to me. Flagstaff has been most kind to me. I have seen it grow from five hundred people, mostly men, in 1883, to its present twenty-two thousand. . . ." September 4, 1964, W. H. Switzer's ninety-fifth birthday, was proclaimed as "William Howard Switzer Day" in Arizona by Gov. Paul J. Fannin.

Allen A. Dutton came to Flagstaff in 1883 with the Ayer Lumber Company. He continued with the Riordans, following their assumption of ownership of the mill, until 1916. He was a member of the Territorial Council (Senate) in 1897 from Coconino County, also served as a member of the county board of supervisors, and was one of the first members of the board of trustees of the Northern Arizona Normal School, now Northern Arizona University. He died in 1921. Mrs. Dutton, a cousin of Ed Ayer, died in 1918. Their survivors were two daughters, Mrs. C. H. Coble and Mrs. I. F. Wheeler, and a son, Charles A., who lived for years in Kingman.

William Roden, Sr., came to Flagstaff from Missouri by way of Texas in

1884, and engaged in the cattle business. He died in 1897 at sixty-nine. His son, W. D. Roden, born in 1870 in Texas, was active in ranching until 1907, when he sold his interests to Babbitts. The Roden range was northeast of Flagstaff near Grand Falls on the Little Colorado, bordering on the Indian country. He had frequent brushes with Indians and renegade white rustlers, but managed to prosper and retired at an early age. He spent winters at Phoenix and La Jolla, summers in Flagstaff at a home on West Cherry. He was colorful, strong-willed, generous, self-reliant, typical in many ways of successful stockmen throughout the West in early days. Once he pointed out that his Flagstaff front yard had a flourishing cover of gramma grass, which played such a vital part in the stock business here in early days. He thought it more beautiful than the conventional clover. He died of heart disease in 1941. He had been a member of the Flagstaff Knights of Pythias Lodge since 1902, members of which officiated at his grave-side. He was survived by his wife, Marjorie Frost Roden, and a four-year-old daughter, Maryellen.

Ralph Henry Cameron was one of three brothers who came to Flagstaff in the 1880s and played active parts in the community's affairs. He was born in Maine in 1863, and came to Flagstaff when he was twenty, working in the forest, raising stock, and running a general merchandise store with a partner, John Lind. They sold the store to Babbitt Brothers in 1889, following which Lind joined the Babbitt organization and Cameron went into politics.

Cameron was sheriff of Coconino County three terms in the 1890s, was dele-gate to the Republican National Convention at Saint Louis in 1896, was member of the Coconino County Board of Supervisors in 1905–07, and served as chair-man; was elected as Arizona Territorial delegate in the Sixty-first and Sixty-second Congresses, serving to February 18, 1912, when his term expired four days after Arizona had gained statehood, to a degree through his efforts. He supervised the building of Bright Angel Trail into Grand Canyon, and with his brother Niles operated the Last Chance copper mine below the rim. He was elected United States Senator from Arizona in 1920 and served until March 1927 after being defeated for re-election, and was defeated again when he sought the office in 1928. His mining interests took him to North Carolina, Georgia and California. The eighty-nine-year-old pioneer died of a heart attack in 1953. A son, Ralph, Jr., died a few months before the father, who was survived by his wife, Betsy, and a daughter, Catherine, of Washington, District of Columbia. The settlement of Cameron on Highway 89 north of Flagstaff was named in his honor.

Niles Cameron, Ralph's brother, was born in Maine in 1861, and came to

Flagstaff in 1886. He engaged in sheep raising, then went into the mercantile business. About 1889 he went to Grand Canyon, where he located the Last Chance copper mine, and with Ralph located the Bright Angel Trail into the Canyon. During the last years of his life, he lived at the Canyon and was in charge of the trail. He was also involved in other mining ventures with brother Ralph. He was active in early years in the Masonic Lodge. He died in 1918, survived by his stepmother, Anna Cameron, brother Ralph, and half-brother Burton A., of Flagstaff.

Burton A. Cameron was born in 1874, also in Maine. He came to Flagstaff in 1887 with his mother, Anna. He worked for Babbitt Brothers for twenty-five years, also worked with his brothers in the copper mine at Grand Canyon, and assisted in construction of the Bright Angel Trail. He served as Coconino County Assessor from 1906–12, the last county assessor of Territorial days. He also served two terms on the Flagstaff City Council. He was a member of the Masons, was a Past Exalted Ruler of the Elks, a member of the Arizona Pioneers Historical Society and other groups, and was active in Republican party affairs. In 1889, he married Frances Clift Cummings, in Flagstaff. She died in 1939. He was survived by three sons, B. A., Jr., Harold L., and George A. A grandson, Bill, was for years publisher of the *Verde Independent* at Cottonwood.

The story of the extraordinary Babbitt family and its involvement in Flagstaff and all of northern Arizona began in 1886 and continues into the 1970s. David and Catherine Babbitt farmed on the outskirts of Cincinnati. They had seven children. A boy died as an infant, a girl lived to maturity and died after a brief career as a teacher, and the five remaining sons grew to manhood and all of them were to play a part in Flagstaff's history.

The brothers were David, born in 1858; George, 1860; William, 1862; Charles, 1865, and Edward, 1867. The father died in 1869 and the mother moved her family to Cincinnati. In due time David and George established a small grocery business. Soon William and Charles joined the older brothers in the venture. The store was located across the street from a three-story residence occupied by a leading Cincinnati businessman, Gerard H. Verkamp, his wife and nine children. The Babbitt youths were soon acquainted with the Verkamp girls and the parents. Within a period of five years, beginning in 1886 after David and William moved to Flagstaff, David would wed Emma; Charles, Mary; and the youngest brother Edward, Matilda. Brother George nearly married the fourth Verkamp sister, but instead wed Philomena Wessel, daughter of a wealthy Cincinnati lumberman. In 1915, William wed Elizabeth Roche, an employee of the Babbitt firm in Flagstaff.

After hearing glowing reports about opportunities in the West from a salesman, Jim Veasey, the brothers became interested in seeking their fortunes there, particularly in the cattle business. In 1884 they sent David out on a scouting expedition. He visited ranches in Colorado, Wyoming, New Mexico, and other areas. In due time he returned to Cincinnati without having found the proper opportunity. For more than a year the brothers worked hard developing their grocery business. Early in 1886 David and William took another trip, this time to the Southwest, armed with a draft for $20,000 resulting from sale of some Cincinnati property, and letters of introduction to prominent men, including Dr. D. J. Brannen of Flagstaff. They first visited New Mexico, but did not find what they sought. A railroad clerk at Albuquerque suggested they take a look at Flagstaff, said to be booming.

They stepped off the train at Flagstaff in the predawn of April 7, 1886, only a few weeks after a fire had leveled most of the business community. Dr. Brannen advised them, discussed opportunities, and helped them find a herd of cattle. Within a few days they had purchased something over a thousand head from Messrs. Hesler and Warren. Price was $17,640, a major part of their capital. They quickly adopted as their brand, CO— (CO Bar), standing for Cincinnati, Ohio. Within a few weeks they were joined by Charles, who would devote most of his long life to the livestock interests. They purchased more stock, leased land, took up a homestead, and built a cabin in the little valley now covered by Lake Mary. When David married in the fall, Emma's father gave the couple a $10,000 wedding present, then offered to advance in excess of $50,000 if the Babbitts could find a good merchandising opportunity in the West.

With a slump in cattle prices, the stock operation was limited, so George secured a place as bookkeeper with the pioneer Flagstaff merchant, P. J. Brannen. Looking for opportunities, David soon opened a building material business in a frame building he erected on the northwest corner of San Francisco and Aspen, a site which would be the center of Babbitt operations for scores of years. George purchased a small confectionery and restaurant on the front street and in due time added a soda fountain, the town's first. He had a partner whom he soon bought out. William and Charles continued to handle the stock interests. In due time David bought out the general store owned by Ralph Cameron and John Lind. A fine building of stone replaced the frame building which had housed the building materials business. George disposed of his business, and in 1889, the brothers joined to organize Babbitt Brothers Trading Company. They soon bought out the general merchant, Brannen, and were on their way to bigger things.

The youngest brother, Edward, was associated with the others in Flagstaff in 1887-88, then returned to Cincinnati to study law. He came back to Flagstaff in 1891 and did legal work for the firm, then became Coconino County probate judge, served in the Territorial Council, and in the mid-nineties again returned to Cincinnati to practice law.

The Babbitts very quickly became the leading merchants in the community, and continued to add to their livestock operations. In time they purchased the A-1, the Hashknife, and other big outfits. Other businesses and enterprises were added. In twenty-five or thirty years they would be operating department stores in Flagstaff, Williams and Kingman; wholesale houses at Prescott and Flagstaff; a garage in Flagstaff; many Indian trading posts; and running thousands of head of stock. In 1915, their beef crop brought $1,500,000. They formed a livestock loan company which in the 1920s loaned $5,000,000 in Arizona and California. The company had its ups and downs, booming with booming times, faltering during panics and depressions, but made its way along under the guidance of the brothers, then their sons, then their grandsons and grandsons-in-law.

George Babbitt was a good businessman, but generous and gregarious, and enjoyed a fine home, good clothes, an elegant carriage and, compared with David, was easy-going. "George is our rich brother," David would smile. George Babbitt was tremendously popular, and was for many years high in the councils of the Democratic party in Arizona. He was named one of the three trustees when the Territory proposed to erect a reform school here in the 1890s. Under his chairmanship, negotiations were carried out to secure the land, and in due time a stone structure was erected. The reform school never materialized, in part due to opposition from the people of Flagstaff; but the structure became the nucleus of Northern Arizona Normal School, of which Babbitt was also a trustee, which in time became Arizona State College, and then Northern Arizona University. His son, George, Jr., also was of major service to the institution through his efforts in raising funds for the Student Union Building.

George died of a heart attack in 1920 while visiting in one of the county offices. Mrs. Babbitt died in 1948. Their children were Bertrand, who spent most of his life in the stock business; Margaret (Mrs. T. E.) McCullough; Herbert, Flagstaff businessman and stockman for many years; George, Jr., who devoted years to real estate and investments, and served as Flagstaff postmaster; and Eunice (Mrs. I. F. Veazey). The beautiful George Babbitt mansion on northeast hill was one of the city's showplaces for many years. It was destroyed by fire in the 1950s.

David Babbitt devoted his energies to the direction of the company's widespread holdings, working closely with the brothers. Oldtimers who knew him describe him as quiet and unassuming; but he was devoted to his business and was a highly capable executive. He was the oldest of the brothers, had strong qualities of leadership, and from the beginning was one to whom the others looked for decisions. He carried much of the responsibility for operation of the large concern, but found time to serve Flagstaff as mayor in the 1890s. Mrs. David Babbitt died in 1899. For many years the daughter, Gertrude, kept house for her father. He died in November 1929. The David Babbitts had four sons and two daughters: Raymond G., Edwin, Joseph and David, Jr., and Gertrude and Elaine.

Ray and Joseph played important parts in direction and management of the firm. Edwin's special interest was a garage and automobile agency. David, Jr. was with Ed for a time, then operated an automobile agency in Phoenix.

Ray and Rose Babbitt's son Ted (R. G., Jr.) has for many years directed the mercantile part of the business, and their son James has operated the garage and automobile agency founded by Edwin Babbitt.

Joseph and Viola Babbitt's children include five daughters and a son, Joseph, Jr., a Flagstaff attorney; the daughters are Imogene (Mrs. Lou) Bader, Mary (Mrs. Ralph) Bilby, Betty Jo (Mrs. Michael) D'Mura, Rayma (Mrs. Norman G.) Sharber, and Teresa (Mrs. Charles) Reddock. Sharber served for nine years on the Arizona State Board of Regents, and Bilby succeeded him on the board in 1974. Bilby also became president of Babbitt Brothers Trading Company in 1975.

Many members of the family have worked in community affairs, served on the city council, been active in the politics of both parties, and have held important responsibilities in banks and other important enterprises.

William Babbitt, who came to Flagstaff with David in 1886, devoted his interest to the livestock part of the holdings. He directed the company's holdings in Kansas, bought and sold cattle, and loved the range. He played no part in the mercantile aspects of the operation, nor did he have any interest in politics. He was described by oldtimers as a smiling, friendly, kindly man, a real oldtime cowboy and rancher. He died in 1930, and his wife died in 1946. They had no children.

While Charles was primarily a stockman, particularly in the early days, he was a keen businessman, and his counsels were respected and followed by the firm for many years. He was well versed in the management aspects of the mercantile part of the company's activities. He enjoyed trading and buying and selling cattle, and while astute in his dealings, was more concerned about the game of business than the accumulation of wealth. He was very good in dealing with the Indians at the trading posts and in livestock deals. While he was a kindly man, few ever bettered him in exchanges.

Charles lived in Flagstaff for seventy years, dying in 1956 at the age of ninety. On the sixtieth anniversary of his arrival in Flagstaff, he was interviewed by the *Sun:* "Times have changed a lot, but if I had it to do over, I believe I'd follow the same course. Young fellows starting out today have plenty of new kinds of problems, and I'm not so sure that we could come out sixty years from starting these days, the same way we have now, but I'd sure be willing to try," he said.

Charles' wife preceded him in death. Survivors included sons Paul J. and John G., and a daughter, Miss Helen. A son, James E., died in 1944, and another, Charles J., Jr., also died before his father. Son Paul, an attorney, has been active in direction of the Babbitt firm for many years, and grandson Paul is now active in the firm; another of Paul's sons, Bruce, is [in 1976] attorney general of Arizona. James served in the State Senate in the late 1930s and early 1940s. He succumbed to a heart attack while on a hunting trip. He played an important part in the affairs of the company and was a leading figure on the political scene in the state during his years in the senate. Babbitt Hall on the university campus recognizes his important services to that institution.

Charles' son John has always been directly interested in the livestock phases of the firm's operations. However, when appointed to the senate to complete his brother James' term, he was then elected on his own, and demonstrated qualities of leadership and served Arizona well, particularly the college. He was a member of the Board of Regents for sixteen years, during a time of great growth and problems at the three state institutions. In recognition of his invaluable services, he was granted an honorary doctorate in 1966, when Arizona State College became Northern Arizona University.

A native of England, whose extraordinary skill as a mechanic and machinist was demonstrated over and over again in Flagstaff for seventy years, was Stanley Sykes. He was born in London in 1865, attended a technical college, and served an apprenticeship in a London machine shop, then emigrated to the United States with his brother Godfrey in 1884. The brothers were in the cattle business in Kansas for a time, then came to Flagstaff in 1886, where they opened a machine and repair shop. They also ran some cattle in the Little Colorado River area.

Stanley married Beatrice Switzer, daughter of W. A. Switzer, who came here in 1883. The Sykes had two sons, Guy and Harold, and the latter served this community as mayor.

Stanley assisted in setting up the dome for the twenty-four-inch telescope at Lowell Observatory in 1894, and for many years served as instrument maker at that famed institution, building the driving clocks for the telescopes and other equipment. He was an outdoorsman and gardener, and was a highly talented painter in watercolors and oils. At one time he planned and carried out a boat trip from Phoenix to Yuma, perhaps the only time in history this has been done. When they ran out of water in the Salt River, he and his companion, Charlie McLean, portaged their boat. Dr. E. C. Slipher of the Observatory here once said: "He [Sykes] is the finest mechanic I have ever met. He could do anything with metal that anybody else could do with wood or any other material. He had an excellent background knowledge of science. . . ." Sykes died in 1956 at the age of ninety-one, and Mrs. Sykes died in 1969.

Other brothers who came to Flagstaff in the mid-eighties and remained to play important roles in the community for many years were Timothy A. and Michael J. Riordan. Tim, born in Chicago in 1858, came to Flagstaff in 1886 at the suggestion of another brother, D. M. Riordan, who was general manager of the Ayer Lumber Company. He quickly made a place for himself in the operation, assuming added responsibilities as the years passed.

When D. M. Riordan purchased the Ayer interests in 1887, and the Arizona Lumber Company was formed, Tim became superintendent, and they were soon joined by the other brother, Michael J., born in 1865, who operated a branch commissary for the firm at Williams. A few weeks after the purchase the mill was destroyed by fire. Undaunted, the Riordans busied themselves rebuilding, and soon had a much finer and larger mill to supplant the one which had been brought here by ox team in 1881–82. In 1893 Tim and Mike with F. W. Sisson entered into an agreement to purchase the interest of D. M. Riordan, and the name of the firm became Arizona Lumber and Timber Company, with Tim as president and Mike as secretary.

In 1889 Tim married Caroline Metz of Cincinnati, whose father was a prominent tobacco grower and merchant. In 1893 Mike married Elizabeth Metz, sister of his brother's wife. A third sister, Alice, came west to visit in 1891, and spent the remainder of her life here, living most of those years with M. J.'s family. She started the first parochial school, and taught there until it was taken over by the Sisters of Loretto in 1899. Alice died in 1959.

In 1903 T. A. Riordan conceived the idea of building a lake south of Flagstaff. The dam was placed across a narrow part of what in earlier days had been the Clark ranch. The lake, named Mary in honor of Tim's daughter, became an important factor in Flagstaff's municipal water supply, particularly following construction by the city in the 1940s of an additional dam forming Upper Lake Mary. The Riordans also constructed an electric light plant which served not only their own properties but the community. They were also in the livestock business, and the Riordan name appeared in lists of directors of a number of financial institutions. In 1905 the brothers built the two large, elaborate homes on Kinlichi Knoll south of the city, still landmarks on the Flagstaff scene.

During World War I Tim was food administrator for Arizona under the direction of Herbert Hoover. He traveled widely and made eight trips abroad, including one around the world. He had rather extraordinary administrative abilities and made a success of most ventures. Tim died in 1946 in Los Angeles, and was buried in the Flagstaff Catholic Cemetery. Mrs. Riordan died a few years before him. They had two daughters, Anna, who died in 1927, and Mary, for whom the lake was named and who married Robert L. Chambers of Los Angeles. The Chamberses were popular and respected residents of Flagstaff for many years. Mary died in 1970. In 1976, her husband still occupies one of the Kinlichi Knoll mansions at the age of eighty-four.

Mike Riordan, who came to Arizona as a health seeker, took active part in many business ventures. He had wide interests in art and literature, traveled widely, wrote many articles for magazines, kept meticulous journals, and wrote a history of the Catholic Church in Flagstaff, published in the *Sun* shortly before his death and since circulated in booklet form. Mike Riordan died in 1930, and his wife in 1954. Their children were Blanche, Arthur, Clara, Robert, Richard, and one who died in infancy.

F. W. Sisson, born in Illinois in 1862, graduated from Knox College with honors in 1884. After a couple of years with a manufacturing company in Peoria, he came to Flagstaff and assumed a position with the Arizona Lumber Company. He was associated with the Riordans for many years, and served as treasurer. He was married in 1888 to Mary Willcox. He was a student of literature and art, and experimented with photography, producing scenic views of great beauty. He liked outdoor sports, rode a bicycle, played tennis, and rode horseback. He died in Los Angeles of ptomaine poisoning in 1908.

A transplanted Texan, J. W. Weatherford, born in 1859, came to Flagstaff in 1887 and, during his forty-seven years here, did a number of worthwhile and interesting things, including building a sightseeing road to Doyle Saddle and around the Inner Basin on the San Francisco Peaks. In 1878 as a youth of nineteen, he was in the business of supply agent for mining camps in Arizona. After a sojourn of a couple of years in Mexico with a mining company, he returned to Arizona and very soon thereafter found himself in Flagstaff. He served for a time as deputy sheriff, and established a mercantile business and operated it for twenty-three years. He built the Weatherford Hotel, a Flagstaff landmark, and a place of great elegance in the early 1900s. He erected other buildings, including an opera house which is now occupied by the Orpheum Theater. In 1920 he started building his toll road up the Peaks, completing it in 1926.

In his early years here, Weatherford played an active part in the establishment of the Normal School. He was active in the Democratic party but held elective public office only once, in 1887, when he served as justice of the peace. He was a charter member of Flagstaff Elks, carrying card number four. In 1884 he was married to Margaret McGratton. They had one son, Hugh. Weatherford died in 1934.

E. M. Doe, born in 1850 in Vermont, was one of Flagstaff's pioneer attorneys, coming here in 1887 as a partner of W. G. Stewart, a prominent figure on the political scene who was active in bringing about the creation of Coconino County. Doe was appointed Coconino County's first district attorney. For many years he was attorney for Saginaw Southern Railroad Company, Saginaw Lumber Company, Arizona Central Bank, and the Santa Fe Railway. He was a member of the Constitutional Congress preparatory to establishment of the State, but would not sign the constitution, considering it too radical. In 1909, President Taft named Doe as district judge and member of the Territorial Supreme Court. He was a close friend of Dr. Percival Lowell, founder of Lowell Observatory.

From Henry Ashurst's diary, we learn that Doe was six feet tall and erect, carried a sword cane and could fence, had reddish hair and a heavy carnelian moustache, smoked (and chewed) cigars. He enjoyed sumptuous formal dinners and rare vintages, liked to gamble, was courtly in manner, was subtle and ingenious, and in Texas in early days had killed a man in self-defense. As a child he had a cockney nurse who gave him an interesting accent. He ran away from home at fifteen and spent some months in Germany. Doe varied the style of his apparel. On one occasion in 1893, Ashurst saw him in attendance at the Territorial Supreme Court wearing a cutaway coat and a crimson Tam O'Shanter. He was an intellectual and a bon vivant, bohemian and gourmet. He liked to fish and hunt.

Elias S. Clark, born in 1862 in Maine, came to Flagstaff in the 1880s and read law under Doe's supervision. He was admitted to the bar, became district attorney at Flagstaff in 1897, moved to Prescott, and in due time became Territorial Attorney General, serving from 1905–09.

A colorful personality who graced the Flagstaff scene for sixty-eight years

E. M. Doe, attorney, district judge, supreme court justice (1850–1919).

John Clark, who came to the Flagstaff area in 1876 (1839–1923).

was George Hochderffer, born in 1863 in Illinois. According to a story handed down in the family, President Lincoln came through on a campaign tour when George was but eight months old, and shook his hand, calling him "that little rebel [Democrat]." Hochderffer took pride in that story, and in later years said he had shaken hands with every American president from Lincoln to Harry Truman with the exception of Andrew Johnson.

He arrived in Flagstaff in 1887 with his father, Frank J. Hochderffer, and a brother Frank, Jr., in a covered wagon drawn by a team of mules, en route to California. They got here shortly after one of the fires which recurrently leveled much of the business section. As they knew how to make brick, they busied themselves for a time, then resumed the trip to San Francisco, this time by train.

In time they returned to Flagstaff. George was active in ranching and farming, and also was town marshal as well as soldier, botanist, writer, traveler and artist. Through his efforts, Company I of the National Guard was established here. He was active in politics, was a Democratic precinct committeeman for sixty-nine years, and attended many national Democratic party conventions. He knew all of the community's pioneers and colorful characters well, made records of much valuable historical data, and incorporated a lot of it into a book which was published after his death, *Flagstaff, Whoa!*

As a botanist Hochderffer collected specimens in various parts of the continent. As an artist he produced many fine oil paintings. He traveled widely. In his later years he lived at Cottonwood. There, shortly after his ninetieth birthday, he fell and hurt himself. A few days later he called on a friend from Flagstaff who had a winter home in Cottonwood. He walked up to the door carrying a cane under his arm. Asked about it, he said, "The doctor told me to carry this thing, so I'm doing it." He was tall, military in bearing, and looked and acted every inch the colonel, which he was in the guard.

Although born in Illinois, Hochderffer had a German accent acquired from his parents, and this, combined with his naturally hoarse voice, made his speech sometimes difficult to understand. He was courtly, dignified, humorous, and eagerly interested in all things around him. Although a Catholic by birth and training, in mid-life he entered the Masonic fraternity. When he died in 1955 at ninety-one, a Catholic friend asked a priest to recite the rosary for Hochderffer, which he refused to do. The friend proceeded to do so himself. By his request, Hochderffer had Masonic funeral services. His children were George, Jr., Mrs. May Fair, and Frank, who died during World War I.

Thomas E. Pulliam, born in Arkansas in 1861, was married in 1884 to Lida Anna Freeman, and came to Flagstaff in 1889. He was county recorder for four years, county supervisor two years, sheriff three years, and justice of the peace two years. For three years he served as superintendent of the State Industrial School at Fort Grant. He was a Flagstaff city councilman for seven years and mayor for two years. He was appointed to the board of visitors of Northern Arizona Teachers College. He was active in the Elks and Masons. They had five children, one of whom was Clarence T., who served Flagstaff faithfully and well as city clerk for forty-five years, from 1919 until 1963.

The Ed McGonigles came to Flagstaff in 1888 to visit wife Mary's brother, John Cooney. They liked Flagstaff and stayed. Ed worked as yard foreman for the Arizona Lumber & Timber sawmill for five years, then for twenty years as superintendent. He and associates then opened another mill, the Flagstaff Lumber Company, which many years later became the property of the Cady Lumber Corporation. His brother Charles, who followed him here, was killed in a logging accident. Ed McGonigle was involved in construction of the first Lake Mary Dam and also in the building of the later, larger dam. The McGonigles had three children, Susan, who married John J. Britt of Flagstaff; Clara, who assisted her father in operation of the Lightning Delivery for years, and Veronica, who died in 1919. McGonigle was elected to the Arizona Assembly in 1928. He died shortly thereafter.

J. E. Jones, an attorney, came to Flagstaff in 1888 at the age of thirty. A native of Tennessee, he lived as a child in Arkansas. He studied law with a brother, R. H. Jones, who also later became a Flagstaff resident. J. E. was married in 1880 in Arkansas to Sarah Scarborough. They had five children: Fenton E., Mrs. Mina B. Campbell, William C.; Zella, who married Frank Harrison, Coconino County Judge in the 1930s, and Charles C. All were raised in Flagstaff.

While his energies were channeled to the practice of law here in the early days, he had an interest in the Flagstaff *Democrat* weekly newspaper in the late 1880s and early 1890s, through foreclosure of a mortgage.

He served Coconino County as superior court judge in the 1910s and 1920s, presiding over many notorious trials including the Nash and Indian Miller murder cases. His most noteworthy trial was that in which the will of Dr. Percival Lowell, founder and benefactor of the observatory, was contested by the widow. The Lowell will had established a perpetual trust for the benefit of the institution. The case involved an estate of about $2,500,000. He ruled in favor of Lowell's trust, and was upheld by the Supreme Court on appeal by Mrs. Lowell. Judge Jones was a member of the Odd Fellows, the Knights of Pythias, and related groups. He died in 1929.

Daniel Lorain Hogan, a colorful, humorous and useful citizen who died in

1957 at age ninety after having lived here sixty-six years, was a native of New York. He worked in construction, helping erect many of the earlier structures on the university campus, and also served as a deputy sheriff. During the Spanish-American War he was a member of Teddy Roosevelt's famed Rough Riders in a group from Arizona headed by William (Bucky) O'Neill of Prescott. He regaled generations of Flagstaff residents with stories about happenings in that war. He was survived by sons Ernest J. and Thomas H., and a daughter, Mrs. Lora Mae Dunnam.

These, then, are some of the pioneers who settled in the pine-forested wilderness around the San Francisco Peaks in the decade of the 1880s, and made the community of Flagstaff something more than a name.

# CHAPTER VII

# Flagstaff's Flagstaffs

THE SEVERAL VERSIONS of what we may call the Flagstaff legend agree that the community received its name from a flagstaff. Differences have to do with where it stood, by whom it was erected or prepared, and when; whether it was a standing tree trimmed of its branches, or a pole planted in the ground, or lashed to a standing tree; and who applied the name Flagstaff to the community and when.

In general the stories are not necessarily in conflict, although they have generated some argument from time to time. Some of the difficulty has resulted from the fact that nearly always two different matters were under simultaneous discussion: 1) the flagstaff or flagstaffs, and 2) the naming of the town. Further difficulty has arisen from the mistaken idea that there could be only one "real" flagstaff and that the community could be named on only one occasion.

It is certain that there were three poles or trimmed trees which could have been used to fly flags in the immediate Flagstaff vicinity in the early 1880s; in the summer of 1887 a fourth, over one hundred feet high, was erected in a prominent place by the Grand Army of the Republic; in the 1890s another pole was erected by a local National Guard unit; and as an expression of the patriotic fervor accompanying the Spanish-American War in 1898, contributions were solicited to erect a very impressive flagpole which its promotors promised would be the tallest and fly the largest flag in the Territory.

But the only poles or trimmed trees which concern us here are the three which were in evidence in the very early 1880s, each of which has been claimed by early settlers as the flagstaff which gave the town its name. The matter of Flagstaff's flagstaffs is a bit complicated, and to simplify the discussion we will give names to these three flagstaffs around which the stories have grown.

The flagstaff erected by the second Boston party in 1876, on what later became known as Clark Ranch, in the general area of present-day Flagstaff Junior High School and China Canyon, we will call the "1876 flagstaff"; the trimmed tree which some oldtimers say stood near Antelope Spring in what became known as Old Town, and from which a flag is said to have flown, we will refer to as "Old Town flagpole"; and the trimmed tree which stood near the railroad right-of-way at the foot of Switzer Mesa until it was cut down about 1888, we will call "East tree."

We open our discussion with data relating to the East tree, because it has been widely reported and believed to be the "original" flagstaff, and because we know that on one of the occasions when the community was given the name Flagstaff, this tree was in the mind of the namer. It would be misleading to refer to this tree by the name with which it is usually designated, Beale tree, because there is not a scrap of evidence that Lt. Edward Fitzgerald Beale, on his several trips through this area in the 1850s, trimmed out such a tree or was even near its site. The Beale wagon road ran a considerable distance north of this point, not far from the present-day routing of the natural gas pipelines which cross the area near Mt. Elden. And we do not call it a flagstaff because no one has ever claimed that they saw a flag on it, in spite of the fact that it was frequently referred to as a flagstaff.

The connection of the name of Lieutenant Beale with the East tree seems to have been made for the first time by George H. Tinker, editor of the weekly *Arizona Champion,* in one of a series of promotional articles he published in January 1887, and reprinted in pamphlet form, "A Land of Sunshine." The booklet had wide distribution and was republished in hard cover in 1969 by Tinker's grandson, Ben, thus further perpetuating the Beale story. Tinker's 1887 piece flatly stated without evidence that Beale's party had passed over the spot where Flagstaff now stands, "camped at the eastern extremity of the present town, his men [cutting] the limbs from a straight pine tree, on which to run up the . . . flag. The tree still [1887] stands there shorn of its limbs, and gave the name to the town of 'Flagstaff' when the first settlement was made here more than a quarter of a century later."

The East tree's location at a considerable distance from any of the springs, although it was in an area where water sometimes stood in potholes in the rock, suggests that it was not intended as a flagstaff at a camp site. Its location at the edge of what became the railroad right-of-way, at the beginning of a curve, gives some credence to the idea that it might have been prepared for some railroad construction purpose. General Palmer's 1867–68 railroad survey followed a line about three miles north of this point. "Yet in 1867 members of the [Palmer] party camped near the site of Flagstaff, while members were exploring the canyon country to the south. This party might have stripped one of the trees, although there is no record or tradition of the event," says Dr. Harold S. Colton. It's not impossible that it was prepared by engineer Kingman's survey crews as late as 1881. Lopping the branches from a tall pine tree is not a task to be undertaken lightly. It would be hard, dangerous work, chopping or sawing branches eight to twelve inches in diameter from a tree while managing to maintain a foothold aloft.

Over a period of many years the *Arizona Champion* and its successor, the *Coconino Sun,* published articles and letters relating to the flagstaff or flagstaffs and the naming of the town. Thoughtful citizens were concerned over the conflicts in accounts coming from responsible sources, and attempts were made to resolve the problem.

One such attempt was made on December 3, 1926, when the *Sun* published an article by George Hochderffer, who came to Flagstaff in 1887, and who for the rest of his life would repeat his view that the East tree had been prepared as a flagstaff by Lieutenant Beale and that it was this flagstaff which gave the community its name. He says flatly that the East tree had been trimmed by Beale's survey party. "The tree had been dead many years when I first saw it in 1887 but it was still standing, firm but somewhat worm-eaten. In January 1888, this flagpole was cut down by a well-known character of that time, Old Bismarck. It was consumed as firewood in Sandy Donahue's saloon. I selected some of the wood at the time and have it now in my possession. I also have a rolling pin made of the wood by a brother of mine and presented to my wife as a wedding present. I am sure that at that time it was the general belief that this was the flagstaff of Flagstaff. I have never heard the story contradicted until about 1896—eight years later. . . ."

Hochderffer, in his researches, made two visits to San Pedro, California, to consult pioneer Peter J. Brannen about the flagstaffs and the naming of the town. In his book he quotes the following statement by Brannen:

> In the spring of 1881 a meeting of citizens was called. These citizens met in the P. J. Brannen tent store for the purpose of selecting a name for the newly established post office. Marvin Beal offered the name of Antelope City after the Old Town Spring, known as Antelope Spring. Ed Whipple suggested the name Flagpole after a flagpole that at the time was lashed with rawhide to the top of a tall pine tree near the spring. [Old Town flagpole]. However, the name Flagstaff offered by Mr. Brannen was finally accepted. This name had been inspired by a tall pinestaff, known as the Lieutenant Beale flagstaff [the East tree], which stood near

and within a few feet of the present-day Shell Oil tank on the railroad right-of-way. [Thus] Flagstaff became the name of the post office and the city.

No doubt this is substantially what happened. There are corroborating statements by men who were present at the meeting that Brannen did urge the name, Flagstaff, for the post office. But Brannen also confirms the existence of Old Town flagpole—and states that Ed Whipple had *that* pole in mind during the discussion! But of course the "newly established" post office to which Brannen referred had to have a name in order to be established—and that name was Flag Staff. Months before this meeting, a mail route between Prescott and present-day Winslow had been set up with Flag Staff as one of its stops. On March 25, 1881, the Prescott *Miner* reported:

> The new mail route recently established between Prescott and Brigham City, on the Little Colorado River, via the San Francisco Mountains, is now in full blast and is being run by Messrs. Kerens & Griffith three times a week, and furnishes mail at the following places along the route: Chino Valley, McCullum's 52 miles from Prescott; Volunteer Springs, 78 miles; Flag Staff 93 miles; Turkey Tanks, 105 miles, and thence to Brigham City. The mails leave Prescott Tuesdays, Thursdays and Saturdays at 9 A.M. Returning, they leave Brigham City Mondays, Wednesdays and Fridays at 9 A.M., arriving in Prescott Wednesdays, Fridays and Sundays at 11 A.M. This is the most available route at the present time between Prescott and points in Apache County and Western New Mexico. The route is one of great importance, as it will be the means of furnishing the army of railroad builders with letters and papers from all parts of the globe; it will also be a great accommodation to ranchers and stockmen along the line.

This mail route no doubt was established in February when Thomas F. McMillan, first permanent settler, was named postmaster. In April 1973, National Archivist James Rhoads advised United States Senator Paul J. Fannin of Arizona:

> The records of the Post Office Department in the National Archives show that the post office at Flagstaff was established on February 24, 1881, in Yavapai County [later in Coconino County], Arizona. Thomas Mc-Mellon [the spelling shown consistently in the postal records], who was

appointed postmaster on that date, and Alfred D. Young, who was appointed on May 9, 1881, both declined. Patrick B. Brannen was then appointed on May 23, 1881.

We have found no correspondence with Thomas McMellon or Alfred D. Young in the postal records. These records do not explain the origin of the name of the Flagstaff office nor do they show that it was ever known by any other name.

Very probably the meeting of citizens to discuss a post office and town name was called by P. J. Brannen after P. B. Brannen's appointment on May 23. P. B. Brannen was senior proprietor of the newly established tent-store at Antelope Spring. His nephew, P. J., who operated the store, was never postmaster, although he certainly performed the duties as the new post office was located in a corner of the store. And later, as the *Arizona Champion* reported on October 4, 1884, a petition was circulated in Flagstaff urging P. J.'s appointment as postmaster. But the position went to a James R. Kilpatrick, a competitor of the Brannen mercantile establishment, a month later. Subsequent postmaster appointments went to Dr. D. J. Brannen in 1887, George H. Cook in 1889 and Thomas J. Ross in 1893.

Thus, it appears that P. J. had merely urged formalizing a name that was already being used for the post office. Nor, of course, was he the first to apply the name to the community itself, although the story has been repeated many times that he was. For as noted earlier, the Yavapai County Board of Supervisors had officially designated Flag Staff as a voting precinct in the fall of 1880, some seven months before the meeting in Brannen's store. And two years before that, J. L. Harris had found the name Flagstaff already in use for the McMillan homestead and so recorded it in his 1878 land survey map of the area.

Samuel King, bookkeeper for the Brannen general store in early days, on a visit to Flagstaff in 1920 declared that the East tree was the "right" flagstaff. King married Sadie Hawks, daughter of the pioneer J. F. Hawks family which ran the community's first rooming house or hotel. On April 2, 1920, the *Coconino Sun* published an item reporting that the Kings had left here thirty-five years before, which would make it about 1885. They visited Flagstaff oldtimers, one of whom was John W. Francis. The item declared:

> Both Mr. King and Francis declare that there is a mistaken idea as to the exact location of the old pine tree that was trimmed and used for a flag by the first settlers; they claim that it was located close to the present Union Oil station [later the Shell Oil bulk plant] and not at or near Old

Town Spring in the west end of town. They tried to settle the question, but were unable to find the old stump of the tree.

This reference, of course, is to the East tree.

Hochderffer repeated his claim favoring East tree in articles in the *Sun* over a period of years. In April 1937, he and W. H. Switzer, who had come to Flagstaff as a boy of fourteen in 1883, looked for evidence of the East tree. They found a stump which they were both sure was the remains of the tree. Switzer's family had lived a short distance from the site, and he told this writer on several occasions during the course of a friendship which extended from the early 1940s until his death shortly before his ninety-eighth birthday in 1967, that he was positive they had found the right stump.

The two oldtimers loaded up the stump and shipped it to Dr. Andrew Ellicott Douglass, founder of the laboratory of tree ring research at the University of Arizona, Tucson. Dr. Douglass was an old friend of the two men. He had lived in Flagstaff in the 1890s and early 1900s, working at Lowell Observatory. He took a personal interest in dating the stump. Douglass advised Dr. Colton, director of the Museum of Northern Arizona, in a letter dated August 20, 1942, that he believed the tree may have been cut down some years after 1890, and also that the tree showed a small ring for the year 1877, suggesting it might have been injured in some way that year or a year earlier. He added: "My longtime recollection of a stripped tree placed it near Old Town Spring on the west side of the valley bottom." Here, of course, Douglass is referring to Old Town flagpole.

So much for the East tree. No one of record ever saw a flag on it, but it was certainly a prominent landmark in Flagstaff in the 1880s. Who did the laborious job of lopping off its limbs, and for what purpose, we do not know. But we have the word of the pioneer Flagstaff merchant, P. J. Brannen, that he had East tree in mind when he recommended the name, Flagstaff, at the meeting in his store in the spring of 1881.

Now for the Old Town flagpole:

The daughter of one of the first settlers in Flagstaff gave the story of the naming of the town as she had been told it, in an interview appearing in the *Coconino Sun* on December 16, 1927:

> Mrs. William Friedlein, who was a tiny girl when her father, Marvin Beal, and her uncle Frank arrived with the first tent settlers in Flagstaff in 1881, tells the story of the naming of Flagstaff as she heard it.
>
> One night about a year after the family arrived her father came into

their little tent home and requested that her mother hurry with supper because there was an important meeting that night. The purpose of it was to decide upon a name for the rapidly growing cluster of buildings grouped around the spring at Old Town.

There were about ten men present, of the probable twenty male inhabitants. Popular opinion at first favored the obvious name of Antelope City after the spring which was known by that name at the time.

The name of Flagstaff was finally selected and this is how it was thought of. There is an old stump now, according to Mrs. Friedlein, to be seen near Old Town Spring which is honored that our present modern city was named for it. In early days when wagon trains across the country depended upon water holes there was always some conspicuous signal left for the next expedition. A tall tree had a large square of canvas floating in the top to direct caravans to the water beneath it. It was called the Flagstaff far and near and thus it was most logical that the settlement around it should be included in the name, according to the majority of the pioneers present. And so they adopted the name by acclamation.

What happened to the tree is another story. Some years after it was cut down for spite, so Mrs. Friedlien's story goes, by a town bum and floater who was sore because citizens refused to longer furnish him free meals. An indignant vigilance committee, met in solemn conclave, gave him his choice of hanging or leaving town between suns. He left.

So here we have evidence that the very early settlers, the Beals (not to be confused with Lt. E. F. Beale), felt that the flagstaff for which the town was named was Old Town flagpole. The Beals always lived very near the site in Old Town.

On December 7, 1928, the *Coconino Sun* interviewed Ed Whipple who, as noted previously, opened the first saloon in Old Town during the winter of 1880–81. He repeats the story of the meeting at which the town was named or renamed by P. J. Brannen and adds:

The spring at the west end of town [Old Town] was then called Flagpole Spring, later known as Old Town Spring. It was so named because a flagpole had been put up some time before by the militia boys when they came through here. It was about fifty feet long and was put in the top of the tallest pine tree nearest the spring. This pole could be seen from any high ground for miles around and thus the spring was named Flagpole Spring. . . . The original flagpole fell down shortly after I came

here and later there were so many flagpoles that they were no longer a
landmark. The original one had been laced to a tree by rawhide thongs,
which was some job. The militia boys used to be around this country a lot
in those days to keep the Indians in line and keep them from doing any
damage. . . .

Further evidence regarding the presence at Old Town of a flagpole comes
from the Rev. J. T. Pierce, the community's first permanently assigned pastor,
who arrived in 1883. On April 12, 1929, the *Coconino Sun* published a report of
a picnic held at Long Beach attended by many Flagstaff oldtimers at which
Pierce recalled his years here. Upon being questioned as to whether the flagstaff
was a pine tree or a raised pole, he answered: "Both. I remember it as a young
pine, stripped of all branches, and a pole spliced to its top to which the flag was
fastened. It stood close by the spring in Old Town."

John Lind, who came to Flagstaff in 1881, stated in a letter to Charles J.
Babbitt, the Flagstaff merchant and stockman, many years later, that upon his
first entrance to the community he inquired of a man named Jim Black where
he would find water for his horse and the answer was, "Ride straight west and
you will see a flag flying from a flag pole and there you will find the spring."

Mrs. Wid Raudebaugh, daughter of pioneer lawman John Francis and
granddaughter of Marvin Beal, said in later years that both her grandfather and
father had always told the family that the original flagstaff was at Old Town
Spring. (But on April 2, 1920, Francis is quoted along with King as stating that
the East tree was the original flagstaff.)

Charles C. Stemmer, for many years postmaster at Cottonwood, who was
raised in Flagstaff in the 1880s and 1890s, in an article written for the seventy-
fifth anniversary edition of the *Sun* in 1959, stated:

> On July 4, 1876, a party of soldiers camped at the site of the town just
> beginning. They stripped a fir tree of bark and floated the American Flag
> from the top, thus giving the name to the new town. There has been
> much discussion about the location of the tree used by the soldiers. Along
> about 1896, I was told by Mr. Marvin Beal, uncle of Mrs. Lotta Beal Gil-
> lette [the first white child born in Flagstaff], that the tree used for a staff
> stood a little northeast of Old Town Spring.

Who erected Old Town flagpole? Sometimes we are told that it was done
by the militia boys. Sometimes it has been suggested that it was the original
1876 flagstaff erected by one of the Boston parties. We have one story purport-

ing to be an eye-witness account. Albert Franklin Banta was a colorful figure in early-day Arizona, and seems to have been present almost every time anything happened. He was involved with a number of early newspapers, including those at Holbrook and Saint Johns, and claimed to have been a soldier in the military escort with the first Territorial Governor, John Goodwin, on his trip to what became Prescott, the Territorial Capital, in 1863–64. In a letter published in the *Coconino Sun* on April 9, 1920, he stated:

> Many silly stories have gone the rounds of the press, anent the origin of the name Flagstaff, some more or less romantic. The following is a true version of its origin, by one acquainted with the facts.
>
> In 1881, the writer left Saint Johns with a team of four mules and wagon for the grading front of the Atlantic & Pacific Railway, then west of Canyon Diablo. The same year a couple of fellows purchased a quantity of "red-eye" or "sheep-dip" at Prescott; going to Antelope Spring, near the present site of the city of Flagstaff, they put up a log cabin and opened up their booze joint.
>
> As usual a few "tin-horns," and disreputable thugs made the joint their headquarters. The 4th of July, 1881, coming on, the whole outfit got gloriously drunk; therefore, immensely patriotic, and decided they must have a flag. With the available material present, they made a non-descript flag out of anything to be found. The flag was four feet long and two feet in width. The next thing was a pole, and a small pine tree was suggested. However, one of the party proposed to climb a nearby pine tree, and with a hatchet cut off the limbs as he ascended the tree. This done, the flag, previously fastened to a stick, was taken to the top of the tree and with a piece of rope and a bit of twine made fast to the top of the tree. Naturally, not one of the drunken bunch even dreamed they were giving a name to one of the beautiful cities of Arizona. That historic flag-tree was about forty feet eastward of the "saloon." The writer camped in the flat east of the cabin, and the grading outfit of Mr. Price was about half a mile further east. However, the "society" of Antelope Spring did not appeal to me, and after a couple of days I took the back track for St. Johns.
>
> After the general elections of 1882, the writer passed the place, going to Prescott, as a member of the 10th legislative assembly, and the same non-descript flag still fluttered from the top of the pine tree; and in 1884 —possibly in 1885—the remnants of that flag could be seen. . . .
>
> The foregoing are the facts in regard to the tree and its location, and

the events incident thereto, as the writer was on the ground, and speaks of his personal knowledge, all other "cock-and-bull" stories to the contrary notwithstanding.

A. F. Banta.

Prescott, April 6, 1920.

My Dear Colonel [Fred S. Breen, editor]—I send you the above (historical) facts in order to forever (if possible) put to rest any further silly rot about that pine tree and its location, and to show there was little or no romance about the whole matter.

A. F. B.

We have no data purporting to be firsthand, other than Banta's, as to the circumstances surrounding the trimming or erecting specifically of Old Town flagpole. But as we have shown, there is plenty of evidence that there was such a pole at the Old Town Spring location in the early 1880s.

Now for the 1876 flagstaff—or flagstaffs. As we have seen, in the spring and summer of 1876 two groups of young New England men—the Boston parties—journeyed westward with the idea of colonizing along the Little Colorado River. The groups, traveling a month or more apart, found in turn that the promised land had already been taken over by Mormons from Utah. So in both cases the parties pressed on westward toward San Francisco Mountain. While the first Boston party was camped at the head of Canyon Diablo, the leader, Major Griggs, rode ahead and returned to camp with word that he had found a beautiful valley at the foot of the San Francisco Peaks. Immediately plans were made for a few men to press on ahead. In that group were Griggs, George Loring, who wrote many letters home to his wife recounting the party's adventures; Loring's pal, Horace E. Mann; and perhaps four others, S. L. Tillinghast, Frank Reilly, C. F. Hayes and J. H. Tourjee.

The small group of six or seven men arrived at Griggs's chosen spot on May 7. It probably was near one of the springs in Antelope Valley, future site of Flagstaff. The men were disappointed in the location. The leader had meantime found a more desirable site which was seven miles nearer the mountains, and the men arrived there on May 9. It was in Fort Valley.

McClintock tells us that Mann was "very definite" about the following:

While waiting for the main party, this being late in June, 1876 [we know that he and the others left the general area at the end of May or first of June] and merely for occupation, the limbs were cut from a straight pine tree that was growing by itself near the camp. The bark was cut away, leaving the tree a model flagstaff and for this purpose it was used, the flag being one owned by Tillinghast and the only one carried by the expedition. The tree was not cut down. It was left standing upon its own roots. This tale is rather at variance with one that has been of common acceptance in the history of Flagstaff and the date was not the Fourth of July, as has been believed, for Mann is sure that he arrived in Prescott in June.

The flag-raising was a memorable occasion for the men involved. Members of the first Boston party, including those who arrived at the site after the flag-raising incident, would naturally assume in later years that it was their flagstaff which gave the community its name. They were long gone when the second Boston party showed up in late June and raised a flag on the Fourth of July.

The names of many of the men comprising the Boston parties are known [Appendices A and B]. There are communications from party members appearing in Flagstaff and Prescott newspapers over a period of many years. First of these was published September 8, 1888, in the *Arizona Champion* at Flagstaff, only twelve years after the original flag-raising:

Norwich; Ct. Aug. 30, '88

Editor *Arizona Champion,*

Thinking that it might be interesting to your readers, to know that the tree which was trimmed for the flag-staff from which your town took its name, was cut down and planted by three of the Boston Coloney [*sic*], April, 1876, your humble servant being one of the three, who erected the flag-staff planted a piece of coin with the motto, "In God we trust" under the butt of the tree. I remember while we were in camp at this place, a bear came out of the woods some distance from where we were. The flag was floating from the staff. One of our party, who had a field glass, saw the bear was much surprised to see the flag, and stood for some time viewing the beautiful visitor. He then lazily trotted off into the woods again. I have heard of "the lion running from the U.S. flag" but never a bear. Hoping your town will grow and blossom as "The Rose of New England,"

I am Fraternally yours,
J. H. Tourjee

On September 21, 1888, Tourjee also wrote a letter to the Prescott *Journal-Miner,* which appeared on October 3. He covered about the same ground as in his letter to the Flagstaff paper, with a bit of additional comment: "I was informed some time ago that the country in and about the San Francisco Mountain was being peopled up fast, and was interested in reading the history of Flagstaff [probably the Tinker articles of January 1887] especially where it spoke of Lieutenant Beal's [sic] party planting a tree in that section when they were surveying in 1853, which they had used for a flagstaff. That tree was cut down by the Boston colony, and planted near the spring, before the settlement began, in 1876. . . ."

The next letter appeared in the December 30, 1921, issue of the *Coconino Sun:*

> Marlboro, N.H., Nov. 28, 1921.
> Postmaster, Flagstaff.
> Dear Sir: In the spring of 1876, I went into Arizona by way of Holbrook—think that was the name—up, or rather down the Little Colorado to Canyon Diablo, then up to a small valley at the base of the San Francisco Mountain. At the lower end of the valley, around a small spring we layed out a town, but our grub gave out and we were obliged to get out.
> Now, what I want to know, is Flagstaff at this same place. Now, I would thank you very much if you would tell me all about where you are located—also, where is the place called Angell?
> Thanking you for any favor you may do me, I am,
> Very respectfully,
> C. F. Hayes.

In 1918 F. J. O'Reilly, a member of the first Boston party, revisited Flagstaff. On September 6, the *Coconino Sun* interviewed him, stating that he was with the original party of Bostonians who came through here in 1876 "and who put up the flag on a tree at Old Town Spring, from which Flagstaff derived its name." This location of the flagstaff raising at Old Town Spring may have been supposition on the part of the news reporter or editor; it is more likely that O'Reilly couldn't recall the exact location. After all, he had not seen the area for more than forty years, and many changes had taken place. We will find a bit later that the visiting Bostonian's statement is also referred to as proof that the flag-raising took place in the China Canyon area.

The *Sun* also remarked regarding O'Reilly's interview:

> Mr. O'Reilly's account of the founding of the town of Flagstaff differs somewhat from the account given by Carpenter [J. A.] Wilson, who was

a member of the party and who made Flagstaff his home for many years afterwards up to the time of his death. Mr. O'Reilly claims that six of the party left the main party at Canyon Diablo, this six coming to Flagstaff, where they camped among the pines on the hillside near the spring and that on May 1st, May Day, they trimmed up the tree and hoisted the flag.

Mr. Wilson's account of the affair differs in that he said the whole party camped there and that the tree was trimmed up and the flag hoisted on the Fourth of July, 1876, which has been the accepted version of the affair among the old residents and pioneers.

The two accounts differ because O'Reilly was with the first Boston party, and Wilson with the second—and both had flag-raisings. The men were telling the story the way each remembered it.

In an interview with the other Flagstaff newspaper, the *Northern Arizona Leader,* on September 13, 1918, O'Reilly told substantially the same story as had appeared in the *Sun* the week before. But he recalled the names of five of the six in the advance detchment of the first Boston party as John Heath, John Wilcott, John Murphy, William Webster and himself, plus one other whose name he could not recall, with no mention of either Loring or Mann.

We know the second party was at the Mormon settlements along the Little Colorado on June 23—and they headed for San Francisco Mountain as soon as they learned that the first group had gone there.

The Centennial flag-raising that took place on July 4, 1876, at the site of later Flagstaff, was certainly performed by members of this second Boston party. There is impressive evidence that it took place in the area which we now de- scribe as west of Flagstaff High School, near a cabin erected by McMillan, who had arrived a few months earlier. Second Boston party members in later years agreed that their party had cut down a pine, trimmed it of its branches, placed a coin bearing the motto, "In God We Trust" in the bottom of a hole, and planted the flagstaff which they used for the Centennial flag-raising.

Probably the first mention of the incident in print appeared in the Prescott *Journal-Miner* on March 2, 1886. Flagstaff had been in the news with reports of a fire which had razed most of the business community. Adjacent to a report concerning the fire losses, the Prescott paper said:

> The origin of the name of the town of Flagstaff is not generally known, except to a few. The incident which gave it its name, is as follows. On Independence Day, Centennial year, 1876, a small party known as the Boston colony, consisting of Geo. C. Webster, J. A. Wilson, Robert Ker-

reir [Kennedy] and others, while marching through the country went into camp on the site of the present town. At that time there was no habitation near. Overflowing with the patriotism characteristic of the true American citizen and particularly of the Bostonian, they decided to celebrate the day in American style. To do so they cut down a tall pine sapling, stripped it of its foliage and bark and erecting it in a perpendicular position, unfurled from it the stars and stripes. On breaking camp they left the flagstaff standing, and a few years later, when the line of the railroad was located there and a town established, it was given the name of Flagstaff in honor of the liberty pole still standing, which had been created by this Boston colony.

Here the *Journal-Miner,* apparently unaware that there had been two Boston parties and two flag-raisings, lumps together Webster and Kennedy of the first group with Wilson of the second group as members of the "Boston colony." Wilson is the only one of the three who could have been present at the Fourth of July flag-raising. Probably the other two remembered that their group had raised a flag, and did not recall that it had taken place in May. Robert Kennedy was one of twenty-two disgruntled first Boston party members who signed a letter to the Boston *Herald* from "San Francisco Mountain" on May 20, 1876.

On February 15, 1894, the *Coconino Sun* discussed the flagstaff matter, and stated that the sources of its information were Thomas F. McMillan, Frank Hart and Slow Wilson. Those were very good sources. We know that McMillan and Hart were here in 1876. We know that Wilson was a member of the second Boston party. At any rate, the *Sun* reported:

> The commonly accepted story that Lieutenant Beale and his escort trimmed a pine tree and ran to its top the stars and stripes on a certain Fourth of July on the site of Flagstaff, proves, on investigation, to have been due to the imagination of some newspaper writer, and not to the facts in the case. It is probable that Lieutenant Beale celebrated the nation's birthday in the San Francisco Mountains, but the spot was not near the present location of Flagstaff.
>
> From such early settlers as Frank Hart, of Oakland, Cal., Thos. F. McMillan, the wool grower, of this place, and J. W. [*sic*] Wilson, the contractor and builder, of Flagstaff, the facts which led to the naming of this place are ascertained.
>
> A few days before the Fourth of July, 1876, a party of settlers on their way from Boston, Mass., to Prescott, Ariz., were camped at T. F. McMil-

The northern portion of the original homestead on which T. F. McMillan settled in 1876 is now occupied by a residential area, extending from Navajo road northward into the vicinity of the Northern Arizona Pioneers' Historical Society Museum. This photo shows the area, and what we know as Highway 180 or Fort Valley Road, as it appeared at an early time.

This narrow rocky defile (China Canyon) through which North Bonito Street now passes, is very near the site of the first settler's cabin and the scene of the July Fourth, 1876, flag-raising by the second Boston party. In early days the ends of the canyon were closed off with rail fencing and it was used as a corral.

lan's corral, near the spring on what is now known as John Clark's Ranch just north of town, is located. The party decided to rest for a few days and concluded to celebrate the 100th birthday of our Republic amid the pines of Arizona.

A suitable pine tree was chosen and it was trimmed and smoothed by the carpenters of the party, among them J. H. [*sic*] Wilson, now of this place. The top of the staff was ornamented with a gilt ball.

The flagstaff was raised on the morning of the Fourth of July, 1876, with the proper ceremony. A piece of money, a nickel, we believe, was deposited at the bottom of the hole, and the flagstaff was raised and the stars and stripes floated from the top during the stay of the party, which was some two weeks longer.

Frank Hart and T. F. McMillan, who were both in this section at the time, say that the flagstaff stood for several years and finally decayed off at the ground and fell down. But the location was known by all the old settlers as "The Flagstaff," and with the advent of the railroad and the locating of a station here it was called Flagstaff.

The Lieutenant Beale party passed through this section in 1855, and it is a well-known fact that a pine tree after trimming ceases to grow and decays. So it is not even probable that the tree was standing when the first settlers came to the San Francisco Mountains ten [twenty] years later.

The town obtained its name appropriately in either event, but the evidence that the celebration of the Boston party here on the Fourth of July, 1876, gave the name to the town of Flagstaff is fully corroborated by old settlers who are still living, and the *Sun* tells for the first time the true story of how our beautiful town was named.

The Prescott *Journal Miner* challenged the *Sun*'s claim that this was the first telling of the story, referring to its report March 2, 1886, which appears above. The *Miner* said the information came from Robert Kennedy, described as a member of the Boston party and a resident of Prescott for many years. The *Sun* published an item headed, "We Stand Corrected."

A man who claimed to have been a member of the second Boston party was Thomas Edward Cleland, who went on to California and settled. In 1947 his widow, who had heard him tell many times about the raising of the flagstaff here in the wilderness, visited Flagstaff and this writer interviewed her. She said her husband's party left Boston May 1, 1876, and arrived at the present site of Flagstaff some time in late June or early July 1876, and stopped over for a couple of weeks to rest their teams. When they came into the area, they found a tall tree, or stump, which had been cleared of branches, or had in some manner been marked or cut so that it was distinctive. Mrs. Cleland said her husband told her that the men trimmed a smaller, slim tree, and lashed it with rawhide to the other tree, thus making it a flagstaff. They had a fine, big American flag with them which they had brought from Boston, knowing that they would be some-where in the wilderness on July 4 and wishing to be prepared for a suitable celebration.

The statements by McMillan and Hart, both of them living in this area dur-ing the summer of 1876, and of Wilson, who was a member of the second Boston party, are quite strong evidence that the Fourth of July flagstaff was near McMillan's cabin in the China Canyon–high school grounds area.

Al Doyle, the pioneer scout and guide, wrote an article about the naming of Flagstaff for the *Northern Arizona Leader* of Flagstaff, appearing on June 25, 1920. He gave details no doubt as he had heard them from earlier settlers. He said the party had "camped at a beautiful spring just a little north of the present town of Flagstaff," which would put it in the McMillan corral–China Canyon area. He repeated the usual details, with the added color that the group enjoyed a feast of deer, antelope, elk and wild turkey, celebrating the Centennial at the point where they raised a tall, slender pine and raised the flag, which had been found in one of the traveler's trunks.

In the same issue, the editor said that Doyle's story about the flagstaff raising had been questioned, but that it had been authenticated by members of the Bos-ton party on a visit to Flagstaff in later years who "[identified] the location of those Fourth of July services, and the spring beside which they occurred. This spring is located on the property of John Clark, just north of town, and all indi-cations point to Mr. Doyle's story as the authentic version of the naming of Flagstaff." The reference was probably to the visit here in 1918 of Frank O'Reilly and a companion.

Charles Clark, who came to Flagstaff as a boy in 1883 with his father, Asa, gave his version of the matter in the July 5, 1929, issue of the *Coconino Sun:*

There were three trees here at one time that were trimmed into flag-poles, was the statement last Saturday of Charlie Clark of Grand Canyon, former merchant here. . . .

"The original flagpole, or flag tree, was not far from the first house ever built here, the double log cabin built by Bill Hull a short distance northwest of the present City Park Lake, and the flag tree was southwest of the cabin two or three hundred yards, in an open space in the timber. I lived in that cabin two years.

"The tree was trimmed by a party of railroad surveyors and a flag erected there on the Fourth. The spring alluded to is more of a seep. There is an immense supply of water close under the surface there and in 1886, when Old Town Spring went dry, I supplied Flagstaff with water, at 50 cents a barrel, which we drew from a six-foot well and which we couldn't pump dry.

"There never was a flag-tree at Old Town Spring. Later there were two others, however, one in the east part of town and one on railroad land near Beaver Street and not far from where the old G.A.R. Hall stood.

"My uncle, John Clark, came here in the '70s [1876] several years ahead of the railroad, and from him, Senator Ashurst's father, Bill Ashurst, Tom McMillan and others I often heard about this original flag tree. In fact, it stood there then and I remember when it was cut down for wood, I think by Johnny Love, who lived with my family a couple of years. I know to a certainty that that was the original Flag-pole.

"Probably my statement won't settle the controversy, but the facts are as I state them."

On December 3, 1926, the *Sun* published an article by George Hochderffer presenting the data we have already offered regarding his view that the so-called Beale tree (East tree) was the original flagstaff, but with the following additional information:

Flagstaff had the name when I came here [1887]; yet as there are so many different opinions as to just how it came to get that name, I suggest that the few left calling themselves oldtimers get together to fight it out, or rather to tell what they know about it, and then permit the newer population to decide which is the most plausible story. . . .

[When I arrived] Asa Clark and his son, Charlie, then a boy of eighteen, were batching in the old McMillan cabin, also known as the Hull cabin.

Bill Hull told me some years later that this cabin was the first structure of any kind erected in Flagstaff. He also pointed out the spot where the flagpole had been raised the historical Fourth of July, 1876, by the Boston party, of which Slow Wilson was a member. The spot is near the center of . . . the . . . baseball ground in City Park. . . .

Naturally the staff raised July 4, 1876, near the Clark Ranch Spring is of historical value; yet in my opinion, the name came from the Beal [*sic*] staff that was on such a prominent knoll for so many years, while the Clark Spring staff raised was not in such a commanding position.

I was told by Bill Hull that the Clark Spring staff had been taken down soon after for the five dollar gold piece that was supposed to have been placed at the bottom of the staff. The coin, however, proved to be a quarter of a dollar when found.

Howard H. Weidner, a lifelong resident of this community, grandson of John Marshall, one of the first settlers, told the writer in April 1973, that his grandfather always said that "the" flagstaff was near China Canyon in the City Park area. M. J. Riordan, pioneer lumberman and a leading figure in Flagstaff for many years, told his version of the flagstaff story in *The History of the Catholic Church in Flagstaff,* which he wrote shortly before his death on October 7, 1930. It was published in the *Coconino Sun* on December 5, 1930:

> Flagstaff was not even a name on July 4, 1876 . . . when a passing Boston party of sturdy adventurers broke a branch from a tree for a flagpole near the John Clark Spring and unwittingly christened the future town, for as a community gathered around Old Town Spring, by common consent the settlement became known as Flagstaff, in reference to that flagpole and to the ceremony that took place around it on the hundredth anniversary of the Declaration of Independence. At that date the only actual settlers in the neighborhood were Thomas McMillan and Frank Hart. . . . It was not until the fall of 1881 that a post office was opened with Mr. P. J. Brannen [*sic*] as first postmaster, and it was only then that the name Flagstaff became a fixity—"a local habitation and a name."

Members of the McMillan family were never in doubt regarding the raising of the flag on July Fourth, 1876, nor where it happened. McMillan often repeated the story of the Fourth of July flagstaff to his family. His son, Donnelly, told this writer in an interview appearing in the *Arizona Daily Sun* on August 28, 1954, that his father often pointed out the spot where the pine tree was trimmed into a flagpole to help a group of settlers celebrate July 4, 1876. "He had a wagon yard and horse corral for travelers near the spot," Don McMillan said. He located the site of the pole as a little to the south and west of Marshall School—the China Canyon area.

At a meeting of the Pioneers Society on May 28, 1906, McMillan made a statement regarding the flag-raising on July 4, 1876, and definitely fixing the location. But the minutes do not tell us what it was. However, with all of the McMillan family statements, there can be no doubt that it was in the area later pinpointed by McMillan's son Donnelly. McMillan's daughter, Mary Edith (Mamie) Fleming, a lifelong resident of Flagstaff, repeated the story many times, and in an interview appearing in the *Arizona Daily Sun* on February 29, 1968, she too located the Centennial Flagstaff in the China Canyon area. McMillan's stepson, Arthur J. Anderson, who was about seven years old when his mother married McMillan in 1888, also confirms the story in a family memorandum. He heard it many times from his stepfather.

In Chapter III dealing with the Boston parties we quoted John Bushman, one of the leaders of the Mormon colonists, as stating that in the spring of 1877 after having camped for several days in Fort Valley near Leroux Spring his group traveled southeastward about seven and a half miles and came to a very rich valley "and camped at a spring for dinner. The Boston colonists put up a liberty pole 1876." This would be the second Boston party's July Fourth, 1876, flagstaff at the McMillan (Clark) Ranch in Antelope Valley.

In the early years the name of the town often appeared as two words, Flag Staff. Harold Longfellow, for many years a resident of Flagstaff and Sedona, a collector of mail covers and cancellations, has [in 1976] one showing the post office's name as "Flag Staff" with the cancellation date of November 24, 1881.

Before becoming Flag Staff or Flagstaff, the area also had other names. The first Boston party laid out a townsite in Fort Valley in May 1876, chose lots, set up some corners, and named the town Agassiz in honor of the great scientist for whom one of the Peaks is named. Members of the group also wrote letters home showing their location as San Francisco Mountain. The vicinity of the original town of Flagstaff was long referred to as Antelope Valley. We find in the Prescott *Miner* of May 6, 1881, another name that didn't stick:

> BEACHVILLE—This is the new and interesting name given to Flag Staff on the line of the A. & P. R.R. The name is of course in honor of C. W. Beach, of the *Miner,* who camped at the place in 1864 with the first citizen freight train that came into Arizona from the East.

There are many variations on the flagstaff stories. One credits the cavalry, another the militia, another a government expedition with raising the flag on that historic Fourth of July. And there is even one purporting to be an eyewitness account, claiming that the naming took place in 1868! The story appeared in the *Sun* on July 26, 1929, quoting Daniel Campbell of Prescott, father of former governor Thomas E. Campbell. The elder Campbell said he was here as a member of a military expedition, and that they had found a tree which "had been struck by lightning."

All the limbs had been chopped off and the bark had been peeled off. It was a big tree. General Devvin looked at it and said, "Well, Flagstaff would be a good name for this locality, don't you think," Ed Burke, one of the scouts, said, "Yes, I think that would be all right." And so it was named!

Perhaps the most comprehensive earlier attempt to settle the question of Flagstaff's multiple flagstaffs came in 1942 when the Chamber of Commerce set up an Historic Landmarks Committee for the declared purpose of determining "which tree at Flagstaff was the first one to fly the United States Flag and the one from which Flagstaff derived its name." The committee members, including a number of pioneer residents, investigated the various claims, debated them at length, and finally arrived at a compromise decision which favored the East tree site, but also recognized the Old Town Spring and 1876 Clark Ranch sites [see Appendix C]. This did not resolve the question, of course, but in fairness to the committee members, it must be noted that much of the evidence we have presented in the preceding pages was not available to them at the time.

From this new evidence, gathered in the course of researching this book, we can draw more definite conclusions. It now seems certain that the first Boston party raised a flag at their camp in Fort Valley in May 1876; that the second Boston party raised a Centennial flagstaff on July 4, 1876, in the Clark Ranch area; that some sort of flagstaff or flagpole stood near Old Town Spring in the early 1880s; and that the East tree's only claim to fame is that P. J. Brannen had it in mind when he suggested the already familiar name of Flagstaff for the post office, and thus the community, in late May 1881, although no one has claimed that they ever saw East tree in use as a flagstaff.

The weight of the now available evidence—from recollections of residents of the area in 1876, from records and memories of members of the Boston parties, from the observations and records of the Mormon Bushman and Hunt group of travelers in 1877, and from the fact that the name Flagstaff as descriptive of the immediate area was already in use in 1878, as recorded in J. L. Harris's land survey made that year—strongly indicates that the name came from the second Boston party's flagstaff raised on July Fourth, 1876, near China Canyon, to mark the nation's one hundredth anniversary.

# THE YEARS OF ESTABLISHMENT

# CHAPTER VIII

# Lumber and Livestock

IF FLAGSTAFF WAS FATHERED by the railroad, then its mother was the lumber industry which caused the town to be established where it was and provided important economic nurture for many years.

It is true that the first settlers came here to raise stock five or six years before either the railroad or the sawmill were in evidence. But without the accessibility to supplies and markets provided by the railroad, and the sawmill payrolls, there would have been comparatively little growth and development.

It is interesting to speculate about what it would have been like here at Antelope Spring today if Ed Ayer had built his sawmill in some other forested place along the line of the railroad. Perhaps Flagstaff would never have become big enough to have a post office. And what if the railroad had followed some other line across northern Arizona?

In spite of the great importance of the sawmill in Flagstaff's early days, the town fortunately never was a single-industry community. Down through the years, with changing times, the economic weight has shifted about, but the base has always been diversified. However, the sawmill was very important in early days, as its successor mill is important in our day, and scores of Flagstaff families trace their beginnings here to fathers, grandfathers and great grandfathers who came to work for the mill.

Flagstaff's first sawmill began operations in mid-August 1882, some two weeks after the arrival of the railroad. As noted earlier, it was an enterprise of Chicago industrialist Edward E. Ayer, who held contracts to supply ties and lumber to the Santa Fe and the Mexican Central Railroad and an option from the Santa Fe on eighty-seven square miles of timbered land south and west of what was to become Flagstaff. Hamilton's 1884 guidebook tells us:

One large mill near the town employs over 250 men, and has a capacity of 120,000 feet per day. Last year [1883] this mill turned out over 20 million feet of lumber . . . the establishment is one of the most perfect of the kind on the Pacific Coast being provided with planers, shingle machines, etc. To look at the immense piles of magnificent clear lumber stored in the yards, the visitor might well imagine himself in the piney woods of Maine or Wisconsin.

The sawmill was powered by steam which required liberal supplies of water. Consequently while the mill was being built, a pipeline was laid from O'Neill Springs eight and a half miles south, and from other smaller springs, to the mill site. The O'Neill Springs area in later years became known as Pump House Wash and so it is known to oldtimers today. It is now within the area of Kachina Village subdivision.

While Hamilton reported that the mill had two hundred and fifty employees, we read in the *Arizona Champion* of February 23, 1884, that it had twice that many, and used five to six hundred animals. The article notes that the total payroll included men working for subcontractors. It is likely that the mill regularly employed around two hundred fifty men. On occasion, extra help would be employed. The *Champion* article adds that Ayer's main business was manufacturing lumber for export but that the mill was also furnishing lumber for domestic trade and also made boxes for the California fruit industry.

Ayer was president; his close associate, Lot P. Smith (not the Mormon leader with a similar name), was vice president; the general superintendent was J. A. Wakefield, and his assistant was Ayer's brother, Henry C. The firm had at least two other smaller mills in operation at various times. Ayer spent $150,000 establishing the mill. No doubt it made money, and he may well have gotten his money back within a year or two. His problem was that the sawmill required too much of his time, and his other interests were of more importance.

His biographer, Frank Lockwood, tells us that when Ayer was looking about for a man to go to Flagstaff and take full charge, he remembered an extraordinarily well-written business letter he had received from the agent at Fort Defiance in charge of the Navajo Indians, a young man named Denis Matthew Riordan. Ayer contacted the Department of the Interior, and asked about Riordan. He was told that the young man was very much the best agent in the department, and that he was receiving $1,500 a year. Ayer requested that Riordan, then in the East, call on him in Chicago on his way back to Arizona. A week later they met and were mutually impressed. Riordan was tall, muscular, handsome, obviously intelligent, and well-mannered. Ayer was a man of great ability and character with an intuitive feeling for the qualities of others.

The original Flagstaff sawmill was built in 1882 by E. E. Ayer, the machinery being hauled in by ox-teams from Canyon Diablo before the railroad had been built to Flagstaff. D. M. Riordan, who had been general manager for Ayer, purchased the mill in early summer, 1887. Within a month, it was destroyed by fire.

D. M. Riordan (far left with vest and white shirt) quickly erected a new mill pictured here, greater in capacity and more complete in every way, including the large wooden water tank (left) which was equipped with pumps and hose for fire-fighting.

"Do you want to work for me?"

"What do you want me to do?"

"I want you either to go to Aguas Calientes and start a lumber yard there that I am contemplating, or to Flagstaff and take over the management of my sawmill."

"Why Mr. Ayer, I don't know anything about the lumber business."

"Well, I'm blamed glad you don't. I've had all the experts I want."

"What would be your terms?"

"If you will go to Flagstaff I will give you $2,500 a year, all expenses for your wife, children, and nurse, will furnish you a house, and pay your traveling expenses when you are away from home. And if you prove successful, I will advance you."

Said Riordan, "I accept!"

Riordan left that night by train to assume his duties and so the Riordan family entered the Flagstaff scene. In later years, Ayer said about Riordan: "He proved one of the very best managers that I ever had, and a most charming personality—one of the squarest, most honest, and efficient men that I ever knew." This is indeed high tribute, coming from a man of Ayer's stature. On April 12, 1884, the *Champion* reported that Navajo Agent Riordan had resigned. On May 10 it reported that J. A. Wakefield had resigned as boss of the Ayer mill, and that D. M. Riordan had succeeded him.

Matt Riordan was born in Troy, New York, in 1848, son of a carpenter; he had few opportunities for schooling. The family moved to Chicago in 1852. As a youngster he enlisted in the Union Army four times during the Civil War, and was caught and brought home each time by his father. Finally in 1864, at the ripe age of sixteen, he enlisted for the fifth time and got into the field. He was discharged in 1865. He worked as a freight brakeman on the Rock Island, then went with the firm which became Marshall Field & Co. In 1868 he went west, worked in Wyoming and Utah, then with some companions bought a six-horse team and wagon and started for Nevada. He then found himself running a lumber yard at Carson City. Later he was in Virginia City working as a miner at $4 per day. In a few years he was running a quartz mill near Bodie, and gaining valuable management and office experience. He made a little money and with two others put up $40,000 for a copper mine near Bisbee, Arizona. He saved money and made some lucky turns in mining stocks. He then had a silver prospect near Tucson. He went to Prescott and became acquainted with F. A. Tritle, territorial governor, and with Tritle and F. F. Thomas had the United Verde property under option, but had to let it go for lack of $14,000. Out of his friendship with Tritle he was offered the Navajo agent job at Fort Defiance. He was with the Indians from early 1882 to early 1884.

Some time after taking over the Flagstaff sawmill operation he brought his brother, Timothy A., into the organization. A bit later the brothers were joined by a third brother, Michael J. We read in the *Champion* on March 5, 1887, that the company was opening a branch commissary at Williams under Michael Riordan's charge and that the company would have a hundred men working there during the summer.

D. M. Riordan made a success of the sawmill operation, and Ayer offered him a job in Chicago at $10,000 a year as manager of part of the Ayer enterprises. Riordan said he would rather make a success of the Flagstaff mill and get $1,000 a year than to be in Chicago at $10,000. Ayer offered to sell Riordan the mill. Matt explained that he had only six or eight thousand dollars saved, and had no capital for such a venture. Ayer said: "Matt, I want you to go back to Flagstaff and inventory my property at a fair valuation and send me your notes due in one, two and three years at six per cent." (Normal interest at that time was ten per cent.)

"But of course you will want a mortgage on the plant."

"No, Matt, I do not. You couldn't run the mill without more money. You will have to mortgage it to run it. It's insured, of course, and I shall not ask you for any security whatever—only the insurance if it burns."

Riordan said later that within two months he had lost $18,000 through the failure of customers, and dropped $40,000 more in the Arizona Mineral Belt Railroad, the line which proposed to build from Flagstaff south to Globe and on to connect with the Southern Pacific. Only forty miles or so was ever built.

The new Riordan firm was the Arizona Lumber Company, established on June 20, 1887, with D. M. Riordan as general manager and principal stockholder, and his brother T. A. as superintendent.

On July 16, less than a month later, the mill was destroyed by fire. Fortunately the evening was quiet, and a rain had fallen that day. The men labored heroically and managed to confine the loss to the main structure, saving the yards and other buildings. The *Champion* in its issue of July 23 said that the structure with the lumber it contained represented a loss of nearly $100,000. The insurance on that part, the paper, said, was less than $20,000. It added that Charley and Ed Greenlaw, who were running the mill on a contract, also lost heavily. (They would continue in business, operate other mills in connection with the Riordans, and the Greenlaw name is commemorated in one of Flagstaff's most modern business areas on a site where a Greenlaw sawmill once stood.) D. M. was in Chicago when the fire occurred, and T. A. was at a branch mill near Bellemont. "But in their absence General McDonell, A. A. Dutton, Ed and Chas. Greenlaw, the employees of the company and a large number of citizens of Flagstaff did all that could possibly be done in fighting the flames and as shown, did it successfully . . . ," the paper reported.

Preparations were made to rebuild immediately. One of the smaller mills at Rogers Lake was brought in and set up near the ruin, where it operated until a new mill was built. D. M. advised his associates from Chicago that he had secured ample finance, and that he was preparing to ship two new mills immediately. The paper said that the company would then have five mills running. It added that the business had been built up through the untiring energy and able business ability of Maj. D. M. Riordan, "and the people here have confidence that with his hand at the helm the present destructive fire will only prove a temporary check in its growth. . . . The mill has been of incalculable benefit to the town and the interests of both are so closely bound together that any serious injury to . . . the company . . . could prove a great disaster to Flagstaff."

On July 30 the *Champion* reported:

> Great credit is due to Mr. T. A. Riordan for the prompt and energetic work by which he has succeeded, in only two weeks . . . in bringing the heavy machinery of the sawmill, including engine and boiler from Rogers Lake and setting it up . . . the mill saw will commence revolving Monday morning.

By October Riordan also had a thirty-thousand-foot-a-day mill running full blast at Volunteer Prairie, employing twenty-five to thirty men. Six carloads of lumber a day were being shipped from that point.

An important part of the business was the commissary. In 1887, sales were running from $11,000 to $16,000 a month. This part of the operation was apparently very profitable, because by 1888 the commissary at Flagstaff had become the wholesale and retail division of the Arizona Supply Company and was running a full two-column ad every week in the *Champion* listing all sorts of merchandise, from groceries to clothing, and from implements and tools to confections. The big ads ran for some months, then ceased; it may be that the Riordans decided to concentrate on lumber. But the company store continued to operate until about 1930.

With all these sawmills going, the output must have been around one hundred twenty to one hundred thirty thousand feet a day. How much money did the mill make? What did the payroll amount to? The answers to these questions are not easy to come by. The operators were always reluctant to discuss such figures. In the years after 1897 when T. A. and M. J. bought out D. M.'s interest, they frequently claimed that they were making no, or very little money, and ran the mill mostly to provide employment for their people. However, during those years they both lived in what could be considered baronial style; and it was apparent that they managed to keep the wolf quite a distance, perhaps some light years, away from their door. All such data could probably be dug out of the mill's records which are now mostly a part of the Northern Arizona Pioneers' Historical Society Collection in the Special Collections Department of Northern Arizona University's Library. But our purpose here is to take a quick look, and get on with the history of the community. So, doing some horseback arithmetic with a knowledgeable Arizona lumberman, we arrive at some guesses:

First of all, Matt Riordan apparently had no trouble paying Ayer for the mill in the three-year period, with the insurance assist, a total of $145,000 with interest. And probably he was at the same time paying off loans for rebuilding the mill; so he was handling pretty sizable sums. If the mill had a capacity of a hundred thousand feet a day, and if it ran an average of two hundred days a year, both very low figures, it produced at least twenty million feet a year during the 1880s. If lumber sold for $10 to $45 per thousand, at an average of perhaps $25, this means that Ayer and later the Riordans were grossing around $500,000 a year, to say nothing of the earnings of the commissary. If, as our industrialist friend suggests, we figure that payrolls then as now took forty per cent of the gross receipts, the employees were getting about $200,000. If there was an average of two hundred fifty of them, it would mean an average of $800 per year per man, which would come to $20 per week for forty weeks, and this agrees with other data we have on wages in northern Arizona in the 1880s. Hamilton's invaluable guide book tells us that in 1883–84, in Yavapai County, miners earned $4 per day; blacksmiths, $4 to $6; bricklayers and masons, $5 and $6; clerks, $50 to $100 a month plus board; teamsters, $40 to $70 per month and board; and day laborers, $2 to $3.50. A lot of the labor around the logging camps and at the mill and in the yards was common labor.

The $200,000 payroll taken from $500,000 leaves $300,000. Operating expense, insurance, repairs, replacement, would probably take from $100,000 to $150,000 of this, leaving a gross profit of around $150,000. This would vary, of course. But note that there was no income tax; that property tax was a small item and so was stumpage. We do not know what Ayer and then the Riordans paid the Atlantic & Pacific, or Santa Fe, for stumpage, but it must have been very little. After the national forests were established, the figure in the 1900s ran around $1 per thousand. Today timber taken from national forests in Arizona may run from $53 to $60 per thousand for stumpage, and sells for $170 per thousand. An income of $150,000 per year would seem about right for Ayer, and later the Riordans. The Riordans certainly managed to accumulate at least a million dollars or so apiece during the forty or more years they owned the mill.

The January 1, 1887, issue of the *Champion* reported that the office of the company was connected by telephone with three points—the town of Flagstaff, the branch mill at Rogers Lake, and a spur on the railroad five miles distant.

During early 1888 the Riordans were charged with trespassing and cutting timber on government lands, a matter finally resolved in their favor.

In March 1888, the Arizona Lumber Company held a stockholders' meeting and D. M. Riordan was elected president and manager; T. A. Riordan, secretary, and F. W. Sisson, treasurer. Work on the new mill was pushed. On June 2, the *Champion* reported that during the previous week the fires were lighted for the first time. Every effort was made to reduce danger of fire:

> The engine is an immense Atlas Corliss, having a four foot stroke and a 48-inch cylinder. This engine is without exception the finest piece of machinery ever brought into Flagstaff. The main pulley is 14 feet in diameter and both this and the engine were placed on foundations of five feet of solid masonry. . . .
>
> The main building is 130 feet long by 30 feet wide with two additions on the sides running nearly the full length and 24 feet in width. . . .
>
> A reel of hose long enough to reach any of the buildings is kept constantly attached to the pump in the engine room . . . just outside is a large tank with a capacity of from 45,000 to 50,000 gallons and this will as much as possible be kept full at all times. . . .
>
> Not only the people of Milton, but those of Flagstaff, will welcome the sound of the whistle, that was in the days of "Auld Lang Syne," the only public sentinel announcing the dawning and dying of the day . . .

The mill whistle would continue to signal work days, noon breaks, and fires for scores of years, as familiar to generations of Flagstaff residents as the voice of a neighbor.

It took D. M. Riordan until the mid-nineties to get the sawmill and related operations running the way he wanted.

"I decided to put into effect a profit-sharing plan that I had thought over for years, the idea having been suggested by Edward Everett Hale. It would be too

Major J. Wesley Powell, Civil War veteran and famed one-armed Colorado River explorer, with Riordans. *Left to right:* Mrs. J. Harry Hoskins and son, Arthur C.; Miss Alice Metz at gate; Hoskins's maid; Mrs. T. A. Riordan and daughter Mary, later Mrs. Robert L. Chambers, for whom Lake Mary was named; Mrs. F. W. Sisson and daughter Marjorie; Major Powell; Mrs. E. E. Ellinwood and daughter Cornelia, later Mrs. Sam Morris; T. A. Riordan and D. M. Riordan.

long a story to tell you. . . . It is sufficient to say that my effort ended in a heart-breaking conspiracy among the beneficiaries; and rather than endure the con-tinuing disappointment, I disposed of my remaining interests at a sacrifice and left that region, completely cured and freed from illusions on profit-sharing in this country under present social conditions."

When D. M. Riordan's remarks appeared in print in 1917, M. J. pasted a copy in one of his voluminous scrapbooks, with added comment: ". . . [the remarks are] accurate as to relation of events. They took place . . . but I put no reliance on the reasons assigned for them . . . he assigns the reason for his selling out . . . to 'a conspiracy among the beneficiaries. . . .' There was nothing of the kind. He sold simply because he was sick of Flagstaff and was living at Macon, Georgia, leaving [us] to run the . . . concern. He nagged us to death . . . he could never do anything which was not all done in his own way without attrib-uting to others some low motive. . . ."

At any rate, D. M. sold his interests to his two brothers, and there was a cool-ness between them during the years following. Matt Riordan was offered and refused the presidency of a railroad; did some mining exploration; traveled; played an active part in mining, including Arizona; and directed mining oper-ations for the General Electric Company. At the beginning of World War I he was selected by President Wilson to carry $4.5 million to Europe on a boat sail-ing over dangerous waters to provide aid for American refugees in Europe. His later years were spent in San Francisco. He died July 12, 1928. His wife preceded him in death. They had three daughters, Helen, Marie and Elizabeth. When Matt Riordan was Navajo agent, he selected Chee Dodge as a young Navajo who showed promise of becoming a real leader, and did what he could to assist him in his career. Dodge became probably the most able and most highly hon-ored Navajo leader in the history of the tribe. Matt Riordan was a man of extraordinary qualities, as Ayer had divined. He was intelligent, hard-working, thoroughly honest, and was respected by other leading figures in America for more than a half-century.

While lumbering was an important industry for Flagstaff in the early days, so were railroads, and not just the Atlantic & Pacific line. While bridging, grad-ing and track-laying crews were slowly pushing the Atlantic & Pacific railhead across northern Arizona in 1881 and 1882, what must have been a frequent and optimistic, or at least hopeful, topic of conversation in Flagstaff's stores and saloons and along its single street was the proposal to build a branch railroad southward to Globe.

The idea appealed to a lot of knowledgeable people, and as the years passed

would gain considerable support—but not enough. It was a very ambitious proposal, and the costs of the one-hundred-sixty-mile line through forbidding terrain would have been immense, but it was not an impossible pipe dream, and if
the cards had fallen in a little different way, it would probably have been built.
At is was, about seventy miles of grade was completed, seventy feet of tunnel
through the rock at the Mogollon Rim was dug out, and forty miles of rails
were laid.

The proposal originated with Col. James W. Eddy, a successful Chicago
attorney who had served in the Civil War and held a seat in the Illinois Legislature for some years. Eddy started work on his idea in 1881, before the Atlantic
& Pacific had completed its line across Arizona. He recruited Gen. A. A.
McDonell of Globe, a skilled engineer. He then went after financing, and
zeroed in on the officials of the Atlantic & Pacific, who agreed to buy some of the
bonds of the Arizona Mineral Belt Railroad. Eddy needed a lot more capital,
but felt that the Atlantic & Pacific would come across in due time if he could
show that the project was making progress.

The major physical obstacle was the Mogollon Rim, where the grade had to
rise two thousand feet in a few miles. The answer which General McDonell
came up with was a thirty-one-hundred-foot tunnel cutting down through the
rock. Work was started, and the tunnel was driven about seventy feet, by which
time Eddy had spent $55,000, all of his cash. But by this time, the Atlantic &
Pacific was in financial straits and could not help. So work stopped, but Eddy
didn't. It is quite probable that if the Atlantic & Pacific had been on a sounder
financial basis in the early 1880s it would have supported the project, in which
case the line would have been completed.

There was concern at Flagstaff that the Mineral Belt would tap the Atlantic
& Pacific at a point about four miles east of town, and if that happened, the
business section would have to move and in time the site of Flagstaff would be
abandoned. On February 16, 1884, the *Champion* called attention to the fact
that the railroad company had sold lots here and the people had bought them in
good faith, and it called on the Atlantic & Pacific to settle the question permanently. In due time this was done and the Atlantic & Pacific said it would
build a fine station at Flagstaff plus other improvements. The connection between the Atlantic & Pacific and the Mineral Belt as finally determined was
right in the middle of present-day downtown Flagstaff.

On November 28, 1885, the *Champion* reported that the outlook for construction of the Mineral Belt was brighter. The item said the estimated cost of
the first seventy-five miles from Flagstaff would be $975,000, that the sale of

bonds had realized $600,000, and quoted Eddy to the effect that the balance would be forthcoming soon. Spirits soared in Flagstaff. Some leading citizens had already invested in the venture. But the $600,000 which Eddy claimed had already been raised by sale of bonds did not materialize. In early 1886 he worked out an agreement with the Atlantic & Pacific by which the latter agreed to subscribe $200,000 in Mineral Belt stock, and this was later hiked to $400,000. They would pay this sum $25,000 at a time, as each five miles of railroad was completed, and they would gain controlling interest when the line was finished.

But Eddy did not have the money to start construction, so that he could complete five-mile sections and start receiving $25,000 checks from the Atlantic & Pacific.

Late in 1886 Eddy succeeded in getting Francis E. Hinckley, a Chicago capitalist, to put up a bit more than $100,000 to get the job underway, in return for $345,000 in Mineral Belt bonds. It is probable that the officials of the Atlantic & Pacific were not advised of the details of Hinckley's involvement. With $345,000 in bonds, he would have a big voice in operation and management of the line, and would possibly even constitute a threat to the Atlantic & Pacific's control.

Enthusiasm and optimism were in the air, however. The hard-headed, knowledgeable manager of the Ayer Lumber Company, D. M. Riordan, joined with others and on December 31, 1886, organized yet another company to build another railroad, this one from Flagstaff to Grand Canyon. Officers included J. S. Morris, president; D. M. Riordan, treasurer; S. A. Bickley, secretary, and the directors included Morris, Riordan, Riordan's brother T. A., Colonel Eddy and General McDonell of the Mineral Belt, plus two very worthy and substantial Flagstaff citizens, P. J. Brannen and P. P. Daggs.

On March 12, 1887, the *Champion* reported that the legislature had passed a bill exempting the Grand Canyon Railroad from taxation for a period of six years from date of completion. The paper painted a rosy picture of how business would boom during construction and forever after as tourists flocked in to see the Canyon. "Flagstaff has a great future before it and every one should strive to help it forward and to help those who are trying to help us."

An example of the attitude prevailing in Flagstaff in 1886-87 appears in a letter written by Eddy's son George to the Aurora, Illinois, *Beacon* and reprinted in the January 15, 1887, *Champion:*

> Flagstaff . . . exists on its natural advantages, having the finest country
> on the whole A & P tributary to it; and not even a disastrous fire as the

business portion passed through last year can cinch out its merchants, but they build better than ever. P. J. Brannen alone has paid $100,000 in freight to the A & P, and yet the depot here is nothing but three box cars, while I saw on the Mohave desert in southern California, at a station called Fenner, as large a depot as the one at Englewood. I write all this to show the disadvantages Flagstaff has gone through in its growth and still stands at the head of the list, and with a larger business and a better country surrounding than any other town between Albuquerque and San Bernardino; while with reasonable help by the railroad it might have been a place of 5,000 or so and the emporium of northern Arizona. Well, now the A & P people have awakened themselves and intend to make up for lost time, and will now build the finest passenger depot between Kansas City and Los Angeles, a good freight house, a repair shop, a round house, large stock yards, help to build waterworks, and give the place a boom.

The Atlantic & Pacific was making promises rather than laying out money for Mineral Belt construction. Few of the things it was then about to do for Flagstaff according to the above happened, and those only after the passage of years.

With Hinckley's money, Eddy put in the "Y" connecting the Mineral Belt with the Atlantic & Pacific at Flagstaff early in 1887 and started laying rails southward. On February 5, 1887, the *Champion* reported that two hundred men were employed on the railroad job. Seven cars of rails had arrived, nineteen cars were en route from Emporia, "and about one hundred loads on the way somewhere this side of New Orleans, so that a steady and sufficient arrival is now assured . . . the rails are of English manufacture and are rusty and weather-beaten from long exposure on sea and land." There were weekly progress reports. The right-of-way pushed on out into the forest, more rails arrived, and on March 26 the paper said that ten miles and fifty-one feet of the railroad was completed. May 14 the report was that fifteen miles of track was down. On July 9 the paper said that twenty-four miles of track had been laid, and that the grade around Mormon Dairy Lake was being constructed:

> The traffic of the road is already very heavy, far exceeding the expectations of the promoters of the line. At a point near Mormon Dairy there are over one hundred tons of wool now waiting shipment . . . the road is also kept busy bringing in logs for the Arizona Lumber Company, and ties for shipment east and west, while a large traffic has been developed in

fire wood, this fire wood is shipped to Los Angeles, where it is mainly used for brick making.

During the summer as construction progressed, optimism grew. It was even said that the Chicago and Rock Island Railroad would build a line from San Francisco to the Colorado River, where it would connect with the Flagstaff and Grand Canyon line. Eddy announced that he would extend the Mineral Belt south from Globe to Tucson and on into Mexico. And there was to be a branch line twenty-five miles long to serve the United Verde Mines at Jerome. If all this came about, Flagstaff would become a major transportation and industrial center.

September 17, 1887, the *Champion* reported that forty miles of track was in place and that traffic was increasing, and was sufficient to pay cost of operating both freight, passenger and construction trains.

But the October 22, 1887, issue of the *Champion* reported that work had stopped. Eddy had spent all of Hinckley's $100,000, and had gone to the Atlantic & Pacific for the $175,000 that was due at the rate of $25,000 for each five miles completed. But the Atlantic & Pacific said the requirements had not been exactly complied with, and refused to pay. There was no money for the payroll:

> Suit will be commenced at once against the A & P . . . and all necessary efforts will be made to recover from the company under the contract. President J. W. Eddy and Mr. McDonnel [*sic*] of the Arizona Mineral Belt road, will do all in their power to make it comfortable for the men who worked on the road and who have money due them for construction, work and material. All the tents are to be taken to Flagstaff and put at the disposal of the men for the winter.

A committee of local stockholders headed by Dr. D. J. Brannen investigated and stated that the Mineral Belt had indeed not met all legal technicalities, but that the Atlantic & Pacific was bound in good faith and fair dealing to pay. But the Atlantic & Pacific didn't agree. It is probable that the problem was the big block of bonds given to Hinckley in exchange for his $100,000 without Atlantic & Pacific approval. It also may be that officials of the Atlantic & Pacific had some complicated maneuver in mind aimed at ousting Hinckley, and for that matter Eddy and others. At any rate the following appeared in the May 19, 1888, issue of the *Champion:*

> A special train containing Superintendent Gaddis, of the Atlantic & Pacific and Messrs. Banks, of Boston, Brittain, of New York, Edward W.

Kinsley, of Boston, and Baring, of the noted London banking firm of Baring Bros., and others, stopped in Flagstaff last Wednesday. During the day the party made a tour of inspection over the Mineral Belt RR, and expressed themselves as highly gratified with the condition and prospects of the road. In the evening the entire party, with Mr. E. S. Gosney, of St. Joseph, Mo., visited the *Champion* office and spent an hour in conversation concerning the town, its advantages, and attractions. Concerning the Mineral Belt, Mr. Kinsley, who is a heavy stockholder in the Santa Fe and President of the Aztec Land and Cattle Co. [Hashknife] stated that there need be no fear about the road, and while not positively saying that work would be commenced immediately, left no ground for doubt as to its completion in the near future. The gentlemen stated that they would return in a few weeks and make a visit to the Grand Canyon as well as other points of interest in this vicinity. The *Champion* has never made any idle talk, but is free to say that from the conversation with Mr. Kinsley, it believes that work will be resumed very soon on the Mineral Belt Road.

But it wasn't. Hope faded, flickered, flamed, and faded again, but the Atlantic & Pacific refused to come across with the $175,000. The already completed forty miles of Mineral Belt track opened up some freight traffic—but the company lacked rolling stock and the Atlantic & Pacific refused to supply any. At this point, the Mineral Belt leased their line and facilities to Frank E. Foster, president of the Arizona Wood Company, which was cutting and shipping train loads of cord wood to the West Coast. Foster was also a director of the Mineral Belt.

Finally in 1888 Hinckley, Foster and Riordan combined forces and filed suit to gain possession of the property. The court ordered the few items of rolling stock to be offered for sale to cover delinquent taxes. The Hinckley-Foster-Riordan combine put up $895 for the locomotive and other cars, all of which were then transferred to the Arizona Lumber Company. It appears that Hinckley expected in due time to gain possession of the entire Mineral Belt line, if Eddy failed to raise the money to pay the bills and complete construction.

There were labor liens amounting to about $40,000. After various complicated legal maneuvers, in December 1888, Yavapai County Sheriff William J. Mulvenon offered the entire Mineral Belt property at auction to satisfy these liens. P. J. Brannen, the pioneer Flagstaff merchant, offered $40,000, and D. M. Riordan, on behalf of himself and Hinckley, then offered $40,440, and as highest bidder took possession. It may be that Brannen entered his bid on behalf of Riordan. Riordan and Hinckley then incorporated as Central Arizona Railway Company and said they would use the line for logging, and also extend it on toward Globe as finances permitted.

There were further legal maneuvers. Riordan announced in 1890 that the plan was to extend the road not only southward, but also northward to Lee's Ferry and on to connect with the Utah Central. If all of these plans had materialized, railroads would have come into Flagstaff from five directions: east and west, via Atlantic & Pacific; north and south via the Mineral Belt line which later became the Central Arizona Railway Company; and northwest, the Flagstaff and Grand Canyon Railroad. But then money was not available, and the nationwide panic of 1893 stopped the dreaming. That year the company stopped paying taxes except on the twelve miles near Flagstaff, being used for logging. Hinckley withdrew. And the next year the track extending on past the twelve miles was taken up and sold to the Santa Fe, Prescott and Phoenix line.

The Flagstaff and Grand Canyon Railroad, proposed in 1886 by Riordan and others, surveyed a line to the South Rim, but there was no construction. A railroad to Grand Canyon did make sense, and in due time the Santa Fe built one from Williams, locating it there largely because of the efforts of William (Bucky) O'Neill of Prescott, who was interested in some mineral deposits which a line from that point would serve.

D. M. Riordan said later that he had "dropped" $40,000 in the Mineral Belt at a time when he was just getting started as purchaser of the Ayer Lumber Company, suggesting that he considered it a loss. However, the Mineral Belt track was used for many years to haul logs to the mill, and branches were run out from it into various parts of the forest. It probably was a very good investment for the Riordan interests, when all was said and done.

The third major industry for Flagstaff in the early years, and the first in point of time, was of course ranching. A comprehensive history of the livestock industry in this area is not within the scope of this book. That vast and colorful subject deserves extensive separate treatment, and at least a general outline is already available in the writings of Bert Haskett, formerly with the United States Bureau of Animal Husbandry in Arizona. His most valuable works are two comparatively short articles, "Early History of the Cattle Industry in Arizona" appearing in the October 1935 issue of *Arizona Historical Review* and "History of the Sheep Industry in Arizona" appearing in the July 1936 issue of the same quarterly. Also much color, authentic detail and historical fact was compiled and published by Earle R. Forrest who worked as a cowboy for one of the major cow outfits in this area in the early 1900s. There is much data too, in that goldmine of contemporary records, the files of the Flagstaff newspaper.

The Flagstaff area was an important part of the wild and woolly West of the 1880s and 1890s. This was the land of the big sheep operations, and perhaps the largest of all, Daggs Brothers & Co., had their offices in Flagstaff. One of the two largest cattle outfits, the A-1 (Arizona Cattle Co.) operated out of Flagstaff, and the vast range of the giant Hashknife outfit (Aztec Land & Cattle Co.) ran around southeast and south of our immediate area. The Hashknife had its headquarters near Holbrook, but its cowboys and bosses had frequent occasion to visit Flagstaff. Southward two or three days ride lies Pleasant Valley, where twenty or more men died in the war between the Grahams and Tewksburys, a bloody vendetta sometimes described as a sheepmen's and cattlemen's war—which, up to a point, it was.

The cowboys, outlaws and lawmen who have become a vital part of the legend and folklore of America once jingled their spurs along our wooden sidewalks, bellied up to the bars along Railroad Avenue, bought guns, ammunition and supplies from Brannen, Kilpatrick, Salzman, Cameron & Vail and Babbitts'. Al Doyle, who appears in fictional form in some of the works of Zane Grey, was a stockman who lived in a pleasant two-story brick home on Birch Avenue, and his barn and corrals were on the site now occupied by the Flagstaff City Hall. John Francis, the model of the cool, capable, heroic western sheriff, in very early days ran a saloon in Old Town, filled in as a teacher in the one-room school, and in later years, as a lawman, nearly always got his man. In even later years he ran a garage in Flagstaff. There were others, just as authentic, and also valued as community leaders, but few were as colorful as these two.

The great majority of stockmen devoted their energies to managing, improving and marketing their flocks and herds, and had no inclination for the dramatic violence depicted in countless later western stories and films. Most of the real frontier stockmen built homes, raised families, and served their community. A rather surprising number traveled about the country, and some spent months now and then in milder climates. Many were familiar with fine hotels and business houses, including the banks, in major cities east and west.

While sheep had been driven through northern Arizona between California and New Mexico from very early times, the first permanent sheep ranch in the northern part of Arizona was established in 1868 by James Baker near the butte which is named for him in the Mogollon Rim country, about sixty miles south of Flagstaff.

Sheep raising in the immediate Flagstaff area, as reported in an earlier chapter, began in 1876 with arrival of Thomas F. McMillan from California, David F. Hart, and James O'Neill. Very soon thereafter came John Clark, followed by William H. Ashurst with a band of sheep from Nevada. Then came J. F. and W. A. Daggs with herds, and they were soon joined by a third brother, P. P. The Mormons who settled on the Little Colorado in 1876 had some sheep and cattle. They built woolen mills at Sunset (Winslow) and Moencopi (Tuba City) but these ventures were not successful and were abandoned. Others who came with sheep in early times were Henry Fulton, John Elden, and John Clark's brother, Asa. Charles H. Schulz was here with sheep as early as 1880.

The Daggs brothers were the biggest operators, and it is said that at times they ran as many as fifty thousand head. In 1882 they brought in some purebred Vermont Merino rams at a cost of from $100 to $600 each to improve their flocks. They produced some fine sheep, and had no trouble selling their young crossbred rams; in 1886, they sold a thousand for prices ranging from $6 to $12 per head, when sheep were generally priced at $2.50 to $3.75 a head. Other efforts were made to improve the herds in this area, and a distinctive Arizona sheep was developed, predominantly of American and French Merino blood.

During the 1880s most of Arizona was open range except for the Indian reservations. Sheep summered in the lush meadows of highly nutritious native grass in the upper country, grazed their way to lower elevations in the fall, and returned in the spring. In the early years sheep were raised only for wool, and prior to the coming of the railroad the wool was freighted either eastward to the terminus of the railroad at Trinidad, Colorado, or westward to the Colorado River, where it was barged to points where it could be shipped by boats to Boston and other important wool markets. The railroad made sheep raising not only more profitable and easier, but it also became possible to ship lambs and mutton to distant markets.

Profit from a well-tended flock of sheep could be quite handsome. Profits of fifty per cent a year were not unusual, and some enterprising and fortunate men got their original investment back the first year. There was little expense involved in running the stock, as grazing was free on the public domain and sheep herders were paid only very nominal sums. During the 1880s wool prices were generally good, partly as a result of protective tariffs. Herds increased rapidly, and more and more men entered the business, many of them with no qualification other than the itch to make some money as rapidly as possible. By the end of the decade all ranges were taken, part of them by cattlemen whose business was also growing rapidly. There was some competition between sheepmen and cattlemen, and between rival flocks and herds as the pressure on the range mounted. However, there was no clear-cut, black and white differentiation between sheepmen and cattlemen. Some stockmen, notably Babbitts, were both, and many stockmen had firsthand experience with both sheep and cattle.

Haskett tells us that outside Indian reservations, in 1870 Arizona had 803 sheep; in 1876, 10,000; in 1880, 76,524. In 1885 it was estimated that Arizona had 680,000 sheep, most of them in the north and north-central areas of the Territory. Haskett says that in 1890 there were 698,404. On January 1, 1887, the *Arizona Champion* estimated that there were one hundred fifty thousand sheep in the San Francisco Peaks area alone, worth on the average $2.75 each. Five or six months later this figure was revised upward to two hundred thousand. The *Champion* also reported that Arizona fleeces would average from seven to eight pounds, would bring $1 a fleece, and that two million pounds of wool was produced here in a single season.

Herds owned by the Navajo, Hopi and other Indians also grew rapidly. Their stock was generally of inferior quality, shearing half as much or less than the improved herds elsewhere. The Indians were even more careless than others in damaging their grazing lands, and some areas were irreparably ruined.

With the astronomical increase in numbers of sheep and outfits, growing competition with the cattlemen for the no longer limitless range, the scarcity of water, plus problems of marketing and shipping, the sheepmen came together for discussion, settlement of disputes among themselves, and made some attempts to present a united front in matters concerning their industry.

It's probable that even as early at 1882 the handful of sheepmen in our area got together to discuss common problems. We find notices in the *Champion* as early as October 1884 and April 1885 of formal meetings. On May 1, 1886, that newspaper published two-thirds of a column reporting on a meeting of the Arizona Sheep Breeders and Wool Growers Association at Flagstaff. They elected Henry Fulton, president; J. B. Tappen and R. Kinder, vice presidents; C. H. Schulz, secretary; J. F. Daggs, corresponding secretary, and Walter J. Hill, treasurer. But earlier sessions had been called by McMillan. The May 1, 1886, session produced resolutions protesting low wool prices, high freight rates, and also vigorously protested "the taking possession of large extents of the public domain . . . without warantie [*sic*]" by the big land and cattle companies.

But these were still very good years for the sheepmen, and fortunes were made. Some of the money went into comfortable homes. Some went into local enterprises including stores and markets; the bank building which still stands on the corner of Leroux and Santa Fe Avenue was built by McMillan, and he lived in an apartment there for some years. The sheepmen played parts in the organization of the banks. Daggs brothers had fingers in many enterprises. Hill, who had prospered with a big sheep outfit at Volunteer Springs, built an imposing residence and stocked a library with finely bound classics. He and others traveled, invested in enterprises elsewhere including mines, took an interest in civic affairs, and improved their holdings.

When it had become apparent in the late 1870s that the railroads would be built across Arizona and soon, not only sheepmen but cattlemen saw the opportunity, and small herds moved into Arizona's vast, lush pastures from both east and west. In a brief historical sketch in the January 1, 1887, issue of the *Champion,* we read that the first cattle were brought into the general locality in 1877 by John Wood, who drove seventy-eight head into the Mogollon Mountains. Baker, who brought sheep to the Mogollon Rim, also had cattle.

When the Mormons came to the Little Colorado Valley to settle, they brought cattle with them, mostly dairy stock. In 1878 Lot Smith, one of the Mormon leaders, and a group of forty-eight men and forty-one women from the settlements went to the large, shallow lake twenty-eight miles southeast of Flagstaff, which soon became known as Mormon Lake, and built three log cabins and handled a herd of one hundred fifteen dairy cows, making butter and cheese. The Mormon Lake operation in due time would also have herds of range cattle.

It will be recalled that in 1877 John Young, son of Brigham, had dispatched a small expedition from the Mormon settlements on the Little Colorado to Leroux Spring, north of Flagstaff, to establish a claim to its water. Then in 1881, after securing contracts to furnish ties for the railroad and for grading right of way, he led a party of about sixty men and some women to the vast open park near the spring and established a camp of small cabins and tents. Rumors of Indian unrest led him to build a long, low cabin, which formed one side of a fort, the other three sides being a stockade of double-length railroad ties set in the ground on end. This fort Young named Moroni for an important figure in the Book of Mormon. In due time, with completion of the railroad, Young used the fort as headquarters for the Moroni Cattle Company, the first large cow outfit in the northland.

Earle R. Forrest, in July and August 1943, wrote a series of articles for Flagstaff's *Coconino Sun* dealing with his experiences as a cowboy employed by Babbitts in the early 1900s. He was stationed at the fort built by Young, later owned by Babbitts. Forrest says that in the loft of the building he found old records of the Moroni Cattle Company including checks drawn on the Second National Bank of Santa Fe, beginning in 1881 and extending to 1885. Forrest

Two views of the fort which gave Fort Valley its name. It was built in 1881 by John W. Young to shelter tie-cutters working under contract with the Atlantic & Pacific Railroad. The camp was originally a group of tents and cabins, but with reports that the Apaches were restless, Young built the stockade and named it Fort Moroni. It later became headquarters for the Moroni Cattle Company and later, the Arizona Cattle Company.

tells us that Young had become associated with some eastern capitalists, and the original Moroni Cattle Company became the Arizona Cattle Company, the famed "A-1 Bar" outfit. Young severed his connection with the A-1 in 1885, about the time he left the area because of warrants charging polygamy.

Central office of the A-1 was in New York City. President was John C. Dela Vergue; vice president, Henry R. Don der Horst; manager and director, Ellis Wainwright; treasurer, C. L. Rickerson, in whose honor the fort was renamed; secretary, H. W. Guernsey, and superintendent, Charles Goven. In the fall of 1885, Goven was replaced by Capt. B. B. Bullwinkle, and in the May 14, 1887, issue of the *Champion* we learn that Goven was bookkeeper. The A-1's range ran from south of Flagstaff in the area of today's Lake Mary, north to the Grand Canyon, and from the Little Colorado to Ash Fork. It covered eight hundred seventy-five square miles, but A-1 had title to but a fraction of this if we can call one hundred and thirty-two thousand acres a fraction, which was purchased at fifty cents per acre from the railroad. It consisted of alternate square miles, running fifteen miles one way, twenty-four the other, a part of the vast acreage granted to the railroad by Congress as a subsidy for construction.

From Forrest's July 23, 1943, article, we learn that the A-1 had invested more than a million dollars in their operation, including land, cattle, horses, improvements, etc. At the peak, A-1 ran as many as sixteen thousand cattle.

The A-1's superintendent, Bullwinkle, was an extraordinary figure, worthy to appear in the colorful scene of the Flagstaff community in the 1880s. He had spent most of his life as a fireman in Chicago, and was there during the Great Fire in October 1871. For years he was captain of a private firm known as Chicago Fire Patrol, which worked with light buggies and fast teams, attempting to get to fires before the fire department in order to salvage merchandise and other articles before they either burned or were ruined by water. In the fall of 1885 he disposed of a trucking and teaming business, and in the last week of December came to Flagstaff and took charge of the A-1.

A story about Bullwinkle providing us with a fascinating glimpse of life in Flagstaff as it was lived by the prosperous stockmen in the 1880s, appears in a May 9, 1887, item in the *Champion:*

> One of the editor's friends dropped in this week and told us a story about a poker game Saturday night between Capt. B. B. Bullwinkle and Frank Vanderlip, local cattlemen.
>
> Vanderlip had no money with him but plenty of cattle and an immense desire to play poker with Captain Bullwinkle. The latter is known

for his great natural resources, and he swept away the seemingly insur-
mountable difficulty by proposing a game of one steer ante, two steers to
come in, and no limit. They played on this basis. The captain dealt and
Vanderlip antied one steer. Both came in and the game opened with four
steers on the table. The captain drew two tens and caught an unexpected
full, while Vanderlip passed out.

The third was a jack pot, and it took three deals to open it. Vanderlip
finally drew two jacks and opened the pot with a fine breeding bull,
which counted six. The captain covered this with five steers and a two-
year-old heifer, and went him twelve better. Vanderlip, who drew another jack, saw the twelve cows and went him fifty steers, twenty two-
year-old heifers, four bulls, and twenty-five heifer calves better. The captain looked at his hand and placed upon the table six fine cows, five bulls,
one hundred two-year-olds, fifty prime to medium steers, and with a side
bet of a horse to cover the bar bill. Vanderlip made his bet good with an
even two hundred and fifty straight halfbreeds and twenty-four mustangs
and the NE ¼ of the SW ¼ of Section 10, Township 24, Range 2 east,
and called. The captain held three aces, and put in his hip pocket seven
hundred sixty-two steers, heifers, etc., and a big stock ranch.

Bullwinkle loved fast horses, and had many of them at the headquarters
ranch. Oldtimers said that he nearly always raced to town, attempting to better
his own time. The May 14, 1887, issue of the *Champion* tells of his death, in a
long article headed "His Last Ride." He was racing along for a business appointment when, shortly after passing the Lockett place a couple miles north
of town, his horse fell and fatally injured him. Joe and Henry Lockett saw the
accident happen, and rushed to the scene. They took him to the Lockett home,
and very quickly both of the town's doctors, P. G. Cornish and D. J. Brannen,
were at his side. He died a few hours later with his wife and fourteen-year-old
son present. A grand funeral was held with the Masons in charge, and the body
was shipped to Chicago for burial. The article said that he had worked wonders
in straightening out the affairs of the company, fencing certain areas, erecting
buildings at the home ranch, getting the company's cattle all on its own land,
and installing a telephone between Fort Rickerson and Flagstaff, etc. He was
obviously a very popular man in the community. Said the *Champion:*

> His familiar face was seen upon our streets almost every day and no
> man could have been taken away from our midst that would have been
> more missed. . . .

When Bullwinkle suffered his fatal fall he was on the way to Flagstaff to meet Maj. Henry Warren, general manager of the Hashknife, who had come by train and was to be in town only a few hours. This was the other big cattle company, having perhaps forty thousand head. It began operations in 1885 with purchase of land from the Atlantic & Pacific Railroad. This huge block of land was forty miles wide and ninety miles long, extending from Holbrook to Flagstaff, mostly on the south side of the railroad. At times its stock ran over a much larger range. Haskett tells us that the principal owners were John H. Simpson, president; Henry Kinsley, secretary, and E. J. Simpson, manager, all of Weatherford, Texas. The Seligmans of New York and the stockholders of the Atlantic & Pacific were also members of the firm, because of the land turned over to the cattle company. George H. Tinker's promotional articles which appeared in 1887 in the *Champion,* reported that the Aztec Land & Cattle Company, Ltd., was chartered under New York state laws; that the office of the company was at Holbrook; that Warren was vice president and general manager; that Simpson was ranch superintendent; that Kinsley was assistant treasurer, and F. A. Ames land agent.

The company shipped about forty thousand head of Texas cattle and unloaded them along the right-of-way from Holbrook westward. The Aztec Company owned a lot of timber, and in 1887 there was talk that they might establish a sawmill and possibly erect a slaughtering and refrigerating establishment at or near Flagstaff. The firm was known as the Hashknife because of the shape of its brand.

Haskett tells us that these two big firms, despite being amply financed, did not prosper, and that their cattle gradually diminished in numbers until they were forced to retire from business:

> After they had retired from the field it was found that a number of small outfits had sprung up from nowhere and prospered amazingly on ranges adjoining these companies. It was claimed at the time that a saddle horse and rope was all that was needed to start a cattle outfit on the Hashknife and A-1 ranges.

Heavy overgrazing, particularly by the Hashknife, caused serious damage to the vegetation and top soil, and huge areas once covered by nutritious native grasses became barren wastes.

But while the biggest operators failed to prosper, many others did succeed. Hamilton tells us that a man starting with a hundred head could increase his herd thirteen-fold at the end of five years. Beef cattle in 1884 were worth from

A cowboy of the real West. Frank Livermore, foreman for the Arizona Cattle Company (the A-1 outfit), whose headquarters was in the Fort Valley area. Livermore was typical of the working cowboys in the days of the big cattle spreads. Not much glamour, but plenty of savvy about stock.

seven to eight cents a pound, neat, and stock cattle were usually rated at about thirty dollars a head. The cattle in our area, and other parts of Yavapai, doubled to seventy-five thousand in the two years between 1882 and 1884. Most of them were shipped or driven from Texas, Colorado, California and New Mexico. Hamilton notes that the ranges were filling up in 1884. Stock dotted the range as far as one could see, and herds being driven to the stockyards for shipment were a common sight; hitching rails along the streets were lined with cow ponies, and cowboys strode and swaggered about, most of them with revolvers strapped to their thighs. The July 24, 1886, issue of the *Champion* reported:

> Last Saturday evening some 1,200 head of cattle were herded within the northern limits of our town, and their constant bellowing, mingled with the cries of the cowboys, kept up such a racket throughout the night that sleep in the vicinity was impossible. Next morning the cattle were driven right through the main street, of which they held possession for over an hour to the detriment and obstruction of all other travel and business, while there were better and more feasible routes on either side of town. The cattle were rendered frantic by the unusual sight of houses, engines, cars and a labyrinth of railroad tracks and only the utmost efforts on the part of their drivers prevented a general stampede. We do not know who directed this drive, but hope such an outrage will not happen again.

Cattle were omnipresent and important. The number of cattle in Arizona for various years, as reported on the tax rolls, showed huge gains yearly up to 1891. Haskett expresses the view, generally supported by knowledgeable oldtimers, that the assessment rolls showed perhaps half of the actual stock on the ranges. Those on which taxes were paid in the Territory in 1883 totaled 168,973. In 1885, there were 267,899, and of these, 89,688 were in Yavapai County. In 1887 the Territorial total stood at 446,838. The peak year seems to have been 1891, when the total was 720,941 on the tax rolls, and if Haskett and other oldtimers are right, there were actually about a million and a half!

On May 3, 1885, the *Champion* noted that fifty thousand calves would be branded in Yavapai during the spring roundup. A significant item had appeared a few weeks earlier, March 21, which stated that the courts had decided that barbed wire could not be used unless adjacent owners approved, and that such wire along roads would render erectors liable for injury. The coming of wire marked the beginning of the end of the open range.

With so many cattle, rustling was a major problem. Unbranded calves without cows (mavericks), were fair game for ambitious cowboys intent on building up their herds. Sometimes the cows were killed, then the calves branded and driven away so that the owner of the cow would be unable to prove the parentage of the calf. The cattlemen were organized in the Mogollon Livestock Protective Association which dealt with freight rates and other problems, and also, theft. Early in 1885, the *Champion* commenced the weekly publication of registered brands, with a standing offer of $500 reward for information leading to conviction of rustlers. Publication of brands was to continue to be a feature of western weekly newspapers in livestock areas for many years, indeed, well up into the 1920s. Study of these brands is most interesting for those who have learned the nomenclature, and the recitation of the distinguishing burns and ear-marks rolls from the tongue of a real cowman with the cadence and color of poetry. And there is frequently an undercurrent of humor in this lingo of the brands. These marks, burned into the cow's hide, were not only a means of establishing ownership, they also served as a sort of coat of arms. Many owners to this day take great pride in them. Cowboys, ranches, any part of an outfit might be described as belonging to the CO Bar, the Hashknife, the Slash JV, or whatever.

Editor A. E. Fay of the *Champion* championed the cattlemen's cause and published all available news which would interest them. In his issue of April 11, 1885, we read that he had been chosen as secretary of the Mogollon Association. Officers included W. H. Ashurst, president; William Munds, vice president; and J. F. Daggs, treasurer. The *Champion* was declared the association's official newspaper, in which all notices would appear.

Note that J. F. Daggs was an important figure in this group; he and his brothers also operated the biggest sheep outfit in the area, probably in the entire Territory, and they were leaders in the Wool Growers Association. The Daggses for a time also operated a slaughterhouse, and a wholesale and retail meat market at Flagstaff.

The feud between two families in Pleasant Valley south of the Mogollon Rim, the Grahams and the Tewksburys, was in a limited sense a war between those who ran sheep and those who ran cattle, but there were other important factors. Both had been in the cattle business, and it seems probable that they first fell out over the division of cattle they jointly stole from Jim Stinson. There is good reason to believe that the precipitating factor was the appearance in what had hitherto been a range exclusively used by cattle, of a big herd of sheep under the management, probably partial ownership, of the Tewksburys in 1887. It has been pretty well established that the sheep came from the Daggs brothers of

Flagstaff, who had plenty of money and were constantly on the lookout for more range for their growing flocks. Forrest wrote what is probably the definitive work on the feud.

From Forrest we learn that in 1926 the secretary of the Arizona Pioneers Historical Society at Tucson wrote to P. P. Daggs, long retired and living in California, asking for his memories of the war. He answered:

> I know you would not be unkind enough to lure me into anything for which I would be captured and shot at sunrise. I have one consolation: the enemy will not do it. They are all "sleeping with their boots on."
>
> I ought to know something about the "Tonto Basin War." It cost me ninety thousand dollars. General Sherman once said, "War is hell." He was right.

The Graham-Tewksbury feud started in 1886 and came to a close a decade later when Edwin Tewksbury, last of his clan, was charged with the ambush and murder of Tom Graham, tried twice, and finally released. There were perhaps twenty deaths resulting directly from the feud. A grisly incident which has been the basis of many highly colored stories and films occurred when the Grahams surrounded a Tewksbury cabin in the early morning hours and coolly shot down John Tewksbury and William Jacobs as they started out for horses. The Grahams continued firing at the cabin for hours, with fire returned from within. As the battle continued a drove of hogs started devouring the bodies of Tewksbury and Jacobs; the Grahams did not offer a truce but continued shooting. Suddenly John Tewksbury's wife came out of the cabin with a shovel. The firing stopped while she scooped out shallow graves for her husband and his companion. Firing on both sides then resumed, but no further deaths occurred, and after a few hours the Grahams rode away.

Then a couple of days later occurred a dramatic confrontation. Andy Cooper, a member of the Graham faction, was in Holbrook, where he openly boasted that he had shot both Tewksbury and Jacobs, which was very probably true. Sheriff Commodore Perry Owens of Apache County, who had a warrant for Cooper's arrest on an earlier charge, rode into town. He learned that Cooper was there, and Cooper learned that Owens had arrived. Cooper went to the Blevins home where he was staying, saddled his horse, then reentered the house preparatory to leaving ahead of the sheriff. At this point Owens came on the scene with a loaded rifle and with his pistol on his left side with the butt forward, a novel way of carrying a gun. But Owens was noted for his facility with arms. He came to the door and Cooper pushed it open a few inches.

Owens demanded that he come with him. Cooper refused, and stepped back in the house. It seems very unlikely that Cooper did not have his pistol in his hand, under the circumstances. Owens fired, hitting Cooper who staggered back into the room. Almost simultaneously John Blevins came to the adjoining door and shot at Owens, but the shot missed and killed Cooper's horse. The sheriff swung his rifle and put Blevins out of action, breaking his arm. The sheriff then stepped back into the street.

At this point a fourteen- or fifteen-year-old youth, Samuel Houston Blevins, picked up Cooper's pistol and ran out the door. Owens shot him and he died in a few minutes. Owens then sighted a fourth man, Mose Roberts, slipping out of a window on the side of the house. Owens shot him through the body, and he died very soon, too.

This is very probably the most famous shooting affray in northern Arizona's history. It has been dealt with in fictional form many times.

Sheriff Owens died at Seligman May 10, 1919, many years after he had retired as an officer. He is buried in Flagstaff. His widow told this writer in a letter written in 1944 that Owens wanted to be buried in a small plot near his home at Seligman, but after his death she felt his grave would be better cared for if she brought him to Flagstaff. "Commodore," incidentally, was Owen's given name.

In a long column of local news items appearing in the *Champion* on April 10, 1886, appears a most significant paragraph—the first mention of the Babbitts in Flagstaff:

> David Babbitt and brother [William] of Cincinnati are visiting Flagstaff. These gentlemen are here for the purpose of visiting and inspecting cattle ranges with a view of purchasing and are the guests of our popular townsman, Dr. D. J. Brannen.

On April 24 appeared the following:

> The Babbitt Bros. of Cincinnati have purchased from Messrs. Hesler and Warren about 1,200 head of stock, consisting of 800 cows, 35 fine grade bulls, 200 two-year-olds, and about 200 yearlings. The cattle purchased are all first class stock and in fine condition. We are informed by a prominent stockman that he considers this herd one of the best in this vicinity and considers that the gentlemen have made a cheap and excellent purchase.

On July 7 the paper reported:

We invite the attention of our readers to the brand, CO Bar, and other brands of the Babbitt Bros. who have recently settled in our neighborhood with a band of some 1,800 head of fine cattle.

Only ten months after David and William Babbitt arrived in Flagstaff and bought the Hesler-Warren herd, they joined with W. H. Ashurst and the A-1 people in shipping seventeen cars of beef to Los Angeles. The *Champion* reported on February 18, 1888, that Ashurst's cattle average 1,154 pounds; A-1's, 1,088, and Babbitts', 1,070, and that they received three cents per pound.

In September 1888, we learn from the *Champion,* a petition had been sent to the agent for the Navajos at Fort Defiance, requesting that he keep the Indians off the Coconino Forest:

> These Indians have stolen a good deal of stock [cattle] and sheep from owners in this section and unless they are prohibited from trespassing in this section, serious trouble is anticipated as the stockmen do not propose to endure it any longer.

The Indians were having trouble finding grass for their sheep, too.

By the closing years of the decade there were far too many sheep and cattle and far too many outfits, and each year more and more animals came in from other states and territories. On December 1, 1888, the *Champion* reprinted the following from William O'Neill's Prescott stock paper, *Hoof & Horn:*

> Many stockmen are beginning to realize that the number of cattle that are being shipped into this Territory . . . will compel them to seek new pastures. Many portions of the Territory are now overstocked to an alarming extent, and the continual driving of stock here places the future pasturage for stock in a very important condition. All available ranges where a natural supply of water can be had are now located and settled upon, and those seeking ranges are compelled to either buy or intrude on other parties' property.

The easy days of open range and quick profits were drawing to a close. This does not mean that no more money would be made in this area in stock; indeed, the Babbitts were only getting started and nearly ninety years later their families would still be running profitable ranches. Some large fortunes would be made in the years after 1890, particularly during the war years. But increasingly the stock business would be in the hands of highly skilled professionals who knew best how to utilize the available range, water, and capital.

The heavy overstocking of the late 1880s greased the skids for the coming calamity of the 1890s. In 1891 and 1892 the area was seared by a devastating drought. Then, when it finally rained in 1893 and grass started growing again, there was a nationwide financial panic. Stock sold at giveaway prices, and all marginal and many substantial stock outfits gave up the ghost. Only a few—the highly skilled, the lucky, the well-financed, survived.

The original settlement at Antelope Spring which became known as Flagstaff. When New Town was started a mile east following completion of the railroad in August 1882, this became known as Old Town. Most of it was destroyed by fire in July 1884. The top view looks west, and the bottom one is the same scene looking east. There were also a few cabins, tents and light frame structures scattered about in the woods nearby.

# CHAPTER IX

# Building and Rebuilding

THE ORIGINAL FLAGSTAFF SETTLEMENT near Antelope Spring, soon to be known as Old Town Spring, got its start in the winter of 1880–81 with erection of a couple of structures, a log cabin housing Ed Whipple's saloon and restaurant, and a tent to which was soon added a log cabin, quarters for the general store of P. B. Brannen & Co. This store in due time would accommodate the first post office.

As the railhead moved slowly westward across the Territory early in 1881, large gangs of workers were stationed in camps along the right-of-way, and tie-cutters were busy preparing for the coming of the rails. The contractors needed supplies, and the men had money to spend. Other establishments soon joined Brannen and Whipple. By the summer, there were a number of saloons and gambling establishments as well as retail stores. The Prescott *Miner* reported in mid-September that "a dance hall has been started in Flagstaff. Here is another revenue of $100 per month for the county."

There are a few photographs of the original community, or at least of the row of cabins, tents and frame structures which comprised most of it, taken after the railroad reached Flagstaff early in August 1882, and prior to July 1884, when much of it was destroyed by the first big fire. We know that the one appearing at the top of the opposite page was made by Ben Wittick, Albuquerque photographer, who visited the area in March 1883. A somewhat similar photograph was submitted in February 1922 by the *Coconino Sun* to a group of oldtimers for identification. Included were William Freidlein, James Lamport, Dad Willis, Ed Whipple, W. H. Switzer and Mrs. C. A. Greenlaw. It was their opinion that the buildings, running from left to right, beginning with the gable-ended structure just to the right of the tent, were Court & Hanner's saloon; an unidentified saloon and dance hall; the Log Cabin saloon owned by Banjo Bill Dwyer and Adam Conrad; P. B. Brannen & Co.'s log cabin and tent; a place described as a "Jew store," which may later have become Browning's saloon;

Beal's restaurant and/or hotel; John Drain's saloon; and finally, the J. H. Hawks bakery and restaurant. The oldtimers said that the Log Cabin saloon was later owned by Bill Bailey. (There are frequent references in the early and mid-eighties to a James Bailey—perhaps the same man.) Which one of these structures if any was the original Whipple saloon was not stated.

W. H. Switzer told the writer on a number of occasions in the 1950s and '60s that when he was a fourteen-year-old youngster delivering milk in 1883, one day he ran up the steps of one of the saloons and saw a man lying with a sack over his head. Billy kicked the sack away, then fled in horror. He had seen that half the man's head had been shot away. He learned that the man had been prowling around the night before until he came in contact with Deputy Sheriff W. S. Dykes with a shotgun. The body had been left on the porch until a coroner's jury could be summoned.

The street on which these places fronted was a very rough wagon road and at its western extremity near the spring it ran into the Overland Road. Shortly after the railhead arrived at Flagstaff, the Atlantic & Pacific established a depot three-quarters of a mile northeast of the settlement on the south side of the tracks at a site now occupied by the Santa Fe freight office. It consisted of two boxcars, later three, one serving as living quarters for the agent whose duties also included operating the telegraph. Probably there was a platform of heavy planks.

With the location of the depot thus settled, the Brannens decided to move from Antelope Spring and erect a new building close to the depot. In the summer of 1883 they started construction of a one-story stone structure on the north side of the tracks and immediately opposite the depot. The walls were up by early September. By late October the building was complete and the move was made, and Brannen was in Albuquerque buying merchandise. Charles F. Kathrens was chief salesman and Samuel S. King bookkeeper. The building cost $10,000, a lot of money in 1883.

The Brannens found the move comparatively easy because they had little investment in the cabin and tent at the old location. Some of the other establishments did not find it as easy, because they had erected more permanent structures, including some false-fronted frame buildings. It is understandable that they were loath to abandon these, wherever the depot might be. However, some firms followed Brannen and some new ones were established, and they built facing the railroad tracks and on both sides of Brannen's. By the winter of 1883–84, the new community was being called "East End" or "New Town" and the original community was designated as "West End" or "Old Town"—this latter name still in use by the grandchildren and great-grandchildren of the settlers.

On October 25, 1883, the first Flagstaff newspaper, *The Flag,* made its appearance. Its columns revealed that Flagstaff had four general stores: Brannen; Leon Brannie & Son in Old Town; Dewitt C. Newell whose location we are not sure of, but probably in New Town; a new place in New Town owned by Daniel A. Murphy, who had formerly been a partner in a firm known as Stevens & Murphy, in Old Town. *The Flag* also reported that James Wilson, formerly of Holbrook, had come to town and that day had driven the first nail in the new building which was also to stock general merchandise. The firm would be known as Barth & Wilson. Murphy still had some interest in Old Town, perhaps the remainder of the Stevens & Murphy venture, because when fire razed Old Town in 1884 his loss was listed as $500 for goods. Flagstaff was booming.

The weekly *Flag* was established in a new building in New Town under the guidance of Henry Reed. It would fold up in about six months and the equipment would be moved to Holbrook where it would produce the *Times. The Flag* was supplanted in Flagstaff by the *Arizona Champion* which started life in Peach Springs in September 1883, and moved to Flagstaff between issues and produced its first issue here on February 2, 1884. The *Champion* later became the *Coconino Sun,* which in 1946 gave birth to the *Arizona Daily Sun.*

The first issue of *The Flag* advised that the previous Monday at 1 A.M. the first through train to California had steamed triumphantly up to the Flagstaff boxcar depot, to be greeted by the hearty cheers of those who stayed awake (no doubt in the saloons) to witness the event. Time from Albuquerque to Needles, five hundred and seventy-four miles, was twenty-eight hours.

In late September the Prescott *Courier* quoted Sheriff Henkle as stating that Flagstaff had about fourteen business houses, that new ones were starting almost every week, and that Flagstaff would grow to be a very large town.

While the *Champion* was being published at Peach Springs it regularly featured news reports from Flagstaff in increasing volume as the weeks rolled by. From one column in late 1883 we learn that Spinney & McLean had built a two-story hotel in New Town and would open it with a social hop in mid-November, that Wilson & Barth had opened their new store which had a second story and that the second story had also been used for an opening hop. The paper in early December advised that Kilpatrick & Co. had erected a large building in New Town to accommodate another general store—the town's sixth. The editor noted, "Room for more, Gentlemen." Early in 1884 readers learned that

H. H. Hoxworth & Co. were building "one of the largest stores yet put up in Flagstaff," 25 x 60, and would sell hardware, tinware and furniture, with opening scheduled for February 1. An item also noted that a large bear had wandered into town, possibly attracted by P. J. Brannen's slaughterhouse.

Flagstaff's original hotel, The Pioneer, operated by F. L. and M. S. Beal, was in Old Town. There were three restaurants; one operated by E. S. Shiprell; one by the pioneer settler, J. F. Hawks in Old Town; and the third was the Oriental operated by J. W. Spafford. Eugene Turner was the only attorney. J. A. Marshall, whose wife Eva would teach the first school, and James M. Sandford were the justices of the peace. Thomas Tobin had the blacksmith and wagon repair shop. John Sanderson dealt in fruits and confectionery. The Black Brothers ran the livery, sales and exchange stables. D. J. Brannen, the town's only doctor, had just opened the drug store in New Town. There were a number of saloons, including Gregg & Gregory, Hickerson & Prescott, Carter & Osborn, all probably in New Town, and in a row running along the single street. W. M. Laughlin had a saloon in Old Town, which would escape the fire of July 1884. Others, probably in Old Town, were John Francis, Stanley & Coakley, James Bailey, Sterling, Feisley and Mother Dolan. A. L. Brock & Co. were carpenters and builders. New Town had grown rapidly after Brannen started the ball rolling.

In the 1880s Patrick Hamilton's promotional guidebook dealing with Arizona was subsidized by the Territorial government. The 1884 edition, no doubt containing data compiled in 1883, reported that there were two towns, Old and New Flagstaff, with a combined population of six hundred; that the newer part was build on both sides of the railroad; that most structures were of wood but one large merchandise establishment was of dressed stone; that there were a half dozen stores, as many saloons, etc.

Actually there were three towns, the third being "Milltown," which surrounded the Ayer Lumber Company plant a half-mile south of Old Town and a mile southwest of New Town. It was wholly owned by the company. In 1883–84 it included a large boarding house for employees, an extensive commissary which for the first few years furnished merchandise to the mill employees at cost, possibly a necessary inducement to bring in and keep the necessary skilled workers; and there were many frame structures. Milltown in due time became Milton and had its own rules, most noteworthy being that liquor could not be sold in its environs. It would have graded streets and sidewalks. The mill was landlord, sole employer, banker and in a sense the local government. It continued as a separate community until 1920 when it successfully petitioned to join the Town of Flagstaff.

In February 1884, the *Champion* with prophetic vision stated that "the time is not far distant when Flagstaff will be the point of supply for all of the smaller towns within a radius of hundreds of miles."

The building boom was not limited to New Town. New structures were going up in Old Town. By May, Yavapai County had built a jail for the growing community, and almost simultaneously the Flagstaff Brewery started producing beer. We more or less resist the temptation to link these two developments. While the brewery was doing well, the Flagstaff Bottling Works was also busy, producing soft drinks and soda water.

Prices in the store were high, but not as high as formerly. We read that men's suits sold for $10.00-$25.00; shoes, $4.00-$7.00; ladies' kid shoes, $2.50-$4.00. Canned fruit sold for thirty-five cents, vegetables, twenty cents. Wholesale prices seem to have been about half the retail price. Wholesale meats included beef at eight-and-a-half cents; mutton, eight cents; pork, fourteen cents; and fresh antelope and deer, seven cents.

The July 8 *Champion* reported that fire had leveled most of the business section of the town of Williams, thirty miles west. Flagstaff was generous with aid for the stricken community. And then it was Flagstaff's turn. In the early hours of Tuesday, July 22, occurred the first of the community's major fires. This one almost completely wiped out Old Town. "The fire is attributed to carelessness on behalf of a female in the dance hall, who knocked over a lamp," the paper reported.

## RED RUIN

### *Nearly the Whole of Old Town Laid in Ashes*

Early Tuesday morning a fire was discovered in old town by James Bailey, in the rear of Drake's dance hall. He immediately gave the alarm, and although he had a large building close by, before proceeding to move his goods personally, went from house to house to wake up the occupants. The fire had gained too much headway to be extinguished, and as it was sure to sweep the whole row west, the wind blowing from the east, the owners at once commenced moving out their goods, but the flames sprang from building to building with such rapidity, that in some instances the owners had barely time to get out with the clothes they could get on. The fire went clear down the row, and aside from Beal's and McLaughlin's buildings, the old town is a thing of the past, as those who had enough left to build with are coming to new town.

The following is a fair estimate of the loss, including buildings, as we could gather: Mr. Drake, $200; John Francis, $600; Stanley & Coakley, $600; J. Bailey, $1,000; Dan Murphy, on stock, $500; Mother Dolan, $500; Sterling, $299, and Feisley, $150; upon which there is no insurance.

Two days after the fire Marvin Beal sold his place to Drake who had been burned out. Drake immediately turned the former saloon and eating place into a dance hall. Dance halls must have been profitable, because as we noted a bit earlier Yavapai County was receiving $100 per month for a license to run such an establishment. Bailey, whose place had been burned, was busy rebuilding, and would soon open the new Lone Star saloon next door to New Town's Blazing Star saloon. A note stated that "Will Murphy deserves credit for saving the band instruments at the fire."

The warning was not lost on the merchants of New Town. We read that:

> Our townsman, Harry Hoxworth, had been selected by the business men along Railroad Avenue to act as night watchman for a period of six months. The extreme danger of fire in the long row of wooden buildings facing the railroad, had rendered this action necessary, and in the selection of Harry to guard the property by night, they have made a most excellent choice, as he is largely interested, owning a valuable store building in the center of the block. Sober, honest and faithful, our people need have no fear of a conflagration, as he will his "vigil keep."

Fires and the continued growth of the community underlined the need for adequate water supplies. Water was being hauled in barrels from Old Town Spring, from the railroad's water tank which was supplied by tank cars, and from as far away as Leroux Spring in Fort Valley. "The matter of a liberal supply of water for Flagstaff is becoming a serious question. The railroad company is drawing the reins on the people, and perhaps sooner than we think, will cease to be as liberal in respect to supplying water as heretofore. Our citizens should be looking for a supply of water from some other source," the newspaper had warned weeks before the fire. In the following winter the editor again emphasized the necessity of a proper water supply, suggesting a system of dikes and basins to catch the runoff from summer rains and melting snow, and that $1,500 would be sufficient to purchase pipe and construct a reservoir to properly utilize the water from Antelope Spring, pointing out that that amount was paid out every month at the rate of $1 per barrel during the dry season. In March one of the old settlers, a Mr. Rumsey of Old Town, got himself into trouble by shutting off the spring. "He thought it a good scheme to appropriate Antelope Spring to his own use and proceeded to fence it by placing logs around it. He was arrested

First building erected in what became New Town is at the right, Brannen's Pioneer general
store, built in the summer and fall of 1883. Along with most of New Town it was gutted by
fire in February 1886, but rebuilt, and stands today on the northeast corner of Santa Fe Avenue and San Francisco Street. The James Vail structure at the left was also destroyed in the
1886 fire, was rebuilt, then razed by another major fire in July 1888, finally rebuilt of brick,
and stands today.

A view of New Town about 1888 after its rebuilding following the 1886 fire. Brannen's store
is near the center, in front of and to the left of the church. Dr. D. J. Brannen's drug store is to
the right of the general store. Just to the right of the railroad water tank is what appears to be
the walls of the Bank Hotel building nearing completion, which stands today on the northwest corner of Santa Fe Avenue and Leroux Street. To the right of the water tank and near
the tracks are three box cars with steps, the railroad depot; note the shipments of goods piled
on the ground nearby.

for the offense, but a compromise was effected and he was released by paying costs of suit and promising to remove the obstructions from the spring," the *Champion* noted. During the fall, with the memory of the fire still sharp in people's minds, the *Champion* reported that the Atlantic & Pacific Railroad might pipe water from the big spring on the San Francisco Mountains into Flagstaff. "In that event some of the enterprising citizens of Flagstaff should organize a water company to supply the town," the paper said. But that pipeline was not to be built for a long time.

Building continued and the community grew. In July the post office became a money order office. Perhaps of greater interest was the report that Ben Taylor had renewed his lease on the roller skating rink and that it would remain open every day. That rink would become of considerable importance soon, when it would be used as a storehouse for food and clothing donated for the sufferers from another fire which would destroy much of New Town. This fire occurred on Sunday, February 14, 1886. The *Champion* office was among structures destroyed by the blaze. The *Journal-Miner* at Prescott ran a report on the conflagration on February 17, but the *Champion* did not resume publication until February 27, when it made up for lost time by running four full columns of news about the fire, led off by the following headlines.

## FIERY FLAMES

---

Destroy the Business
Section of Flagstaff

---

Wm. Bidinger Burned To
Death and Cremated
In the Ruins

---

Over Thirty Buildings
Destroyed In As
Many Minutes

---

A Night of Terrors to
The Little Moun-
tain City

---

In Which Nearly 100

People are Made
Homeless

———

All of the Stores And
Their Contents Re-
duced to Ashes

———

Leaving Inhabitants
Without Means Of
Sustenance

———

Only Twelve Thous-
and Dollars of the
Loss Insured

———

Winslow Nobly Responds
To the Needs Of the
Fire Sufferers

———

By Sending A Car-load of
Provisions Within a
Few Hours

———

Other Places Follow with
Prompt and Generous Aid

———

Work Already Commenced Towards Rebuilding The Town

———

According to the detailed *Champion* report, John Vining, night telegraph operator at the railroad depot, went out on the platform in front of his office for a breath of air shortly after 4 A.M. He saw a flicker of flame coming from in back of the post office. He ran up the street kicking doors as he went and in a few minutes the street was full of people. The fire spread rapidly. There was no water and all set to work to salvage what they could. Within twenty minutes of Vining's alarm, the whole block, from Gold (Leroux) Street eastward to San Francisco was in flames. It was hoped the destruction would halt there, but in a few minutes the flames leaped the street and swept around the stone building housing Brannen's. It then raced on eastward, destroying everything. As the crowd watched, the flames then broke out in Brannen's. Flames had also swept northward, destroying buildings on both sides of North San Francisco. "Then the sun rose, seeming more bright than usual, in this land of sunshine, and lit up a scene of smouldering desolation from the post office corner to the eastern limit of town."

The saddest sight the dawn revealed, the *Champion* reported, was the charred body of William Bidinger. He had perished in his room in the back of Berry's saloon. He was about twenty-five, and unmarried. "The funeral took place on Monday, and although no relatives followed the body to the grave, a long line of mourning citizens testified to the high estimation in which Billy Bidinger was held," the *Champion* said. The flames were first discovered issuing from the roof of a Chinese restaurant in Berry's building and, as feeling against the Chinese was more or less endemic in Western American communities at the time, the Orientals were sharply questioned. Sam Kee, owner of the restaurant, said that he and his assistants had been awakened by the fire and had fled. The *Champion* opined that if the Chinese had given the alarm at once, the fire might have been controlled; the paper also suggested that the Chinese might have started the fire deliberately, a suggestion believed by more than a few, evidence of the trauma which the conflagration had inflicted on the community.

As the townsfolk wandered about the smoking ruins early Sunday morning increasing anger was expressed against the Chinese. Finally a meeting was called and early in the afternoon twenty or thirty men went in a body to Hop Sing, acknowledged leader of the Orientals, and instructed him that all Chinese were to leave town within twenty-four hours. Most of them departed that evening on the westbound train, "leaving only two or three in town to settle up, or who owned property they wanted to dispose of. But on Tuesday several of them came back again and went to work." Another meeting was called. Some of those attending defended the Chinese and urged that they be allowed to remain, but when a vote was taken, all but three men present voted that the Chinese must go, and a committee of five was appointed to see that the decision was carried out. The paper reported:

> Some difficulty was experienced by the committee at the Ayer Lumber mill, where several Chinamen are employed as domestics. The difficulty of obtaining white help made the residents of mill town object to parting with the servants, but this hitch was arranged by the Chinamen at the

mill town being allowed to stay until female domestics could be procured to fill their places.

In the months following, the evicted Chinese drifted back to Flagstaff and reopened their restaurants and laundries. But more than a year later, on May 21, 1887, the following appeared in the *Champion* with an editor's note that it had been handed in for publication:

> FLAGSTAFF, A.T., May 5th, 1887: You are hereby commanded to get the Chinamen who reside in your houses in new town out of same inside of ten days or suffer consequences.
>
> COMMITTEE

> FLAGSTAFF, May 16, '87.—In answer to the above anonymous letter received this A.M. written by a person or persons styling themselves "Committee" on the Chinese question, I have only this to say. That if another spasmodic eviction of Chinese is to convulse Flagstaff, *let it be so,* but don't think for a moment to bulldoze me by such letters, much less to make me your servant. Every man, woman or child our government welcomes to our ports, so far as I am concerned, shall know the meaning of *Three Cheers for the Red, White and Blue.*
>
> MRS. A. S. GONZALES

Considering the stature of the men who served on the committee following the disastrous 1886 fire, it is unlikely that they would deliver an anonymous letter such as the above. So probably it was the work of someone with a grudge against the Chinese, or against Mrs. Gonzales. At any rate, Mrs. Gonzales, who was the former Mrs. Emma Treat, sounded a clear call for reason in the community at a time when not much of it was being applied to the Chinese question.

Estimates of property losses in the 1886 fire totaled about $100,000, with P. B. Brannen & Co. reporting the largest loss—$40,000—and J. R. Kilpatrick's mercantile establishment the second largest—$10,000. Only the Brannen and Kilpatrick firms carried any insurance, but coverage amounted to only $10,000 and $2,000 respectively, far less than the estimated losses.

On the day of the fire, a telegram came from Winslow stating that $300 had been contributed by the large-hearted residents of that town, that provisions and supplies had been purchased, and that the help would arrive in a car attached to the evening train. Denver also contributed generously, as did towns along the Atlantic & Pacific line and in southern Arizona. A relief committee was appointed to handle distribution. It included Messrs. P. P. Daggs, J. W. Spafford,

B. B. Bullwinkle, W. H. Ashurst and J. R. Kilpatrick. W. G. Stewart was named secretary and Henry C. Ayer treasurer. G. Hoxworth, H. Pierce and W. E. Lockwood and many others including Sam Black assisted in distributing. Ayer Lumber Company donated $500 in money but reserved the right to distribute it, and also reduced the price of lumber used in rebuilding by one-third.

Rebuilding started at once, the *Champion* reported:

> Before the smoke of the fire had passed away, preparations were being made to rebuild. The first man to do any business in new quarters was Sam Shannon, who ran up a small tent in front of the ruins of his old habitation. J. R. Kilpatrick at once commenced building at the back of his former store, a frame structure in which he will do business for the present, and when a new building is erected on the former site, this place will be used as a storehouse. Daggs Bros. & Co. are erecting two temporary buildings, one on the lot formerly occupied by J. Donahue, the other where the hotel was. The last will be opened as soon as completed, as a meat market. J. N. Berry and the irrepressible Dan Coakley arrived in town from Kingman on Tuesday. Very soon a temporary building was run up opposite Berry's old stand, and Dan was dispensing liquid consolation to the sufferers. J. F. Hawks has a temporary building completed on the site of his former restaurant, where he is furnishing meals for his boarders. Sam Shannon has also commenced to rebuild.
>
> J. R. Kilpatrick, J. N. Berry, Dan Murphy, G. Hoxworth, A. Gonzales, W. J. Hill and Prentiss & Vail, will commence to rebuild in a few days. P. B. Brannen & Co. are awaiting the examination of the ruins of their building by the insurance inspector before they decide when and where they rebuild. It will be but a short time before the destroyed portion of the town will be rebuilt and in a more substantial manner than it was before this disaster.

The big fire, Bidinger's death and the fear of the alien Chinese were not the community's only interests that week. On the same page with the report of the conflagration we learn that G. K. Miller would deliver another lecture at the schoolhouse Wednesday at 8 P.M., and his subject would be "Mind and Matter." We also read that a number of Flagstaff people went to the ball at Williams Monday evening, that the fire had cancelled plans for the proposed G.A.R. ball on Washington's birthday, that the stockmen were planning their annual meeting, and that Sheriff Mulvenon had been in town.

Winter storms hampered rebuilding, but the community's determination never faltered. A year later, the *Champion* could proudly report that the twenty buildings destroyed by the fire had been replaced by more than seventy—and some of these were built of brick. "This is a large growth for one year and starting, as it did, under such disadvantageous circumstances (almost every man in town having lost all he had) it is a wonderful resurrection from such a disaster." The fire had again underlined the necessity for better supplies of water. In May the railroad installed a pipeline from Old Town Spring to the tank near the depot, and in July the company installed a pipeline to the tank from Rogers Lake, nine miles to the southwest.

Fire struck the community again on May 11, 1886, with the destruction of five houses in Old Town. The mill whistle gave the alarm shortly before noon. High winds fanned the flames, destroying part of a barn belonging to J. H. Rumsey, an ice house belonging to the estate of J. N. Berry, a dwelling belonging to J. H. Prime, and occupied by a Mexican family; a small house belonging to Frank M. Beal, McLaughlin's residence, and an unoccupied house belonging to G. A. Woods. "All of the property was old and not of any great value" reported the *Champion* on May 14. The fire was believed to have been started by sparks from a passing railroad engine.

In May 1886, P. J. Brannen started sale of lots in the Brannen addition, in the southeast portion of the community. Ads appearing in the *Champion* showed that the town now boasted four general merchandise stores, eight saloons, four eating establishments, two banks, two barber shops, two meat markets, a shoe shop, a photography shop, a paint shop, two blacksmith and wagon shops, a laundry, a brewery, a jeweler, two contractors, a saddle shop, a drug store, a sundries shop, and a furniture store. Professional cards indicated there were four attorneys, three physicians, and two justices of the peace and notary publics.

The community's ramshackle railroad depot, consisting of a couple of old boxcars, had long been a subject of complaint and ridicule. In mid-summer a group of leading citizens met with the Atlantic & Pacific's general manager, J. H. Scott, to discuss the matter. Scott told the group that his company owned six hundred feet of land on both sides of the railroad right-of-way; that much of the business section was really on railroad land; but that his company would relinquish its rights to all land on the north side of the tracks if the squatters occupying places on the south side would enter into agreements to lease their sites for a period of three years. If this could be done, Scott said, his company was ready to build a fine new depot. Soon the *Champion* reported that all of the southside squatters had entered into lease agreements with the exception of two, and that work would get underway on the new depot, "to be the best built and largest depot on the line of road furnishing sufficient accommodation for the offices and freight departments of the Atlantic & Pacific road, the Mineral Belt and the Grand Canyon road, when the latter is completed."

As the community rebuilt, business boomed and optimism prevailed. There was talk of establishment of a bank, and soon plans were underway to get one going. Early in February 1887, the community learned that it would have not one bank, but two—the Arizona Central Bank with J. H. Hoskins as manager, and the Bank of Flagstaff, the president being W. G. Stewart. Both would open on February 19, but the Arizona Central under difficulties—its safe and fixtures had failed to arrive. Apparently the problem was not insuperable.

In March 1887, a year after the fire, the Los Angeles *Times* published a long article dealing with Flagstaff in the form of an interview with an unidentified observer. It was reprinted in the *Champion*. It reported that Flagstaff was booming because of the market for lumber, and because of the arrival of the Arizona Cattle Company with fifteen thousand cattle and the Aztec Cattle Company with thirty thousand, that there were numerous smaller outfits, all doing well, and that about a hundred thousand sheep ranged in the mountains near Flagstaff. The population of the community, including Mill Town, was estimated at one thousand. The fire of the year before was mentioned, and the community's extraordinary rebuilding efforts were praised. It said the community had three large general merchandise stores, that a school was flourishing, as were churches, and that the community had a good newspaper, the *Champion*. The tone of the article was enthusiastic about outlook for completion of the Mineral Belt Railroad to Globe, and the projected railroad from Flagstaff to Grand Canyon. The piece also mentioned the cliff dwellings (presumably Walnut Canyon), Oak Creek Canyon's trout fishing, and the climate was described as the most wonderful in the world. The article wound up with the statement that a thousand men could find ready employment around Flagstaff. Similarly complimentary but briefer remarks about Flagstaff appeared in a Phoenix paper, reprinted in the *Champion,* pointing out that the proposed Flagstaff first class hotel would accommodate "those seeking relief from the heated portions of the country."

David Babbitt, busy with his brothers in running the cow outfit, continued to scan the Flagstaff horizon for opportunity in the summer of 1887. The brothers were experienced in retail business, particularly groceries. But the grocery and general merchandise field was pretty well occupied in Flagstaff, so David opened a lumber and building material business in a small frame structure on San Francisco Street a block north of Brannen's. That corner, occupied by a large two-story building, continues to be the headquarters of Babbitt operations to this day [1976]. Brother George arrived from Cincinnati where he had been winding up the family's affairs. Neither the ranch nor the lumber yard had an opening for another man, so George found a job as bookkeeper for P. J. Brannen. G. A. Bray, successful Prescott merchant, announced on August 20 that he would open a new store on San Francisco Street with clothing, boots and shoes, hats and caps. The paper might have mentioned, but didn't, that Bray had been a member of the Boston party which visited here in early summer, 1876. Many years later he would become Flagstaff's first mayor.

On August 15, 1887, the ever-present danger of fire was again brought home to Flagstaff. What the *Champion* of August 20 described as a "dastardly attempt to burn the town" was averted by the chance discovery of flames taking hold of the back part of a Chinese restaurant owned by Sam Lee. Shortly after midnight Alfred Graham, en route home, saw the reflected light, gave the alarm, seized a bucket of water which was taken from him by R. E. Dressler, who ran to the blaze; other assistance arrived, the flames were extinguished, and evidence of deliberately spilled coal oil was found on the corner of the roof and the wall, along with a broken bottle which apparently had contained the oil.

When the townspeople learned that a deliberate attempt had been made to burn the structure, the businessmen met and offered a $500 reward for information leading to conviction of the guilty party. The Chinese again came in for the blame, at least indirectly. A committee comprised of Dr. D. J. Brannen, T. G. Norris, J. W. Francis, E. J. Gale and G. H. Tinker was named "to draw up some resolutions toward taking steps for removing the Chinamen from Flagstaff." The committee's resolution stated:

> Whereas on the morning of the 16th of August an incendiary attempt was made to destroy our town by fire and Whereas it is urged that this attempt grew out of a prejudice against the Chinese now in our town, and in fear of a repetition of the dastardly act being again attempted, and Whereas we are credibly informed that all fire insurance policies now in force will be cancelled unless measures are taken at once for the detection and removal of the cause of this attempted fire. Now therefore, be it resolved by the citizens of Flagstaff in mass meeting assembled, that in view of the facts above mentioned, we earnestly solicit and request all Chinese engaged in business in our town to close their respective places of trade and for all time hereafter abstain from all further business in our town.

A second committee, consisting of Francis, E. F. Odell and Max Salzman, informed the town's Chinese residents of the passage of this resolution, and set a deadline of September 1 for their departure. The eviction order drew a protest from the Chinese consul in San Francisco.

Almost a year later, anti-Chinese feeling surfaced again briefly in the columns of the *Champion*. On June 23, 1888, the paper published the following communication:

> Editor: Not wishing to be called a kicker, but at the same time I feel as though it is but right to express the feeling of a majority of the business men on Railroad Avenue.
>
> Within the past two weeks Chinamen have been permitted to rent and engage in business on our main street. Our citizens know that on account of the Chinese an ineffectual attempt was made last year to set fire to the town. Those of us who are so fortunate as to have insurance know that if they are permitted to remain, the insurance agency will cancel our policies. It behooves our citizens to consider this matter and if it is policy for the sake of a few dollars to jeopardize our town. Let us hear from others on the matter.
>
> Citizen and Taxpayer

However, when the community was again visited by fire only two weeks later, there was nothing in the newspaper to indicate that the presence of the Chinese had anything to do with it.

By November the Arizona Central Bank was progressing, but the Bank of Flagstaff had apparently turned up its toes. The bank's new stone building, seven lots and two wooden buildings had been sold under foreclosure of mortgage, the purchaser being Ralph H. Cameron.

In November the *Champion* again emphasized the need for water development:

> One of the most important necessities that Flagstaff requires at present is a good and ample water supply. By this we mean a system of water works. Water sufficient to supply a town with a population of 50,000 could be easily brought from the Smith Spring, by pipes, and a reservoir could be built at small cost. The water could be sold at a much lower figure than at present and a better and more ample supply obtained. There is an opportunity for some energetic man who is willing and has some spare cash to invest to realize a handsome profit on the capital invested, by bringing water into this town.

On December 24 the *Champion* noted that the new Los Angeles City Hall would be built of stone taken from a quarry two miles from Flagstaff. The issue of the paper appearing on the last day of 1887 reported that Messrs. Cameron and John H. Lind were buying the Kilpatrick store, adding that both had experience in both the stores of Brannen and Kilpatrick, and that they were "pleasant, agreeable and courteous gentlemen, and well known." The big sawmill had operated a commissary for employees from the beginning. During 1887 and 1888 it ran large ads in the *Champion* seeking to attract retail business from town.

Flagstaff was agog and aglow after reading in the January 28, 1888, *Champion* that the community might very soon have electric lights. George D. Nagle, president, and E. M. Sanford, general manager of the Jasper Electric Light Company, met with local citizens and made their proposition, and "by noon our businessmen had more than complied with their demands." Sanford left for San Francisco to buy the equipment. But three weeks later readers learned that the project had struck a snag. Sanford published a notice that the expense of lights here would be double the first estimate, "as it will require two separate plants, one an arc and the other an incandescent plant, and in order to assist in the erection of a plant, a subscription to the capital stock has been placed in the Arizona Central Bank for those who wish to subscribe for the capital stock, paid up at one dollar a share." On March 17 the *Champion* reminded the community of how fine it would be to have electric lights, and asked, "where is the company that was to erect the lights at once?"

In the late winter and early spring of 1888 a number of developments were reported in the *Champion*. Dr. J. M. Marshall, a dentist, arrived from St. Louis and opened up a practice. The paper also reminded the community of the need for a forty-room hotel, reporting that negotiations for such a facility were pending. And a couple of weeks later the community learned that the new railroad depot was progressing rapidly, "of which the *Champion* feels a right to be proud, after the long and persistent fight it had made to secure depot facilities for the people of Flagstaff." In late April J. W. Weatherford established a hack line between Flagstaff and Milton, making round trips every half hour, fare, fifteen cents each way.

The need for a reliable water supply continued to be a matter of major concern. A public meeting was scheduled for April 5 to hear plans for establishment of a stock company to improve the spring at Milton and run its water into a tank or reservoir from which pipelines would be extended through the principal street. While the matter was being considered, the community on July 2 observed an overwhelming argument in favor of the proposal—another major blaze. The Saturday, July 7, 1888, issue of the *Champion* headlined:

## OUR BIG BLAZE.

---

### Flagstaff Again Visit-
### ed by the Red
### Destroyer

---

### Railroad Avenue Business
### Houses Swept Away

---

### Cleaned Out and Busted,
### But Not Discouraged.

The good people of Flagstaff were wrapped in slumber. The streets were entirely deserted. Even in the saloons the drowsy god which holds the sleeper in tenacious delicious embrace in this matchless climate, had wooed the last lingering devotee of Bacchus to indulgence in its irresistible charms. The gray shades of dawn were just beginning to relieve the sombre sway of night, and quiet unusual to Flagstaff prevailed. Suddenly

### THE SHARP CRACK OF A PISTOL

shivered the sea of silence, and the red glare of flames laughed at the feeble attempt of dawn to dispel the shades of night. A score of men leaped to discover the cause for the shooting and the next instant as many throats swelled in unison with

### A HOARSE YELL OF "FIRE"!

This was precisely what was the matter, for a glance showed the building occupied by C. F. Taylor as a saloon to be enveloped in flames....

The fire quickly swept both eastward and westward through the row of structures fronting on what is now Santa Fe Avenue between Leroux and San Francisco, precisely the same area leveled in the fire of 1886. It did not leap San Francisco, at the corner of which stood the Brannen Mercantile building, rebuilt after the first big fire. The fire fighters managed to prevent the flames from spreading north along San Francisco and Leroux (then Gold Avenue). T. A. Riordan of the big sawmill led many of the fire fighters, and bravely stood high up on the burning Donahue building emptying buckets of water on the flames. The efforts were without avail.

Immediately following the fire, rebuilding commenced, and construction of a water distribution system along Railroad Avenue got underway. Pipe was being laid to convey water from the railroad's supply at a spring eight miles south, and the system would be under management of J. M. Simpson. Another company was laying pipe from Clark's Spring a mile north of town and was erecting a reservoir. "Flagstaff will thus be plentifully supplied with water, and more secure from fire," the *Champion* concluded. In a few weeks it was reported that Simpson was pushing the work with vim, and had a force of men running pipes from the main line into the different stores and saloons on Railroad Avenue, and "the old water barrel will soon be a thing of the past." At the end of the month Simpson published a note stating that fire plug keys could be found at Citizen's Bank, Cameron & Lind's, Bayless Bros., J. Salzman, J. Sanderson, "To be used in case of fire only." But this was only a start. It gave some protection to business establishments along the front streets. It would be many years before running water was available throughout the community.

Optimism prevailed. While Simpson was busy laying his water main up the front street, it was learned that a new bank would open on September 5. It would be known as the Citizens Bank and would temporarily occupy the building formerly used by the Bank of Flagstaff, now defunct. As soon as a new two-story stone building could be completed, on the northwest corner of Railroad and Gold, the bank would occupy it. Thus the beginning of a structure which would continue to play a part in Flagstaff for many years—the Bank Hotel building, still in use and still owned [in 1976] by descendants of the builder, T. F. McMillan, the Fleming brothers, his grandsons.

The new Citizens Bank with capital stock of $50,000 would be headed by E. S. Gosney as president; David Babbitt, vice president; and John Vories, cashier. Directors would be these three plus William Munds, H. Fulton, J. F. Daggs and C. H. Schulz. Stockholders would also include John Marshall, Dr. E. M. Schaeffer, J. Salzman, W. M. Fain, C. C. Goven, Allen Doyle, J. T. Munds, P. P. Daggs, Dr. D. J. Brannen, James A. Vail and J. W. Francis, certainly a prestigious roster.

Through the late summer and fall, 1888, rebuilding the burned-out establishments was pushed. The *Champion* reported:

> The gaps in the burned out district are fast being closed up. The store of Jim O'Neill, on the old site, is about completed, Bayless Brothers will have their barbershop ready for occupancy in a few days, Wash Henry has moved into his new Gem Saloon, and next to him is about finished a fruit store for C. A. Keller and Al Stout. The stone building of J. J. Donahue is rapidly rising, joining which, on each side, will be erected brick

buildings by D. A. Murphy and James Vail. The burned block will thus
soon be covered with better buildings than were the old ones. It is the
intention of Messrs. Murphy, Donahue and Vail to make their buildings
as near as possible fire proof.

During the summer of 1888, George Babbitt, who for the past several months
had been keeping books for P. J. Brannen, joined M. F. Jennings in a confectionery and notions store on San Francisco Street. David Babbitt's lumber yard
prospered. In late 1888 he moved the small frame structure to another lot and
started work on an impressive two-story stone building, thirty-five by seventy
feet, to accommodate his growing business. In due time this building would be
enlarged until it occupied more than a quarter of a block.

In the early months of 1889, business was good, jobs were plentiful, new
establishments were opening up or were in the planning stage, and the outlook
for Flagstaff's future was bright. In March, P. J. Brannen, the pioneer merchant,
moving to attract business in view of his many competitors, added the services of
a dressmaker. George Babbitt soon bought out his partner, Jennings, and in the
spring ordered a new marble soda fountain costing $650, "and will dispense that
cooling beverage to his many patrons during the coming hot weather." In April
the Citizens Bank which had opened its doors only seven or eight months before, announced that it was consolidating with the Arizona Central Bank because the field would not accommodate two such institutions. Deposits were
transferred to the Arizona Central. E. S. Gosney, who had been at the helm,
would wind up the bank's affairs.

A major concern of the community during the late 1880s was the lack of
property titles. After persistent effort by the town's leaders, the national Congress in the spring of 1889 enacted a measure setting aside three hundred twenty
acres for a Flagstaff townsite. The response to this was, as would be expected, a
large public meeting in June. As usual a committee was chosen to work out
details of transferring title to individuals, and again as usual the committee immediately got busy. Members included J. B. Tappan, C. H. Schulz, F. E. Foster,
J. R. Kilpatrick and Al Doyle. A survey was made under the committee's direction. Lots, blocks, and streets were designated. The committee had been asked
by the public meeting to leave a park of at least thirty acres, and also set aside
Old Town Spring "either as a wide street or small park."

To carry out the efforts aimed at clearing townsite titles, funds were needed.
T. F. McMillan, J. F. Daggs and Henry Fulton had advanced $1,300 in cash. It
was repaid by the townsite committee in due time, with a small interest pay-

ment. Active in all of these community activities were the familiar figures, the merchants, the stockmen and others. Mrs. Emma Gonzales, who was interested in property on the south side and who had protested the eviction of the Chinese following the earlier fire, sued to block the move aimed at transferring titles in the townsite. This provided some headaches, and perhaps some entertainment. But her efforts failed.

During Flagstaff's early years, milk supplies could usually be secured from a neighbor with a fresh cow. In June 1889, A. P. Gibson of Old Town started regular daily milk deliveries, assuring his customers that he would deliver only the genuine article.

Fire struck again, on June 1, 1889, when the wholesale warehouse of the Riordan Mercantile Company at Milton, the sawmill company town, was destroyed. The company had a water system, which proved its value; the blaze was prevented from spreading to the mill and many other buildings. The loss was estimated at $50,000. Only a month later, on the night of Saturday-Sunday, July 6–7, the "fiery fiend" visited the community again. The July 6 *Champion* carried a one-paragraph report under this headline:

DOUBLE BLAZE.

———

Our Town Again Visited By
the Fiery Fiend.

———

Two Fires in one Night Which Cause
The Loss of $50,000 Worth of
Property.

———

THE DEPOT IN ASHES.

The brief item stated that the alarm was given about 1 A.M. Sunday, July 7, by pistol shots. Those responding found that flames had already taken possession of two residences belonging to Messrs. Dan McGonigle and George Woods. The fire was brought under control after having done an estimated $1,200 in damage. Then at about 6 A.M. the Atlantic & Pacific Railroad depot caught fire and burned to the ground with loss estimated at $50,000. How the fire originated was not known. If one notes the dates, the question comes to mind, how did the *Champion* get a story about two early Sunday fires into its issue dated the previous day—Saturday? Probably as follows: The four-page newspaper had been printed, folded, addressed and placed in the post office sometime Saturday. Sunday morning the publisher, no doubt having spent part of the night helping fight the fires, went to his office where the still-standing four-page forms rested either on the makeup stone or on the little press. He pulled out a few inches of type from a prominent spot, set the headlines and the brief report, inserted the new type in the chosen place, re-locked the forms and then printed additional copies of the previous day's issue of the weekly paper for distribution Sunday. In his following issue, published on Saturday, July 13, having had the whole week to write a report and set it in type, he gave the details.

He tells us that the blaze started shortly after midnight in a frame building owned by G. A. Woods, caused by the carelessness of the occupants who left a lamp burning. The flames quickly spread to the buildings adjoining on both sides, one used by McGonigle as a saloon, the other the residence of Mrs. Stemmer. We are told that through the untiring efforts of the assembled citizens and the valuable assistance rendered by the Little Giant double action pump recently purchased by a few of the citizens, the flames were finally controlled.

Fires notwithstanding, however, business prospered in the growing community. Quarrying sandstone was by now an important industry and in August 1889 the Arizona Sandstone Company was paying $500 a day freight on stone shipped for construction purposes to points as distant as Omaha. In September J. M. Simpson, who had been builder and manager of the water system designed primarily to protect front street business houses from fire, sold it for $3,500 to N. Ross. In mid-fall Gruner & Dillman were putting up a two-story stone structure to house their brewery. November snow storms slowed work on the new Babbitt building and an addition to Dr. D. J. Brannen's drug store.

Then at the end of November occurred a momentous event in the history of Flagstaff and the development of Babbitts'. David Babbitt bought out the store of Cameron & Lind and announced that he would buy all goods in carload lots and give his customers the benefit. This was the entrance of Babbitts into general merchandising, a field in which they would lead northern Arizona for scores of years to come. Along with the goodwill and merchandise, David Babbitt acquired the services of Cameron's partner, John Lind, who would manage the hardware end of things for Babbitts' for thirty-eight years.

Following this important step the Babbitts quickly took an even more significant one. On the last day of 1889, Babbitt Brothers Trading Company was established. David and Charles invested $25,000 each; George $10,000 ($6,000 on a ten per cent note) and William, $5,000. A few years later they formalized their partnership agreement, spelling out responsibilities: David would be general supervisor, direct buying, and sales on credit, and no transaction of importance

The five Babbitt brothers, *left to right,* George (1860–1920), Charles J. (1865–1956), Edward (1867–1943), William (1862–1930), and David (1858–1929).

would be made without his consent. George would supervise grocery sales, keep an eye on other departments, and assist in the office. Charles would superintend the butcher business, keep records of stock slaughtered, supervise care of horses and stock, and superintend hauling and delivery. Each was to draw $100 per month. William was given no duties nor salary as his responsibilities were with the CO Bar cattle.

On February 1, 1890, Babbitt Brothers' first newspaper advertisement appeared in the *Champion:*

BABBITT BROTHERS
Flagstaff, Arizona
WHOLESALE AND RETAIL DEALERS IN
Groceries, Provisions, Boots, Shoes,
Hats, Drygoods, Notions, Glass, Hair,
Cement and Plaster of Paris
AGENTS FOR MOLINE WAGONS AND
NEW HOME SEWING MACHINES

The Babbitts would continue to add lines, including drugs, automobiles, undertaking parlor, indeed everything the community needed or wanted. (The saying was prevalent in Flagstaff in the 1930s when the writer arrived here, that Babbitts would provide everything you needed, "from the basket to the casket." Their prominence in livestock operations was recognized in another witticism: "In northern Arizona, even the sheep say, Baa-bbitts.")

Freight, mail and passenger service was halted for several days in late February 1890, when floods took out a couple of hundred of feet of track east of Winslow. The high water also took out the telegraph line. The water was so deep that it was difficult for men to get in to replace the washed-out track.

While much of the new construction in Flagstaff was of brick and stone, most of the community still consisted of wooden structures, fire protection was still makeshift and inadequate, and the "fiery fiend" continued his destructive visits. On March 28, 1890, another major blaze consumed a block of business houses. The April 3 *Champion* reported:

Fire started last Sunday morning about 4:10 in the rear of C. H. Clark's merchandise store, which part was used for the storage of coal oil. The flames soon spread and the adjoining building on the south (Sawyers hall), which was used by F. Fairchild soon caught, then G. A. Bray's store, when the flames crossed over to the opposite side of the street, and consumed the whole of it. There was very little water to be had and of course all the work that could be done was to save other buildings which were in danger. The wind was very high, but fortunately blew in the right direction, or the fire would have consumed half of the town.

The origin of the fire was certainly the work of an incendiary, as no fire could have possibly started in this locality otherwise. After and during the fire there was considerable stealing going on, and Deputy Sheriff Black, made two arrests (Mexicans) who were tried before Justice Weatherford and sentenced to 40 days each.

John G. Tinker, editor and publisher of the *Champion,* had the questionable pleasure in his issue of June 7 of reporting that his residence had been completely destroyed by fire the day before. High wind fanned the flames and made it impossible to save the contents. Loss, $1,000. On June 12, a fire in Old Town did about $2,000 damage. Consumed were J. H. Rumsey's barn, together with a fine team of horses and a calf; the blacksmith shop of Frank Rumsey with all his tools; Mrs. Steinway lost her house with all furnishings, saving only a trunk and a stove. The community's citizens loyally came to help, and managed to keep the fire from spreading further. Cause was sparks from an engine passing on the nearby tracks. While some parts of the business community had been piped for water, much of the town was still dependent on the barrel, filled regularly by B. O. Bayless, usually at the rate of fifty cents to one dollar per barrel.

The Bank Hotel was acclaimed as one of northern Arizona's most popular resorts, and the *Champion* noted on August 16 that a new cook had been engaged, and the resulting meals could not be excelled. In the same issue of the *Champion,* it was reported that a good board sidewalk had been built from town to the schoolhouse. The sawmill company furnished the lumber, the school board the nails, and a subscription was taken up to pay for the labor. The schoolhouse was located on what is now the northwest corner of Northern Arizona University campus. During the summer, too, George Babbitt completed what the newspaper described as one of the neatest as well as most convenient residences in town. This structure stood on the northeast corner of Cherry and Leroux, and was razed during 1974 to provide additional downtown parking.

Late in 1890, as business boomed and it was becoming certain that Coconino County would be established during the spring by the Territorial Legislature, Babbitt Brothers vastly expanded the size of their building, adding on both the north and west sides. Part of the second floor would become Babbitt Opera Hall, meeting place for many organizations, the scene of dances and other social affairs, and presentation of plays, both professional and amateur. Shortly after establishment of the county a considerable part of the second floor was rented for county offices. Soon the Babbitts found themselves with their first Indian trading post, Red Lake. In years to come this part of their business would grow mightily, until in due time they would operate seven such establishments.

During the spring of 1891 the businessmen of Flagstaff were concerned with two issues: Establishment of a Board of Trade which many years later would become the Chamber of Commerce, and the continued need for more adequate water supplies. The Board of Trade was organized in May, with such prestigious names involved as Attorney W. L. Van Horn, Dr. D. J. Brannen, and D. M. Riordan. This group, widely supported by the business community, would in a few years cooperate generously with Dr. Percival Lowell in founding his observatory here. In June the *Champion* again focused attention on the water matter:

> THE WATER QUESTION. What Flagstaff needs more than anything else is a good system of water works. For domestic use the present supply is not abundant but is got along with. But for irrigation or fire purposes there is no water supply, whatever. Water in abundance can be obtained by going to the San Francisco Mountains for it. It is conceded by all our citizens that Flagstaff cannot permanently prosper without an adequate supply of water. With an inexhaustible supply within our reach there is no good reason why we should not have it. . . .

In August the townsite committee let contracts for grading streets and building bridges. Successful bidder was Frank Foster, who was paid $600 for grading and bridging Railroad Avenue, $158 for Aspen Avenue, and $116 for Birch. For $200 the community had secured from the Railroad Company forty acres of land on the far south side of town for a cemetery. A part of the cost was met by the lodges. It was necessary to clear the area, and a contract was let to Messrs. Ferguson and Hart. "They are working like beavers and after they finish their work the cemetery will present a different picture. . . ." the *Champion* reported. In due time many graves, some dating from the earliest years, were moved from the old Flagstaff cemetery just north of Old Town in what is now a part of City Park. George Hochderffer said some were left, and traces of them gradually disappeared, and some of those very old graves are under the tennis courts.

Sandy Donahue, proprietor of the Senate saloon on Railroad Avenue in the approximate location of the later Commercial Hotel, won plaudits by building a gravel sidewalk from his place to the railroad depot—first sidewalk in Flagstaff other than those made of planks. Those stepping off the train and wanting to

The Bank Hotel building, which in early days provided not only hotel facilities but also accommodated the Arizona Central Bank, was a major meeting place in the late 1880s and 1890s for major social events. It was also Flagstaff terminus for the Grand Canyon stage.

keep at least their feet dry were inevitably led to Sandy's place. It must have been a good investment because a few years later Sandy rebuilt it with rock.

With establishment of Coconino County and Flagstaff as the seat in April 1891, Flagstaff could look back over a decade of growth and progress rarely if ever equalled in the Territory and this in spite of repeated major fires. Population had increased from a handful in 1880 to more than fifteen hundred. (Williams had also grown, from a settler or two in 1880 to about five hundred.) The new county, occupying an area which a decade before had only a very few hundred residents, now boasted four thousand. The 1891 assessed valuation was nearly two million dollars, and as the *Champion* pointed out, the "real value is without doubt three times this amount."

The *Champion* did some bragging on behalf of its town, and county:

> [Flagstaff] is the business center of a vast country rich in grazing, lumbering, agricultural, mining and other resources and capabilities. It is peopled by energetic, progressive Americans. It has two newspapers, a sound bank, a live Board of Trade, three building associations, a public reading room and library, four halls, nine secret societies, two militia companies, good schools, two good churches, good hotels, restaurants and lodgings, fine business blocks and residences, and refined society.
>
> It has the best [railroad] station on the A. & P., for 500 miles, and is the initial point of the Central Arizona railroad, constructed 30 miles, and to be built to Globe, Tucson, and Phoenix. . . . The products of our extensive lumber mills, located here in the center of the largest virgin pine forest in the United States, find markets all over Arizona, New Mexico and Southern California, reaching into Kansas and Mexico.
>
> Our quarries furnish forth a beautiful pink building stone of fine texture and great crushing power, and with rapidly widening markets. . . . [Flagstaff] has within its vicinity a hundred thousand acres of fine agricultural lands, producing without irrigation fine crops of all grains and vegetables. . . . The healthiest climate on earth for man and beast, and with our immense good ranges are raised cattle, horses and sheep in great numbers. . . . We export annually thousands of carloads of lumber, stone, lime, brick, cattle, horses, sheep, wool, vegetables, merchandise, etc.

The editor goes on to list some of the tourist attractions, almost as an afterthought. But in a few decades these natural wonders such as Grand Canyon, Oak Creek, and the prehistoric Cliff dwellings, would have more economic significance for Flagstaff than the sawmills, quarries and stock industry combined.

# CHAPTER X

# Molding Minds and Morals

NO SOONER HAD THE PIONEERS found a means of providing a living for themselves and families in and around the raw, new little settlement at Antelope Spring at the foot of the San Francisco Peaks than they immediately went about setting up the institutions which would educate their children, administer spiritual guidance and inspiration, and provide the amenities of formalized, organizational contact between like-minded citizens. Individuals and families of similar backgrounds, religious preferences, interests and attitudes met, talked, planned, and with surprising rapidity established the structures they needed. The school and churches came first, filling the basic requirements. Then came the lodges.

Reporting all of this was the community newspaper, which at its sometimes best was the medium of general communication, the bearer of tidings, the public billboard, the crystalizer of attitudes, the forum where individuals gained attention, recognition, sometimes reprobation; the sounder of alarms, the mirror of the community's life. It was the community newspaper that reminded the settlers from greatly varied climes that they now constituted a community—and that community was Flagstaff.

There was only a handful of school-age youngsters in Flagstaff in 1882, among them the families of Frank and Marvin Beal and J. F. Hawks. Apparently the parents prevailed on P. J. Brannen, the pioneer merchant, acting postmaster and community leader, to assist them in having a school established, the first move toward which would be to form a school district. We learn from Yavapai County records that on November 22, 1882, P. B. Brannen, P. J.'s senior partner, a long-time Prescott resident and prominent businessman, persuaded the board of supervisors to take this action. The new district was given the number 24. In October the board had approved a school district for Williams—No. 23.

Establishment of the district meant that some funds would become available to pay the expenses of running a school, and also that there would be some standards or requirements for the classroom. However, the amount of money available for new districts was so small that for years contributions were solicited to pay the teacher's salary.

We are fortunate in having a few paragraphs about the start of the Flagstaff school written on February 1, 1938, by Mrs. Eva Marshall, the first teacher. Bessie Kidd Best, Coconino County Superintendent of Schools from 1929 to 1972, asked Mrs. Marshall to write about her early days at the school:

> It was about January 10, 1883, that I began teaching in a little log house half way between "Old Town" and where the first school house was built. There was a fireplace in it and Mr. Henry Ayers [of the Ayer Lumber Company] used to send mill blocks to keep us warm. We had to keep the door open, as there was only one small window. Mr. Marshall with some help made seats and desks.
>
> The trustees were P. J. Brannen, Marvin Beal and one other. I cannot remember his name. [The files of the Arizona *Champion* indicate that by the next fall, it was W. A. Switzer.]
>
> That fall [1883] the school house was built and we dedicated it Thanksgiving evening. It is needless to say the house was packed. It was the first meeting ever held in Flagstaff.
>
> We were then a part of Yavapai County and school funds came from Prescott. Then I remember we got word there were no more funds and Mr. Ashurst [W. H. Ashurst], father of Senator Ashurst, said he would pay my salary, for a while, to keep the school going. He was anxious to have his children in school.
>
> At the time we started there were only six or seven, but soon there were more, in fact, in less than a month. I had to wait months before getting any salary.
>
> When the school house was built the citizens paid nearly all the amount. If I remember right, the county paid part.

In 1905 Miss May Hicks, student at Northern Arizona Normal School, wrote a paper on the history of the Flagstaff school. She may have gotten some of her data from Mrs. Marshall, who was still in Flagstaff, and who became Flagstaff postmaster in May 1906. Miss Hicks' paper appeared in the *Coconino Sun* on November 25, 1927. She tells us that the first school opened in a rude log hut situated in Old Town, but after a short time Mrs. Marshall refused to teach unless another location could be found, because "there was a great deal of promiscuous pistol shooting" in Old Town which interfered with class work. Mrs. Marshall does not mention this. However, Miss Hicks wrote only twenty-two years after the school first opened, and should have had access to firsthand reports. At any rate she wrote that after a month the board procured a log house on the south side of the tracks some distance from the saloons and pistol play. This cabin must have been the one that Mrs. Marshall mentions in her memoir. Her description would place it west of present-day Milton Road.

The W. A. Switzer family came to Flagstaff in September 1883, and a son, William H., fourteen years old when the move was made, told the writer in an interview in September 1961 that he, two sisters, and a brother attended that log cabin school the first fall they were here. He said the cabin was an empty tie-chopper's cabin, and that with the arrival of the Switzer children there were enough pupils to make it possible to have the school. He also recalled that it was located between Old Town and what is now the university campus.

Miss Hicks wrote that when the school first opened seats were shingle blocks and the youngsters furnished their own firewood. "At one time fuel was lacking and school closed for two days." She says there were thirteen pupils, but sometimes fewer, and that the first term closed June 30, 1883.

Families with children who attended the school in early years, and some of them in the mid- and later 1880s, were the Marvin Beals with four daughters and two sons; the Frank Beals with two daughters and a son; and the J. F. Hawks family with three daughters and three sons. Early pupils also included the son and daughter of the teacher, Eva Marshall, and husband Jim.

There were three J. Marshalls here in the early days: J. A. (Jim) Marshall, who was Justice of the Peace and also did some ranching, and whose wife was the first teacher. Their children were George and Cora. The second was John Auterson Marshall, who was also a stockman, and later became Flagstaff water superintendent. These Marshalls had two children, Charles, who was to be a Flagstaff barber for many years, and Josephine, who married Hayes Weidner. The third, J. M. Marshall, was a dentist.

The Territorial government was aware of the new little school at Flagstaff, because *The Flag* of October 25, 1883, reported that the state superintendent of public instruction had been in town looking after public school interests. On November 13, 1883, the *Champion,* then published at Peach Springs but featuring a regular column of Flagstaff news, reported that a new and roomy schoolhouse was being erected between New Town and the Ayer mill. This would be the frame structure Mrs. Marshall mentions in her memoir. At first it consisted of a single room.

The schoolhouse was erected on the light rise at the north end of the present [1976] university campus, about where the Student Personnel building stands, a structure which for many years housed NAU's Training School. Perhaps the one-room schoolhouse was located there to get the students as far as possible from the noise and violence of the town's row of saloons with their many pistol-packing (and shooting) patrons, but possibly the Ayer mill officials might have encouraged this location because of its convenience for their employees. It's probable that Ayer donated some part of the lumber used in its construction. We know also that the Brannens, who had been instrumental in having the school district established, did what they could to push the growth of the community toward the south side of the railroad. They owned land there, and later in the 1880s would sell lots in the Brannen addition, in the southeastern part of what is now known as downtown Flagstaff. It would seem that Switzer's references to his attendance in the log cabin school had to do with the term which opened in September 1883, at the time the Switzers arrived here, and up to Thanksgiving, when the new frame structure was dedicated.

On December 8, 1883, the *Champion* reported in its Flagstaff news column on the Thanksgiving evening gathering:

> The dedication of the new school house by the scholars of Mrs. Marshall's school, aided by the presence and assistance of many of the ladies and gentlemen of the place, was an enjoyable affair, as was the dance on the evening following. It is highly creditable to Flagstaff that these social gatherings are attended by such numbers of its best people—ladies and gentlemen of refinement and culture.

The last issue of the *Champion* published in 1883 gives us this glimpse of the Christmas season in the little town:

> The Christmas Festival, under the direction of Mrs. Marshall, was a successful and pleasant affair. Many young hearts were made glad by toys and presents and many of the older hearts grew young again in administering to the fancies of the young folks. Some little pleasantries were indulged in and presents were made to old as well as young. Eugene Turner received two bars of soap, &c.

The January 12, 1884, issue of the *Champion* stated that "Mrs. Marshall's school opened Monday, her fourth term in the district." According to her memoir of many years later, her first term had been in the spring of 1883—so the term beginning early in 1884 would be her third. The January 19 issue of the paper reported that attendance was thirty-five and that Territorial funds amounting to $244.41 had been apportioned for the Flagstaff school. Yavapai County's total was $6,927.45. On February 9 the community learned that Mrs. Marshall had become ill and that John Francis, a graduate of a normal school, would take her place. "Mr. Francis will make a good teacher," the *Champion* said.

The money provided by the Territorial government for the Flagstaff school ran out in early spring. On April 26, 1884, the *Champion,* now being published at Flagstaff, reported:

> The public school closes next week. The proposition to vote a special tax for the purpose of paying the indebtedness and continuing the school was voted down by the residents of the precinct. It is not probable that there will be a public school for some months to come.

But the hat was passed, and apparently the term was continued, although possibly quite abbreviated. We read that W. H. Ashurst gave $25.

In the spring of 1884, incidentally, Miss Ida Rawson opened a private school, charging $2.50 per pupil.

Flagstaff was agog when it was learned in the fall of 1884 that a warrant had been issued for arrest of J. A. Marshall* on complaint of M. S. Beal, charging him with embezzlement of school taxes for the district. Deputy Sheriff Dykes found Marshall at Holbrook, took him in custody and hailed him before Justice J. W. Spafford, who set his bond at $1,000. On November 29, a statement in the *Champion* by Thomas McMillan, M. S. Beal and W. M. Fain, explained that Marshall had been elected special assessor and collector of school tax, and had collected about $200; that he failed to turn the money over to the county treasurer within the time specified by law; that no demand was made upon him to produce the money until this time had passed; that he was asked about the matter and acknowledged that he had used the funds, and had asked a citizen of Flagstaff to lend him the money to replace it, and backed up his appeal with the threat to skip town. Marshall was acquitted by the court in Prescott, apparently after making good the shortage.

Shortly after start of the fall term in 1884, the public school trustees installed a new blackboard, four by twenty-eight feet in size. Mrs. Marshall continued her duties as teacher and taught through the spring term of 1885. In July the people of Flagstaff learned through the newspaper that under a new school law, all public monies for schools in the future would have to be raised by direct taxa-

*Husband of the teacher, Eva Marshall.

tion in the various school districts, and that there would be no Territorial appor-
tionment as before. But there would be no school tax unless the levy was approved by the taxpayers of the district. Flagstaff would for a time attempt to
finance its school by donations.

After completing the spring, 1885, term, Mrs. Marshall taught for a time at
an apparently temporary school at Mill Town.

In August the new teacher, W. L. Van Horn, applied a "much needed" coat
of paint to the building, and on September 5 the *Champion* said that the term
had opened with thirty-eight students. On December 5, 1885, Van Horn advised
that sixty days of school had been completed, that average attendance had been
thirty-five with a total enrollment of fifty-eight, that there had been seven hundred fifty-eight cases of tardiness, and that two students—Obed Frye and Eva
Ashurst—had been neither tardy nor absent for a month.

In December the newspaper reported that the attorney for the Atlantic &
Pacific had been in town and had paid the special school tax of $672 levied
against the railroad's property. "The judge spoke very kindly of our people, and
said his company was ready at all times to contribute a liberal share toward
schools along its line. This puts our school on a solid financial basis, clearing it
of debt."

On June 13, 1885, the *Champion* reported that there were a hundred and
forty-seven school-age children in the Flagstaff district. But we note that not
more than one out of three of these was in school.

In June 1885, the *Champion* recommended the following for school trustees:
George Hoxworth, W. H. Ashurst and J. F. Hawks, "all of whom have children
of school age and pay school tax and are interested in school matters." Those
elected included Hoxworth, A. A. Dutton and W. A. Switzer. Van Horn continued to teach the school apparently through the fall term of 1886. Then he
established a law practice and would continue active in that profession for
some years.

Money to run the school continued to be a problem. In February 1886, the
*Champion* expressed the view that the "only remedy for this condition is to call
a special election of the district for the purpose of assessing a tax to meet the
requirements." In the same issue the paper reported that the closing was a great
inconvenience and disappointment for the families who had moved from rural
areas to town during the winter to enroll their children in school. The trustees
launched a drive for donations to operate the school. The campaign produced
$240 plus pledges for more. The Ayer Lumber Company contributed $50 "on
condition that no attempt would be made to impose a tax," the *Champion* said.

This view of Flagstaff Public School is believed to date from 1887. If so, the man in the back row right is probably the teacher, G. Y. Crothers. Two of the women in the back row may be his assistants, Misses Flora Weatherford and Clara Coffin. Enrollment at that time was about forty, which seems to tally. Henry F. Ashurst, later United States Senator, is said to have been a pupil at the time. He would have been thirteen years of age, and may be the boy in the third row, near the center, with the doorway behind him.

G. D. Crothers became teacher on January 1, 1887, with forty pupils. The school board, the *Champion* noted, "is composed of Messrs. Hoxworth, A. P. Gibson and A. A. Dutton." Later that month the probate judge fixed the appropriation for the school at $700.40 for the current year. "The funds will be used to the best advantage, especially the odd .40 cents," the *Champion* remarked. The judge's action suggests that the district would now finance its school by a tax levy.

Early in 1887, with increased enrollment, it became necessary to partition the single schoolroom.

An interesting item in the October 1, 1887, *Champion* states that the county school superintendent, Judge O'Neill, had settled the rival claims of Miss Flora Weatherford and Miss Clara Coffin to serve as assistants to Crothers; Miss Weatherford would teach three months, to be followed by Miss Coffin for a similar period. "This seems to be an amicable settlement of the difficulty which satisfies all concerned." Miss Hicks tells us that the two gave such satisfaction that the next year Miss Weatherford became principal and Miss Coffin became her assistant.

In the spring of 1887 the school became so crowded that the trustees invited bids for a new wing, and by May 21 it was completed and ready to use. In 1888 Miss Laura Fulton opened a kindergarten, charging $15 per quarter, but it was in operation for only three months.

On August 17, 1889, the *Champion* reported that the voters of the school district would vote three days later on a proposal for a special tax to raise $6,000 for the purpose of erecting a new brick schoolhouse. The issue carried sixty-one to 6, and Van Horn was elected assessor and collector of the school tax, but the frame structure built in 1883 would serve for many more years.

In the fall of 1889, the public school principal was L. L. Kiggins, with Misses Clara Coffin and Jennie Crothers as assistants. The enrollment was eighty-eight: twenty grammar class, thirty-six primary, and thirty-two intermediate. In September a *Champion* reporter visited the school and found it "doing just fine," noting that among improvements were a number of single desks.

In November the townspeople met with Maj. J. W. Donnelly, assistant land commissioner of the Atlantic & Pacific, regarding a site for a school. He said the company would donate one block of twenty-four lots for the purpose. But he also noted there were some persons in Flagstaff who thought that the railroad was using its influence to the detriment of the town, and denied this was the case, declaring that company officials "had been throwing all their influence for the prosperity of Flagstaff." This program would be held in abeyance for a time, he added.

For the school year 1890–91, J. W. Ross was principal with Jennie Jordan as assistant. In June 1891, school census marshal W. A. Switzer reported that there were two hundred and ten children between the ages of six and eighteen in the district. For the coming term, H. Weims was named principal, Miss Charlotte Wirtz and Mrs. B. F. Olney, assistants.

Soon the community would recognize the need for additional school facilities, and Emerson High School would be erected. However, by the late 1890s high school students would be attending classes at the Normal School and Emerson would be used exclusively for grade school students.

The spiritual as well as the educational well-being of Flagstaff's citizens also received early attention. In July 1883, the Rev. Nathan L. Guthrie of Prescott was sent to Flagstaff by the Methodist Conference to see if the community was ready for a church. During his month's visit he preached the town's first sermon in the boarding house at the sawmill. In reporting back to the Conference on his Flagstaff experience, he apparently stressed the rather urgent need of the community for some uplift and the likelihood that a church would be supported, for very soon the Conference dispatched the Rev. John T. Pierce, twenty-two, who had left college in Iowa because of poor health and had come to Chino Valley north of Prescott where he preached and taught school and attempted to regain his health. The youthful minister served all communities along the Atlantic & Pacific from Holbrook to Mineral Park, then the seat of Mohave County. His headquarters were in Flagstaff. Schoolhouses were used as meeting places in other communities, with the exception of Mineral Park, where he used the courtroom.

Shortly after arriving in Flagstaff, Pierce went to the railroad land department and pointed out that he needed three lots for a parsonage and church. The railroad offered to give him two lots if he would buy one for $25. He raised the money quickly from among the "boys," which in those days meant the habitues of the saloons. He built the parsonage facing west on Leroux, where the Sprouse-Reitz store is now [1976]. Also we learn from Dr. Garland Downum of Northern Arizona University, who wrote a brief history of the Federated Community Church in 1956, that for a couple of years, Pierce and the Rev. I. M. Ashley, a Congregationalist, preached on alternate Sundays in the schoolhouse.

With Pierce's departure in 1885, the church was taken over briefly by the Rev. J. G. Eberhart. Soon the Rev. Guthrie returned for three years. We learn from Downum's history that the congregation grew rapidly, and the church was incorporated in 1886. A decision was made to build a church on the northeast corner of Leroux and West Aspen on the lots purchased by the Reverend Pierce, and the structure was completed in nine weeks. It was thirty by fifty feet, and would seat three hundred, and had a very high tower, perhaps forty feet. It was the first church building along the line of the Atlantic & Pacific in Arizona. The *Coconino Sun* of January 15, 1887, reported that "some gentlemen of the town have clubbed together and raised enough money to send for a bell to be placed in the tower of the new church." In the same issue we read that a box supper was given at the schoolhouse to aid the church. In May the bell arrived; with the swinging apparatus it weighed twelve hundred pounds, the bell alone weighing nine hundred. On May 25 it rang for the first time, to summon the congregation and friends to a supper party in celebration. It rang not only for church affairs, but also as a fire alarm.

In August 1888, Miss Laura Fulton and others joined to give a musical concert and entertainment at the church, the proceeds going toward liquidating the debt on the parsonage. On October 2, 1888, the church was formally dedicated. In November 1889, new furniture was secured and a carpet laid. There were frequent bazaars and other amusements to help defray expenses. At the conclusion of the Reverend Guthrie's pastorate, the church had forty-seven members and seventeen others were in process of becoming members.

In December 1890, the Independent Order of Good Templars organized. This group was sponsored by the Methodist Episcopal Church. Downum tells us that for some time prior to 1891, local Presbyterians met in the Masonic lodge hall over Kilpatrick's store, which was on the northeast corner of Leroux and Santa Fe. It was also reported that services were conducted in the parlor of the Bank Hotel by the Rev. James A. Menaul. The *Coconino Sun* reported on October 15, 1891, that a Presbyterian church had been organized on Easter Sunday with a membership of twenty and that others were preparing to join. On November 19, 1891, the *Sun* reported that the Presbyterians had purchased four lots for $300 from the Atlantic & Pacific, and Downum reports that the railroad company donated two others. A contract was let and work on the building was underway by early December. The paper reported that it would be twenty-six by fifty feet, with a fourteen-foot ceiling, and that the Rev. Robert Coltman, the pastor, was pushing the work and expected to have it completed in January. Coltman had been installed in October, and continued as pastor until 1893.

Many years later the Methodist and Presbyterian churches were to join as the Flagstaff Federated Church, and to this day the church alternates between ministers of the two persuasions.

In an interview in the *Coconino Sun* August 9, 1929, when Reverend Pierce and his wife returned to Flagstaff for a visit, he recalled:

I am pleased to see the attention paid to cultural life in this community. I note with interest your Teachers College, civic clubs, Museum, fine churches and schools . . . Even in the early days there was a large proportion of college-bred people and others with high moral standards, by whom the wild ways of the usual frontier town were greatly modified.

M. J. Riordan tells us in his "History of the Catholic Church in Flagstaff," published in the *Coconino Sun* in December 1930, that there is no record of when the first Roman Catholic priest visited here, but that Father LeBreton, a young French priest assigned at Prescott for a short time, was here in either 1884 or early 1885. It is not known whether or not he said Mass during his visit. Father Gubitosi, a Jesuit stationed at Prescott, came to Flagstaff in the fall of 1886, Riordan says, to secure an affidavit favorable to a non-Catholic Negro who was condemned to death at Prescott. While here, he said Mass in the home of one of the Catholic families. He returned several times that fall and the next spring, saying Mass in homes, "probably at the D. M. Riordan home and at least on one occasion at Charles Kathren's house." Riordan records:

> The first Mass in Flagstaff of which there is accurate record was said by Father Gubitosi in the residence of P. J. Brannen, at what is now the southwest corner of Cottage Avenue and Agassiz Street, the Mass being said on February 4, 1887, at the funeral of Mrs. Michael Brannen, the mother of Peter J. Brannen. The writer was present at that Mass and served it, and the burial, which was probably the first in Flagstaff conducted by a priest, was on a little hill about a quarter of a mile southwest of the site of the old brick church.

A few weeks before the Mass for Mrs. Brannen, the Catholics of Flagstaff met and prepared a letter to Right Reverend Bishop Bourgade at Tucson requesting that a parish be established, that a priest be sent, and pointing out that some assistance would be required in the construction of a church. The letter was signed by John A. Donavan, D. J. Brannen and M. J. Riordan. The Bishop replied that he did not have a priest available, but that he was going to Europe in the spring and would attempt to find one for Flagstaff, along with a gentle hint that Flagstaff must be prepared to support him: "Often in these out-of-the-way towns in Arizona, Catholics forget that the priest needs the necessaries of life. . . . This is not the case in Flagstaff for which I warmly congratulate you." He suggested that they should secure a site for a church.

In June 1887, a meeting of Flagstaff Catholics was held at the Hawks' hotel with Gen. A. A. McDonell, vice president and construction engineer of the Mineral Belt Railroad then under construction, as chairman, with Father Gubitosi as advisor and M. J. Riordan as secretary. The July 2, 1887, *Champion* reported that $1,500 had been raised, that committees had been formed, and the selection of a site would be made immediately. Dr. D. J. Brannen, F. DeC. Pitts, P. J. Brannen, George Babbitt, and a Mr. Johnson were to select the site. Moses Brannen, D. M. Riordan, McDonell and Charles Kathrens were to deal with finance, and a committee of ladies headed by Mrs. P. J. Brannen was to solicit donations. On August 27 the group met again and it was reported that P. J. Brannen had offered to donate the site. He owned much property on the south side of the tracks. The Riordans also owned property on the south side of town. It was felt that establishing the church on the site offered by Brannen would encourage settlement and growth in that area. In his history, Riordan says that the offer "was unfortunately accepted" because the town did not grow that way, but north, and in due time a new church would be built on the north side of the tracks.

While all this was going on, Father Gubitosi said Mass in the schoolhouse. Riordan tells us that whenever he came, the young people would circulate the news, then gather the necessities, providing fuel, arranging seats, setting up an altar, laying out linen "and perhaps occasionally securing a few flowers."

> It was in this schoolhouse on Sunday, January 29, 1888, that singing at Mass was first attempted. As there was a wheezy organ in one of the classrooms, it was dragged that Sunday into a strategic position, as impromptu choir was organized, by . . . Caroline Metz [who later became Mrs. T. A. Riordan] and hymns were sung during the service to the great delight of the priest and the congregation. . . . Mass was said in a private house on the two following days, January 30 and 31, 1888. Later in the year Father Gubitosi was succeeded by Father Ferrari, another Jesuit.

Under Father Gubitosi, foundations for a comparatively small church were laid in the later months of 1887. Upon Father Ferrari's arrival, he discussed the plans for the church with the local committees and a decision was made to at least double the original dimensions. In the June 9, 1888, *Champion,* we read that the building was under construction, that it would be thirty-six feet wide by sixty feet long, and the spire would be seventy-eight feet high. In August the *Champion* reported that the brick for the structure was being burned and that the walls would be going up soon. "The structure will be handsome, and worthy of the pride of Catholic residents."

Flagstaff's first churches. The Methodist Episcopal Church, top, which stood on the northeast corner of Aspen Avenue and Leroux Street, was built in 1886, the bell was installed in 1887, and the structure was formally dedicated in October 1888.

The first Roman Catholic Church was built on Ellery Street on the southside. Planning got underway for its erection in 1887 and mass was said in it for the first time at Christmas 1888; in commemoration of this it was named Nativity.

Riordan tells us that Father Ferrari did much of the work himself. "He built himself a little shed at the rear of the church where he did his own housekeeping and slept in a chair, and later oftentimes on a pew in the new church."

Mass was said in the new church for the first time at midnight on the morning of Christmas, 1888, and in commemoration of this the church was given the title of the Nativity.

Readers of the *Champion* learned on March 9, 1889, that "A new, magnificent organ is at the depot to be used at the new Catholic church." And on June 29 the paper reported:

> The new Catholic church is one of the finest temples in Arizona and is being finished up in fine style. It will have an iron ceiling, and a gallery in the front of the building. Much credit is due Father Ferrari for this elegant church as he has been untiring in his efforts and worked very hard to build the structure.

On November 16, 1889, the *Champion* announced that the bell would be christened in afternoon ceremonies. There were several speakers. Four ladies and four gentlemen would act as sponsors in the christening: Mrs. David Babbitt, Mrs. T. F. McMillan, Mrs. William Carroll, Mrs. J. Derr, P. J. Brannen, T. A. Riordan, Ed McGonigle and J. F. Hawks. It was named Star of Bethlehem. A translation of the Latin inscription: "My name is the Star of Bethlehem, with my voice clamoring amongst the stars; Glory to God in the Highest and peace to men of good will."

During 1889 Father Ferrari not only served Flagstaff but communities all along the line. He built a church at Needles, and said Mass and administered the sacraments "at section houses, boarding houses, and boarding cars." At Christmas 1889, he announced that the church was already free of debt, and that his mission here was ended. He continued until July 1890 when he returned to Albuquerque, and his place here was taken by the Rev. John J. Dolje, a young Dutch priest who had previously served at Prescott. The July 5, 1890, issue of the *Champion* reported:

> Flagstaff has been erected into an independent parish with a residing parish priest. The limits run along the line of the Atlantic & Pacific Railroad from Prescott Junction to the eastern boundary line of the Territory. The residence and office of the parish priest is to be near the church in Flagstaff, and the other points along the railroad will receive regular visits. Rev. J. Dolje has been assigned the duties of this new parish.

Two weeks later the newspaper reported that Father Dolje had arrived from Prescott, and would reside here permanently as pastor. Father Dolje purchased a house on the southeast corner of Cottage and O'Leary. There he lived with the twin brothers, Michael and Daniel Hennessy, brothers of John Hennessy, who would be a longtime resident of Flagstaff. The twins became interested in entering the priesthood and later went to Belgium for study. Michael was ordained and became pastor at Ocean Park, California, where he lived until 1926.

On June 27, 1891, the *Champion* reported that Bishop Bourgade of Tucson was on a tour of confirmation, and that he would confirm here the following Sunday. The paper, ever ready to promote the area, quoted him as saying that he had been a resident of Arizona for twenty-two years "and thinks Flagstaff and surroundings are the most beautiful and prosperous parts of the territory."

Father Dolje continued in Flagstaff until 1893. While he was visiting in Holland his place was taken by Fr. Felix Dilly. Next permanently assigned priest would be the Rev. Joseph Freri, who arrived on December 5, 1893. During Father Dolje's time, the first board of trustees was established: Dr. D. J. Brannen, David Babbitt, and M. J. Riordan.

Following soon after the founding of the first school and the first churches was the establishment of the first of Flagstaff's lodges. In the decades following the Civil War, fraternal organizations became an increasingly important part of life in the United States. Nearly every Protestant male adult was affiliated with one or another lodge and many with two or more, and there were associated groups for the women.

The lodges served several useful functions. They demanded of their members a minimal level of moral and ethical behavior, at the very least lip-service to accepted standards of honesty and deportment. They also provided social association for men of middle and working class tastes and living patterns, and they gave the card and password bearer admission to circles of like-minded fellows in other communities. Lodges are not as evident on the scene today, but many are still active and perform their functions as they have for scores of years, filling a need for many.

Probably a majority of the men who came to Flagstaff in the 1880s were members of lodges in other communities, and as they met in Flagstaff, they had means of identifying themselves and their new associates. These informal contacts between brother Masons, Odd Fellows, Knights of Pythias and others were the nuclei around which the new lodges were to form. The Railroad Brotherhoods had some ritual and social activity, and there were mentions of their presence during the early 1880s, but their ranks were closed to all but railroaders.

The first move in Flagstaff toward eventual establishment of a local lodge of Freemasons came on May 10, 1884, when a notice was published in the *Champion* calling on all Masons to gather at the schoolhouse on May 12 to discuss Masonic prospects. Some of the Masons who were here at that time and who may have attended that first discussion meeting were members of lodges in Vermont, Kansas, Kentucky, Michigan, Ohio, Iowa and elsewhere. While there were differences in the ritual and other esoterica in the various jurisdictions, which were autonomous, they had in common basic tenets and means of identification and communication.

Another organization with local units throughout the land was the Grand Army of the Republic, membership in which was limited to men who had served in the Union forces during the Civil War. Its purposes and practices were quite like those of later groups such as the American Legion, Veterans of Foreign Wars, and others. In July 1884, the community was notified through the newspaper that a meeting would be held on July 19 to organize a G.A.R. post, and those eligible would be men "who served their country against the rebellion." On July 26 the paper reported that the post had not been formed, but that twenty men had signed up, and that the unit would be called Phil Sheridan Post. During August and September details of organization were worked out. On October 4 notice was given that Ransom Post No. 67 would meet at "Vale" (Vail) Hall, the notice being signed by J. B. Smith, post commander, and J. W. Spafford, adjutant. Plans were made for a grand ball which was duly held on November 5, 1884. Many meetings were held during the winter. In May 1885, the paper commented that the post had fourteen members coming from thirteen states.

The members must have been devoted, because in February 1886, it was reported that they were building themselves a hall on what is now Santa Fe Avenue, west of the Bank Hotel, that it would be eighteen by forty feet in size, would have a cupola at the front complete with a bell to summon the members to meetings, and that the men had done all the work themselves. The post was apparently so successful that on October 16, 1886, notice was made that the Sons of Veterans had met and organized, with Robert Bell in the chair. Taking part were Jerome Ford, Harry Hoxworth, Joseph and Robert Bell, W. A. Dyer, Ev Griffin, Thomas Fry, George C. Morgan, and John Tinker. They immediately applied for a charter, the first in Arizona.

A few days later Mrs. George Hoxworth was elected president of the Women's Relief Corps, also an offshoot of the G.A.R. The Sons of Veterans named their unit Camp Grant. By December they had received a fine fife and drum, "which will be used at meetings hereafter," the *Champion* reported. The Sons and the Relief Corps both met in the G.A.R. Hall. All three organizations continued very active for years. Numerous balls were held. In August 1885, the G.A.R. draped the windows of Hoxworth's hardware store with crepe in mourning the death of Gen. U. S. Grant.

On November 8, 1884, two notices appeared together in the newspaper. One was a call for all Master Masons to meet at the office of the *Champion* on the evening of November 12 signed by J. R. Kilpatrick, a leading merchant; A. E. Fay, publisher and editor of the newspaper; and Walter J. Hill, one of the leading stockmen. The other, worded exactly the same but addressed to Odd Fellows, also bore Fay's and Hill's names, but with C. F. Kathren's name in place of Kilpatrick's. A week later the newspaper reported that a lodge of Odd Fellows would soon be established, and on January 17, 1885, readers learned that the Grand Master had issued a warrant for Flagstaff Odd Fellows to organize. Apparently the Odd Fellows failed to gain sufficient support to establish their lodge on a firm basis, because nothing further about their activity appeared in the newspaper for several years.

The Masons also apparently decided that the time was not yet ripe to seek a charter. Throughout 1885 and 1886 there was no further lodge organizational activity in the new community. Then in May 1887, announcement was made that Lodge No. 8, Knights of Pythias, was to be instituted on May 23, and that Grand Lodge officers from all over the Territory would be on hand for the occasion. The Knights of Pythias got off to a good start and would be very active in Flagstaff for many, many years. The list of charter members as published included many leading citizens [see Appendix D]. They had many business and social meetings during 1887, climaxed in the fall by a grand Thanksgiving ball in which the whole community participated.

On October 8, 1887, the community learned that Flagstaff Lodge, under dispensation, Free & Accepted Masons, was in process of organizing, and that the Rev. N. L. Guthrie, the widely popular pastor of the Methodist Episcopal Church, would be acting worshipful master. This information was reprinted in the Flagstaff newspaper from the Prescott *Journal-Miner,* indicating that Aztlan Lodge No. 1, F.&A.M., Prescott, which had started working as early as 1866 with a California charter, was sponsoring the move for a Flagstaff lodge. The Prescott lodge had gotten together in 1882 with lodges in Phoenix, Tucson, Tombstone, and Globe, and organized the Arizona Grand Lodge.

Late in January 1888, it was announced that the Masons of Flagstaff had received a dispensation and that a meeting would soon be held to organize. "There are thirteen charter members [see Appendix D] and a sufficient number of Masons in the city to form a very prosperous lodge," the newspaper reported. The lodges of which these men had been members were not necessarily in the states of their birth. Some had received the Masonic degrees in Kansas, Idaho, and elsewhere, typical Americans of their generation in that they had traveled about the country looking for opportunities. In April 1888, notice was given that the Masons would meet at least once a month at Kilpatrick's hall, on the second floor above his store. On April 21 the newspaper reported that the Masons had conferred their first Master Mason degree on April 18 on Charles C. Goven, general manager of the Arizona Cattle Company.

Also in April 1888, Flagstaff saw establishment of yet another fraternal group, the United Order of Honor, Flagstaff Lodge No. 151. In August the newspapers reported that Alex Rothenstein, who had traveled about Arizona organizing U.O.H. lodges, was in trouble for mismanaging funds. The *Champion* opined that local men who had paid charter fees, initiation fees, dues and assessments, could charge it all up to profit and loss. The group would continue activities here for a time, then vanish.

Present at Masonic Grand Lodge sessions in Prescott in November 1888, representing the Flagstaff group, were J. E. Burchard and Walter J. Hill. They returned with word that Flagstaff lodge had been formally granted a charter, No. 7. Arizona's original five lodges, listed above, which organized the Grand Lodge, had taken numbers from 1 to 5. No. 6 was granted to Holbrook, which petitioned the Grand Lodge for a charter at the November 1888 session, and having made its request a few days before Flagstaff, saw action on its petition taken up first. A month following the Masonic Grand Lodge sessions, on December 17, the Flagstaff lodge was constituted with Grand Master Morris Goldwater officiating. Exactly fifty years later, on December 17, 1939, Goldwater, eighty-six, returned to Flagstaff for the lodge's fiftieth anniversary. This is believed to be the only time in the history of Freemasonry in America that a grand master has attended the fiftieth anniversary of his own constitution of a lodge.

In May 1888, the Knights of Pythias Grand Lodge was held at Winslow, and many Flagstaff members and their ladies attended. H. W. Gibbons of Flagstaff was elected grand vice chancellor and Max Salzman, grand outer guard. Past chancellor George H. Tinker of Flagstaff moved that the next annual session be held at Flagstaff, and the group passed the proposal.

In July 1888, the newspaper reported that a lodge of the Order of the Eastern Star would be organized here, with J. G. Savage as worthy patron, Mrs. Susan R. Morse as worthy matron, and Miss Lillian Beal as secretary. (To be eligible for membership in the Star, ladies must have a husband, father, grandfather, son or other close male relative who is a member of the Masonic fraternity.)

In January 1889, the Masons gave a grand ball which was a great success, and the Knights of Pythias were busy with plans for Grand Lodge sessions scheduled for May. As the date approached, the entire community was asked to cooperate with the Knights' committee, listing homes where rooms were available for visitors, etc. The event was a smashing success, as reported by the *Champion* in its May 25, 1889, issue. H. W. Gibbons of Flagstaff was elected grand chancellor, J. W. Francis grand master at arms, and Ed Gale as grand inner guard. Events attended by people from all over the community included a concert at the skating rink by the Sixth Cavalry Band from Fort Wingate. Following meetings continuing throughout the evening, a banquet was held at midnight in the wool house. The menu included lobster, chicken, turkey, ham, tongue, strawberries, bananas, oranges, apples, malaca raisins, filberts, and three kinds of cake. Among the guests were people from every part of the community. After the three-hour banquet the Knights returned to their meeting place and spent the remainder of the night performing degree work. This was the usual pattern for such major events. The community, made up largely of comparatively young people, worked hard and played hard.

On August 17, 1889, the *Champion* reported that a lodge of Royal Arch Masons had been organized and that the group was holding its meetings in the hall of Flagstaff Masons. "They start off with every prospect of success. This makes eight different orders in our village," the paper said.

In February 1888, the *Champion* again reported that an Odd Fellows lodge might be organized. But nothing further was heard about this move for more than two years. Then, on June 14, 1890, announcement was made that an I.O.O.F. lodge had recently been organized [see Appendix D] in Flagstaff, that an election of officers would soon be held and that Grand Lodge officers would be present to constitute the new lodge. The election was held June 18. Chosen were C. R. Bayless, noble grand; J. C. Newman, vice grand; A. S. Alvord, secretary; C. H. Clark, treasurer. Elaborate plans were made for the installation and constituting ceremonies, and the lodge was given the number 11.

The ceremonies, on June 25, 1890, included installation of the officers, followed by "the usual courtesy of surrendering the chairs to the grand officers," the *Champion* reported. The names of ten applicants for membership were then read, and the lodge proceeded "to instruct them in the divine lesson of humanity." At midnight the Odd Fellows stopped work long enough to go to the Bank Hotel to partake of a sumptuous lunch "provided for the occasion by our popular townsman, T. J. Coalter, whose establishment is second to none along the Atlantic & Pacific road." Then the group returned to the Masonic hall, rented for use each Wednesday, and work continued until 3 A.M. Then, under good of the order, speeches were made, and the Odd Fellows suspended operations until the following Wednesday. The Odd Fellows continued to be very active with many meetings, pot luck dinners, initiations and balls.

Perhaps the high point in Odd Fellow activity came on June 2, 1891, when a grand ball was staged in commemoration of the seventy-second anniversary of the founding of the order. As reported on June 6, by the *Champion:*

> About nine o'clock the guests began to gather in large numbers and at 9:30 more than sixty couples entered the Grand March, which was led by Miss Ella Hawks and Phil Brannen, and when the first quadrille was called twenty-five additional couples swelled the already large crowd of merry dancers. The scene was a charming one, the elegant toilets of the young ladies adding much to the brilliancy of the affair. . . . Many handsome bouquets of flowers were worn by the ladies. It was, without doubt, the most pleasing and successful affair of the kind ever witnessed in Flagstaff. Good music was furnished by the Coconino Orchestra. . . . each and every one appearing to lay aside the duties and cares of every day life for the time being, and entirely giving themselves up to the delightful pleasure of dancing. At midnight about one hundred couples repaired to the Bank Hotel, where Mine Host Coalter served a most sumptuous repast. The dining hall was profusely decorated with [flowers].
>
> After supper they went back to the ball and continued to dance "until glimmers of dawn made their appearance. . . ."

Guests were present from nearly all northern Arizona communities.

On July 25, 1891, the *Champion* reported that a lodge of Knights Templar, a Masonic body, would probably be organized soon. On August 22, 1891, the paper reported on establishment of still another group:

> On Wednesday evening last a lodge of the Independent Order of Foresters was instituted at this place. . . . The new lodge starts out under most favorable circumstances, and with a good membership. The officers elected and installed included George Hochderffer, W. L. Van Horn, C. L. Smart, Fred Leix, William H. Switzer, B. M. Spencer, C. P. Ruffner, W. C. Phillips, Aaron George, N. G. Layton, E. S. Wilcox and W. S. Decloss.

In years to come other groups would organize, but some would fall by the wayside. Masons and Odd Fellows would continue operations without interruption up to the present [1976].

But perhaps the strongest tie binding the fledgling community of Flagstaff together, and linking it with other communities in the Territory, was the press. Moreover, the files of the *Arizona Champion* and its successors, the *Coconino Sun* and the *Arizona Daily Sun,* which have been appearing regularly for more than ninety years, constitute by far the most interesting and comprehensive source of historical data about Flagstaff. Considering the vicissitudes of many years, with fires, moves, changes of ownership, vandalism and carelessness, the files are remarkably complete. Yet at times there has been some confusion regarding the newspaper's beginnings and early growth.

From the late 1870s through 1883, the Prescott newspapers gave more or less regular coverage to the events going on around the San Francisco Peaks. During the time the railroad was being built and Flagstaff was enjoying its rip-roaring youth, reports on happenings here appeared in nearly every weekly issue of the Prescott *Miner.* P. J. Brannen, the town's first merchant, served for a time as correspondent.

The first newspaper to be published in Flagstaff was *The Flag,* which made its initial appearance on Thursday, October 25, 1883, with Harry C. Reed as editor, and Charles W. Rainhard as manager. Reed was a perennial starter of weekly newspapers: we know of at least five he launched or had to do with in a period of five years. A few weeks earlier the *Arizona Champion,* then published at Peach Springs, had noted in a column of news from Flagstaff that "Colonel Reed, of San Marciel, is putting up a building sixteen by twenty-five to be used as a printing office, from which the *Flagstaff Flag* will be published, to appear in about two weeks." Following the appearance of the initial issue of *The Flag,* the *Champion* described it as neat and newsy. "We think the *Champion* before noticed the genial editor and proprietor...Col. Harry Reed.... [*The Flag*] is as bright and pretty as a child's new copy book, and as large (nearly)." The reference was to the unusually small size, the pages being only about nine by twelve inches. No copies of the twenty-six or twenty-seven issues of *The Flag* seem to have survived with the exception of a single sheet, two pages, Vol. 1, No. 18, dated February 23, 1884, which is in the possession of the writer. Unfortunately these two surviving pages contain no local news matter, but they do contain some local ads.

There are a number of contemporary references to *The Flag,* however, and we have some data from the first issue, republished as a local feature in Flagstaff's *Coconino Sun* on September 12, 1895, stating that the *Sun* had been loaned a copy of the first *Flag* by W. H. Anderson, pioneer rancher and farmer. We are fortunate that Anderson and the *Sun* thus salvaged for us a firsthand glimpse into our community's very early history. In September 1906, Anderson took his valuable copy of *The Flag* to a meeting of the local Pioneers' Society. A minute entry states:

> The Society was presented by W. H. Anderson with a copy of the first paper published in Flagstaff, Vol. 1, October 25, 1883, name of the paper being *The Flag,* edited and published by Harry C. Reed.

In the ensuing years the Society has had its ups and downs, including long periods of inactivity, and somewhere along the line that copy of *The Flag* became misplaced or destroyed. Hopefully it may turn up someday.

The *Arizona Champion,* which was to supplant *The Flag* as the community's newspaper, was first published at Peach Springs on September 15, 1883, by Artemus E. Fay. Fay was born in New York in 1842; became clerk of the House in Pennsylvania in 1875; edited the Titusville, Pennsylvania, *Daily Courier;* was editor of the *Arizona Star* at Tucson 1877–79; established the Tombstone *Weekly Nugget* and edited it during 1879–80; played a part in producing the Dos Cabezas *Gold Note;* was married in 1882 to Amanda Hicklin of California; then moved along to Peach Springs which many folks including officials of the Atlantic & Pacific expected would become the northern Arizona metropolis.

Fay produced a four-page, full-sized paper, well printed and well written. He loyally promoted Peach Springs, but also ran news from other communities along the Atlantic & Pacific line, including Flagstaff. The Flagstaff items were frequently signed "Hal" (J. W. Spafford), an able writer and reporter who not only worked with Fay after the paper was moved to Flagstaff, but later became publisher for a short time. He was a man of many talents and interests. The *Champion* noted on November 3, 1883, that "J. W. Spafford of the Oriental Restaurant was equipping for a day or so in the mountains." A month later the paper reported that Spafford had closed the restaurant and intended to engage in other business. Spafford's interesting and colorful column of Flagstaff items in the *Champion* were usually headed, "Flavored Flagstaff Flutterings Fricasseed For Family Fare."

Fay, publisher of the *Champion,* and Reed, publisher of *The Flag,* were on the best of terms, and had complimentary and friendly things to say about each other. On December 29, 1883, the *Champion* published this good-humored note in its column of "Flagstaff Flutterings":

Colonel Reed, of *The Flag,* boarded the eastern express Monday, and has not returned. He had a dressed turkey under one arm and a suspicious looking bundle under the other. No doubt he has gone to take the role of Santa Claus in some suburban town.

More and more Flagstaff news appeared in the *Champion.* The community was growing rapidly, and the Peach Springs boom was not materializing. In the issue of January 26, 1884, Fay announced he was moving the *Champion* to Flagstaff. He had kind words for his supporters at Peach Springs, then stated:

> We go to a larger field, where there are more people and more business, which makes a large increase in our home trade, and our outside patronage will remain at least the same. . . .

Between issues he loaded his press, handset type, job printing equipment, paper stock, subscription lists, masthead, etc., on an Atlantic & Pacific freight car and moved up the line. His next weekly issue appeared on time at Flagstaff February 2, 1884. While the name of the newspaper was to change a time or two, it was to appear regularly from that time to the present. We could refer to it as the *Arizona Daily Sun's* grandfather or grandmother, because in 1891 it became the weekly *Coconino Sun,* which in 1946 gave birth to the daily. Hence today's *Arizona Daily Sun* is a continuation of the original *Arizona Champion,* by far the oldest business establishment in the community. The *Coconino Sun* still appears on Saturdays, being chiefly a vehicle for legal advertising.

The first Flagstaff issue of the *Champion* reported that the office was located over Hickerson & Vail's saloon, corner of Railroad Avenue and San Francisco Street, a site still occupied by a bar, Club 66. Fay's salutatory:

> The CHAMPION bark is launched this week from Flagstaff harbor, and let the sea be rough or smooth, the ship is well timbered and can weather any storm. For many months we have had an eye on the growth, life and permanency of the town, surrounded as it is by a rich farming country and thousands of acres of grazing and timber lands. We have watched its progress, witnessed and appreciated the enterprise of its business men, and felt no hesitancy in numbering ourselves and our press with a people who have shown by their public spirit the liberality and faith that is in them. It will be our aim to look after the local interests of this portion of Yavapai County, show to our large number of readers the opportunities open for them in this section, and to carefully chronicle all local events of interest that may occur in both town and county; aid and

assist in all public measures looking to the welfare of our people, and lend all honorable efforts that we think will result beneficially to our section of the country. In a word, we are with the people and for the people. We bring to Flagstaff a circulation along the line of the A. & P. railroad from Albuquerque to The Needles double that of any other paper published in Arizona, and we enjoy a large eastern circulation which is rapidly increasing, having the names of those who are eagerly watching the developments of our country. We do not come to Flagstaff to build up anew, but to give to our new field of labor the advantages the CHAMPION can render by its well established business. We hope to present to the people of Flagstaff a paper in which they will take pride; a mirror in which reflects the local sentiment on all questions of a public nature, and if we fail in doing so, then our most confident expectations will not be realized. Whether it be a bon voyage or not, here is our heart and hand.

With the *Arizona Champion* firmly established in Flagstaff but continuing the volume and serial numbers which started in Peach Springs on September 15, 1883—one of the sources of confusion as to the exact age and history of the paper —there came the demise of *The Flag*. On April 19, 1884, after the *Champion* had been appearing here regularly for more than two months, it reported that "Colonel Reed of the *Flag* is again on the wing." And on May 3 appeared the following:

> Our neighbor Colonel Harry Reed has hauled down his colors temporarily preparatory to planting them in another field. Our esteemed contemporary has offers of substantial support in Holbrook, which no discrete journalist in these hard times could ignore.

The same issue also stated:

> Our two leading attorneys who have been assisting Colonel Reed of the *Flag* can say pleasant things to each other. If they do not do so the wags about town do not forget it. It is said that the paper stood Van three weeks but seven days of Sanford as editor made Colonel Harry decide to move. [E. M. Sanford and W. L. Van Horn?]

Reed moved the equipment of the *Flag* to Holbrook and on May 17, 1884, the first issue of the *Holbrook Times* appeared. Reed stated: "We refer with more than ordinary pride to our first issue—the *Holbrook Times,* the successor of the weekly *Flag* which for more than six months was published at Flagstaff." On May 24, the *Champion* had this to say about Reed's new venture:

We have received the first number of the *Holbrook Times,* published at Holbrook, Apache County, by Colonel Reed, the material being the *Flag* office, lately published in Flagstaff. It is a neat four page, five column paper and dazzles the eye with its sparkling local happenings. The Colonel pays the *Champion* a handsome compliment, which we will endeavor to merit. Long live the *Times.*

It's more than probable that Fay had purchased from Reed the list of subscribers and goodwill. Evidence that Fay and Reed had made some formal arrangement when Reed left Flagstaff is contained in a piece in the *Coconino Sun* in the fall of 1895, calling attention to the fact that it was starting its thirteenth year, and that it was "the legitimate successor" of *The Flag* and the *Arizona Champion.*

The relationship between Fay and Reed continued to be friendly in the months following the *Champion's* move to Flagstaff and Reed's move to Holbrook. In the July 12, 1884, *Champion,* we read: "The genial countenance of Col. Harry Reed of the *Holbrook Times* was seen on our streets this week. . . ." On January 31, 1885, the *Times* announced that Reed had closed his connection with that paper and had assumed management of the Saint Johns *Herald.* He later ran the *Apache County Critic* at Holbrook, and then on November 3, 1888, the *Champion* reported that Reed had become editor of the San Fernando *Sun* in California.

Then the bird was on the wing again; on February 8, 1890, the *Champion* reported that "Col. Harry Reed, the man who started the first newspaper in Flagstaff, which was called *The Flag,* paid our town a visit this week for medical treatment. Colonel Reed is now postmaster at Holbrook, Apache County." Some years later the *Champion* reported that Reed had died in California at the advanced (!) age of seventy.

To return to the *Champion.* On April 19, 1884, it reported that J. W. Spafford was severing his connection with the paper, and that for the past several months he had been a constant contributor, a portion of the time filling the position of local editor. The November 8 issue advised that Spafford, justice of the peace, had opened a real estate agency. His ad appeared regularly:

J. W. SPAFFORD. Ranches ranges and mining properties. Collections made, titles examined, and properties visited and reported on, Government claims collected. A fine lot of ranches, large and small, now on hand in San Francisco Mountains, Loans negotiated, Cattle and sheep for sale. Office Gonzales Block.

But Spafford had not entirely severed his newspaper connections and inter-ests. On March 7, 1885, the *Champion* reported that editor-publisher Fay, chief clerk of the Territorial Council (Senate) was at Prescott, attending the session of the Legislature, and that Spafford was getting out the paper. On May 30, 1885, the *Champion* reported that Spafford had spent eighteen days at Grand Canyon with a photographer preparing articles for eastern newspapers. Then on September 26, 1885, we read:

> With this issue of the *Champion* we close our connection with the paper, having sold the establishment, together with the good will, to the Champion Publishing Company, J. W. Spafford, Esq., editor and man-ager. . . . A. E. Fay.

The next issue, appearing on October 3, said:

> This issue of the *Champion* appears under the control of a new man-agement, the undersigned having bought the property from Mr. A. E. Fay, who started the *Champion* about two years ago and has since man-aged it with signal success, contributing much by his journalistic ability and enterprise to the development of the interests of Flagstaff and the surrounding country. . . . J. W. Spafford.

On February 14, 1886, the disastrous fire occurred which wiped out most of the town's business section. The *Champion* office was destroyed with an esti-mated loss of $750. Among many other losses was a $1,000 building belonging to Harry Reed, no doubt the old *Flag* office. The *Champion* failed to appear on February 20, one of the few times in over ninety years that it or its successors missed an issue. The February 27 issue stated: "Although a considerable quan-tity of material was rescued from the flames, the loss from damage has been great, and a heavy expenditure will be required to place the office in working order." The report added that the newspaper publishing and job printing plant had relocated in a building it had formerly occupied, on the south side of the railroad tracks. Equipment used in such plants was comparatively light, and given the availability of plenty of willing hands, could be moved rather quickly.

Apparently, however, the loss sustained in the fire was sufficient to discour-age Spafford, because when the March 27, 1886, issue appeared, the following change in management was announced:

> The *Champion* makes its appearance this week under an entirely new proprietorship and management, the property having been bought from Mr. W. E. Lockwood, the sole owner, who had leased the press and

printing material to Mr. J. W. Spafford, the former manager. The new company will be known as the Flagstaff Publishing Company and will be under the business management and editorial charge of H. G. Temple.

A William Lockwood was an early settler and prosperous stockman, Civil War veteran and member of the local post of the G.A.R. In later years he was shot and killed from ambush near Canyon Diablo. L. T. Bargman was accused of the murder, and tried but acquitted. Perhaps Spafford, wanting to buy Fay's *Champion,* went to the well-to-do stockman to borrow the money. Spafford was around only a few months. On April 7, 1886, the Prescott *Journal-Miner* advised that "J. W. Spafford, late of the Flagstaff *Champion,* will go to Kansas about the first of the month, where he thinks of engaging in railroad construction contracting." When Spafford decided he couldn't make a go of the paper, and chose another field, Lockwood must have turned the property over to Temple. After Temple had produced only two issues, the paper announced on April 10 that it had become the property of George H. Tinker, with Temple apparently remaining as an employee. In the same issue a note appeared requesting advertisers owing money to forward it to E. E. Booth. A month after Tinker took over he was joined by his son, John, who had worked for the *Journal-Miner* at Prescott for three years. As for Fay, we read in the March 27, 1886, *Champion* that he had started a new venture in California called the *Santa Monica Wave.*

On January 1, 1887, Tinker published a lengthy special article dealing with Flagstaff, giving a historical sketch, and a review of business, industry, prospects, leading citizens and other data. The piece was revised and expanded into a booklet, and in due time sold for twenty-five cents per copy. It was titled, "A Land of Sunshine. Flagstaff and its Surroundings." It is an interesting example of promotional journalism of the 1880s. The ads are good sources of information about Flagstaff; the historical data is unreliable; but some of the other material gives us valuable information regarding the leading citizens of the community at the time. It was republished in 1969 by Tinker's grandson, Ben.

In September 1887, Tinker, who produced a fine newspaper, took several weeks' leave of absence and went East to visit his old home in Connecticut and also to attend the G.A.R. Encampment in Saint Louis, leaving the paper in the hands of Temple "who had been connected with the paper for about a year." The October 22, 1887, *Champion* said that:

> Temple . . . on Saturday night without issuing the paper, left Flagstaff stating that he would return the following day, but as he was last

seen at The Needles, and as it is known that he had about two hundred dollars in cash belonging to the office, the supposition is that he had stolen the money and left the country. Before leaving he placed all the books, including the subscription book, in the safe, of which only himself and Mr. Tinker knew the combination, which of course, will prevent copies of this issue from being mailed to subscribers living outside of town. Mr. Tinker has been telegraphed and it is hoped will have returned home before another publication day.

On October 29 the *Champion* rejoiced over Tinker's return, no doubt with the combination of the safe. On November 5 the *Champion* reprinted an item from the *Journal-Miner* stating that Temple had skipped with $400 or $500 of Tinker's funds, and Tinker added a note that to this total could be added "seven hundred more, and as near as can be ascertained after the destroying of books and papers in the office, Mrs. Tinker and children can thank God that as yet they have something to eat."

The newspapers in those days took political affiliations seriously, and very often small communities which could barely provide sustenance for one paper had two, so that both major political parties could have the "voice" they felt a need for. The *Champion* seems to have been Democratic until it became the property of Tinker in 1886, when it became Republican. So it was not surprising that a Democratic paper was established in Flagstaff about New Year's 1888. We read the following in the January 7, 1888, *Champion:*

> We are in receipt of the first issue of the *Frisco Signal,* J. C. Vining, editor and proprietor; E. E. Booth, publisher. In his exordium Mr. Vining does not anticipate a smooth voyage on the seas of journalism, and in that assertion he is perfectly correct. He informs his readers that those who do not coincide in his political views are at liberty to read other portions of the paper, where we suppose he means, politics will not be injected. On the tariff question, the *Signal* puts itself flat-footed, as an advocate for the protection of wool, and concludes by saying: "We have come to grow up with the country, and propose to make some development follow as the result of our efforts." It is a bright, seven-column paper, and typographically it presents a neat and workmanlike appearance. We welcome it to the journalistic field.

Certainly a gracious welcome to a competitor. Associated with Vining at least for a time was E. S. Clark. The *Signal* and the *Champion* did some sparring, but not of a serious nature.

On Monday, July 2, 1888, much of the business section was again destroyed by fire, and going up in smoke was the *Signal* office on the second floor of Sandy Donahue's building located about where the Commercial Hotel later stood for many years. The *Champion,* in its issue of July 7, said that the *Signal* office was "one of the best outfits in the printing line to be found in Arizona." In that same issue the *Champion* reported as follows:

> J. C. Vining, publisher of the *Frisco Signal,* states that he will resume publication in about two weeks. Flagstaff will then have two Democratic papers, as E. S. Clark has issued circulars announcing that on next Friday the *Yavapai Democrat* will make its bow to the public. While the unterrified will thus be plentifully represented, the great and only moral newspaper of northern Arizona moves smoothly onward.

In another column on July 7, 1888, the *Champion* also reported:

> In Justice Crothers' Court on Monday Herbert Steele secured judgement against Vining and Booth, as publishers of the *Frisco Signal,* for wages due plaintiff as editor of that paper. Mr. Steele came to Flagstaff from San Francisco about the first of May, taking the position of E. S. Clark, who had resigned the editorship of the *Signal.* Mr. Vining, in answering the complaint, alleged that Mr. Booth was not and never had been part owner of the Signal, but the evidence adduced showed that up to the time of the recent fire Vining & Booth were equal owners of the *Frisco Signal* and *Winslow News.*

On July 28, 1888, the *Champion* reported:

The rumor that the *Winslow News* would be removed to Flagstaff to fill the position of the burned *Frisco Signal* is probably untrue.

In the same issue appeared the following:

> The first issue of the *Yavapai Democrat* has made its appearance. The editor, equal to the task of pandering to the wishes of the great unwashed, now uses his suspenders as a belt, and when word comes that there is nothing for dinner, he tightens the belt and resumes work. There is no labor half so sweet as that rendered by love.

But on September 15, 1888, the *Champion* said:

The *Yavapai Democrat* since it absorbed the *Frisco Signal,* under the control and management of E. S. Clark, has become one of the newsiest papers in the Territory.

On November 10, 1888, the *Champion* reported that Clark had severed his connection with the *Flagstaff Democrat* and J. E. Jones of Arkansas had taken charge. On December 1, 1888, we read that Clark was now traveling agent for *Hoof and Horn* of Prescott. Jones was an attorney who came here in 1888. He served as probate judge, county attorney, and for years as superior court judge. In an interview appearing in the *Coconino Sun* on February 8, 1929, Judge Jones said, "I . . . acquired the *Flagstaff Democrat* by foreclosure of a mortgage, which others managed for me while I attended to my law practice. . . ."

George H. Tinker died on May 11, 1889, of a heart attack. His obituary said that he was a native of Norwich, Connecticut, was forty-one, and had come to Arizona in 1867. He spent thirteen years in Prescott before coming to Flagstaff. He left a wife and five children. At least one of his grown sons, John, was a newspaperman, and had worked at Prescott and in Flagstaff. Another son, Joe, became a professional baseball player and was the Tinker of the famous "Tinker to Evers to Chance" combination, known to baseball fans of earlier years. John took over management of the *Champion* upon his father's death. There were frequent appeals in the newspaper's columns for payment of bills for advertising and subscriptions; no doubt the Tinkers were having a hard time of it. To add to their troubles young Tinker and his wife became the parents of a daughter who lived only a couple of weeks.

C. M. Funston, who had been editor of the *Mohave County Miner* at Kingman, purchased the *Champion* from the Tinkers in early 1891. On April 25, 1891, the *Champion* apologized for the lack of news in the paper, stating that the proprietor, Funston, had been busy at his duties as clerk of the court in Mohave County, but would soon be back in Flagstaff and would devote his efforts to improving the paper. On May 16, the following appeared:

> Mr. John G. Tinker, who has been a resident of this town for the past five years, left on Thursday for Prescott. Mr. Tinker was accompanied by his family and goes to Prescott to accept a lucrative position on a newspaper of that place.

On May 23, 1891, coincident with the creation of Coconino County, the following item appeared in the last issue of the *Champion:*

> With this issue the old name of this paper *Arizona Champion* is dropped, and it will appear hereafter under the new heading of *The*

*Coconino Sun.* The newspaper outlook in this field, while not as good financially as it would seem, is perhaps as good as at any other county seat in the Territory. We believe that the citizens of this community will liberally support a good live newspaper, and *The Sun* will endeavor to be such. A number of improvements are in contemplation for *The Sun* and they will be made as fast as the patronage will allow. New presses, new type will be added. We ask the help of the citizens of Coconino County in making the *Coconino Sun* such a newspaper as they desire.

On August 15, 1891, the *Coconino Sun* commented:

Our enterprising contemporary, the *Flagstaff Democrat,* has entered upon its fourth year of usefulness in the field of journalism.

Apparently the *Democrat* had changed from "Yavapai" to "Flagstaff" with the establishment of the new county.

Funston quickly showed that he meant business. By early fall he had secured a new cylinder press, paper cutter, and an entire new job office, and was demonstrating that he was determined to improve the editorial and typographical qualities of his newspaper. He was also concerned about quantity—and would soon be able to claim that the *Coconino Sun* had the largest circulation of any paper ever published in Flagstaff. "Advertisers should bear this in mind," he rather pointedly remarked.

# CHAPTER XI

# Flagstaff—A Frontier Town

AS THE 1880S PROGRESSED, Flagstaff's days of violence and frequent sudden death receded, but with occasional reminders that the frontier was not yet completely tamed. As in communities across the land, life in Flagstaff revolved around home, job, business, school, church, lodge, ranch or other enterprise, but here a certain rawness was still in evidence, and only a few miles out from the edge of town was the wilderness. Flagstaff was becoming established as a community, but it was a community on the frontier.

While the people of the town busied themselves with the kinds of institutions, activities and customs they had valued in their home communities, law and order now generally prevailed in the town's few streets, but in a rough and ready form. Highwaymen occasionally robbed travelers; a man going home at a late hour, perhaps from a saloon, might lose his watch and wallet to a masked bandit; cattle rustling was endemic; Indians were still a threat to an isolated rancher or herd; many men, particularly those who worked with livestock, carried pistols strapped to their thighs, and the rifle in its leather scabbard was as much a part of a horseman's outfit as saddle, bridle or slicker.

In September 1883, only a year after the railroad reached Flagstaff, the Prescott *Courier* reported:

> In railroad building times the town was given a hard name by ruffians who frequented it; now the people are as quiet as a Sunday school class, so it is said.

It was quiet, but not that quiet. Mankind in the raw, in the varieties attracted to boom camps and lawless conditions, was still in evidence. In November 1883 the community read this strange item:

> "Blind Jim," well known along the A. & P. line, now makes this town his home. Here, too, is the grave of Stoner, the man killed over a year ago,

[ 285 ]

and for whose murder Jim was extradited from Kansas, and tried and acquitted by the court at Prescott. Jim had been in town but a few days until he got on a spree. Actuated by some impulse that would be hard to account for, he visited Stoner's grave. Placarded on the head-board, he saw his own name as that of the murderer of Stoner. Pulling up the slab, he shouldered the same, and marched into town, swearing vengeance on his enemies. The unnatural and inhuman parade ended by Jim chopping the headboard to splinters with an ax. Flagstaff is fast filling up with orderly, law-abiding and peace-loving citizens. We predict that such un-natural and disgraceful scenes must soon end.

But in the same issue of the *Champion* they learned that Spinney & McLean's new two-story hotel in New Town would open with a social hop. "A general gathering of the elite of the lumber town and vicinity is anticipated. . . ." Social activities were important. By present standards life in Flagstaff in the 1880s was hard, but the people thrived. They had great vitality, optimism and self-confidence.

The homes of the people of Flagstaff were mostly quite small, making them easier to heat with wood stoves. Most homes had a wood-burning kitchen range, and a space heater in another part of the house. Few bedrooms had a direct source of heat. As coal became available, most of it shipped from Gallup a couple of hundred miles east, some people used it, but it was comparatively expensive. Everyone could afford the wood which was so plentiful in the surrounding forest. The kitchen range usually was equipped with a reservoir attached to the side, the source of hot water, along with large vessels on the stove top.

There were no electric lights in the early years. Homes and business establishments generally depended on kerosene lamps, and there were some carbide lights. The gallon "coal oil" can with a potato stuck over the spout as a cork was a common item in the woodshed, pantry or back porch. Sometimes when wood failed to ignite easily on cold mornings, a slosh of coal oil helped. Needless to say this could result in singed eyebrows and explosions.

Breakfast was an important meal and few homes failed to provide a hearty breakfast of meat and eggs, flapjacks, homemade bread and butter, with home-made jams and jellies, plus tea or coffee, and milk. The major meal of the day was dinner, served at noon. It usually consisted of meat, usually mutton, beef or pork, but also wild game; potatoes, sometimes another vegetable or two, home-canned fruit, and pie or cake. The evening meal, "supper," was a bit lighter but by modern-day standards was still substantial.

In all homes there was a lot of hard work to be done. The mother, sometimes assisted by daughters or a hired girl, heated all of the necessary hot water on the wood-stoked kitchen range for washing clothes and dishes. If fortunate they might have a smaller stove for heating water in a laundry room or back porch or shed. The generally prevailing household work pattern in those days was to do the family washing on Monday, which meant not only heating water, but rubbing the clothes by hand on a washboard, then boiling them in a large copper vessel on top of the stove followed by two rinses in big wash tubs, then wringing them either by hand or with a simple rubber-rollered wringer attached to one of the tubs. The clothes would then be hung on lines to dry, sometimes in freezing weather. Tuesdays were generally devoted to ironing with flat irons heated on the wood-burning stove, the hand protected by a cotton or wool pad. Mending and sewing usually occupied the women's time on Wednesdays. Thursday was usually the day for shopping and visiting. The baking day was Friday, and meant the production of enough loaves of bread to supply the household for a week, plus the necessary pies, cakes and cookies. Saturday was housecleaning day and at the conclusion of that weekly chore came the heating of more water for baths for all members of the household, frequently taken in wash tubs on the kitchen floor in front of the flaming range.

Billy's Barber Shop and Baths had bathing facilities: "Everything provided for the ladies, and their patronage is especially solicited," the ad stated. Price was seventy-five cents. Men's haircuts cost thirty-five cents, shaves twenty-five cents. The early Flagstaff hotels did not have baths connected with rooms, but each room would have a wash stand. When plumbing first became available in hotels it consisted of separate bathrooms for men and women, used by all patrons. Towels and soap were placed in individual rooms.

Household ablutions took place in a wash pan which usually rested on a bench near the kitchen door, accompanied by a bucket and dipper plus a bar of soap, very probably homemade. Or the wash bowl might be chinaware, accompanied by a large, heavy chinaware pitcher and an elaborate soap dish, all resting on a stand, usually with oilcloth cover, and perhaps with a mirror on the back. Below and inside the stand would be the large chinaware slop jar or chamber pot, into which the soapy water was dumped. These chambers were also the indoor toilet, used only in emergencies or at night. The household toilet was a privy, a shed built over a pit in the back yard.

Home canning, preserving and drying was done very extensively by most housewives. Cellars would contain shelves for many jars of fruits, vegetables, relishes, etc., as well as some meats. It was a common practice to make sausage in the fall, press it into cakes, fry it well, place the cakes in fruit jars, and then pour the jars full of boiling hot fat. So prepared, meat kept indefinitely. Cellars also contained bins of potatoes and apples and other fruits, and piles of squash and other winter vegetables including turnips. Some homes of course depended on the stores and markets for many of the necessities, but most did some preserving, canning, and storing for winter.

Most homes had back yards occupied by corrals. Horses were used either as saddle animals or to pull light rigs or buggies, the only means of getting about other than walking. Some yards also had a milk cow or two, and some pigs. And there were lots of chickens, and some turkeys and geese. There were piles of manure. Only gradually over the years were sidewalks built, and these were of wooden planks. Streets were dusty in dry weather, deep with mud in rains, clotted with dirty snow and ice in the long winters.

But the people of Flagstaff did not consider themselves underprivileged, or below some statistician's poverty level. Quite otherwise. They were proud of their homes, and women took pride in their housewifery skill. They were not aware that they suffered hardships as result of lack of running water and plumbing. They were living quite as they had lived in other communities before coming to Flagstaff, and at any rate they were living in about the same style as their fellows.

Churches and fraternal groups provided some of the amenities, but this was only part of the cultural, social, and recreational activity. A glimpse at what they were doing in Flagstaff, as revealed in the columns of the newspaper, gives us a feeling of breath-taking activity—and all this on top of the heavy housework which fell to the lot of the women, and the long hours devoted by the men to their jobs or businesses. Reports of balls, hikes, excursions, picnics, hunting and fishing trips, celebrations, observances, jaunts to Walnut Canyon cliff dwellings, Oak Creek and Grand Canyon jostled for space in the paper. Crowded in among such reports were other items, reflecting the rougher side. It was still the frontier:

California Bill is one of Flagstaff's fixtures. Bill is either an old Indian fighter and deserves great credit and indulgence from his fellow citizens, or he is a great bear and should be sent to jail or a lunatic asylum. He is full of scars and wounds, received either while fighting Indians or stealing horses. As it is, he seems a cross between a knave and a fool, annoying ladies and strangers who visit the town, and in the name of decency should be suppressed.

In the fall of 1883 a town brass band was organized under tuition of Professor Watson, who was congratulated for his foresight in leading the amateur players to the distant schoolhouse for weekly practice "instead of asking the citizens to evacuate." Christmas rolled around and its observance was duly reported:

> Christmas was a bright sunny day and our citizens enjoyed themselves in an orderly quiet way. There were some visitors in town. A few windows were smashed, four rough and tumble fights, and a few hundred shots fired, but then there was nothing boisterous to speak of.

Things were quieting down by comparison with earlier times, and the *Champion* signaled the changes:

> His Honor, J. A. Marshall, and the legal talent of our town, have been busy for some days with a number of civil and criminal cases. There is more dignity in our legal proceedings than in many larger places, and the writer can remember when even in Flagstaff there was less decorum than now. It is not many years ago that court was held in a back room of Talbot's saloon. A motion to adjourn to the bar for liquid refreshments was always in order. A hung jury was made unanimous by a game of freeze out or old sledge, and his honor, the Judge, entertained visitors from afar by wrestling with Charley Haws' pet bear. It was this same judge who asked a witness as to his being positive about his evidence: "Why, you —— old fool," replied the witness, "it was as plain to me as a goat on a hillside." But these reminiscences are rendered more pleasant by the knowledge that they are past and that our present court and legal talent are in keeping with our improved condition and the size and importance of our town.

In February 1884 a meeting was held to organize a Literary Society. A report on the first regular meeting took up more than a half column in the weekly newspaper. The program included an address by Judge J. C. Hicks on the purpose of the organization, followed by Mrs. Hicks who delivered an essay on the "Conditions, Fertility and Uses of the Cork Tree." J. W. Spafford gave an address, "The Popular Cry," and the paper said it was received "in a manner flattering to the author." Then a debate was held, subject being: "Resolved, that Chinese emigration should be prohibited to the United States," with W. G. Stewart and Dr. Brannen for, and attorney H. J. Miller and E. M. Sanford against. Not surprisingly, the affirmative won. Then, with an audience still avid for more intellectual fodder, "Attorney Eugene Turner gave a short, lucid address on the same subject." Two weeks later the group gave another program, this time with *three hundred* spectators, and debated the question: "Resolved, that large corporations should not be subject to legislative restriction and control." The affirmative won again. The remainder of the evening was devoted to the performance of a one-act farce.

In June those attending the Literary Society's meeting were well rewarded. The program opened with a business session including reading of lengthy minutes of previous meetings. Entertainment, elucidation, instruction or education, whatever it was, started with a cornet duet, "worthily rendered, and it speaks highly for the progress of the band boys." Then came a "very creditable reading by Miss Carrie Crothers of a poem, 'The Deacon's Potatoes.'" Miss Belle Hoxworth followed with an original essay on "Social Signs." DeWitt C. Newell's renditions of martial airs on the flute were heartily encored. Mrs. James Marshall then read "in a voice and tone that ranks her as an excellent declaimer, Jean Ingelow's sweet poem, 'The Brides of Ingelby.'" Belle Hoxworth and J. E. McCormick sang a love ditty. Mrs. Eugene Middleton recited "The Joiners," a humorous takeoff on secret societies, which was still safe to do because none had yet been organized in Flagstaff. Paul Reidel then played a cornet solo. After these preliminaries the meeting got down to business with the debate on whether annexation of Mexico to the United States was for best interests of both. And again the affirmative won. Meetings of the society through the years followed this pattern, although with a bit more sophistication as time passed.

While the respectable citizens of the community were concerning themselves with cultural and social activities, there were still echoes of the casual violence of early days. The *Champion* reported:

> On the 23rd instant, Shadick, a sporting character, called George Phelps, a stage driver, out of a saloon and shot him, the victim dying instantly. There was a strong threat of lynching, but the prisoner was finally lodged safely in jail. A fast woman was the cause.

The newspaper expressed a view echoing the feelings of the community's respectable townsmen as relating to the cowboys who came to town on sprees and vented their feelings by promiscuous shooting:

> They are bragging, whiskey-drinking bummers who delight in six-shooters, fine horses and saddles. . . . Their aim in life seems to be to have

Flagstaff's "hanging tree" on which the bodies of nine outlaws were found hanging by their necks one morning in the mid-eighties, after a night's work by a local vigilante committee. The tree stood near the west end of Cherry Street in what is now the City Park.

a good time. . . . They delight in disconcerting the eastern tenderfoot. . . .
Nearly all die with their boots on, and no one mourns their death.

Then something happened that gave the community fodder for conversation
for months and years; the people came out of their homes one early morning to
be confronted by a grisly and horrible spectacle: the bodies of nine men hanging
by their necks at the ends of ropes on a big pine tree near the cemetery at the
west end of town. They were card sharps, holdup men, thieves and camp robbers who had plagued the community for months. The officers of the law and
the courts had been unable to deal with the problem. A vigilante committee had
identified the undesirables by its members becoming willing victims of crimes.
Then one night the committee met, rounded up the outlaws and disposed of
them without ceremony at what was referred to as a "necktie party."

For many, many years there were rumors that the committee had included a
number of very prominent and highly respectable citizens, which is quite likely.
There are no unimpeachable records as to this, of course. At that time, and in
the situations then prevailing, it was not considered particularly reprehensible
for citizens to take the law into their own hands, when properly organized, and
when more formal procedures had failed or were inadequate to deal with the
problem.

A reminder that there was still plenty of wilderness surrounding the town
came in a report in July 1885 that there were many grizzly bears about. "Mr.
Wilson was killed by one and his grave was covered with boulders to protect it
from coyotes. The bear came back and moved all the boulders and dug the earth
within a few inches of the body." The community was edified to learn about
this time that Dr. Brannen had taken from a patient in Flagstaff a tapeworm
(or two of them) measuring thirty feet in length. "The patient is doing well
and his appetite is not half as strong as before." There were other distractions
too. The editor of the *Champion* warned some of the town's boys:

> Canning dogs seems to be the pastime of some party or parties un-
> known, but boys, when you can dogs during divine services, that is draw-
> ing the funny line too close to respectability, and the next time it occurs
> we will give your names in full to show people how low you have fallen.

As far back as 1876, as we have seen, the Fourth of July was a special occasion for celebration in Flagstaff, and this remained true during the 1880s. In
1884, for instance, a major program was planned which included a parade and
readings and addresses, followed by races, games and a picnic, with a grand
pyrotechnic display in the evening.

And just before the Fourth of July in 1888, one of Flagstaff's worst fires again wiped out an entire block of front street business buildings. But to expect that this would in any way dampen plans for the big celebration "did injustice to the energy and pluck of our citizens," the *Champion* declared. "Almost before the fire had ceased to blaze, a few spirited rustlers were in the field and by Tuesday evening the original program was in shape, and handbills were distributed announcing the celebration was a 'go.'" The day's activities, including a parade, games, races with prizes totaling $1,000, and picnics, were climaxed with a grand ball.

The next year the community planned an even more elaborate celebration of the glorious Fourth, under the general direction of the Flagstaff Riding and Driving Association, which had found a large area south of the community, put in a race track and facilities for rodeo events, and had raised sufficient support to engage the United States Sixth Cavalry Band to come for the two-day event. The band concert included a grand "entree act" followed by a duet for cornet and clarinet of semiclassical nature; a violin solo; a polka featuring the cornet; medley, "Babes in the Wood"; an orchestral production, and a Mexican dance. Part Two of the program included theme with variations from "Somnambule"; an overture; a gavotte; a mandolin solo; a violin duet; aria from "The Barber of Seville"; and a closing orchestral feature. The Cavalrymen also played for the big dance. The entire community was urged through the columns of the newspaper to join the grand procession each day. The usual speeches, picnics, and other events were featured, punctuated by the popping of firecrackers and the barking of pistols.

In addition to organized entertainment, there were many informal events. In midsummer 1885 the Black brothers introduced croquet at their home and it was very popular. At the same time, seeking another outlet for energy, a move was underway to organize a baseball team. A favorite scene of recreation and entertainment was the roller skating rink, and events sometimes included all-night dances—on roller skates. Oyster suppers were widely popular; sometimes there were taffy pulls; and groups would gather to sing favorites around the accompanying piano or organ. The *Champion* observed: "After nightfall the sound of music issuing from several places of resort impress strangers with the abundance of musical talents with which this city is gifted. The piano, violin, guitar and flute have many adepts, some of them of more than ordinary skill." But it was still the frontier. In October 1885 it was reported that a lad of thirteen, John Fain, had killed a mountain lion and a wildcat, and had sent in the scalps to claim his bounties. During the same month the *Champion* reported:

Flagstaff is said to be very quiet. The truth is that an element that was of no value to the town has been steadily departing for fresh fields, and pastures new, but the solid people remain and business in the future will be more prosperous than it has been.

But in December, Flagstaff newspaper readers learned that Apaches had killed twenty-eight people in the Territory during the previous week. And then the community's quiet was disrupted:

Early Sunday morning some unhung scoundrel made a second at-tempt to blow up the Lone Star saloon of Jas. Bailey. The explosive was placed directly in front of the door and its explosion blew the doors open, shattering a portion of them into splinters about the size of a match.

Bailey's problem was that he had reduced the price of drinks at his bar, and apparently some competitor disapproved. The dynamiter was never caught.

But Flagstaff was becoming more concerned with the amenities. Box-toed shoes became the rage in late 1885, and then came the "satchel bustle." The *Champion* reported: "The rear appendage of a lady's dress is a cavity which serves all the purposes of a traveling bag, large enough to contain a nocturnal garment and toilet requisites. By wearing this improved bustle a lady can avoid the necessity of encumbering herself with any baggage when going on a short visit. Now when you see a woman making a grab for her belongings behind, don't be alarmed, there is nothing busted—she is merely going for a clean hand-kerchief or a pocket looking glass."

Improved dress was becoming increasingly important as citizens prospered and the community grew. Grand balls were staged all during the 1880s, be-coming increasingly elaborate, and providing opportunities for display. On one occasion, a ball in March 1889 which honored the inauguration of Republican President Benjamin Harrison, widely attended by couples from Winslow and Williams as well as Flagstaff, the *Champion*'s reporter devoted a full column to a description of the gowns worn by every lady attending. "The toilets of the ladies were superb and taken altogether it certainly was the finest dressed assemblage Flagstaff has ever had the honor of entertaining," he wrote. We give a sampling:

Mrs. Ralph Cameron, black silk beaded trimming; Mrs. U. Z. Curtis, cream nun's veiling and satin; Mrs. William Glendenning, black lace over black satin; Mrs. G. D. Donnelly, cream satin and wine colored velvet; Mrs. George Babbitt, pink nun's veiling; Mrs. P. J. Brannen, wine colored satin; Mrs. Jim O'Neil, black and old gold satin; Mrs. T. A. Riordan, black lace and pink satin; Mrs.

Parade forming at corner of Santa Fe Avenue and San Francisco Street is typical of such events before the advent of the automobile. Always led by a band, the marching groups would include militia and National Guard units, sometimes fraternal organizations and school classes. Fourth of July parades, such as this seems to be, would lead the way to a park area where a patriotic program would be held followed by a barbecue or picnic, then racing and rodeo events, sometimes athletic contests. Frequently such celebrations lasted two days and were always climaxed by a grand, community-wide ball. Photo *circa* 1890.

William Yaney, brown cloth and plush; Mrs. Max Salzman, black silk; Mrs. J. A. Vail, wine colored cloth and plush; Mrs. Al Doyle, black "cassimere"; Mrs. T. F. McMillan, black silk and lace; Miss Eva Ashurst, cream lace over pink satin; Miss Belle Switzer, gray cloth and blue velvet. The men's clothing was not described, but nevertheless, every man attending was listed.

The custom at all of these affairs was to open with a grand march, usually led by some prestigious citizen and his lady. Dr. D. J. Brannen officiated at some of these. Dancing then continued until midnight or more usually about 1 A.M., when the whole group decamped to the Bank Hotel dining room or other eating place for the banquet. Following is the menu for the Knights of Pythias banquet in May 1889: lobster and chicken salad; turkey, ham and tongue; olives, radishes, celery, tomatoes; strawberries and cream, bananas, oranges, apples, malacca raisins, filberts, almonds, English walnuts; orange, marble and jelly roll cake; and finally, tea and coffee. Then the group would return to the hall and dance until daylight. The Inaugural Ball and the Knights of Pythias Ball of 1889 were grand, but more or less typical of other balls held throughout the decade and like those which would be held in the following decade.

Masquerades were sometimes held. In August 1890, the ladies staged a grand ball dressed in calico dresses, and the men in flannel shirts and pants with no suspenders. Supper was spread about 1 A.M., and as usual, dancing resumed. Shortly thereafter the young men staged a return ball in the opera house, and dancing continued until about 1:30 A.M. when a violin string broke, ending the music. A few weeks later there was a fancy dress ball staged by the Flagstaff Early Hour Dancing Club.

The Flagstaff Opera House was the converted roller skating rink, and the newspaper said that it would seat six hundred, hence was the largest such establishment in the Territory. Half of the proceeds of opening night in the fall of 1887 was donated for purchase of a hook and ladder rig for the volunteer firemen.

Flagstaff was welcoming and enjoying the social graces, but it was still necessary for the *Champion* in February 1887 to remind precinct officers that they should do something about the practice of discharging firearms around the town, particularly at night. It pointed out that the law provided for up to ten days in jail and a fine of $50 for violations. "There is another subject of annoyance which needs some remedy," it added. "Flagstaff is pestered with dogs, big dogs and little dogs, yaller dogs and almost all kinds of worthless dogs and it has been stated recently, some mad dogs. . . ."

In August 1885, at mid-point in the decade, when instruments and equipment for entertainment were not as plentiful as they would become a bit later, the following note of appreciation appeared in the *Champion*:

> The thanks of the Flagstaff Social Club are due, and are hereby expressed to J. N. Berry, for the use of his piano on the occasion of their entertainment . . . The piano was presided over by Mrs. Dr. Hendricks, who discoursed sweet and well-measured music.

The significance of this item, reflecting as it does the tolerant and democratic mood prevailing in the community, is that the piano came from Berry's saloon —where it was used regularly to accompany songs which would certainly not have been on the program at a meeting of the Social Club!

Berry had been a resident since the community's beginnings. He ran a saloon, but had a very good reputation. He was generous, contributed to every worthy cause, was a good citizen and widely popular. But soon he would figure in a night of violence which struck Flagstaff with the force of an earthquake. By early 1887 the people of the community believed that the violence which had marked the early years was passed. True, there were still some pistol-happy cowboys, a few tinhorns, but the community felt that it had lived down its turbulent beginnings. Then on the early morning of Tuesday, January 18, 1887, a man was killed in a saloon brawl, and two brothers were lynched as a result. Flagstaff, which had seen many murders in bygone years, and taken them in stride, was deeply shocked. The men involved were all well known. The feeling would last for many decades.

William Lamb, a generally inoffensive cowboy, was drunk. There were a number of men watching a monte game in Berry's saloon. Lamb began singing. One of the onlookers, George Hawks, a young man with a propensity for gun play, ordered him to shut up. Lamb was infuriated. Soon he calmed down and went outside. After a time, he returned, and continued the row. Eyewitnesses said that at this point George Hawks's younger brother William handed his brother a revolver and said that if he didn't whip Lamb, he would "give it" to George. At this point Lamb was walking across the room headed toward the door. George Hawks ran up behind him and hit him two or three times over the head with the pistol.

"There was general confusion and George Hawks appeared to be making a break for the door. A young man known as the California Kid pinned his arms from behind, Hawks still holding the pistol with both hands," the *Champion* reported. The proprietor, Berry, ran from the counter and endeavored to wrest the gun from Hawks. A pistol shot was heard and Berry cried out. Everybody's attention was on the wounded man. Hawks left the saloon and was seen with his brother running down the street. Berry, shot in the stomach, lingered all day and died in great agony.

After Berry's death the two Hawks brothers, who had been under surveillance all day, were taken and locked in jail. As the building was unsafe, prisoners having frequently escaped from it, J. Y. Crothers and William West were appointed as guards. They walked about to keep warm. Between midnight and 2 A.M. they saw a crowd turning the corner and coming toward them. A rifle was leveled, and they were told to drop their guns and put up their hands, which they did. The mob entered the jail. Crothers and West later said they heard George Hawks pleading that he was not guilty and could prove it. Rapid shots were fired. The masked men came out of the building and scattered.

The guards entered the building and found the body of George Hawks dressed only in his underclothing. He had three bullet holes, one through the head, one through the center of the body and one through his right hand. William Hawks was lying fully dressed on the floor, having been shot twice, one shot having gone through his heart. A broken, burning lamp was kicked out into the street. On the floor was found a rope about forty feet long with a noose at one end. The inquest found the brothers had died from pistol wounds inflicted by unknown persons.

The Hawks brothers were sons of J. F. Hawks, one of the earliest settlers who was highly thought of, and who operated an eating house and hotel in the community almost from its beginning. The Hawks boys did not enjoy their parents' good reputations. George Hawks was notorious for carrying a pistol and fighting. In November 1883, he had a quarrel in a saloon with "Poker Bill" and pulled his pistol. The dispute being adjusted, he was returning his gun to its holster when it was accidentally discharged and wounded a bystander in the foot. In February 1884, he accidentally wounded himself dangerously with his pistol. The brother, William, was considerably younger, and perhaps comparatively inoffensive. Another brother, John, once stepped out of a Flagstaff saloon and for no reason shot a Mexican sitting in a doorway.

Berry's funeral was held Thursday, with Rev. N. L. Guthrie in charge. "In the procession were the Knights of Pythias, the Grand Army of the Republic, the Sons of Veterans, and every citizen of Flagstaff that could ride or walk to the cemetery," the *Champion* reported. The funeral for the Hawks brothers took place later in the day and was attended by a large number of citizens, "who sympathize deeply with the father, brother and sisters of the deceased boys. They were buried according to the rites of the Catholic church, M. J. Riordan officiating." The paper concluded its two-column article: "John N. Berry . . . was one of the best hearted and most liberal men to be found, and those who had been the recipients of his generosity are numbered by hundreds . . . consequently the grief at his untimely and violent death was so general that almost every house was a scene of mourning." All of the saloons in town closed up from the time of Berry's death until after the funeral Thursday. Following the shooting of Berry and lynching of the Hawks brothers, the Prescott *Journal-Miner,* on January 28, 1887, said:

> The Flagstaff lynching is a matter to be greatly deplored by our people. So far as the killing of George Hawks, the slayer of Berry, is concerned, but little regret can be expressed for he had the reputation of being a worthless character particularly desirous of killing some one, in order to become notorious . . . why his brother should have been made to suffer the extreme penalty of his crime is a matter not to be explained.

On June 25, 1887, Flagstaff learned that George Prime, J. Y. Crothers and William West had been arrested for killing the Hawks. Then K. C. Henley was also charged. A week later the paper reported that Prime and Crothers had returned from Prescott after posting bond, and that Henley and West would be freed soon, and in due time they were. Apparently nothing came of the case, for there is no reference to it in the newspapers in subsequent months.

Times were good in 1887 and the Christmas season was a good one for everybody concerned, with many entertainments, church and school programs, and other events. The stores went all out in their offerings of Christmas merchandise. Brannen Mercantile offered many items, including "Scotch bottom, button calfskin shoes" for $3.50 and had men's suits costing from $7.50 up. Brannen's drug store offered silverware, cut and decorated glass, china, peach blown ware, all in latest designs and styles, as well as albums, dressing cases, clocks, note and fancy paper. G. A. Bray took a very large ad in the newspaper to list literally hundreds of items as gift suggestions. His list included clothing, silk handkerchiefs, "gent's" nightshirts, pipes, hairbrushes, sleeve holders, slate pencils, cuspidores, chocolate pitchers, teapots, toys of all kinds including guns, picture frames, rubber dolls, mirrors, toothbrushes, "Parisian busts," teething rings, bird seed, and chamber or toilet sets. His list goes on for two full newspaper columns. Richards, the confectionery man, did a good business, too, and after the holidays reported that he had sold thirteen hundred pounds of candy, many kegs of nuts, and boxes and boxes of fruit. Sanderson's had fresh oysters, no doubt shipped from the Pacific Coast. Price, seventy-five cents per can, size not given. Some ads proposed New Year's gifts as well as or in place of Christmas gifts. As a part of the holiday festivities, the Grand Army of the Republic announced that it would give a free supper at the hall and that the whole community was invited.

As usual the New Year was welcomed in style. "The streets of our town, especially on Railroad Avenue, were well filled with men and boys and right royally did they greet the birth of the New Year, with the firing of pistols and cheers." Three years before, the newspaper said the racket was so great that nothing like it had been heard "since the palmy days of Old Town, when 'Poker Bill' and his associates held nightly revel and rejoined in ungodly glee." On New Year's Day, 1887, a Sunday, services were held at the Methodist Episcopal Church with many attending. Then on Monday, January 2, a holiday, Flagstaff folks made their customary New Year's visits. "About forty of our young men in carriages, carts and on horseback joined together and each one provided with a tin horn made the welkin ring as they passed through the streets on their way to the houses of friends." Among those making calls were the officials of the sawmill and the Mineral Belt Railroad, riding in a big carriage. Going along with them but in his own new patent vermillion dog cart was Captain Bullwinkle, superintendent of the A-1 Cattle outfit. "The only accident which occurred was the upsetting of this brilliantly colored vehicle on Railroad Avenue, spilling some of his friends who were occupants of the jaunting car, but fortunately, the only damage done was to ornament their holiday garments with a plentiful supply of dust," the paper reported. Elegant and elaborate lunches were served. For some of the teenagers an old-fashioned taffy pull was held at the Beal home. "Jim Vail says candy wasn't the only sweet thing he found there," the *Champion* noted.

During the winter and spring the many usual social events were held. Then in May plans were made for the annual community-wide Memorial Day observance, and it was marked by the elaborate planning and extensive activity which characterized all community endeavors. There seemed never to be a lack of willing hands, minds and purses. We read in the May 26, 1888, issue of the *Champion*:

> Following the beautiful example of those patriotic ladies who decked with floral offerings the graves of those heroes whose blood stained the field of Fredericksburg, the 30th day of May in each year has attained National importance as the date designated and set apart for the decoration of soldiers' graves. In conformity to this custom the people of Flagstaff among whom are many who have attained honorable distinction for

valiant services under the old flag, have arranged for the proper observance of the day held sacred to the memory of the comrads [*sic*] who have
been mustered from earthly service into the ranks of the unbroken column in grand review before the Great Commander.

On Wednesday, May 30th, with L. L. Burns as officer of the day, the
following order of exercises will be observed: memorial service at the
G.A.R. hall at 10:30 A.M. sharp. Memorial address by Henry J. Miller,
Esq. After the . . . services at the hall, the march to the cemetery will be
taken in the following order: Flagstaff Cornet Band, School Children,
Chautauqua Circle, Woman's Relief Corps. By the order of J. E.
Burchard, George Hoxworth, L. L. Burns, J. R. Lockett, J. B. Smith,
committee.

A similar program was staged the following year, and the newspaper published a report occupying four full columns, including the Honorable W. G.
Stewart's patriotic speech.

Typical of scores of money-raising events staged over the years was the Catholic Church fair, which continued for three days in October 1888. The Flagstaff
Cornet Band donated its services; as usual, there was plenty of food. And donated items were raffled off, including: a sand-painted carriage robe, an embroi-
dered plush table scarf, a hand-painted sofa pillow, a stone chamber set, a
handsome hanging lamp, a cut glass water set, a six-shooter, a mantel clock, a
silver knife, a fork and spoon, an oil painting entitled *Sunset Scene,* a panel
mirror, with a plush frame, a silver cream jug, a sugar bowl and a call bell on
stand, a hand-painted banner, an album of cabinet photos, a "tite-a-tat" set, a
colored glass counter silver stand, a mustache cup and saucer, and a handker-
chief holder. There was a contest for a gold watch between Miss Nellie Downs
of Winslow and Miss Ella Hawks of Flagstaff. Miss Downs won. The paper
does not say what the contest was. Ralph Cameron, who more than thirty years
later would be a United States Senator, won a gold-headed cane from T. A.
Riordan. That contest was not explained, either. Exhibited and sold was elaborate needlework. There were various money-raising features including the selling of space to write signatures in chance books. The event was generously
supported by Protestants and Catholics alike and the Catholics were publicly
congratulated by the *Champion* for the "good harmonious spirit shown, even in
the spirited contest for that doll, which was won by Miss Grace. We hope to
have more entertainments of this kind in the near future."

But it was still the wild and woolly West in spite of social graces, as Flagstaff learned in March 1889, when it read that an Atlantic & Pacific train had been held up at Canyon Diablo, between Flagstaff and Winslow. The train had stopped at the station. Robbers with six-shooters covered the engineer. They took between $700 and $800 from the express car, overlooking the safe which contained between $125,000 and $150,000. After leaving the express car one of the bandits returned, told the express messenger that he had left his gun in the car and would like to get it. "He stepped gaily into the compartment, secured the weapon, lifted his hat politely and bowed good night to the astonished messenger, who is even yet wondering what ailed him that he did not shoot the robber." Deputy Sheriff James Black, E. A. St. Clair and John Francis of Flagstaff left in pursuit as soon as word of the holdup came over the telegraph wires. Others were also on the trail from Winslow and Holbrook. In April the train robbers were captured near Beaver, Utah, by Yavapai County Sheriff Bucky O'Neill.

The community's Chinese residents, who had been blamed for the devastating fires during earlier years of the decade, found another way of making the news in August 1889, when the *Champion* reported:

> On Sunday night our peace officers made a successful raid on a hop joint kept by some Chinamen in the washhouse known as Hop Sing's, capturing three Chinamen and one white man. They were tried before Justice Weatherford who assessed two of the Celestials $25 and $60 respectively. The others were discharged.

On September 28, 1889, the following appeared:

> NOTICE. All boys, that have been in the habit of throwing stones and clubs at Chinamen, will take notice that hereafter they will be promptly arrested for any unnecessary assault upon Chinamen. James L. Black, Deputy-Sheriff.

We wonder how Deputy Black would discriminate between a "necessary" and an "unnecessary" assault?

The newspaper reported on August 31, 1889, that "Our Chinese colony celebrated in a quiet way their festival of the dead last week, in memory of those of their countrymen who have entered the realm of the pagan deities." And we note in the November 22, 1890, issue that "The Chinamen save a good deal of money in Flagstaff by going along the railroad track with a gunnysack or a basket and picking up chunks of coal that drop from the engine, going along the road. They manage to get enough fuel in this way to keep their washing establishments going." In February 1891, a note appeared, listing Sam Kee and Sing Gee as among businessmen supporting the Methodist Ladies in their public jubilee. While prejudice against the Chinese was still strong, it was moderating.

In the town's earliest years, particularly in the Old Town days, the house-holder went to the stores principally to obtain staples, such as flour, baking powder, tea, coffee, sugar, salt, spices, etc. But as time passed, and as demand and ability to purchase grew, more and more merchandise was added to fill the needs of the people. In 1885, J. Sanderson advertised that he had butter, eggs, also fresh vegetables and fruits in season from both California and the East, and that goods were arriving daily. Marshall and Mehlenpah's meat market re-minded the people of Flagstaff that they stocked mutton, pork, beef, and all kinds of sausage, and wild game in season.

In Flagstaff's early day grocery stores, or more usually, grocery departments in general merchandise establishments, most items came in bulk. Tea and coffee could be purchased in packages, but most people bought tea out of a bin, by the pound, and purchased roasted coffee beans to take home and grind fresh as need arose, but most stores had coffee mills and ground the customer's preferred blend of roasted beans on demand. Cheese came in huge wheels, which were covered with hinged screens. Clerks used to pride themselves on being able to cut off exactly the amount of cheese the customer ordered, a half pound, pound or more. Cookies and crackers came in bulk. Pickles and sauerkraut came in kegs and barrels, and orders were ladled out as required. Plug chewing tobacco was much in evidence. There were no, or very few, cigarettes, but there was a lot of pipe tobacco and cigars. Dipping snuff was popular with men whose work kept their hands too occupied to handle a cigar or pipe. Many cowboys chewed tobacco. All public places and many homes provided cuspidors, or at the least, a wooden box filled with sawdust for spitting purposes.

By September 1889, Flagstaff was consuming two beeves and from four to five sheep daily, as indicated by sales at the meat markets, in addition to plenti-ful wild game. But the true figure for meat consumption was undoubtedly much higher than indicated, because many people purchased quarters, halves and sometimes whole beeves in the fall for their own use, and also did the same with mutton. Meat could be kept in the colder months for a very long time in cool, ventilated places.

In September 1889, Wash Henry and a party of friends returned from a trip to Oak Creek Canyon with four hundred trout and many pigeons. With such catches, it was no wonder that the editor of the *Champion* pointed out a bit later that Oak Creek should be stocked regularly to alleviate the shortage of fish in the markets, stating that "There is no doubt that the culture of fish in that never-failing stream would be successful." While fresh ocean fish was frequently in the markets, it was not always available. Brannen Mercantile advertised in 1887 that it had California flour for $4 per hundred pounds; potatoes, $1.75; oats, $1.60, an important item when everybody had horses; and corn, $2.15.

In January 1887 a notice in the paper stated that the popular chop house, Coalter and Gale's, would be open day and night, with fresh oysters and lunches served in first-class style. Their bill of fare for a Sunday appears in their ad: chicken soup, baked trout, boiled meats, chicken and cream sauce; entrees were stewed duck, lamb fricassee, roast turkey, complete with the fixings; vegetables included corn, peas and potatoes, and for dessert, lemon or plum pie. In October 1887, the community was advised that a Mr. Richards was preparing to make ice cream and that he had the reputation of making the best of that confection in Kansas City. In the spring of 1889 readers learned that they could go to George Babbitt's for a nice cool drink of soda. Fresh lunch tongue was offered at Fisher's.

An organization which was quite busy during 1888 and for a time thereafter was the Chautauqua Literary and Scientific Circle, another of the Methodist Episcopal Church's many activities. Some distinguished citizens were involved. Old minute books indicate that it had as many as seventy-three members. After disbanding in the fall of 1888, it reorganized and adopted a new name, The Flagstaff Musical and Literary Association. Its program typically included songs, declamations, debates, essays, and additional musical numbers. In March 1889 the debate was, "Resolved: that the teachings of Robert Ingersoll are injurious to the best interests of the United States." The paper didn't say, but it's probable that it was found by this church group that Ingersoll's agnostic teachings were indeed injurious! Sometimes a lecturer would be secured.

Meetings of the Library Association were frequent, with D. M. Riordan as the spark. The formal organization included him as president; D. J. Brannen, vice-president; W. L. Van Horn, secretary, and A. P. Gibson, librarian. It supplanted an even older library group. Riordan alone contributed more than six hundred volumes, "and among them are several which are worth their weight in gold." J. H. Hoskins and Van Horn were to draft rules for the reading room, and D. J. Brannen and W. A. Switzer were named as a committee on periodicals. The reading room was open to all, was well lighted, airy and pleasant as well as comfortably furnished, and was temporarily located in the front room of the Methodist Episcopal Church parsonage. Those who would comply with the rules could check out books to take home. Soon the formal organization in-

A Women's Christian Temperance Union picnic, held in 1890, was largely attended, and among those present were two of the town's major saloon keepers, J. J. (Sandy) Donahue, center, front row, with the long watch chain, and James Vail, upper far right. The future United States Senator, Henry F. Ashurst, appears left of center, immediately behind Donahue.

cluded G. A. Bray, George Babbitt, Prof. L. L. Kiggins, and the Rev. J. H. Gill, as well as J. M. Simpson, J. F. Daggs, P. G. Cornish, T. J. Coalter, T. F. Mc-Millan, David Mitchell and A. A. Dutton.

In addition to the town's other organizations, a Women's Christian Temperance Union group was also established.

Baseball teams were formed and games were played between Flagstaff and Milton. National Guard and militia groups were also popular, with uniforms, marksmanship training, and many social activities.

For a time the gay blades of the community were regaled by shaking dice for the cider, and then calling the turn by making a final shake for the oysters for the crowd. About that same time public notice was given that parties desiring to marry must now take out a license, because the legislature had passed an act to that effect. And on top of countless other social and recreation activities, Flagstaff got the checkers craze and nearly every store in town, according to the newspaper, kept an outfit ready for the accommodation of customers.

The tourist business was increasing. Early in 1890 a stage line to Grand Canyon was launched, its Flagstaff terminus being the Bank Hotel, and Flagstaffians sometimes did some touring of their own. When they lacked for more than a few weeks a major recreational event, such as a ball, the people went by train to Winslow or Williams and sometimes even farther to take part in festivities. At times groups such as the Winslow Amateur Dramatic Club would come to Flagstaff and stage their productions.

Times were changing. The frontier was receding further and further, and there were only occasional reminders of earlier, more dangerous, more exciting times. In August 1889 Flagstaff oldsters were touched when they saw going by on the old Beale road a "Prairie schooner" of immigrants, and "a band of Supai Indians in their fantastic dress of many colors."

In November 1889 Babbitt Brothers completed their new two-story building, and to celebrate a dance was given on the second floor, "attended by all of Flagstaff's society people, who say they had a good time. . . . There was another dance at 'Dad' Hawks's, which was equally enjoyable." Perhaps bored with the customary balls and masquerades, The Early Hour Dancing Club of Flagstaff arranged in early 1891 to stage a "grand Rag and Picnic party" to commemorate Washington's Birthday. Just what Washington had to do with the event is difficult to understand, other than to provide a convenient date for the entertainment. Costumes were to be constructed after comical designs, "for example gunnysacks, tacking, and dry goods of all designs and colors, etc. The ladies and gentlemen of the club will all furnish picnic lunch for the occasion. Nonmembers of the club are invited to do the same. Winslow and Williams are cordially invited to attend. A grand programme of dances will be furnished by N. D. Flores who as a ballroom conductor stands peerless in Arizona."

Important events in the life of the small community were the daily arrival of trains from east and west. Those with little else to do would be on hand as the trains came in, to enjoy the momentary excitement of the locomotive puffing up to the station and see who got off and on. The trains were the community's chief, nearly only, link with the outside world, and so matters relating to train travel and mishaps were interesting news. An amusing item appeared in the *Champion* in January 1889:

> Two trains ran into each other west of here a few miles on Wednesday. The two engines were badly smashed, but outside of that, there was nothing serious.

The evening train from the west failed to arrive on time at 9 o'clock on December 8, 1888, and word soon came over the telegraph that the engine and five coaches had gone over a one-hundred-foot embankment about forty-five miles west of Flagstaff. The engineer lost his brakes, the train went thundering along the track at a wild speed and ditched. Engineer and fireman were cut and scalded seriously. Others were injured. A relief engine was sent out, freight cars were substituted for those in the ditch, the track was repaired and the train resumed its journey.

In August 1889 the editor waxed irritable with the employees of the Atlantic & Pacific, for negligently running their trains too fast and not whistling when going around sharp corners, hence many animals were being killed. Thirteen were killed between Flagstaff and a point two miles west, and a similar number to the east. The community also learned in March 1890 that a locomotive ran a long distance a few days before without a smokestack, a barrel being substituted. A few months earlier an engine went through an open switch in Flagstaff, left the tracks, and off the edge of the bridge into Rio de Flag. "It was a narrow escape for the engineer, who stuck to the engine until she went down. The fireman had already jumped off. The engineer was scalded a little." A large crew spent two days getting the engine out of the ditch and back on the tracks. Damage to the locomotive was estimated at between $2,500 and $3,000.

By September 1889, the newspaper was able to report that Flagstaff was one of the few towns in Arizona which had made steady progress in the previous five years. "In that time it has more than thribbled [*sic*] its population and now presents the appearance of a prosperous little city." Flagstaff had gained a sense of identity and permanency. Those discouraged by the frequent fires had long since moved down the line. The challenge and the difficulties which the community offered in the 1880s had attracted precisely the type of man and woman the situation called for.

Professional entertainers of many kinds now began showing up in Flagstaff; some were simply exploiters of credulity, like the phrenologist who collected fees for feeling bumps on the heads of the townspeople and then predicting their fortunes along with a rundown of qualities of character. In September 1890, the *Champion* reported that the largest crowd ever to assemble in Flagstaff had attended a performance of McCabe and Young's Minstrels at Wood Hall, the gate being about $400. At perhaps twenty-five or thirty-five cents a head, this represented a lot of people.

A popular and frequent visitor in Flagstaff in 1889–90 and thereafter was G. Wharton James, author and lecturer. He gave illustrated travelogues and lectured on such subjects as "Memory and Its Culture," "Wit and Humor" and "A Geographical Description of the Grand Canyon of the Colorado." His Flagstaff sessions were held at the Methodist Episcopal Church, and admission charge was usually thirty-five cents. His lectures were well attended. In 1890, after a number of visits to Grand Canyon, finding that lectures on that subject were welcomed in the communities where he visited, he wrote a small book on the Canyon, contributing his writing skill and asking the people of Flagstaff to pay for publishing it, which they did. "We deem this a move in the right direction for the future of our town and are certainly fortunate in having so able a gentleman write us up," the *Champion* opined in August 1890. The community not only understood the benefits that would accrue to Flagstaff from increased tourist travel to Grand Canyon, but also genuinely liked James' lectures.

Many important figures in the world of science, literature, the theater, music and government visited the community over the years, usually en route to Grand Canyon. Inevitably some of them had contacts with local people, and this tended to generate a climate of appreciation and understanding of the larger world beyond the confines of the mountain community.

In March 1888 Prof. Victor Mindeleff, chief of the ethnological section of the Smithsonian Institution, was a guest of the D. M. Riordans. Another distinguished scientist who visited Flagstaff on occasion, also a guest of the D. M. Riordans, was Maj. J. Wesley Powell, the one-armed Civil War veteran, who was instrumental in establishing a number of important national scientific and research agencies. He was also famous for his daring explorations of Grand Canyon by boat. Because of his association with the local community and because of the part he played in making the Canyon known, the lake formed by construction of Glen Canyon Dam on the Colorado River in the 1950s was named in his honor, a move sparked by the *Arizona Daily Sun*. In June 1888, Charles A. Garlich, working with the ethnologist, Frank Cushing, visited Flagstaff with a party, and in September one of the first of many botanists who would be attracted to the high plateau country appeared in Flagstaff:

> Charles S. Sheldon, professor of natural science in the Missouri State Normal School, assiduously devoted himself during two days to the study and botanical analysis of the plants in the vicinity of Flagstaff. He was amazed at the variety of wild flowers that grew in profusion. Many of them he was unable to classify properly, as their species were unknown to him, and altogether they formed the most interesting collection he had ever made. Not less than sixty specimens were gathered, and yet the plants were not exhausted in their astonishing variety.

The famed biologist C. Hart Merriam spent considerably more time in the San Francisco Peaks area in the late 1880s, and from his researches here would evolve his productive "life zone" theory. Visits by these and other scientific and academic personages played a part in generating a favorable climate here for future developments in such fields.

Flagstaff's days of gun-play and violence were nearly all behind her, but not entirely. Cattle rustlers and thieves were sometimes summarily dealt with. C. C. Stemmer, who spent his childhood and youth in Flagstaff, told the writer that one morning in 1889 or 1890 when he was delivering milk, he saw what appeared to be two men dancing in the road near Railroad Avenue and the center of town. Upon closer inspection, he found two men hanging from the limb of a tree. Both had been riddled with bullets and blood was dripping from the toes of their boots and their fingertips.

William Roden, a rancher whose range bordered on the Navajo reservation along the Little Colorado River northeast of the Peaks, came in and reported that a Navajo chief named Hostine had threatened his life. Judge N. G. Layton issued a warrant. Sheriff John Francis and a posse of seventeen captured Hostine near the Roden ranch and he was brought in, but part of the posse was left surrounded by armed Indians. Hostine was placed under a $2,000 peace bond which was put up by four wealthy tribesmen, and National Guard Companies C and I went out and rescued the posse. No one was killed.

The early months of 1891 in Flagstaff were occupied as usual with a plethora of bazaars, carnivals, balls, meetings of the literary groups, band concerts, militia drills, parties, as well as activities of the many fraternal groups. Memorial Day and the Fourth of July were not neglected. Times were prosperous. In winter months it was possible to rent a pair of "high stepping prancers in silver mounted harness, and the usual number of sleigh bells, hitched to a fancy cutter," at a cost of $5 for the first hour and $3 per hour thereafter.

So ended Flagstaff's first decade. It is easy to smile at the activities and concerns of Flagstaff's Literary Society and other such groups of ninety years ago—but the fact remains that the pioneers were rather extraordinarily aware of values beyond the bare matter of making a living, and they gave our community a special flavor which has lasted through the years.

# CHAPTER XII

# A County Called Coconino

BY THE TIME the small accumulation of cabins, frame structures, huts and tents around Antelope Spring had gained a post office in early 1881, with the big Ayer sawmill under construction nearby, and with the trickle of settlers growing into a small stream, it was evident that there was going to be a permanent town.

Most of the newcomers had roots in long-established communities in New England, the Atlantic states, the South and the Midwest, and instinctively recognized the need for local government, and as always in America, this meant the county. The small Flagstaff settlement was in Yavapai County, which occupied more than a fourth of the total area of the Territory and was larger than many states. The seat of county government was Prescott, a long one hundred plus miles from Flagstaff. Going there on business was no casual errand. The trip by horseback or buggy could take several days, and even after the railroad was built and one could travel half of the distance by rail, it still entailed a dusty or muddy journey for the remainder of the way. A call to appear at the courthouse for jury duty or as a witness presented a hardship. So talk about a new county with Flagstaff as its seat started very early.

The second issue of the first Flagstaff newspaper, *The Flag,* appearing on November 1, 1883, called attention to the desirability of establishing a new county, echoing a view already widely held in the community. A couple of weeks later there was more about the proposal, and the *Champion,* published at Peach Springs, said:

> A citizen of Flagstaff, being called to Prescott as a witness, greets the officer with the same unbounded joy that a man in the interior of the Indian Territory starts for the Federal Court at Fort Smith, Arkansas. Prescott is the city of various distances to the average citizen of Yavapai, and over such roads that it must seem a matter of indifference (and we doubt not he often forgets) whether he is the witness or the criminal.

In late December the Flagstaff correspondent for the *Champion,* J. W. Spafford, wrote that Flagstaff was geographically the center of the proposed new county of San Francisco, "and at this time is enjoying an influx of emigration that will ere long give it in numbers that right it will surely demand, *viz.,* a division of Yavapai County with Flagstaff as county seat."

As was usual in Flagstaff's early days, problems were attacked immediately. On January 5, 1884, the *Champion*'s Flagstaff reporter said that a series of meetings had been held

> . . . for the purpose of forming an association for the division of Yavapai County. . . . The organization had been formed and is governed by by-laws necessary for the advancement and interest of the society and is a permanent organization. That the readers of the *Champion* who reside in Yavapai County may know that it is a respectable institution we need to append the names of its officers. President, Frank Daggs; Vice President, J. H. [*sic*] Wilson; Treasurer, P. J. Brannen; Recording Secretary, H. H. Hoxworth; Corresponding Secretary, H. Reed. Standing Committee on Finance, M. S. Beal, J. R. Kilpatrick, Chas. Hickerson; Executive Committee, J. N. Berry, Dr. Brannan [*sic*], J. H. Miller.

In February the Prescott *Journal* expressed the opinion that strife was already evident among rivals for leadership of the movement, suggesting that partisan politics would kill it. By this time the *Champion* had moved to Flagstaff, and taken up the battle. It reprinted the item from Prescott, then stated that politics did not enter into the movement to create a new county: "Democrats and Republicans alike take hold of the project as one man, and all we ask is a nominee for the legislature from this section, by either of the county conventions, and we will support him to a man. We are not looking for Republican or Democratic platforms in the strife before us." This was largely true, and would continue to be true on through the decade until victory would come in the spring of 1891.

One of Flagstaff's sore spots was the lack of a jail; taking prisoners to Prescott was a lengthy and expensive process. The Prescott *Miner* acknowledged this problem and urged construction of a Flagstaff jail to save the expense.

It was evident to reasonable men throughout Yavapai County that county division was coming and would in the long run be beneficial. The question was, when? Officials and taxpayers were rightfully concerned about what the lines of the new county would be, and about the county's indebtedness. What part of it should be assumed by the new county? There was the matter, too, of the railroad, which represented a major item on the tax rolls—how many miles of railroad should or would go into the new county, and how many would remain in Yavapai? County division presented formidable problems.

The *Champion* continued to publish articles urging county division. The Prescott papers from time to time responded with words of caution, sometimes opposition, occasionally ridicule. The discussion continued through 1884, 1885, and well along into 1886. On July 28 that year the Prescott *Journal-Miner* reported that the Flagstaff county division plan was well underway, and that it might find support in other parts of the Territory. It marshaled some arguments against the idea, the chief one being the expense to Flagstaff area taxpayers of setting up a county government and providing all of the needed offices. "We regret that agitation of the question has commenced and trust that the good sense of the people will not allow it to stir up political dissensions nor sectional jealousy," the paper said. The *Champion* continued to print the usual arguments favoring the proposal, and republished comment from other Arizona newspapers that agreed.

Early in January 1887, with the Territorial Legislature soon to convene, a public meeting was held at Flagstaff schoolhouse. Addresses urging creation of the new county were made by W. G. Stewart, Col. J. W. Eddy, Thomas Mc-Millan, S. S. Acker, D. M. Riordan, P. J. Brannen, W. H. Ashurst, and others, a formidable assemblage of the town's heavy artillery and certainly not a partisan group. Stewart was a Republican stalwart and had served in the Territorial Council (senate) in 1885. Riordan and Brannen were also Republicans. Ashurst was a Democrat and representative-elect, and was preparing to go to Prescott to attend the Fourteenth Legislative Assembly; McMillan and Acker were also Democrats.

Colonel Eddy proposed that a committee of three be appointed to act in the matter. The committee would investigate the question of county taxation and other problems. Elected were McMillan, Riordan and Stewart. The name of William Munds of Upper Verde was added, giving the committee the authority to appoint some other person if Munds did not choose to serve. When word of this reached Prescott, the *Courier* came back with a lengthy piece ridiculing the idea, suggesting that the Flagstaff leaders sought only to secure power for themselves. The paper brought up the matter of costs of running a county, pointed out that Yavapai County's size was no real handicap (although it comprised more than a fourth of the entire Territory of Arizona) and prayed that the citizens of the county, especially those in the Flagstaff area, would not "jump from the frying pan into the fire."

This diatribe in the *Courier* was republished in full in the *Champion* with a rebuttal, which ended with the plea, "Justice demands that the county should be divided." A couple of weeks later the Flagstaff paper would be referring to the "Frisco County Bill," stating that it would be "an advantageous measure to the residents of this section and it will not injure any one—always excepting the Prescott clique. The bill ought to pass on its merits and our 'Bill' [W. H. Ashurst] will do his level best to see it through."

In the 1880s many inhabitants of Flagstaff called the San Francisco Peaks the "Frisco Peaks." Ashurst, who would lead the county division battle in the Fourteenth Assembly, Al Doyle and John Marshall favored the name Frisco County and such was the name by which the proposal was known during 1887–89.

Ashurst succeeded in generating widespread support for the bill. It carried the House by fifteen to eight, but met with a tie, six to six, in the Council, and was thus defeated. The blame was placed on the councilman from Mohave County, E. L. Burdick of Mineral Park, who, the *Champion* indicated, had broken a promise to support the bill. On Ashurst's return to Flagstaff the *Champion* said that he had worked hard and honestly for his constituents and that they appreciated it. He had succeeded in gaining passage of a bill which would exempt from taxation for a period of six years from its completion the proposed Flagstaff and Grand Canyon Railroad.

It was apparent to most of Arizona's responsible citizens that the Frisco County cause was just and would in due time be victorious. The *Champion* promised that it would continue to work for the division with every honorable means, that its cause was non-partisan, and labeled the opposition as "a clique whose only aim has been to benefit themselves at the cost of the taxpayers."

Early in 1888 the Prescott *Journal-Miner* pointed out that during 1887 Yavapai County's justices of the peace drew in fees the sum of $1,070.65, of which $458.05 went to the justices in the Flagstaff precinct. Fees paid for constables in the entire county totaled $3,270.54, of which $2,711.89 was paid in the Flagstaff precinct. It added that the Flagstaff deputy sheriff also received fees. It reported without going into details that fines received from justices' courts were a small sum—but that Flagstaff contributed "her full prorata."

The *Champion* pointed out that "Yavapai County is as large as the State of New York, that [Flagstaff] is its largest precinct, that the county seat is one hundred fifty-eight miles distant, all of which causes combine to make the mileage bills of the precinct unusually large." The Flagstaff paper also noted that construction of a jail in Flagstaff would save much of the money spent on mileage conveying prisoners to Prescott, and "a still more effective remedy would be the creation of a new county in northern Yavapai, and Flagstaff or Williams might be made the county seat. This would entirely relieve the southern portion of the county of all burdensome expense . . . and such a solution . . . would be entirely satisfactory to the citizens of Flagstaff."

This is the first mention of Williams as a potential seat for the new county, and may have been simply a nod in recognition of Williams' growing importance. The people of Flagstaff and Williams were together on the county division cause, and no doubt leaders in both communities recognized that Flagstaff would have the generous edge when it came time to establish the county seat. But Williams was a voice to be considered. The county did build a jail at Flagstaff, of wood, at a cost of $475, but it was far from satisfactory.

Following establishment of the Territory of Arizona in 1863, the first legislative Assembly was held in 1864 at Prescott, and met annually there through 1867. In 1868 the capital moved to Tucson and met there biennially through 1878. In 1879 the Tenth Assembly returned to Prescott and continued there through 1887. But pressures were growing to move the capital to Phoenix. Prescott, the Territorial Capital as well as Yavapai County seat, had its problems which would play some part in the matter of the proposed county to be carved out of the northern and eastern portions of Yavapai.

The Assembly consisted of one councilman from each of the ten counties plus two at large from northern and southern Territorial districts. The House was composed of members elected in the several counties on a population basis. It had twenty-four members. Those elected in the fall of 1888 to serve in the Fifteenth Assembly which would convene early in 1889 included five Representatives from Yavapai County. Two were from Prescott; one, J. V. Rhoades, part owner and official of the Arizona Cattle Company, was from Flagstaff; and two, F. L. Rogers and George P. Thornton, were from Williams. This Assembly would move during the session to Phoenix, which would continue henceforth as Territorial and then State Capital.

Earlier in the decade the leaders of Prescott had become aware of the advantages so evident at Flagstaff of being located on a railroad. A plan led by Gov. Frederick H. Tritle and strongly backed by the United Verde Mining Company, which sought a more economical means of getting its copper ore from the Jerome mines than the fourteen-mule wagons then in use, led to enactment of legislation in the Thirteenth Assembly in 1885 providing for a Yavapai County subsidy to build a railroad from Prescott Junction (Seligman) to Prescott. The promoters sold additional first-mortgage bonds to acquire right-of-way and build the line. The legislation provided that the board of supervisors of the county must pay $4,000 for each mile of standard-gauge track completed, payments to start when ten miles of the seventy-three-mile road had been built. By the beginning of 1887 the line, in part built of discarded lightweight rails secured from the Atlantic & Pacific, was completed. Yavapai County thus added $292,000 to its bonded indebtedness, and this was an important factor in the matter of Yavapai County division. A few years later the Santa Fe would build a parallel line to Prescott, originating at Ash Fork. It was shorter and straighter than the somewhat jerry-built Prescott & Arizona Central. Completed in 1895, it soon supplanted the earlier, county-subsidized line, which disappeared, its rails taken up and used elsewhere. With the help of a tax subsidy the new line was extended on from Prescott to Phoenix, with the final spike being driven that same year.

By the time the Fifteenth Legislative Assembly convened at Prescott in early 1889, soon to move lock, stock and barrel to Phoenix by rail via Los Angeles, the closest railroad connection, the county division bill had a new name: "Coconino." Dr. Colton writes that D. M. Riordan was given credit for the change of name, the reason being that most Arizona counties had been given the names of Indian tribes—Mohave, Yavapai, Apache, etc. The name Coconino had some circulation in the area in the late 1880s. The word, Colton tells us, has been spelled in at least twenty-four ways. It was the name given by Hopis and Zuñis to small groups of seed-gathering, wandering Indians on the Colorado plateau. At any rate Riordan's proposal prevailed, and so the measure and the county-to-be were so named.

The Coconino County Bill passed the House by a large majority, and was soon endorsed by the Council. It then went to Gov. Lewis Wolfley who vetoed it. Early in 1889 President Benjamin Harrison had appointed Wolfley as Arizona's eighth Territorial governor. He won out over a number of aspirants, including former Gov. A. P. K. Safford, whose cause hit the skids when it was revealed that Safford had written a letter to the president of the Southern Pacific Railroad, returning $20,000 of $25,000 given him to bribe legislators, explaining that he had overestimated their greed! Wolfley was subject of much contention and quickly embarrassed his sponsors in Washington.

It appears that his veto of the Coconino County Bill was not because he saw a lack of justice in the proposal but for politically expedient reasons propounded by Prescott lawmakers and political and financial figures. No doubt the Prescott & Arizona Central Railroad construction and the county bonds which paid a share of the costs played a part in the veto. It was a bitter setback for Flagstaff. The *Champion* said on March 23:

The county of Yavapai remains as heretofore, and those who have earnestly wished and endeavored to create the new county of Coconino have only wasted their time and accomplished naught. That the defeat of this measure was owing to "mistreatment" there is no doubt, and there is no question in our mind that the very men who have accomplished it would, if they had followed the dictates of their conscience, declare that the establishment of Coconino County would have been a benefit to all concerned. . . . . It will be two years before anything can now be done . . . and we can only accept the result in a matter-of-fact spirit and hope for a better and more scrupulous body of representatives in the future.

Playing a part in the effort for enactment of the county bill was W. G. Stewart, Flagstaff attorney, who had served in the Council in 1885. "The tax-payers of Flagstaff and vicinity are under many obligations to him for the gallant fight he made to create a new county," the *Champion* said in April. "But notwithstanding the help of other prominent citizens of our town, the present Czar of Arizona said no, and the people left must patiently wait another two years." It's possible that Stewart received financial backing from some of Flagstaff's leaders, perhaps D. M. Riordan and the Brannens, in his lobbying efforts.

Mickey Stewart was senior member of the Flagstaff law firm of Stewart and Doe. United States Senator Henry F. Ashurst described Stewart as "red-headed; weight, 110 pounds; prussic acid wit; born tragedian, brilliant orator who played upon human emotions and prejudices as a virtuoso upon a violin." He had been foreman of a cattle ranch, but abandoned the saddle, lasso, spurs and branding-iron for law books. "He was given to poetry as evidenced by his frequent quotations, and much given to bourbon whiskey as evidenced by his frequent potations." On one occasion, according to Ashurst, Stewart entered Sandy Donahue's saloon, deposited fifteen cents on the bar and called for bourbon; Donahue set out the bottle and an empty glass. According to the custom in those days the patron poured his own drink. Stewart poured himself a full goblet, half a pint, whereupon Donahue said: "That is not water you are pouring out." Stewart replied: "I came here for refreshment, not to be insulted." Donahue said, "And how have I insulted you?" Stewart retorted, "Do I look like a man who would drink that much water?"

B. A. Cameron, a pioneer who came to Flagstaff in the mid-eighties and wrote historical reminiscences appearing in the *Arizona Daily Sun* in August 1946, recalled an amusing story about Governor Wolfley, the veto, and Flagstaff's reaction:

The citizens of Flagstaff were much incensed at the Governor for vetoing the bill, and so, to express their opinion of him, hung Governor Wolfley in effigy. On the cross arm of a telegraph pole across the street [south from the Bank Hotel building near the railroad right-of-way] they swung the dummy, boxes saturated with kerosene piled beneath. It was between daylight and dark that flames shot upward and a few minutes later with the fire burning fiercely, a passenger train pulled up to the station and stopped. The passengers, getting out to stretch their legs were greeted by a fusilade of shots, their eye clinging in horror to the dreadful, dangling form that was being shot full of holes by the bloodthirsty population. Needless to say they lost no time in returning to the safety of the train, while the so-called bloodthirsty citizens were doubled up with laughter.

Flagstaff might have been laughing at the discomfort of the railroad passengers, but it wasn't laughing about the veto. George H. Tinker, editor and publisher of the *Champion* and an ardent Republican, was particularly offended by the Republican governor's act. He wrote that the *Champion* was a Republican paper and had always advocated a division of the county "and we blush to say that we are ashamed that the first Republican governor, under one of the best Presidents the United States ever had, has done to our people an injury irreparable. . . ." Tinker went on to say that he had been absent for about a month, hence was not fully cognizant of the facts relating to the veto, but would get busy and inform himself, and then "show you [Wolfley] up as you deserve. Ta, ta, Governor, you will hear from us next week." That article carried a large headline:

THE NEW GOVERNOR OF ARIZONA AS HIS
FIRST ACT PERPETUATES AN OUTRAGE
UPON THE TAXPAYERS OF
NORTHERN ARIZONA.

The next week Tinker devoted two and a half columns to the matter, worked over Wolfley, recapitulated all the arguments in favor of county division, and touched heavily on the perfidy of Prescott leaders for having indicated two years before that in 1889 they would support the bill, then betrayed their promises. He said that in Wolfley's case, ignorance was no excuse; that Wolfley had been fully informed by Flagstaff's W. G. Stewart, of the "clean, cold, deliberate facts." Wolfley's veto message, claiming that the bill as drawn would not be fair to Apache and Yavapai Counties which would be required to credit the new county with a share of public improvements already existent, Tinker examined and refuted:

> Now there is but little more to be said in regard to the veto of one of the most just and righteous measures ever passed by a legislative body . . . we again reiterate that it is our opinion that when the Coconino bill was vetoed an outrage was perpetrated upon a people who will remember it forever. . . . The mandate has been issued and like the Czar of Russia, must be obeyed. But we would call your attention to the fact that the people of Flagstaff and vicinity are not serfs and will at some future day assert their rights.

It was a fine diatribe, and may have played some part in Wolfley's political demise.

The arguments flared back and forth during 1889. In the *Champion* of May 18, 1889, which reported the death of Tinker from a heart attack, appeared posthumously a long article by him refuting arguments put forth by the Prescott *Courier* in opposition to the county division measure. In this article the matter of the Prescott & Arizona Central Railroad bonds was brought out, and Tinker pointedly remarked that the railroad would not benefit northeastern Yavapai County "a two-bit piece." He pointed out that the proposed division gave Prescott most of the taxable wealth, would give the new county Indian reservations and huge blocks of unimproved and comparatively valueless land, listed the tax payments made by the northeastern area, and compared these with what had been received back in minimum road work and fees for public officials. Early in the new year of 1890, the *Champion* struck a new note:

> It is about time that the people of Flagstaff and Prescott put their heads together to agree upon lines for dividing the County, and we are ready to meet the representatives of Prescott at Prescott Junction [Seligman] at any time to discuss the position and settle upon lines, for we must and will have a new county.

In March 1890, the *Champion* began a series of well-written, humorous articles under the byline "A Tax Payer of Yavapai County," who soon proved to be Al Doyle of Flagstaff. Doyle accused the Yavapai board of supervisors of spending money only on roads directly serving Prescott and neglecting others which led to Flagstaff or Phoenix. He pointed out that the county had gone in debt $288,000 to underwrite the Prescott & Arizona Central Railway a distance of seventy-two miles from Prescott Junction to Prescott, and that all of the taxpayers in the county would share in paying off the bonds and the interest. He said that the courthouse, built twelve years before for $78,000, was also being paid for by taxpayers in the northeastern part of the county, and that a building as good could be built for $20,000. He accused Prescott of buying support of legislators to move the Territorial capital back to Prescott from Tucson, and ended his two-column piece with the suggestion that the old bosses of Prescott should follow the example of the Big Colorado Indians, by heaping mud on themselves and hiding from the sight of respectable people "who come to the county to make homes for themselves, if taxes don't starve them out."

Most of Doyle's remarks were addressed to John Marion, publisher and editor of the *Courier*. Marion fired back a salvo and Doyle waded into him again: "He [Marion] slides over my article as though the seat of his pants was patched with a bacon rind, but did not stop to answer a single item referred to in it." He derided Marion's claim that he was only working for the best interests of all of the people of the county. It was great fun, and provided heart and ammunition for those who would continue to fight for creation of Coconino. Doyle pointed out that if the county issued more bonds to continue building the Prescott railroad, it could easily add another $320,000 to the county indebtedness. This would bring the total expended for courthouse, roads, the $475 Flagstaff jail, and the railroad, to a total of $797,345. "Who wouldn't hurrah for county division?" Doyle asked. "May the Lord have mercy on those who have committed such criminal depredations on the hard-working people of the county. . . . The old lady had better divide the old homestead and send part of her troublesome children out to take care of themselves. Both the affairs of Yavapai and the new county will be easier handled. . . . Well I must close or John Issac Rabbi Moses Marion will bat his brains out against Martin Maier's brewery. . . ."

In late March the *Champion* reported: "Several of our citizens who have visited Prescott say that the citizens of that place are ready to meet a committee from this locality to settle the county division question. It is high time something was done about this matter." A month later a public meeting was called of citizens and taxpayers in the northeastern part of Yavapai County to take action.

During the summer Governor Wolfley asked the Yavapai supervisors to give him a statement of the county's indebtedness. Their report revealed:

Tonto Basin wagon road, 8 percent, due 1897, $6,000. Flagstaff and Verde wagon road, 8 percent, 1890, $4,000. Lynx Creek wagon road, 8 percent, 1898, $10,000. Black Hills and Verde wagon road, 7 percent, 1890, $5,000. Black Canyon wagon road, 7 per cent, 1900, $3,000. Yavapai

County Refunding, 7 per cent, 1908, $143,000. P. & A. C. Railway bonds, 1916, $292,000.

There were also these items: Year's interest due in January, 1890, $32,610; floating indebtedness and interest up to same date, $58,000; and estimated expenditures for the rest of 1890, $26,110.

All of these items totaled $580,000. An abstract of the assessment rolls of the county showed a total value of $5,438,422.15. Livestock represented about a third of this. Railroads were valued at $1,703,037. Patented mines were one hundred and fifty in number and were valued at only $100 each for a total of $15,000.

Members of the committee appointed to meet with a like group from Prescott included D. M. Riordan, William Munds, E. S. Gosney and J. B. Tappan. In early September Wolfley resigned, to the relief of the President and other officials, and John N. Irwin succeeded him. A meeting was called at Prescott about the same time "in the matter of a just and equitable division of the county. . . ." Out of this would come the naming of a committee to meet the Flagstaff group.

A committee composed of citizens from Prescott and Flagstaff met at Prescott last week to consider the advisability of creating the county of Coconino by the next legislature. The committee adopted a resolution favoring county division and designated the line of division, so that the vexed question has been determined and the county division question will not enter into Yavapai County politics this year and when the legislature meets there will be no controversy over the matter. The conclusion arrived at by the committee was wise and just.

The new county of Coconino assumes one-third of the indebtedness of the county, after making deductions for county property. The county property, consisting of the court house and plaza, was appraised at $75,000. Such was the agreement of the committee.

This in substance was the agreement reached by the two groups of taxpayers. Details were published in both Prescott and Flagstaff newspapers, giving legal description of the boundaries, etc. The joint committee members also pledged themselves to carry out the agreement to the letter "in a friendly manner, without antagonism, that the mutual interests of both committees may be observed, and they further pledge themselves to discourage any further segregation of the counties of Yavapai or Coconino." J. C. Herndon of Prescott and E. S. Gosney of Flagstaff were appointed to draft a bill embodying the action of the committees, to be presented to the legislature.

The Sixteenth Legislative Assembly which convened early in 1891 included among its members Herndon, as Council member, and J. A. Vail of Flagstaff in the House. Herndon's bill, "An Act to Create the County of Coconino," was published in full in the *Champion,* occupying three and a half columns. It provided for the boundaries as agreed on by the Prescott-Flagstaff committee a few months previously; authorized the governor to appoint interim county officials; provided that a special election should be held in the new county on the second Tuesday in May 1891, to elect officials and designate a place for the county seat; recognized precinct officials elected in the November 1890 general election, attached Coconino to the Third Judicial District of the Territorial court system and provided for court terms to be held each March and August, transferred legal actions pending in Yavapai County, but relating to matters in the new county, to Coconino's jurisdiction; and provided for transfer of records.

The bill also provided that files relating to the Flagstaff townsite matter should be transferred from Yavapai's Probate Judge to the new county's judge; that the supervisors of Yavapai and Coconino should meet on the first Monday in April 1891, in Prescott, and ascertain the indebtedness of Yavapai at date of passage of the county bill, and that one-third of such indebtedness less $25,000 (one-third of the estimated value of public improvements in the county) should become Coconino's responsibility, and that bonds should be issued to refund the indebtedness; and provided for tax levies for the new county.

When the bill was introduced, the Prescott *Journal-Miner* protested the provision for an election to be held in the new county in May, arguing that the infant constituency should not be confronted with the costs of an election so soon. But no protest was heard from Coconino. There was some pulling and hauling in Flagstaff, as to whom Governor Irwin should name as interim officials. But a contributor to the *Champion* signing himself "Spectator" and sounding suspiciously like Al Doyle, issued a word of good sense. He pointed out that such a move might jeopardize the very existence of Coconino:

> The query is now pertinent, wherein: is a half-breed slate selected for a Republican Governor to act upon, by a clique two-thirds of whom are Democrats, and for their individual and party ends, preferable to such appointments, as the Governor without any local prejudices or interests at stake, might make after due deliberation from amongst our best citizens [?]

The act was passed in early February, and signed by the governor on February 19, 1891. All in all, it was pretty fair. Coconino assumed responsibility for a third of the county money expended on construction of the Prescott branch railway line, something over $90,000; but it gained a lot of miles of Atlantic & Pacific track for its own tax rolls, got a third of tax monies received, pro rata, for 1891; and more important, it gained its primary objective, self-government and the convenience of having county offices near at hand.

Press comment throughout the state was favorable. The Prescott *Courier* suggested that when the supervisors of the two counties met to settle financial and other matters in May, "that upon conclusion of the business the people of this town [Prescott] and county give some suitable entertainment to the 'fathers' of Coconino, 'our daughter' and neighbor."

The Buckeye *Blade* penned a fanciful welcome:

> The youngest daughter of Arizona, Miss Coconino, will shortly don long dresses and make her debut into society, taking a place with her older and cultured sisters. The young lady is reported to be of a tall, stately and commanding presence and possessing a freshness of complexion not equaled by her older sisters. It is said, however, that she lacks that exquisite symmetry of form and development for which her elder sisters are famous. The invigorating and bracing influences of the mountain air have developed in her a dashing and rollicking disposition. It is to be presumed when once admitted into society, under the cultured influence of her sisters, that she will soon become as refined and dignified as they are. When you come out Miss Coconino we desire to be entered on your list of friends.

Republican Governor Irwin could not be accused of partisanship in appointing Coconino County's first officials. Democrats receiving offices included George Babbitt, treasurer; J. E. Jones, probate judge; F. B. Jacobs, surveyor; J. F. Daggs, supervisor. Republicans were Ralph Cameron, sheriff; F. R. Nellis, recorder; E. M. Doe, district attorney; D. M. Riordan and G. P. Thornton, supervisors. The supervisors named A. T. Cornish, a Democrat, as clerk. The governor seemed to have recognized the non-partisan nature of the move to establish the new county.

The special election was held in Coconino County on May 12, 1891, and the Democrats swept the polls, capturing all posts with the exception of recorder and surveyor. The Democratic victory foreshadowed the national Democratic victory in the coming fall, when Grover Cleveland would defeat the incumbent Republican, Benjamin Harrison, 277 electoral college votes to 145. (Four years before, Cleveland had received a one hundred thousand popular vote majority over Harrison, but had lost in the electoral college, 233 to 168.) Coconino's sole winning Republicans were C. W. Bush, recorder, and James Lamport, surveyor. T. G. Norris won over James M. Sanford for delegate to the Constitutional Convention; J. W. Francis defeated Cameron for sheriff; J. E. Jones won over E. H. Simpson for probate judge; H. D. Ross was unopposed for district attorney.

George Babbitt was elected county treasurer, defeating J. L. Davis; victorious candidates for county supervisor were T. F. McMillan, C. E. Boyce and A. T. Cornish, winning over A. A. Dutton, F. L. Rogers and P. J. Brannen. Receiving largest winning majority was Babbitt, who defeated his opponent with a 116-vote margin out of a total vote of 533. Judge Jones won his victory with a margin of 115 out of a total vote of 531. Flagstaff was easy winner of designation as county seat, the vote being 429 to 97. Three Flagstaff residents voted for Williams, but ten Williamsites favored Flagstaff. The supervisors appointed J. M. Weatherford clerk.

Coconino now had newly elected officials but only makeshift quarters for them. The sheriff and the district attorney had offices in the Babbitt building, but the recorder, the supervisors and the clerk of the court were in the Kilpatrick building and the probate judge was apparently using his own office. But by December all of the officials would be settled in quarters in the Babbitt building. "It is a great convenience to the public to have all the county officers in one building," the *Champion* said.

A major and continuing problem confronting the new county was the matter of wagon roads. This was true in most counties. The matter was of such paramount importance that the governing body of some western counties was often referred to as "road commissioners" or "road supervisors." The *Champion* did not neglect its duty to remind the supervisors frequently that roads should be kept in repair and that nothing was of more importance. Williams particularly had been neglected in this regard by Yavapai supervisors. The Williams-Flagstaff road would see improvement, a road would be improved northward to Tuba City, another would be maintained to Grand Canyon, and the road into Oak Creek and the Verde country would also require and receive attention.

Three weeks after the election, the *Champion* pointed out that there was now a new county and county seat, and what was needed now was incorporation of Flagstaff. But that would not come until 1894. Then, characteristically, it would be achieved by holding a mass meeting, agreeing on what was to be done, and directing a petition to the county board of supervisors signed by far more than the required two-thirds of the property owners. Preliminary meetings had been held at least as early as 1887.

The editor of the *Champion* warned the new Coconino County officials not to imitate those of the parent county:

> Yavapai County as is well known has been run by a gang of political tricksters, and been run deeply in debt with no benefit to the people. Let us not follow the footsteps of our mother county in this respect but let every man who is a resident of Coconino County make it his duty to be a "watch dog of the treasury" and see to it that no unnecessary expense is incurred in the management of our county affairs.

While economy was the watchword, some things took precedence, for instance the need for a proper jail. The wooden structure built for $475 by Yavapai County a few years before was completely inadequate. A citizen of the community wrote a letter to the *Champion* calling on the supervisors to do something about the matter. "The present so-called jail is little better than a dog house, and to confine human beings in such a place is an act bordering on barbarism," he averred. "The fact that the building stands flat on the ground with no means of ventilation fills the cells with foul atmosphere which is liable to produce disease. . . ." The supervisors paid $60 per month for a jailor, and he was urged to keep the place as clean and neat as possible, but the supervisors were reminded that they should do something about another jail at the earliest possible date.

In September the board considered sites for a courthouse as well as a new jail, and announced they would make the decision early in October. Favored was what was known as Railroad Square, a block on the east side of San Francisco, and this became the site. Prisoners in the county jail were put to work clearing and grading. The supervisors invited bids for a new jail to be built of sandstone. Late in October after a false start with a low bidder who couldn't post the necessary bond, the contract was awarded to Callihan & Doyle for $2,760. The supervisors also granted a contract to the Pauly Company for $4,870 for steel cells and fixtures. Work was pushed and by Christmas the cells and other items had arrived and it was estimated that the building would be ready for use by mid-January 1892.

Building the courthouse was another matter. It was found that it would be necessary to secure an Act of Congress to give the county the power to bond itself for the purpose. This would take years, but in due time it would be done, and the red Coconino sandstone courthouse would be built that still stands [1976].

THE SHORT DECADE beginning with the arrival of the railroad in the summer of 1882 and coming to a close with establishment of Coconino County in the spring of 1891 witnessed the rapid evolution of a raw and lawless supply camp into a respectable community of homes, institutions and establishments.

During this period the general layout of the town took form; schools, churches and other institutions had their beginnings, mercantile and service establishments increased vastly in number and adapted to the changing needs of the community, the lumbering and livestock industries became firmly established, professional men came to join the town's single pioneer doctor, and many of the families that were to play roles in the community's subsequent history arrived.

The tourist industry, which would become of increasing importance with the passing of the years, was already well underway in the 1880s. From the time that Flagstaff became accessible by railroad, travelers from all over the world came to view the Grand Canyon, the San Francisco Peaks, the beauties of Oak Creek Canyon, and the cliff dwellings in Walnut Canyon.

The academic and scientific institutions which were to become of vast importance in later years did not get their start until the 1890s, but the community's attitudes and values favoring them were already evident in the 1880s.

In looking back on that time we find most striking the great vitality and spirit of optimism which pervaded every phase of personal endeavor and community activity. Oldtimers reminiscing in later years would return again and again to this. George Hochderffer tells us: "In those days when an idea came to do a thing, the thing was as good as begun, done and finished without any preliminaries." This vitality characterized settlement throughout the West in the years following the Civil War. But it was especially evident here, perhaps because opportunities were so evident and abundant, and the ambitious and courageous found that in Flagstaff the odds favored such qualities.

Several times a major part of the town was destroyed by fire, and one gains a feeling that the people of Flagstaff almost exulted in the disaster and the resulting challenge to rebuild, bigger and better than ever. Sometimes buildings were replaced in days or a week or two. This tremendous vitality also showed itself in widespread support for all kinds of social and cultural activity, community celebrations, and an amazing calendar of recreation.

Another striking fact about Flagstaff of the 1880s was the remarkably high level of leadership. Men like Dennis M. Riordan, Dr. D. J. Brannen, John Francis, Al Doyle, Thomas F. McMillan, Judges Doe and Jones, the Babbitts, would have been outstanding in any community. The men who held power in

Flagstaff took their duties seriously but generally with modesty. The level of education and culture among community leaders was comparatively high, and there was a constant and intensive effort on the part of many to educate and improve themselves. The Catholic Riordans who ran the big sawmill prided themselves on their culture. They entertained distinguished visitors down through the years. The community's homes housed a number of fine libraries. The Ashurst family appreciated intellectual attainments, and one of their sons, Henry Fountain Ashurst, became a United States Senator distinguished for eloquence and literary tastes.

This is not to say that the cowboys carried Shakespeare about in their saddle bags nor that faro dealers in the saloons were given to quoting Dante—although it is not impossible that some were quite capable of such things. What it does mean is that Flagstaff, even in its earliest years, never looked upon itself as a small, backward town. Its heroes and ideal citizens were men and women of honor and attainment. The flashy and raffish, the splurgers and sporty, were of diminishing significance in the community's life after railroad building times. Flagstaff didn't honor the killers and tinhorns, the gangsters of early days, as did some communities. Flagstaff in the 1880s would shoot it out with an outlaw or camp thief or stock rustler, but those incidents were a necessary part of building the sort of community its people wanted it to be.

An important factor contributing to the special flavor and spirit of Flagstaff was the fair balance between Protestants and Roman Catholics in community affairs and positions of authority, always marked by tolerance and mutual respect. This may not seem particularly significant today, but it was significant and unusual in early days and many communities over the land were not so fortunate nor so enlightened. The town was also singularly free of political partisanship in matters of community importance.

Another factor in shaping the Flagstaff pattern was that from the very beginning, Flagstaff always consisted of two, and sometimes three, more or less distinct communities or self-sufficient areas, almost separate towns. This caused some problems, but it also generated certain opportunities and provided for a healthful division of influence and power. Another generalization of significance in understanding the special quality which Flagstaff had is that during its formative decades there was always something of an economic balance between the sawmill and livestock interests and the merchants and professional elements.

All of these factors contributed to the fact that Flagstaff in the 1880s did not have a clear stratification in its social life, in the generally rigid patterns prevailing in many midwestern and northeastern communities. Flagstaff citizens found few barriers to their social aspirations, and this generated further vitality and tolerance.

The optimism, fellowship, humor and tolerant skepticism which character-ized Flagstaff life; the respect for the better things, while not disdaining the matter of making a living, or if one's ambitions ran that way, a fortune; the openhandedness, courage, ingenuity and willingness to tackle problems, created a unique community in what a decade before had been a wilderness. By 1891 Flagstaff had firmly set the patterns of community attitude, values and action, which would characterize it for years to come.

Old "Judge" Cozzens wasn't so far wrong when more than a century ago he evoked in his fertile imagination a golden land of promise in the wilderness around San Francisco Mountain—our *Sierra Sin Agua*. But neither he nor any-one else could have guessed then that today [1976] there would be a prosperous, cosmopolitan city of more than thirty thousand thriving at the foot of those same towering Peaks, that for a hundred years have served both as a beacon and a lodestone for people with certain qualities and ideals. Many residents of modern Flagstaff will agree that we do indeed live in the midst of a "Marvellous Country."

## Appendix A

THE FOLLOWING IS A LIST of the members of the first Boston party, as assembled from George E. Loring's journal and letters, and articles in the Boston *Herald*, the Prescott *Miner*, the Albuquerque *Republican Review*, the Boston *Globe* and the *Coconino Sun*, Flagstaff. The number comes to forty-five, which we are told elsewhere was the number of members in this party, if we include the nine-year-old son of the leader, Maj. E. W. Griggs.

| | | |
|---|---|---|
| Batch or Balch, E. | Groveland, Hoffman | Reilly, Frank |
| Bradley, W. H. | Hale, C. E. | Robbins, Capt. Richard |
| Bradley, Wentworth | Harriman, Charles M. | Riley, Thomas |
| Breezer, George | Hayes, Charles F. | Spencer, Pardon |
| Caton, William J. | Heath, J. R. | Sullivan, Wm. |
| Davis | Kennedy, Robert | Taplin, Rev. Wm. |
| Drake, Charles | Kinnet, R. | Tillinghast, S. L. |
| Fay, M. W. | Kirk, E. W. | Tourjee, J. H. |
| Fisk, E. W. | Loring, George Edwin | Wadleigh, Issac H. |
| Fletcher, Robert | Mann, Horace E. | Webster, G. |
| Goodwin, J. Henry | Maxwell, J. Frank | Weed, T. Clement |
| Goodwin, Father of J. H. | Maynadier, Major J. D. | Wentworth, Orson |
| Griggs, Major E. W. | Murphy, J. E. | Wheeler, N. G. |
| Griggs's 9-year-old son | Pierce, M. H. | White, F. J. |
| Gagnon, Abraham | Quiston, Robert | Wilcutt or Wilkit, E. |

## Appendix B

THE FOLLOWING IS A PARTIAL LIST of the members of the second Boston party, as assembled from the letters of Horace E. Mann, William M. Breakenridge's *Helldorado*, and articles in the Boston *Globe*, the Prescott *Miner*, the *Coconino Sun* (Flagstaff), and the *Arizona Daily Sun* (Flagstaff).

| | | |
|---|---|---|
| Abbott, A. F. | Cleland, Thomas Edward | Mellon, Thomas |
| Bray, G. A. | Hemmingway, J. W. | Sinclair, J. G. |
| Bray, T. H. | Hunt, Sam C. | Thayer, S. Curtis |
| Canerty | Lowe, Jack | Webster, Edward C. |
| Chase, F. T. | Mahoney, Denis B. | Wilson, John A. |

There are other names given as members of "the Boston party" but these are not identified as to which contingent they were with, although it is probable they were members of the second party. These names are: Heyer and Heyer, brothers; Hoffman (at El Morro the names of T. P. Hoffman and L. P. Hoffman appear adjacent to another Boston party member, so perhaps there were two Hoffmans); Keating; Kelley, A. C.; Lincoln, Fred; Robinson; Rokhar, C. W.; and Vanarawil.

If these names are added to the fourteen above, about half of the second Boston party is accounted for.

## Appendix C

IN 1942 THE FLAGSTAFF CHAMBER OF COMMERCE established an Historic Landmarks Committee under the inspiration of Dr. Harold S. Colton of the Museum of Northern Arizona, assisted by Chamber Secretary Leo Weaver. Its purpose, as declared in the minutes, was "to definitely determine which tree at Flagstaff was the first one to fly a United States Flag and the one from which Flagstaff derived its name." The committee included B. A. Cameron, C. J. Babbitt, George Hochderffer, John Love, T. A. Riordan, W. H. Switzer, V. M. Slipher, Leo Weaver, W. W. Midgley and Colton. Their several meetings and the resulting developments were duly reported in the *Sun* in issues of July-October, 1942. Minutes were preserved by Colton, and have been found in his archives. This writer made copies in 1973 and placed them in the Special Collections Department at Northern Arizona University Library.

At the July 13 meeting, Cameron repeated the story about the party of "engineers" camped here in 1876. Love flatly declared that Old Town Spring was the site of the first flag-raising and the naming of Flagstaff. Hochderffer repeated his familiar Beale tree story, and read letters from P. J. Brannen stating that the flagstaff he had in mind in naming the town was that one. Switzer reported that he had seen that same tree, *i.e.,* the East tree, for years after he came to Flagstaff in 1883. Colton told the group that McMillan, not Brannen, was first postmaster.

At the July 20 meeting the group visited the East tree, then went to the Clark Ranch site in City Park. There Love pointed out the site of the Bill Hull (McMillan) cabin, and showed them the stump of a tree he cut down in 1885. The minutes quote Love as saying that Clark had often told him that a flag flew from this tall pine, but he said positively he had never seen a flag there. Cameron said he had been told by a man named Wilson (probably John A. Wilson of the second Boston Party) that a flag-raising occurred at the spot on July 4, 1876. "No further proof was presented," the minutes state. The group visited Old Town Spring, and Love pointed out the spot where the flagpole stood and described it as having a diameter of about twenty-five inches, and being forty feet high. "The committee returned . . . with Johnnie Love still declaring that the first flag was raised at Old Town."

In due time the committee decided that the Clark Ranch site should be eliminated from consideration, no doubt because of Love's insistence and Hochderffer's and Switzer's strong position relating to Brannen's statement that he was thinking of the East tree when he named, or renamed, the town in the spring of 1881. The committee would have done well to pay a bit more attention to committee chairman Cameron's remarks regarding the party of "engineers" who camped here in 1876, and his further statement that he had been told "by a man named Wilson" long ago that a flag-raising occurred at the Clark place on July 4, 1876. This writer knew Cameron well in later years. He was a quiet man who was not of a temperament to relish an argument over a matter which he knew about only by hearsay. Of course the others had no firsthand information, either, but they did have strong feelings.

The group adopted a motion by Hochderffer that the "Beale" (East tree) be recognized as the flagstaff or flagpole that Brannen had in mind when he named the town; that an imposing memorial with suitable flagstaff be erected in the parkway north of the railroad track, east of Sitgreaves Street underpass, south of Santa Fe Avenue and west of Rio de Flag, a point approximately equidistant from Old Town Spring and the Beale tree site. To his credit Hochderffer also moved that any marker to be erected should refer to the *three* tree sites, and that each of the three sites should be marked with either a steel or concrete post. A pretty good compromise of a difficult problem. The committee did about the best it could with what it had to do with; it did not have the data regarding the Boston parties, the 1878 surveyor's map with "Flagstaff" plainly printed thereon, the information from the Yavapai County supervisor's 1880 minutes, nor the statements and reminiscences of men who took part in the 1876 events in this area.

A scale model of a monument to accompany a sixty-foot fir flagstaff to be set up at the selected central point was prepared by the well-known artist and sculptor, Robert Kittredge. The war delayed the project, and the plan was pigeonholed in the postwar years. The city finally did erect a galvanized pipe flagstaff at the compromise site, however, and improved the little park around it. Later, a similar pipe flagstaff with a small monument was set up near Old Town Spring. The Clark Ranch site has not to this date (1976) been marked.

## *Appendix D*

CHARTER MEMBERS of Flagstaff Lodge No. 8, Knights of Pythias, instituted May 23, 1887, included:

George Briggs, D. A. Murphy, E. I. Gale, T. J. Coalter, P. G. Cornish, Max Salzman, J. W. Francis, George H. Tinker, Ralph Cameron, John Sanderson, J. A. (Slow) Wilson, G. Fitzgerald, Al Doyle, N. G. Layton, J. Rosenbaugh, F. M. Vanderlip, J. M. Gallagher, J. W. Foren, P. D. Berry, E. S. Clark, C. C. Black, A. B. Boyle, L. L. Burns, J. R. Lane, W. Powell, C. A. Bush, F. DeC. Pitts, J. D. Ford, H. E. Campbell, A. A. Dutton and J. A. Vail.

The thirteen charter members of Flagstaff Lodge No. 7, Free and Accepted Masons, constituted December 17, 1888, were:

Walter J. Hill, J. E. Burchard, C. D. Bell, R. A. Ferguson, Edwin Gorton, D. F. Hart, J. H. Hicks, M. F. Hennings, J. R. Kilpatrick, William Munds, J. W. Sharp, J. G. Savage, and E. N. Woodford.

Charter members of Flagstaff Lodge No. 11, Independent Order of Odd Fellows, constituted June 25, 1890, included:

J. C. Newman, William Mooney, W. A. Diggs, A. F. Alvord, J. F. Michael, C. W. McFarland, Charles R. Bayless, Charles H. Clark, and Asa Clark.

## Illustration Credits

I AM INDEBTED to the following for their gracious assistance in making available photos and drawings:

Northern Arizona Pioneers' Historical Society, Special Collections, Northern Arizona University Library: Dr. D. J. Brannen, p. 143; E. M. Doe, p. 165; Ayer Lumber Co. mill (R. W. Wheeler collection), p. 195; Arizona Lumber Co. mill (Blanche Riordan Chambers collection), page 195; Riordans with Major Powell, p. 201; Bank Hotel and Grand Canyon Stage (Mrs. Louise Corey collection), p. 251; Flagstaff Public School in 1887 (Hochderffer collection), p. 259; Hanging Tree (Hochderffer collection), p. 291; Parade, p. 295; W.C.T.U. Picnic (Hochderffer collection), p. 305.

Museum of Northern Arizona, Colton Library: Lithograph, Antelope Valley, 1867, frontispiece; T. F. McMillan and George E. Loring, p. 77; Atlantic & Pacific Railroad construction camp (Lou Grundell collection), page 133; Frank Livermore (Earle R. Forrest collection), p. 217.

Atchison, Topeka & Santa Fe Railway: Canyon Diablo bridge, p. 133.

Lowell Observatory: McMillan-Clark homestead, page 183.

Museum of New Mexico: Fort Moroni (Ben Wittick collection), p. 213; Old Town Flagstaff (Ben Wittick collection), p. 224.

Sharlot Hall Museum: New Town Flagstaff, p. 231.

The map of Routes and Roads in the Peaks Area (1583–1882), p. 16, is from an original drawing by Meredith Guillet.

## Sources and Bibliography

IN VIEW OF FLAGSTAFF'S UNIQUE ORIGINS, plentiful color, economic importance, desirability as a place to live, and significance in the fields of science and education, it is singular that almost no attempts have been made to compile historical narratives dealing with the area, other than of the most fragmentary kind. Hopefully, this book provides some groundwork for future research, writing and publication of local history.

There is no lack of data. A vast amount is available in the collection of the Northern Arizona Pioneers Historical Society, housed in Special Collections, Northern Arizona University Library; also in Colton Library at the Museum of Northern Arizona; in that institution's publications; in Coconino County and City of Flagstaff records, and elsewhere.

Richest source of data is the files of the *Arizona Daily Sun* and its predecessor publications, the *Arizona Champion* and the *Coconino Sun,* almost intact from 1883. This weekly and daily record of the community's life is available on microfilm and in bound volumes in Special Collections, Northern Arizona University Library; at the Department of Library and Archives, Phoenix; and in parts elsewhere. An index for the years 1883–93, compiled at the Northern Arizona University Library, is now available and additions are planned. There is Flagstaff data in the files of the several Prescott newspapers, particularly in the early decades. There is no simple key to Prescott newspaper files. There were many publications; there were consolidations and name changes, and changes in frequency of appearance. The researcher is referred to two guides for detailed information regarding these and other newspaper files and their whereabouts: Estelle Lutrell, *Newspapers and Periodicals of Arizona, 1859–1911,* University of Arizona Press, Tucson, 1950; and *A Union List of Arizona Newspapers in Arizona Libraries,* compiled by the Department of Library and Archives, Phoenix, 1965.

In the lists below, sources are given by chapter and most are self-identifying.

Most unpublished theses available in Special Collections, Northern Arizona University Library, are to be approached with caution, with exceptions as listed in the references. Data relating to Flagstaff and Coconino County in Will C. Barnes's *Arizona Place Names,* including the 1960 revised edition, should be checked with other sources.

The John Bushman diaries and journals as listed as sources of data for Chapters III and VII are interesting and valuable, as is the May Larson record.

George Hochderffer's *Flagstaff Whoa!,* referred to in several chapters, is a valuable autobiographical record by a pioneer of the 1880s, but does not purport to be a community history. Interesting data, particularly advertisements, are to be found in George H. Tinker's *Northern Arizona and Flagstaff in 1887,* originally published in the *Arizona Champion* in 1887, listed as a reference for Chapter VII. However, the reader is warned that it is unreliable in some respects and is apparently the source of much of the confusion regarding the flagstaff(s) from which the community gained its name.

Bert Haskett's brief histories of the sheep and cattle industries, sources of data for Chapter VIII, are excellent.

While the scarcity of previous systematic compilations of data makes the researcher's task more difficult, at the same time it offers opportunities.

Sources and suggested reading, listed by chapter:

## CHAPTER I—SIERRA SIN AGUA

BARTLETT, KATHARINE. "Notes Upon the Routes of Espejo and Farfan to the Mines in the Sixteenth Century." *New Mexico Historical Review,* vol. 17, no. 1, January 1942.

BOLTON, HERBERT E. *Spanish Exploration in the Southwest, 1542–1706.* Yale University Press, New York, 1930.

COLTON, HAROLD S. "A Brief Survey of the Early Expeditions Into Northern Arizona." *Museum Notes,* vol. 2, no. 9, March 1930.

———. *Black Sand.* University of New Mexico Press, Albuquerque, 1960.

———. "Early Failure to Solve the Water Shortage." *Plateau,* vol. 29, no. 2, October 1956.

———. "The Prehistoric Population of the Flagstaff Area." *Plateau,* vol. 22, no. 2, October 1949.

———. *The Sinagua.* Museum of Northern Arizona, Flagstaff, 1946.

GOETZMANN, WILLIAM H. *Army Exploration in the American West.* Yale University Press, New Haven, 1959.

GRANGER, BYRD C. Will C. Barnes's *Arizona Place Names.* University of Arizona Press, Tucson, 1960.

VAN VALKENBURGH, RICHARD. *Diné Bikeyah.* Navajo Service, Window Rock, 1941.

WAHMANN, RUSSEL. "The Historical Geography of the Santa Fe Railway in Northern Arizona." Unpublished master's thesis, Northern Arizona University, Flagstaff, 1971.

## CHAPTER II—THE AMERICAN EXPEDITIONS

AUBRY, FRANCIS XAVIER. "Diaries." *Exploring Southwest Trails, 1846–1854,* vol. 7 of Southwest Historical Series, R. P. Bieber, ed. Arthur H. Clark Co., Glendale, Calif., 1938. Reprinted by Porcupine Press, Inc., Philadelphia, 1974.

BONSAL, S. *Edward Fitzgerald Beale.* G. P. Putnam's Sons, New York, 1912.

BRANDES, RAYMOND. "Guide to the History of the U.S. Army Installations in Arizona." *Arizona and the West,* vol. 1, no. 1, Spring 1959.

COLTON, HAROLD S. "A Brief Survey of Early Expeditions Into Northern Arizona." *Museum Notes,* vol. 2, no. 9, March 1930.

FAVOUR, ALPHEUS H. *Old Bill Williams.* University of North Carolina Press, Chapel Hill, 1936.

FAVOUR, EVA. "Journey of Arizona's Territorial Party." *Echoes of the Past,* R. C. Stevens, ed. Vol. 2, Prescott, 1964.

GOETZMANN, WILLIAM H. *Army Exploration in the American West.* Yale University Press, New Haven, 1959.

JACKSON, W. T. *Wagon Roads West.* University of California Press, Berkeley, 1952.

MARION, J. H. *Notes of Travel Through the Territory of Arizona.* D. M. Powell, ed. University of Arizona Press, Tucson, 1965.

MOLLHAUSEN, BALDWIN. *Diary of a Journey From the Mississippi to the Coasts of the Pacific.* 2 vols., London, 1858.

MORISON, SAMUEL E. *The Oxford History of the American People*. Oxford University Press, New York, 1965.

PALMER, W. J. *Report of Surveys Across the Continent in 1867–68 on the 35th and 32nd Parallels*. W. B. Silheimer, Philadelphia, 1869.

PARKHILL, FORBES. *The Blazed Trail of Antoine Leroux*. Westernlore Press, Los Angeles, 1965.

WHIPPLE, AMIEL W. *Report of Explorations for a Railway Route Near the 35th Parallel of N. Latitude From the Mississippi to the Pacific Ocean*. Vol. 3, Pacific Survey Reports, 33rd Congress, 2nd Session, Senate Executive Document 78, Washington, D.C., 1856.

*See also:* Senate Executive Document 59, 33rd Congress, 1st Session, 1853 (Sitgreaves report); House Executive Documents 124, 35th Congress, 1st Session, 1857 (Beale's report), and 90, 36th Congress, 1st Session, 1859 (Ives's report); and files of the *Arizona Champion* (Flagstaff), 1886, and the *Arizona Miner* (Prescott), 1864–66.

## CHAPTER III—THE BOSTON PARTIES

BREAKENRIDGE, W. M. *Helldorado*. Houghton Mifflin, Boston, 1928.

BUSHMAN, JOHN. *Diaries,* part 1, 1871–1889. Typescript copy, George S. Tanner Collection, Special Collections, Northern Arizona University Library, Flagstaff.

———. *Journal, 1867–1889*. Microfilm of typescript, Special Collections, Northern Arizona University Library, Flagstaff.

COZZENS, S. W. *The Marvellous Country*. Boston, 1873.

FONTANA, B. L. Personal communication to Katharine Bartlett, Museum of Northern Arizona, Oct. 31, 1961. In this letter Fontana, field historian at the University of Arizona, says that editions of Cozzens's *The Marvellous Country* appeared in 1873, 1875, and 1876, and that Cozzens also wrote a fictional book, *The Young Silver Seekers; or Hal and Ned in the Marvellous Country,* published in Boston in 1882.

HOCHDERFFER, GEORGE. *Flagstaff Whoa!* Museum of Northern Arizona, Flagstaff, 1965.

LARSON, MAY H. *Our Move From Utah*. 1933. Typescript, George S. Tanner Collection, Special Collections, Northern Arizona University Library, Flagstaff.

LORING, GEORGE E. Journal and letters, Loring Archive, Arizona Historical Society Collection no. 237, Tucson.

McCLINTOCK, J. H. *Arizona*. 2 vols. S. J. Clarke Co., Chicago, 1916.

———. *Mormon Settlement in Arizona*. Phoenix, 1921.

PETERSEN, C. S. "Settlement on the Little Colorado, 1873–1900." Unpublished doctoral dissertation, University of Utah, Salt Lake City, 1967.

———. *Take Up Your Mission: Mormon Colonizing Along the Little Colorado River, 1870–1900*. University of Arizona, Tucson, 1973.

VERBEEK, K. W. "The Mechanisms of Emplacement of the Marble Mountain Laccolith, Flagstaff, Arizona." *Plateau*, vol. 45, no. 2, Fall 1972.

*See also:* Files of the Albuquerque *Republican-Review,* 1876; *Arizona Citizen* (Tucson), 1876; *Arizona Daily Sun* (Flagstaff), 1947; *Arizona Miner* (Prescott), 1876; Boston *Daily Globe,* 1875–76; Boston *Herald,* 1875–76; *Coconino Sun* (Flagstaff), 1908; and the Douglas *Dispatch,* 1927.

## CHAPTER IV—THE FIRST SETTLERS

ASHURST, HENRY F. *Up in Coconino County.* Pasadena, 1957.

HASKETT, B. "History of the Sheep Industry in Arizona." *Arizona Historical Review,* July 1936.

HINTON, R. J. *Handbook to Arizona.* San Francisco, 1878.

HOCHDERFFER, GEORGE. *Flagstaff Whoa!* Museum of Northern Arizona, Flagstaff, 1965.

KELLY, ROGER E. "Flagstaff's Frontier Fort." *Plateau,* vol. 36, no. 4, Spring 1964.

MCCLINTOCK, J. H. *Arizona.* 2 vols. S. J. Clarke Co., Chicago, 1916.

The Pioneers Society of Northern Arizona, minute book, entry of April 12, 1905. Northern Arizona Pioneers Historical Society Collection, Special Collections, Northern Arizona University Library, Flagstaff.

MURPHY, RALPH. "I Was There When the Old Fort Was Built." *Plateau,* vol. 36, no. 4, Spring 1964.

*Portrait and Biographical Record of Arizona.* Chicago, 1901.

U.S. Census Office. *Report of the U.S. Decennial Census, 1880.* Washington, D.C., 1881.

WILLSON, R. *Pioneer and Well-known Cattlemen of Arizona.* 2 vols. Phoenix, 1956.

*See also:* Files of the *Arizona Champion* (Flagstaff), 1887–88; the *Arizona Daily Sun* (Flagstaff), 1947, 1949, 1954; the *Arizona* (Daily) *Miner* and *Weekly Miner* (Prescott), 1872, 1880–82; the *Coconino Sun* (Flagstaff), 1906, 1921, 1923, 1926, 1928, 1932, 1939, 1941–42; and *Plateau* (Museum of Northern Arizona) for October 1956.

## CHAPTER V—THE COMING OF THE RAILROAD

ASHURST, HENRY F. *A Many Colored Toga.* University of Arizona Press, Tucson, 1962.

Atlantic & Pacific Railroad Construction Records, 1881–82. Atchison, Topeka & Santa Fe Railway Co., Chicago.

HOCHDERFFER, GEORGE. *Flagstaff Whoa!* Museum of Northern Arizona, Flagstaff, 1965.

MCCLINTOCK, J. H. *Mormon Settlement in Arizona.* Phoenix, 1921.

WISEBY, H. A., JR. "A History of the Santa Fe Railroad in Arizona to 1917." Unpublished master's thesis, University of Arizona, Tucson, 1946.

*See also* the files of the following newspapers, particularly for the years noted: the *Arizona Champion* (Flagstaff), 1887; the *Arizona Miner* (Prescott), 1880–81; the Albuquerque *Daily Golden Gate,* 1880; the Albuquerque *Journal,* 1881; the *Coconino Sun* (Flagstaff), 1901, 1921, 1923 and 1926; and the Prescott *Courier,* 1882.

## CHAPTER VI—PIONEERS OF THE EIGHTIES

The material in this chapter was drawn primarily from obituaries and other articles and news reports relating to pioneer settlers of Flagstaff in the 1880s appearing in the *Arizona Champion* and its successors, the *Coconino Sun* and, after 1946, the *Arizona Daily Sun.* The files of these Flagstaff newspapers, dating back to 1883, are preserved in the Special Collections Department of Northern Arizona University Library. Other sources include:

ASHURST, HENRY F. *A Many Colored Toga.* University of Arizona Press, Tucson, 1962.

COLTON, HAROLD S. "Trailing the Lost Mines of the Padres." *Plateau,* vol. 13, no. 2, October 1940.

HOCHDERFFER, GEORGE. *Flagstaff Whoa!* Museum of Northern Arizona, Flagstaff, 1965.
SYKES, GODFREY. *A Westerly Trend.* Arizona Pioneers Historical Society, Tucson, 1944.

## CHAPTER VII—FLAGSTAFF'S FLAGSTAFFS

BUSHMAN, JOHN. Diaries, Part I, 1871–89. Typescript, George S. Tanner Collection, Special Collections, Northern Arizona University Library, Flagstaff.
COLTON, HAROLD S. "How Flagstaff Was Named." *Plateau,* vol. 15, no. 2, October 1942.
———. "Flagstaff Historical Sites Committee File," Flagstaff Chamber of Commerce. Colton Library, Museum of Northern Arizona, Flagstaff.
HOCHDERFFER, GEORGE. *Flagstaff Whoa!* Museum of Northern Arizona, Flagstaff, 1965.
LARSON, MAY H. *Our Move From Utah, 1933.* Typescript, George S. Tanner Collection, Special Collections, Northern Arizona University Library, Flagstaff.
RHOADS, J. B. Letter to Paul J. Fannin, April 3, 1973, in possession of author. Rhoads is director of the National Archives and Record Service.
RIORDAN, M. J. "History of the Catholic Church in Flagstaff," *Coconino Sun* (Flagstaff), Dec. 5, 1930.
TINKER, GEORGE H. *Northern Arizona and Flagstaff in 1887.* Arthur H. Clark Co., Glendale, Calif., 1969.
*See also* the files of the following newspapers, particularly for the years cited: the *Arizona Champion* (Flagstaff), 1884, 1887; the *Arizona Daily Sun* (Flagstaff), 1954, 1959; the *Coconino Sun* (Flagstaff), 1894, 1918, 1920–21, 1926–30; the *Northern Arizona Leader* (Flagstaff), 1918, 1920; the Prescott *Daily Journal-Miner,* 1886, 1888; and the Prescott *Miner,* 1881, 1894.

## CHAPTER VIII—LUMBER AND LIVESTOCK

FORREST, EARLE R. *Arizona's Dark and Bloody Ground.* Caxton Printers, Caldwell, Idaho, 1936.
HAMILTON, PATRICK. *Resources of Arizona.* 3rd edition. San Francisco, 1884.
HASKETT, BERT. "Early History of the Cattle Industry in Arizona." *Arizona Historical Review,* October 1935.
———. "Early History of the Sheep Industry in Arizona." *Arizona Historical Review,* July 1936.
LOCKWOOD, FRANK C. *The Life of E. E. Ayer.* University of Arizona. A. C. McClurg & Co., Chicago, 1929.
RICKARD, T. A. *Interviews With Mining Engineers.* Mining & Scientific Press, San Francisco, 1922.
SYKES, GODFREY. *A Westerly Trend.* Arizona Pioneers Historical Society, Tucson, 1944.
In addition material has come from David Myrick, writer on railroads, San Francisco; from Mrs. Commodore P. Owens in form of personal communications to the author on various dates in 1944; and from the files of the *Arizona Champion* (Flagstaff), 1884–88, and the *Coconino Sun* (Flagstaff), 1943.

## CHAPTER IX—BUILDING AND REBUILDING

ELLIS, BRUCE T., ed. "A Ben Wittick Item." *El Palacio,* Santa Fe, June 1958.

HAMILTON, P. *Resources of Arizona*. 3rd edition. San Francisco, 1884.

SMITH, D. "Babbitt History." Unpublished manuscript in possession of Babbitt family, 1965.

SMITH, STUART J. "Arizona Wagon Roads North of the Thirty-fourth Parallel, 1851–81." Thesis in preparation, Northern Arizona University, Flagstaff, 1976.

In addition material has been drawn from a printed announcement of the Citizens Bank, 1887, in the possession of the author; and from the following newspapers, particularly for the years cited: the *Arizona Champion* (Flagstaff), 1883–91; the *Coconino Sun* (Flagstaff), 1895, 1922, 1928, 1939; and the Prescott *Courier,* 1883.

## CHAPTER X—MOLDING MINDS AND MORALS

DOWNUM, GARLAND, PH.D. *Brief History of the Federated Community Church*. Privately printed, Flagstaff, 1956.

HICKS, MAY. Early History of Flagstaff Schools. Paper, Northern Arizona Normal School, 1905. Published in the *Coconino Sun* (Flagstaff), Nov. 25, 1927.

HOCHDERFFER, GEORGE. *Flagstaff Whoa!* Museum of Northern Arizona, Flagstaff, 1965.

RIORDAN, M. J. "History of the Catholic Church in Flagstaff." *Coconino Sun* (Flagstaff), Dec. 5, 1930.

In addition data have been taken from the minute book of the Pioneers' Historical Society of Northern Arizona, specifically the Sept. 24, 1906, entry, Northern Arizona Pioneers' Historical Society Collection, Special Collections, Northern Arizona University Library; and from the files of the *Arizona Champion* (Flagstaff), 1883–89; the *Arizona Daily Sun* (Flagstaff), 1961; the *Coconino Sun* (Flagstaff), 1895, 1929; and by reference from *The Flag* (Flagstaff), 1883–84.

## CHAPTER XI—FLAGSTAFF—A FRONTIER TOWN

Material for this chapter has been drawn primarily from the files of the *Arizona Champion* (Flagstaff), 1883–91; the Prescott *Courier,* 1883; and personal communications from pioneer residents of Flagstaff during the decade of the 1880s, notably W. H. Switzer, George Hochderffer and C. C. Stemmer.

## CHAPTER XII—A COUNTY CALLED COCONINO

ANDERSON, L. "Railroad Transportation Through Prescott." Unpublished master's thesis, University of Arizona, Tucson, 1934.

COLTON, HAROLD S. "How Coconino County Received Its Name." *Plateau,* vol. 31, no. 2, October 1958.

WAGONER, JERRY J. *Arizona Territory, 1863–1912, a Political History*. University of Arizona Press, Tucson, 1970.

Material may also be found in the files of the following newspapers, particularly for the years cited: the *Arizona Champion* (Peach Springs), 1883–84; the *Arizona Champion* (Flagstaff), 1884, 1886–89, 1891; the *Arizona Daily Sun* (Flagstaff), 1946; *The Flag* (Flagstaff), 1883, by reference; the Prescott *Courier,* 1886, 1889; the Prescott *Journal,* 1884; the Prescott *Journal-Miner,* 1886, 1888; and the *Arizona Miner* (Prescott), 1884.

## Acknowledgments

I ACKNOWLEDGE DEEP OBLIGATION to William G. Hoyt, M.A., managing editor of the *Arizona Daily Sun* for eight years, now an historian, and acting public information director, Northern Arizona University. He gave generously of his energy and free time, served as a sounding board for ideas, made valuable suggestions for developing and recasting parts of the manuscript, provided advice and assistance in editing, and also read proofs. He was a warm enthusiast and at the same time a hard-headed editorial critic. I am grateful to him for believing that the project was worthwhile and should be completed.

I acknowledge special indebtedness to Miss Katharine Bartlett, M.A., curator, Colton Library, Museum of Northern Arizona, for generously making available her resources relating to the Boston parties, for helpfulness in finding sources, and for reading and correcting parts of the manuscript.

A special word of acknowledgment is due William H. Lyon, Ph.D., chairman of the department of history, N.A.U. As we stopped to exchange greetings one snowy day in 1972 he suggested that I attempt such a project. He read early chapters, then the completed manuscript, and offered encouragement and counsel.

I am obliged to John W. Irwin, M.A., librarian-archivist, Special Collections, N.A.U. Library, for research assistance, reading the manuscript, correcting errors, offering valuable suggestions, and for his enthusiasm.

I am grateful to J. Lawrence Walkup, Ed.D., president, N.A.U., for continuing encouragement, for reading the manuscript, and for initiating establishment of a review committee of distinguished staff and faculty members, including Lewis J. McDonald, Ed.D.; Robert C. Dickeson, Ph.D.; Richard O. Davies, Ph.D.; Andrew Wallace, Ph.D., and James W. Byrkit, Ph.D., whose reports have led to sponsorship of this book by the University.

I am grateful to the above for reading all or parts of the manuscript, and particularly to Drs. Dickeson and Wallace for suggestions, but the book as it appears is my work alone.

I appreciate the kind encouragement I have received from Paul and John Babbitt; Bruce Babbitt, Arizona attorney general; Ralph Bilby, member, Board of Regents of Arizona Universities, and his wife, Mary; Henry Giclas, president of the Northern Arizona Historical Society; Mrs. Rayma Sharber; and two newcomers to Flagstaff, Hermann Bleibtreu, Ph.D., director, Museum of Northern Arizona, and Don W. Sellers, M.D.

A list of those to whom I am indebted must include Gladwell G. (Toney) Richardson, my first Flagstaff friend, a source of information about early times and families. His kindnesses over more than thirty-seven years have been many.

I am deeply obliged to Kathryn Howard, B.S., whose professional skill, deep interest and enthusiastic application have proved invaluable in preparation of the index. A word of special thanks is due Mrs. Penelope Halstead, who patiently typed the manuscript, corrected errors, and raised questions which led to improvement of certain passages and the recasting of one chapter.

I thank Steward J. Smith, B.S., for sharing information on early wagon roads; Barton A. Wright, M.A., curator, Museum of Northern Arizona, for assistance in platting early routes, and Angel Gomez, P.E., for checking correlations of data. I appreciate the generosity of David F. Myrick, San Francisco, in sharing lumbering and railroad construction data. I acknowledge favors by Joseph M. Meehan, Jr., B.S., curator, Northern Arizona Pioneers' Historical Society. I am indebted to my old friend, Meredith Guillet, for preparing the map of routes and roads. In production phases at Northland Press I have met with unfailing courtesy and generous assistance on the part of every member of the staff. I am particularly grateful to Robert O. Jacobson, M.A., for his beautiful rendition of the maps, and to Stanley D. Stillion, compositor, for consistent willingness to be helpful, and for his patience.

I thank the other friends, too numerous to list, who have helped in many ways, and who themselves know how they have contributed.

Last but not least I thank my wife, Barbara, for ever-willingness to discuss procedures and plans; for valuable suggestions; for reading the several drafts; for reading and re-reading proofs; for sharing with me a love for our community, and for her limitless patience and never-failing kindness and encouragement.

In addition to credits given in the text I acknowledge with thanks permission to quote from the following:

Museum of Northern Arizona, Harold S. Colton, *The Sinagua,* 1946; George Hochderffer, *Flagstaff Whoa!,* 1965; *Museum Notes,* vol. 2, no. 9; *Plateau,* vol. 15, no. 2; vol. 22, no. 2; vol. 29, no. 2.

*New Mexico Historical Review,* Katharine Bartlett, "Notes Upon the Routes of Espejo and Farfan to the Mines in the Sixteenth Century," 1942.

Yale University Press, William H. Goetzmann, *Army Exploration in the American West,* 1959.

Porcupine Press, Inc., reprint, 1974, of *Southwest Historical Series,* vol. 7, pub. 1938 by Arthur H. Clark Co.

Westernlore Press, Forbes Parkhill, *The Blazed Trail of Antoine Leroux,* 1965.

John Bushman Family Association, *John Bushman Journal and Diaries.*

Oxford University Press, Samuel Eliot Morison, *Oxford History of the American People,* 1965.

The University of Arizona Press, Tucson, the following: Charles S. Peterson, *Take Up Your Mission,* copyright 1973; J. H. Marion, *Notes of Travel Through the Territory of Arizona,* ed. Donald M. Powell, copyright 1965; H. F. Ashurst, *A Many Colored Toga,* copyright 1962.

# Index

Arizona State College: 159, 161; *see also* Northern Arizona Normal School and Northern Arizona University

Arizona Supply Company: 198

Arizona Wood Company: 207

Arson: *see* Fires

Ash Fork, town of: 113, 125, 131, 147, 214, 316

Ashley, Rev. I. M.: 261

Ashurst, Eva: 258, 296

Ashurst, Henry Fountain: 90, 92, 103, 145, 146, 164, 186, 254, 259, 305, 317, 327

Ashurst, Sarah Bogard (Mrs. William Henry): 90, 92

Ashurst, William Henry: 90–92, 103, 104, 127, 186, 210, 219, 222, 236, 254, 257, 258, 313, 314, 327

Ashurst Lake: 90, 103

Ashurst Run: 90

Attorneys: 101, 159–61, 164, 165, 167, 228, 237, 250, 258, 276, 282, 290, 317, 323, 324

Aubry, Francois Xavier: 21–23, 37; Aubry Canyon: 23; Aubry Cliffs: 23; Aubry Hills: 23; Aubry Landing: 23; Aubry Spring: 23

Awatovi: 12–14

Ayer, Edward Everett: 106, 114, 115, 130, 131, 134–36, 140, 147, 150, 155, 193–97, 199, 200, 202

Ayer, Henry C.: 194, 236, 254

Ayer Lumber Company: 127, 131, 134–36, 140, 142, 147, 150, 153, 155, 162, 193–97, 204, 208, 228, 234, 236, 254–56, 258, 311; *see also* Arizona Lumber Company and Arizona Lumber & Timber Company

Aztec Land and Cattle Company (Hashknife): 159, 207, 209, 216, 238

Babbitt, Bertrand: 159

Babbitt, Betty Jo (Mrs. Michael D'Mura): 160

Babbitt, Bruce: 161

Babbitt, Catherine: 157

Babbitt, Charles J.: 157, 158, 160, 161, 176, 246–48

Babbitt, Charles J., Jr.: 161

Babbitt, David: 157–60, 221, 222, 238, 243, 244, 246–48, 267

Babbitt, David, Jr.: 160

Babbitt, Edward: 157, 159, 247

Babbitt, Edwin: 160

Babbitt, Elaine: 160

Babbitt, Elizabeth Roche (Mrs. William): 157

Babbitt, Emma Verkamp (Mrs. David): 157, 158, 160, 266

Babbitt, Eunice (Mrs. I. F. Veazey): 159

Babbitt, George: 157–59, 239, 244, 246–49, 264, 304, 306, 323, 324

Babbitt, George, Jr.: 159

Babbitt, Gertrude: 160

Babbitt, Helen: 161

Babbitt, Herbert: 159

Babbitt, Imogene (Mrs. Lou Bader): 160

Babbitt, James E.: 160, 161

Babbitt, John G.: 161

Babbitt, Joseph: 160

Babbitt, Joseph, Jr.: 160

Babbitt, Margaret (Mrs. T. E. McCullough): 159

Babbitt, Mary (Mrs. Ralph Bilby): 160

Babbitt, Mary Verkamp (Mrs. Charles): 157, 161

Babbitt, Matilda Verkamp (Mrs. Edward): 157

Babbitt, Paul J.: 161

Babbitt, Paul J., Jr.: 161

Babbitt, Philomena Wessell (Mrs. George): 157, 159, 294

Babbitt, Rayma (Mrs. Norman G. Sharber): 160

Babbitt, Raymond G.: 160

Babbitt, Raymond G., Jr. (Ted): 160

Babbitt, Rose (Mrs. Raymond G.): 160

Babbitt, Teresa (Mrs. Charles Reddock): 160

Babbitt, Viola (Mrs. Joseph): 160

Babbitt, William: 157, 158, 160, 221, 222, 246–48

Babbitt Brothers Trading Company: 104, 156, 157, 160, 161, 209, 246, 248, 249; Babbitt Brothers building: 246, 249, 306, 324; cattle and sheep business: 156, 158–61, 211, 212, 221, 222, 238,

226; banks: 164, 237, 238, 243, 244, 252; barber shops: 237, 243, 287; blacksmiths and wagon repairs: 228, 237, 249; breweries: 237, 246; carpentry: 228; Chinese laundries: 118, 235, 302, 303; Chinese restaurants: 118, 234, 235, 239; clothing stores: 152; confectionery: 158, 228, 244, 299; contractors: 117, 182, 237; dance halls: 124, 225, 229, 230; delivery services: 167; department stores: 159; dressmakers: 244; drug stores: 144, 228, 237, 246, 248, 299; fruit stores: 228, 243; furniture: 228, 237; garages: 159, 160, 209; general merchandise and dry goods: 109, 118, 120, 125, 135, 158, 225, 227, 238, 246, 303; groceries: 135, 238, 248, 303; hotels and rooming houses: 142, 146, 150, 163, 173, 227, 228, 236, 238, 241, 249, 250, 252, 263, 286, 287, 298; ice houses: 237; jewelers: 237; laundries: 237; liquor and beer: 132, 229; livery stables: 228; lumber, building materials and hardware: 155, 158, 228, 238, 246, 269; machine and repair shops: 161; meat markets: 142, 151, 219, 236, 237, 303; mercantile: 90, 136, 157, 160, 163, 173, 235; milk deliveries: 245; newspapers: 227; opera houses and theatres: 164; paint shops: 237, photography shops: 237; real estate: 159, 237, 277; retailing: 225, 238, 241; restaurants: 103, 110, 119, 140, 148, 158, 225, 226, 228, 230, 236, 252, 273, 274, 298, 304; roller skating rink: 232, 271, 293, 296; saddle and harness shops: 155, 237; saloons: 103, 110, 112, 119, 124, 125, 127, 136, 140, 141, 145, 146, 151, 175, 209, 225, 226, 228, 230, 234, 237, 243, 246, 250, 275, 294; second hand stores: 152; shoe stores: 152, 237; slaughterhouses: 228; soda fountains: 158, 244, 304; soft drinks: 229; sundries: 237; trading posts: 159, 161; undertaking establishments: 103, 248; wholesale houses: 159; wool sales: 60, 119, 128, 147

C. A. Clark & Co.: 152
C. P. Head & Co.: 128
California Bill: 288
California Kid: 297
Callihan & Doyle: 325
Camels: 32, 33, 35, 36, 41, 95, 108
Cameron, Anna: 157
Cameron, Betsy (Mrs. Ralph): 156, 294
Cameron, Bill: 157
Cameron, Burton A.: 157, 317
Cameron, Burton A., Jr.: 157
Cameron, Catherine: 156
Cameron, Frances Clift Cummings (Mrs. Burton A.): 157
Cameron, George A.: 157
Cameron, Harold L.: 157
Cameron, Niles: 156, 157
Cameron, Ralph Henry: 156–58, 209, 240, 241, 246, 301, 323, 324
Cameron, Ralph, Jr.: 156
Cameron, town of: 14, 156
Cameron & Lind: 243, 246
Camp Apache: 62
Camp Clark: 45
Camp Pomeroy: 45
Camp Verde, town of: 12, 90, 100, 125
Camp Whipple: see Fort Whipple
Campbell, A. H.: 25
Campbell, Colin: 151
Campbell, Daniel: 151, 189
Campbell, Hugh E.: 25, 142, 151
Campbell, John: 68, 69
Campbell, Madie Christman (Mrs. Hugh E.): 151
Campbell, Mary Luella (Mrs. John B. Duerson): 151
Campbell, Mina B. Jones: 167
Campbell, Thomas E.: 189
Campbell, W. H. Hugh: 151
Campbell-Francis Sheep Company: 142, 151
Canyon de Chelly: 89
Canyon Diablo: 11, 26–28, 33, 36, 45, 64–66, 74, 111, 129, 130, 134, 150, 177, 178, 180, 181, 195, 279, 302; bridge at: 124–26, 129–31, 133, 134
Carillo, Veronica Salas: 150
Carlton, Gen.: 45